D0968599

Opposition and Dissent in Contemporary China

Opposition and Dissent in Contemporary China

Peter R. Moody

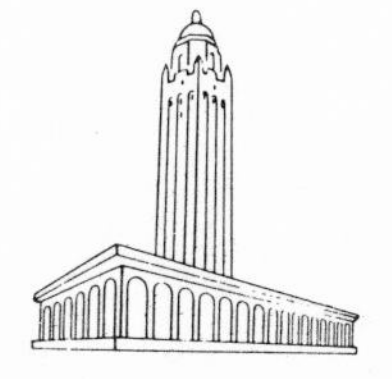

Hoover Institution Press
Stanford University • Stanford, California

The Hoover Institution on War, Revolution and Peace, founded at Stanford University in 1919 by the late President Herbert Hoover, is an interdisciplinary research center for advanced study on domestic and international affairs in the twentieth century. The views expressed in its publications are entirely those of the authors and do not necessarily reflect the views of the staff, officers, or Board of Overseers of the Hoover Institution.

Seven Popeye cartoons by Bud Sagendorf, October 1967, are reprinted by permission of King Features Syndicate, Inc.

Hoover Institution Publication 177

International Standard Book Number: 0-8179-6771-1
Library of Congress Catalog Card Number: 77-72054
Printed in the United States of America

To my father
and to
John, Joseph, Benjamin, and Rebekah

Superior and inferior fight a hundred battles a day.

HAN FEI-TZU

Contents

Preface

This study, basically completed in July 1976, does not discuss events beyond the Ch'ing Ming riots of April of that year. Readers of the official Chinese press since the Cultural Revolution had become used to month after month of monotony, relieved by widely scattered weeks of frantic activity occasioned by a major meeting, a new campaign, or a mysterious purge. The year 1976 broke this pattern. First came the death of Chou En-lai, followed by the second purge of Teng Hsiao-p'ing, then the April riots. The latter part of the year saw the death of Chu Te (an event of little political importance, except to emphasize the passing of an era), the horrifying earthquakes in north China, the death of Mao Tse-tung, and (perhaps politically most significant of all) the purge in October of the more articulate establishment radicals: Wang Hung-wen, Chang Ch'un-ch'iao, Chiang Ch'ing, Yao Wen-yuan—the gang of four. The purge of the gang of four was accompanied by the triumph of Hua Kuo-feng.

Despite these rapid developments, I have made no major changes in the text. Given the fluidity of Chinese politics since the death of Mao, any revision I might make at this point stands no more chance of being correct than does the original text. Also, this study is not intended to be a newspaper, and I do not think that the developments since the summer of 1976 substantively affect my analysis of opposition and dissent.

I make this last statement with some diffidence. The analysis of Chinese politics in this book is largely based upon official interpretations by the Chinese themselves, and in contemporary China each new ruler who mounts the stage provides his own reinterpretation of past events. The new interpretations are not necessarily more valid than the old, but they are not necessarily invalid either; and the analyst should, within reason, take them into account. It is only fair to indicate where, according to newer interpretations, my analysis might be wrong. For example, I interpret the strange 1975 campaign against *Water margin* as a move by the establishment radicals—the gang of four—against Teng Hsiao-p'ing, since in the spring of 1976 the regime was identifying Teng as the target of this campaign. Certain pronouncements in December 1976, however, seem to hint that the real target of this radical campaign was Hua Kuo-feng. The later interpretation does make a certain amount of sense. The campaign criticized "surrenderism," and it is hard to see how Teng, an "unrepentant capitalist roader," had ever surrendered to anyone (except, one might argue tendentiously, to the Soviets). The campaign might have been an attack on Hua—who, presumably, prior to that time had been an ally of the radicals—for caving in to the opinions of the likes of Chou En-lai and Teng Hsiao-p'ing. The new interpretation is not necessarily valid, of course, particularly since Hua seems currently to be attempting to arrogate to himself some of the achievements of Teng.

My analysis of the campaign to criticize Confucius may be more seriously in error. I analyze that campaign as in part a rational modernist criticism of radicalism. In December 1976, however, the gang of four were accused of using the campaign as a pretext to attack Chou En-lai. In this book I argue that the campaign was in fact a complex one, a common carrier for many of the various factions in China; that it began as a pro-Chou attack on the radicals, but that it was co-opted by the radicals for their attacks on Chou. Should the regime come to repudiate the campaign, claiming that it was entirely of radical inspiration, my confidence in my interpretation would be shaken. Unfortunately, such a claim would not in itself falsify my interpretation (an indication of how far from scientific rigor are analyses of current Chinese politics): the function of official interpretations is to serve the current political situation, not to reveal the truth. The evidence for my interpretation comes from some of the language used in the campaign and from statements made about the campaign by various Chinese dissidents, and any reinterpretation must take such evidence into account. As it happens, the campaign had not, as of December, been repudiated. It was still being attributed directly to Mao (still without quoting Mao directly on the campaign), with the additional argument that it had been distorted by the gang of four. This, I think, is consistent with my interpretation. If it turns out that my analysis is wrong, there may be methodological value in allowing the error to stand (with an indication of the possibility of error), along with the erroneous reasoning, that we might avoid similar errors in the future.

To see that the time concerning which I speculate in the conclusion has already arrived is a little disconcerting, particularly since it is still difficult to see which, if any, of the speculations have any merit. One wonders whether the radical tendency has been decisively defeated; if it has, the analysis of Chinese politics in terms of the tendencies discussed so much in this book may cease to be applicable. The gang of four were the radical ideologues but did not constitute the whole of the radical tendency, and at first glance their purge seems to be in part a consequence of their betrayal by their allies on the Politburo. But by January 1977 some of these high-ranking inarticulate leftists were themselves being attacked on wall posters. If the radical tendency has been eliminated from the leadership, Maoist-like radicalism may still persist for some time among certain segments of society as an oppositional stance. As such it may be able to free itself from some of the contradictions and hypocrisy that attended it as a ruling ideology.

While this study does not predict the defeat of the gang of four—I think, indeed, that it overestimates their political strength—it does at least point to it. It shows the increasing isolation of the establishment radicals and the increasing hollowness of their position. To end this study with the Ch'ing Ming riots seems a little anticlimactic, but the anticlimax may be merely dramatic, not substantive. These riots sum up the dissent of the past and indicate the nature of the dissent to come. From a historical perspective they may prove to be more important than I had guessed. One conclusion of this study, that we are entering a period in which opposition and dissent in China will become increasingly obvious and felt, may turn out to be corroborated.

This study was made possible by a Peace Fellowship for the 1975/76 academic year from the Hoover Institution on War, Revolution and Peace—allowing me a year in a pleasant climate, with access to ample research materials. I wish to thank in particular the curators and staff of the East Asia Collection and Dennis Bark, executive secretary of the National Fellows program. Conversations with the following have contributed to my thinking on the problem of opposition and dissent in China, at times in ways they would perhaps neither recognize nor accept: George Breslauer, Esther Kingston-Mann, Paul Marantz, Charles Price Ridley, David N. Rowe (my mentor), Yu-ming Shaw, and Yuan-li Wu. I also wish to thank Marty Zupan for an intimidating weeding-out of the sloppinesses of the original manuscript, and two anonymous readers of the original manuscript for their constructive criticisms, which I hope I have taken seriously enough. It is a custom among academicians to thank their spouses for bearing with the foul temper and familial neglect that, one gathers, accompany scholarly research. I am not sure, however, that I was any more of a pain while working on this project than I normally am, and in any case my gratitude to Peggy transcends all words or occasions. I only wish I could limit the *buts, howevers,* and *other hands* to her satisfaction. Naturally, for doing what I ought not to have done, and leaving undone what I ought to have done, I alone am responsible.

South Bend, Indiana
January 1977

1

Conflict and Opposition

Some might think that a study of opposition and dissent in contemporary China would be a refreshingly brief, if uninteresting, work, adequately summed up in one sentence: There is none. There is not in China, and never really has been, the sort of institutionalized toleration of opposition and dissent found in liberal states.[1] We may, however, take as a starting point a commonplace from Robert Dahl: "No government receives, indefinitely, the total support of the people over whom it asserts its jurisdiction."[2] More generally, it would seem that politics, whatever else it may involve, always involves conflict. The Chinese Legalist philosopher Master Han Fei remarks that superior and inferior fight a hundred battles a day; Plato, a thinker whose notions of politics are rather more exalted than Han Fei's, has Socrates remark, once he is well launched into his description of the ideal state, that he and Thrasymachus have become friends now. We may take as an axiom that opposition is involved in all politics. Since China is now ruled by a totalitarian or revolutionary regime dedicated to implementing thorough social change, we might even expect that the level of opposition in China would be unusually high, although not always superficially apparent.[3]

THE CONCEPT OF OPPOSITION

Some seem to hold that the Chinese regime represents the true interests of the Chinese people, the general will, as it were. If such views (some of which are discussed in the second chapter) are at all valid, then under some systems of thought we might doubt the *propriety* of opposition to the regime or even the propriety of its study, but this says nothing about the fact of opposition. In any case, those who rule China do claim to perceive opposition to themselves and their policies. Given the structure of Chinese politics, however, it is sometimes difficult to say just what should be considered opposition. In liberal societies there is usually (but not always)[4] a fairly clear distinction between the ins and the outs, between government and opposition. In nonliberal societies this distinction may not be so clearly defined, a vagueness in the interests both of the rulers and of those opposed to them. What those in power claim to see as opposition may not really be opposition, and "whenever the opposition is deprived of all legitimacy, it has to appear in the shape of agreement."[5]

Frederick Barghoorn defines opposition in the Soviet Union as the "persistent and—from the official view—objectionable advocacy of policies differing from or contrary to those which the dominant group in the supreme CPSU control and decision-making bodies . . . have caused these bodies to adopt."[6] The notion of opposition as persistent and objectionable is a useful one. Advocacy of policies that are not in fact adopted, prior to a decision being made, should probably not in itself constitute opposition, nor should technical objections to policies when these are *merely* technical and are so construed by others. In China, however, it is not clear that there always is a dominant group within the regime. There has often been, apparently, some kind of factional balance of power embedded within a vaguer division the Maoists call the two lines. Thus, most students agree that in the early 1960s Mao Tse-tung and the party bureaucracy were at odds. Which side should we consider to be in opposition? Each had sufficient grounds for considering itself the proper locus of authority. The answer, perhaps, is "both."

Given the nature of regimes like the Chinese, it is probably not useful to take too narrow a view of what constitutes opposition. Barghoorn distinguishes several types: factional, sectoral, and subversive. Factional and subversive opposition present no real conceptual problems, particularly if factional opposition can be said to be that directed against a dominant group or coalition. Much opposition in China, however, might have to fall under an expanded notion of sectoral opposition: opposition in which the actors seek to "maximize the values and promote the interests of their particular professional or institutional groups."[7] More generally, in this case we may construe opposition as the activity of interests working at cross purposes with other interests, without assuming that any specific set of interests dominates the system as a whole.

H. Gordon Skilling's categorization of opposition in communist systems overlaps Barghoorn's but puts more stress on the intensity of opposition:

> Integral opposition: opposition to the system as a whole.
>
> Factional opposition: opposition "carried on by individuals and groups within the highest organs of the Party of government, although support may be sought in broader social or political groupings."
>
> Fundamental opposition: "opposition to, or severe criticism of, a whole series of key policies of the regime, based upon crucial differences in standards of value, without, however, a rejection of the communist system itself."
>
> Specific opposition: opposition to "specific policies, without a rejection of the regime or its leaders, or its basic policies in general."[8]

This is useful as a general beginning framework—as a way of forming initial notions of the nature of opposition—although it breaks down once we look at the specifics of oppositional interests and movements in China. In practice, opposition is dynamic: integral may mellow into specific opposition (or disappear entirely), and frustrated specific opposition might grow into integral. A faction may sometimes seek fundamental change (which is to say, the categories may not be mutually exclusive). Sometimes what appears to the outside analyst as specific or fundamental opposition (or no opposition at all) may be treated by the regime as integral opposition (a demand, say, for the restoration of capitalism). Since opposition does in fact have to appear in the shape of agreement, it is difficult to say with certainty whether the regime is wrong in such an assessment.

Opposition, in sum, is a *dangerous* activity, and one that can take different forms. It involves more than simple disagreement with policies; it should include at least some sort of attempt to act on that disagreement—at least to the extent of making it known. Opposition is a political act, designed to change policies or power relationships. It also implies that there is something to oppose. A faction may act against those who dominate certain institutions or against policies accepted by other factions or groups, or interests may encroach upon the spheres of other interests. Moving beyond the elite, opposition is resistance (active or passive) to policies accepted by the bulk of the elite. Should politics become utterly chaotic, there would probably be no more point in speaking of opposition; instead we would have unstructured fights. Moves against the power positions of specific leaders constitute opposition when the moves are bound up with forms of policy or with ideological opposition, at least as a pretext. That is, this study is confined to instances of *principled* opposition, excluding personal hatreds and clashes of ambition which are merely that.[9]

THE CONFLICT APPROACH

Since this is a study of opposition, it is perhaps appropriate that it treat politics in terms of conflict. One may view society as a coherent system naturally tending toward stability (system maintenance); alternatively, one may postulate that "all units of social organization are continuously changing unless some force intervenes to arrest this change."[10] According to Ralf Dahrendorf, it is power which arrests change, and the struggle for power which brings it about:

> Power always implies non-power, and therefore resistance. The dialectic of power and resistance is the motive force of history. From the interests of those in power at a given time we can infer the interests of the powerless, and with them the direction of change. . . . Power produces conflict, and conflict between antagonistic interests gives lasting expression to the fundamental uncertainty of human existence, by ever giving rise to new solutions and ever casting doubt on these as soon as they take form.[11]

It is perhaps not necessary to take *conflict,* as Dahrendorf seems to, as an ontological statement of what politics is (or, for that matter, to agree that the interests of the powerless tell us anything whatsoever about the direction of change). Nor is the conflict approach used here as a model or even a theory in any rigorous sense. Rather, it is simply an orientation toward the study of Chinese politics, but one that should lead to the correction of the empirical and normative deficiencies of what have been in recent years more popular and respectable approaches to Chinese politics, particularly studies focusing upon Chinese political culture.[12] Functionalism, from which the focus on political culture is derived, is conventionally accused of having a conservative bias, and this is perhaps true regardless of the nature of the political system studied. Thus, we will be told in effect that the authoritarian nature of the political system in China somehow conforms to the culturally induced values and needs of the Chinese people (and therefore—the normative implication—what might be bad for us is fine for the Chinese; different strokes for different folks). This emphasis, as a general rule, would seem to ignore certain obvious realities.

> To maintain and transmit a value system human beings are punched, bullied, sent to jail, thrown into concentration camps, cajoled, bribed, made into heroes, encouraged to read newspapers, stood up against a wall and shot, and sometimes even taught sociology. To speak of cultural inertia is to overlook the concrete interests and privileges that are served by indoctrination, education, and the entire complicated process of transmitting culture from one generation to the next.[13]

A stress on conflict, then, should help to give a more realistic view of Chinese politics. The quotes from Barrington Moore (directly above) and Dahrendorf, as well as the general tone of the discussion so far, should make it clear that there are normative as well as empirical reasons for the stress on conflict. Fashions have changed in political science, and it is perhaps no longer necessary to apologize for displaying normative concerns.[14] It may be appropriate, however, to attempt to outline the normative view of politics that I think subtends this study, thus making explicit what would otherwise remain implicit.[15]

The point of this study is not to berate certain American academics nor, really, is it to criticize the current Chinese regimes. I hope, however, that it could serve in some way as a critique of totalitarianism. Crudely put, the basic point is that the political order by itself—bluntly, power—cannot provide a standard of right and wrong: the political order is itself subject to judgment according to standards not its own. This, of course, is banal enough, even archaic. It is a reflection of a political tradition that, according to Hannah Arendt, ended with Marx:

> The end came with Marx's declaration that philosophy and its truth are located not outside the affairs of men and their common world but precisely in them,

> and can be "realized" only in the sphere of living together, which he called "society," through the emergence of "socialized" men.[16]

If society sets the standards, there are no standards by which society can be judged. The totalitarian strain in contemporary political thought and action (a strain hardly confined to those countries having totalitarian regimes) denies any absolute standard independent of society—or the power of those who rule it. The problem here is not how values are generated, but, rather, how they are validated—and this is not a problem amenable to empirical investigation. But the denial of the existence of absolute standards seems to entail the denial of *any* noninstrumental judgment of value and, pragmatically, leaves us naked to the assaults of power. The liberal and traditional bromides against the growth of total power seem increasingly unconvincing, not in the sense that they lack merit, but in the literal sense that they no longer seem to carry much psychological conviction. The conflict approach—itself indifferent to any claim about absolute standards—may at least help to serve as a critique of the pretensions to total power.

The stress in this study is almost entirely upon this critical function of the conflict approach. It is possible, of course, to value conflict for its own sake; to do so may generate magnificent political theory.

> For good examples are the result of good education, and good education is due to good laws, and good laws in their turn spring from the very agitations which have been so inconsiderately condemned by many. For whosoever will carefully examine the results of these agitations will find they have neither caused exiles nor any violence prejudicial to the general good, and will be convinced even that they have given rise to laws that were to the advantage of public liberty. . . . every free state ought to afford the people the opportunity, so to say, for their ambition. . . .[17]

Dahrendorf gives a liberal statement of this Machiavellianism.

> Power produces conflict, and conflict between antagonistic interests gives lasting expression to the fundamental uncertainty of human existence, by ever giving rise to new solutions and ever casting doubt on them as soon as they take form. . . . Because we cannot recognize what is true and just, we need competition in science and politics, and competition thrives only if it is built into certain institutions.[18]

All of this is probably valid as far as it goes. But it seems clear that the conflict approach by itself cannot provide much valid positive normative political theory. If the current order cannot be said to be self-evidently just, neither can justice be automatically imputed to those opposed to it. If ambition is the motive for conflict, it is also a clear motive for seeking to eliminate conflict once one has the advantage, and in the absence of normative reasons not to do this, the only question is a prudential one (whether one can safely overturn the laws or institutions).[19] In any case, if might does not make right, it is hard to see why impotence should (as Dahrendorf, particularly, seems to imply). And, as Machiavelli was so fond of reiterating, once the fight is joined, it is resolved by strength, not by goodness.[20]

The dominant Chinese ideology since the Cultural Revolution has in fact been built upon a positive version of the conflict theory—the theory of continuous revolution under the dictatorship of the proletariat. The revolution is always developing. Each new stage embodies its own contradictions, and these give rise to struggle. We cannot view the process as a whole, and therefore, as far as we are concerned absolute truth, the sum total of innumerable truths, can never be known. Still, in the Chinese (and general Marxist) theory, it is somehow possible to speak of the laws of history.[21] The struggle follows a pattern:

> In the socialist era cow-devils and snake-spirits ceaselessly jump up to cause chaos, and the proletariat ceaselessly sweep them away. Great chaos under heaven leads to great order under heaven: this also is the law of development of class struggle.[22]

The Chinese approach to struggle is somewhat different from the Russian one, where opposition, "at least on the overt level," is concealed and depreciated.[23] In China the amount of real struggle may be exaggerated. Also, if Mao is to be believed, struggle will go on forever, even in the stage of communism:

> With the arrival of communism will there be no more struggle? I don't believe it. With the arrival of communism there will still be struggle between the old and the new, between the correct and mistaken. Tens of thousands of years hence mistakes will still be unsatisfactory and will be unable to stand.[24]

All of this can be construed in a liberal sense, but such a construction would be wrong.

It is difficult for any ruling group to base its claim to rule purely upon the purported fact of eternal struggle. While struggle is an important component of the Chinese ideology, this struggle is not, in Dahrendorf's terms, built into institutions. At the same time, however, the conflict is not unchanneled: it takes place under the "dictatorship" (that is, arbitrary class rule) of the "proletariat." This is a necessary part of the theory, since those who articulate it want not only the dynamism of struggle but also control over the struggle's outcome. Temporary concessions may be made to the bourgeoisie, but in the long run there is no coincidence of interests between them and the proletariat. In practice this seems a kind of pseudoconflict: the picture is not one of some spontaneous play of ideas and social forces, in either anarchic or institutionalized fashion, but rather, the arousing of opposition and the dictatorial crushing of that opposition—forever.

The critical use of the conflict approach allows us to view this sort of ideology from the underside, as it were, from the point of view of those on the receiving end. The ideology provides an absolute standard of rectitude for those who win, as long as they continue to win; and those who are defeated have nothing at all to appeal to. The dictatorship precludes any appeal to law; nor are there any universal moral criteria that, in theory, the victors feel they have to respect. As Chairman Mao teaches us, "In class society, there is only class nature; there is no human nature that transcends class."[25] The loser cannot appeal to any general human standard, but neither can he, in practice, appeal even to his own class standing. In contemporary Chinese thought class is a metaphorical concept (as, to a certain extent, it probably is in Marx). Where, for example, are there any operating landlords in China today? Class is not defined so much in terms of objective social criteria as by ideology: a proletarian is one who has proletarian thought.[26] There is a nice dialectical circle here: moral claims or criteria are interpreted as ideology; ideology is a reflection of class standing; and class standing, in its turn, is defined by ideology.

The purpose of this study, again, is not to provide any blanket condemnation of the current Chinese regime; in comparison with most Third World regimes its record, in most respects, positively shines. Nor, given the mores we operate under today, is it the business of a foreigner either to praise or to condemn the regime as such. A focus on Chinese unhappy with various aspects of the regime certainly implies no blanket endorsement of the criticisms they make. It *is* part of the purpose of this work, however, to provide some sort of critique of totalitarianism. In a totalitarian regime, unlike a liberal or a traditional regime, there are in principle no criteria accepted by those who hold power whereby those subject to this power may criticize or resist it. This problem is hardly confined to China—totalitarian modes of thought proliferate as a result of the "terrifying problems that face us in the world today,"[27] and the Chinese version of totalitarianism is hardly its least attractive form. In the face of totalitarianism a traditional critique would seem to become empty moralizing, while a liberal critique would be simply irrelevant (if the criterion for political action is the will of the people, what can be said about a regime able to create the will of the people to order?). The conflict approach provides some minimal leverage. It allows us to look at those who are unhappy and to spell out their case. History too often is victors' history—in China today, explicitly and systematically so. We may do well, then, to attempt a systematic survey of the interests and ideas of those who have lost.

2

Pictures of Chinese Politics

Facts notoriously do not speak for themselves, but require interpretation; and interpretation, in turn, must be tested against the facts. In the study of contemporary China it is extremely difficult to form a coherent interpretation of events, since the facts and their relationships often seem to change from month to month, even from day to day.[1] But in order to make sense of these rapid, apparent changes, some sort of general interpretation whereby they may be explained is necessary.[2] As might have been gathered from the previous chapter, the interpretation used here is partly based upon the totalitarian model,[3] although the concept here is used to refer to a manner of thinking rather than as a strict explanatory model. Although the concept is no longer as popular as it once was, the political and moral problems raised by totalitarianism remain; and the concept is also helpful in giving insight into the particular problem of opposition and dissent in China. This chapter attempts to sketch an outline of totalitarianism as a manner of thinking, to show the relevance of that manner of thinking as a guide to the conduct of politics in China, and to show how the totalitarian manner of thinking fits in with the particular structure and process of politics in China.

THE CONCEPT OF TOTALITARIANISM

Totalitarian is often taken as a term describing a type of regime and is approached through an attempt to determine its essence (for example, the use of terror, the presence of a leader, rule by a single party, legitimization through a specific ideology, and the like) or to abstract the common characteristics of, say, Hitler's Germany, Mussolini's Italy, and Stalin's Russia. The concept is perhaps somewhat tainted by its use in a system of counter-ideology during the early period of the cold war, and it has been attacked as vague, subject to multiple definitions, unable to discriminate among distinct phenomena, and often simply not descriptive of what goes on in the systems labeled totalitarian.[4]

The abstract concept itself is probably inadequate as a description of any particular regime. For example, if fascism is not a totalitarian ideology, then nothing is—if only because it was under Mussolini's approving aegis that the term *totalitarian* was coined. But there seems to be near-universal agreement that Fascist Italy was not a totalitarian system. Even in Germany, Hitler did not gain full control over the army or the churches, and some journals were for a time able to maintain a certain editorial independence.[5] All writers on totalitarianism seem to admit the presence of factions in totalitarian regimes, but if totalitarianism is taken as a descriptive model it is hard to see how such things could be.

The term, then, is misleading if taken as a descriptive one. But much of the writing on totalitarianism is not written in a positivist vein, and it is perhaps obtuse to treat it as if it were. Hannah Arendt, for example, is criticized for allowing moral criticism to supersede her analysis of totalitarianism.[6] But moral criticism (joined with an analysis of some aspects of those regimes that adopt the philosophy she deplores) is precisely the point she is trying to make. Theories of totalitarianism seem based upon a view of the nature of politics that has normative as well as empirical consequences. In an analogical fashion, it is perhaps useful to see totalitarianism itself as a normative political position, although most who share it would (now) probably prefer to call it by some other name. A totalitarian regime would then be one dominated by persons who have a totalitarian view of politics and who are determined to carry out their program. Germany, Italy, Russia, and China, in their totalitarian phases, are no doubt very different from each other; but there are similarities (not identities) in the thought styles of their ruling groups. It would be surprising if these opinions of the rulers have no concrete consequences whatsoever, but what these consequences are is a matter for empirical inquiry—and in conducting the inquiry, there is no need to assume beforehand that the opinions of the rulers or of anyone else determine everything that happens.

Among those who admit the legitimacy of the concept totalitarianism there seems to be general agreement that the totalitarian style of thought is largely a modern one, or at least that the self-conscious attempt to carry out a totalitarian program is a modern endeavor.[7] In part this is because only in modern times do rulers have the technological capacity even to think of attempting programs of total control, but it is also possible to see totalitarianism as one possible reaction to the problems resulting from modernization itself. David Apter says, "Reason applied to human affairs is the foundation of modernity." Partly because of technological developments, but also contributing to those developments, new ways of life open up and old ways and values lose their persuasiveness. "All around us new moral communities are being established, and the context of moral fulfillment is modernization."[8] This would seem to be deficient as a moral theory, since if morality is defined in terms of modernization, the process of modernization is itself apparently beyond moral judgment. Nevertheless, in its somewhat vague way, Apter's statement may be a good empirical description of the moral problem of communities caught up in the process of modernization.

"Rationality," of course, implies the ability to choose, and "self-conscious concern with choice has led to an attitude of experiment and invention that has changed man's entire outlook. Nature became controllable. Human affairs could be seen as ultimately explicable."[9] But this would seem to imply that our attitude toward modernization is founded on a delusion, since if reason in this sense teaches us anything at all, it is that reason in this sense does not provide ultimate explanations. In an ultimate sense, human affairs are probably no more explicable than nature is brought under control. It may, of course, be possible to acquire the physical means to make human affairs fit an explicable pattern, but in this case it is misleading to speak of self-conscious choice, at least for the bulk of humanity.

The problem is, different people will want different things: "Men will, in principle, see more than one alternative as plausible."[10] This implies that modernization will intensify *conflict* rather than moral community. The premise of modernization as described by Apter would seem to be that modern man is able to control his own destiny. But given the increase in disagreement, plus the feeling that matters can be brought under control, there will be a tendency for disparate groups or persons to try to bring about control through political means, particularly as the older methods of conflict resolution become obsolete. This means politicization: "Most discontents in the modern world are not political, but politicized."[11] Politicization is a product of conflict and leads to more conflict; and the greater the amount of conflict, the less control anyone has over anything.

The last phrase is tautologous, but the implications of this triviality are sometimes not followed through. The totalitarian mode of thought seems to be a way of avoiding some of the antinomies that arise from social, technological, and intellectual change. Thus, what are originally taken as descriptive theories may be translated into visions:

> For all the vast multi-lingual literature on Marxism, I have not found Marx's specific ideas on the economy or on politics useful for understanding contemporary political economy. Yet I find myself again and again drawn to the Marxian vision which still captures the minds of millions of people. . . . The secret of Marxism's resilience is what Marx thought it was: a vision or theory grounded in human reason and not divine revelation that teaches there is moral purpose and inevitability to history.[12]

The theory is gutted of concrete content and turned into a vision, the vision in turn being equated with reason. If there is inevitability to history, reason cannot disclose it. God is shown the door, but moral purpose (which is sometimes equated with inevitability, although perhaps not here) now is derived from history. But part of the basis for this vision is the idea that morality is an epiphenomenon of history, a reflection of changing group interests . . . We begin to move into the dialectic.

If a theory is a product of social action—an idea espoused by modern schools other than Marxism—then it changes with the social conditions. But if action is to be grounded in theory (reason), then something must be unchanging. This something is provided by the theory translated into vision, the vision providing "that restless sense of purpose [which] motivates all revolutionary movements." The vision allows revolutionaries to avoid "false consciousness," to distinguish "what is from what ought to be."[13] The theory arises out of action and provides a guide to action, its *ought* reflecting a future *is*. Theory is tested in practice and thus changes with practice—and the change is not random but directed toward a (more or less) set ought. Moving beyond pragmatism, this ought is not, and cannot be, subject to correction by practice. As it graduates to vision, theory changes from a purported description of reality to a program to make reality accord with itself. Reason has been displaced by will. The authoritarian imposition of a vision may not in itself be totalitarian. What *is* totalitarian is the ability to use this vision arbitrarily. Since the vision is allegedly based on objective theory, those who rule may claim that whatever they do is objectively furthering the realization of the vision; and since the theory cannot be tested against reality, the rulers are subject to no constraints other than prudential ones.

The totalitarian mode of thought, then, is arbitrary. An analysis of what we are becomes translated into a program to make us just that. The will to create a society fit for men to live in becomes an attempt to create men fit to live in whatever society is in fact produced: "The problem is to design a world which will be liked not by people as they now are, but by those who live in it."[14] This means, in effect, that what we in fact value (much less what we ought to value) is irrelevant to the construction of the new society—after all, it is a society for new men. Insofar as totalitarian thought conceives of human beings as artifacts of other human beings, it is dehumanizing and its application an "assault on the very nature of man."[15]

REVOLUTIONARY SOCIETY

The totalitarian mode of thought is not confined to exotic peoples, to faraway places with strange-sounding names. Elements of totalitarian thought are accepted in democratic societies[16] and, given the increased ability of some people to control the behavior of other people, there may even be a secular trend toward totalitarianism. In the industrialized countries such totalitarianism would probably not be revolutionary and would thus be different from the Chinese variety. The Chinese variety of totalitarianism, however, does have an increasing share of admirers in other countries, although most of those admirers would probably not like the exact sort of thing done at home. The Chinese system seems to have an appeal to certain apparently good-hearted but unreflective rulers (President Nyerere, President Ford, and President Marcos and his Lady) who see colleagues apparently able to do much good work for subjects who are both enthusiastic and docile. The system also has an appeal to some whose general benevolence is combined with a lack of empathy and political sagacity, as with one Jesuit visitor:

> As I watched the people rising and retiring early, enjoying their few simple pleasures, relying on one another for help and encouragement, convincing each other of goals and means, living an ascetical life in the Spartan society cut off from the rest of the world, I could not help but think of the new China as a huge Jesuit novitiate of the 1930's where the people, like Jesuit novices, worked diligently, intently, and sometimes awkwardly, at developing their virtues.[17]

This is touching enough, although, since reference to the supposed ends of the two situations is omitted, one catches the surprising implication that a Jesuit sees no distinction between Chairman Mao, or even the liberation of mankind, and God. This also seems to be a manifestation of the American—perhaps general Western—inability to see Chinese as human beings in their own right.[18] Not all people choose to become Jesuits, and Jesuits do not remain novices their whole lives. A way appropriate for a self-selected group (and, for the Jesuits, for a limited period of time) is a questionable image of the good society, and the attempt to apply this model to society as a whole has unappetizing consequences.

The sentiment expressed in the quoted paragraph—combined with a reaction against the simplicities of the cold war, a distaste for the American adventure in Asia, and sympathy for the wretched of the earth—can be developed into a more systematic affirmation of the current Chinese regime and its works. A case can be made, for example, that the Maoist stress on restricted consumption, a communitarian ethic, and egalitarian distribution, while a far cry from what utopians of an earlier age looked forward to, represents, given the realities of the world, the best hope for human well-being.[19] Part of this affirmation may involve the contention that the Chinese system is democratic, not in the Western sense, but in a more basic sense. The Chinese system is in fact what the people's democracies of Europe pretend to be. It is a revolutionary system in which the people have stood up; it is a nonelitist system in which the leadership represents the interests of (the great majority of) the people. The leadership is not only accepted by the people but is subject to popular control as well. This model deserves examination because it is a friendly version of the old totalitarian model; and if it is empirically and normatively valid, it would imply that the subject of this study—opposition—is not worthy of consideration, thus refuting virtually all of the commonplaces generally held about politics.

The basic concept of the revolutionary society model is the mass line. The line and direction, as the Chinese put it, is "from the masses, to the masses." The party discovers the needs and desires of the masses, systematizes them, converts them into policy, and leads the masses to their attainment, consulting with the masses over the means of implementation. The mass line was developed by the party in its years before coming to power, and its evolution is described by Mark Selden in his excellent study of the Yenan period.

> The mass line emphasis on forging close links between leadership and the people represents a synthesis of major insights drawn from guerrilla experience. The claim to leadership in a people's war rests on responsiveness to popular needs and aspirations which are learned through constant contact with the people. In the final years of the resistance these principles were applied to the development and transformation of Chinese society.[20]

This, however, is perhaps more complicated when examined than when stated. Some sorts of Marxist theory may imply that the needs, if not the aspirations, of everyone who counts are the same; but this implication is probably wrong. Also, and here Marxists are almost certainly correct, needs and aspirations are subject to change. But the Marxist practitioner has his vision of what these changes should be. From Selden's work it is clear that changes in policy mainly followed the convenience of the party (e.g., what would be the more advantageous policy, given the current relationship with the Kuomintang) rather than the felt desire of the population ruled by the party.[21] The function of the mass line seems to have been to cause a "feeling on the part of the masses that they were involved in revolutionary social change," rather than to cause them actually to participate in the formulation of policy.[22] The role of the party is not simply to summarize and reflect popular needs and aspirations but also to determine what they should be and to shape actual needs and aspirations to this ideal pattern. The mass line, like what Selden calls the bureaucratic method (allegedly favored in the Soviet Union), is a technique of control, and its superiority over the bureaucratic method is in its effectiveness, not its democracy per se. If the mass line functions as a technique of control, we must admit the possibility of a conflict of interests between the controllers and the controlled. It is even plausible to argue that this divergence of interests is wider today, when the party has the power to attempt to implement its vision, than in its old days as an opposition group, when it had an interest in articulating and redressing widely felt grievances and demands.[23]

Mass-line democracy, unlike liberal democracy, is often held to be nonelitist, although one might think that any group which refers to fellow human beings as masses shows itself by that fact to consider itself an elite. *Elitist,* of course, has different meanings. In China, cadres are supposed to lead simple lives, not be arrogant, not demand special privileges, persuade rather than boss, and in general share the daily lives of the masses. To varying degrees at varying times, some cadres do no doubt live up to this ideal. That a ruling group lives a Spartan life is in itself, of course, no guarantee of its democratic sentiments—as the Spartan case demonstrates; but in China there is a genuine commitment to the goal of producing, over the long run, an egalitarian society through the elimination of economic distinctions among the different sectors of society. But to produce economic equality would seem to require great inequalities of power; and in fact, since power is a relational concept, it probably does not make sense to speak of equal power in the way we can speak of equal wealth. If everyone has equal power over the same set of issues, this is tantamount to saying no one has any power. To produce radical change requires a great degree of power and perhaps also the concentration of that power in a disciplined group. Radicalism in itself may or may not be always totalitarian, but it would seem always to be elitist.[24]

This elitism is seen in the ways in which the Chinese rulers approach the problem of producing social change. There is, for example, in Chinese Marxism the concept of the malleability of man.[25] Whatever its metaphysical validity, this cannot have egalitarian implications when used as a guide to policy. The metaphor implies that all persons *can* become the same; but the image is of one man hammering another into shape, the desires of the latter being, by hypothesis, a matter of indifference (he may or may not want to undergo the process, but the idea is that in the end he will be glad he did). Since some may find this prospect unpleasant, there is again potential for conflict.

Richard Pfeffer has tried to reconcile the elitism inherent in a radical program with the democratic implications of the mass line, basing his argument on the concept of needs. This does not, of course, refute the contention of elitism but shows that it does not matter, since it cannot be avoided. ''If social scientists accepted the necessity for a revolutionary vanguard, they would have to accept severe restrictions on democratic control.'' ''Necessity impelled the Chinese leadership in the 1940's and the 1950's and impels the Maoist leadership today.''[26] There is an ''essential necessity'' for institutions that convince the people they are being ''served'' by in fact serving them.[27]

The emphasis on needs is probably heretical from a radical Maoist point of view, which sometimes stresses the ability of subjective factors to shape circumstances; and it is apolitical, since politics implies that there is at least some choice. This, however, does not mean the emphasis is misplaced. Nonetheless, the argument from necessity remains difficult to evaluate. If all things move according to some iron necessity, we cannot determine this by empirical means. From a normative point of view, an emphasis on postulated human needs may be one way of moving beyond the aridities of positivism, positivism perhaps being fine for determining the efficient causes of political actions but limiting insight into what is really important.[28]

The trouble is, however, that *need* is often simply a fancy synonym for *want*. It is more impressive if we can say we need something, rather than merely want it. But the two words imply different things. Our wants may be unrestricted, but our needs are always relative to some goal. We *need* food if our goal is to survive, but we do not need to survive—we merely *want* to. Pfeffer, however, seems to postulate a free-floating need for revolution. The question then becomes: Whose need? Obviously, not that of those killed in the revolution or, if the term is to retain any content, those who believe on balance that they have suffered from it. Perhaps revolution is a need of the poor, but it is not self-evident that their needs could not have been served in other ways. It seems most sensible to say that the Maoist leadership *wants* revolution and feels it *needs* to do certain things to get it. Since others may want something else, conflict is possible.

Pfeffer points to a certain circularity in his argument: revolution is to serve the people, but it is necessary to persuade the people that they are being served. He argues that the interaction between elite and mass through the mass line means the circle is not vicious—that there is mutual adjustment. In response to the question whether the masses can reject Maoist policies, Pfeffer answers, "Yes in practice, but no in theory."[29] The rejection in theory is impossible because as far as the leadership is concerned, the interests of the masses are *defined* in terms of Maoist policies. But it is possible that the institutions for mass consultation that Pfeffer describes may evolve to the point where they are able effectively to formulate and enforce policies reflecting the spontaneously felt interests of segments of the local populations. The policies that might come about this way would probably not be very Maoist, on the whole. As the system becomes less elitist, it would also become less radical, reflecting more the existing structures of interests.

James Chieh Hsiung has performed the useful exercise of attempting to formulate systematically the logic of the revolutionary society approach. Hsiung more or less patterns his discussion after Anthony Downs's economic theory of democracy, but he argues that, unlike the system described by Downs, the Maoist system puts no constraint on the achievement of a Pareto optimum, or at least "optimality." China has a "command economy" and thus need not worry about conflicts of interests. Also, the Maoists assume the "corrigibility of men in an edifying social environment," and the way the system is structured allows them to build this environment. The Chinese political problem is simply the "enforcement of social rationality promoted by the Party." The central planners make decisions unencumbered by the need to placate private interests, the decisions being made "in accordance with the goals found in the system's prevailing norms." These norms, in turn, are set by the central authority—the party or the chairman of its Central Committee. The party does, however, lack perfect information and therefore engages in "constant dialogues with the masses.'' Also Mao, unlike Stalin, likes the masses and ''turns against the Party operatives when the latter's excessive power stands in the way of the masses' productive zeal or of achieving optimality.''[30]

This analysis displays in rather naked form the circularity characteristic of totalitarian thought. Rationality is taken to mean ''in accordance with the norms of the system,'' and the party sets those norms. The use of the party's norms as the standards of rationality isolates those standards from any rational criticism and also prevents a rational evaluation of the rather frequent changes in the norms. Those who might be unhappy with the party can have no rational foundations for this attitude. Thus, the general good may require particular sacrifice, so ''dissent or even opposition from those individuals or groups called upon to make sacrifices ceases to be a meaningful indicator of the falsity or non-success of the policy itself.''[31]

We might quarrel with Hsiung's use of the term *Pareto optimum* (a ''situation in which it is not possible to increase the utility of anybody without decreasing someone else's utility'').[32] The Maoists do not claim to aim at anything like a Pareto optimum (they favor the interests of the laboring people over the class enemy); Hsiung's Maoism requires sacrifice, whereas the Pareto optimum does not; and Hsiung speaks of a Pareto optimum independent of any convergence of individual preferences. This criticism, however, is probably an ''unfair and unwarranted definitional game.'' After all, one may specify that one will call the offspring of a cat ''puppies,'' and only the inattentive are likely to be misled. It would be preferable to focus instead on Hsiung's weaker definition of optimality: ''the achievement of such goals as the equitable distribution of costs and benefits of collective goods.''[33]

It is hard to break away from the circularity of the argument, since it is the circle that furnishes the definition of the key term *equitable*. But if any leeway at all be allowed, it is not clear that the Maoist polity has any decisive advantage over Downsian democracy in achieving equity. A democracy, according to Downs, will not achieve a Pareto optimum if the government is somehow able to benefit a majority more than it would be benefited under optimal conditions; the government, in search of votes, will choose to gouge a minority in order to benefit a majority. If the government stupidly decides to seek an optimum anyway, it will be overthrown in the next election by the opposition, which will have made its pitch to a majority not as well off as it could possibly have been.[34] The elegance (and satirical force) of Downs's argument derives from his assumption that politicians are interested in power, not programs; and I think an examination of Hsiung's model shows that the criterion there is also power, not any optimality.

Since the central planner both decides rationally—according to his norms—and determines what constitutes rationality, his main problem is to insure that he continue to be in a position to set the norms. Hsiung speaks of collective rationality, but his analysis remains in a utilitarian framework, although it is a somewhat curious kind of utilitarianism. If the collective rationality means nothing but the will of the party, it is a redundant concept. If it is to mean anything else, within a utilitarian framework the contention of James S. Coleman is probably right: "The utility of the collectivity is a meaningless quantity."[35] In spite of his postulation of the people as an entity somehow transcending persons, Hsiung still forms his argument in terms of personal advantages: for example, given the rewards for accepting the party's norms and the sanctions against appearing to behave in a self-seeking way, the rational, selfish, greedy economic man will have a strong incentive to behave altruistically.[36] Hsiung's position would seem to be that of the Legalists, which is a kind of inverted utilitarianism. Both Legalism and utilitarianism are atomistically individualistic in their anthropology. Both assume we are self-regarding, that we feel our own pleasures and pains; and both assume there is no moral order beyond pleasure and pain, broadly defined. The utilitarian wants to make a society in which individuals are able to achieve the greatest possible pleasure consistent with the pleasure of other individuals. For the Legalists, individual pleasures and pains, through the manipulation of reward and punishment by the ruler, are brought into harmony with the public interest (*kung*), the public good being defined, not in terms of private desires, but in terms of the power interests of the ruler—the continuation of his ability to stipulate rewards and punishments.[37] The Legalists would agree with Coleman's solution to the problem of collective decisions: power becomes the scale for the interpersonal comparison of utilities. "An actor can fully control an action only if he has total power greater than the value of the action and is willing to employ all his resources toward gaining control of it."[38] The amount of resources one is willing to put into the exercise of power is a measure of the utility of the result. The Communist Party of China (CPC) certainly desires control, and the mass line can be seen as a technique for acquiring it. Notions of optimality and rationality are redundant, being amply covered by the will of the party. This does not imply, of course, that those who run the party in China are indifferent to whether anyone benefits from their rule; rather, it simply means that the concepts of optimality and rationality have no function in Hsiung's model.

The analyses of the revolutionary society school do certainly show the irrelevance of Western models applied to China and also give insight into the goals desired by the Chinese elite (although it is unlikely that any Chinese communist would feel completely comfortable with the sympathetic Western reconstructions of his position). The approach has certain deficiencies, however. It is probably not really meaningless to speak of collective interests apart from individual interests, but this can only be done in terms of an ethical theory. What is equitable, for example, is not a question of fact in the same way that Mao Tse-tung's year of birth is a question of fact. Hsiung has "eschewed ethical questions''[39] and in the process begs the real question. His analysis, through its attempt at formalization, shows clearly what seems to be implicit in other interpretations of Chinese politics in terms of the mass line. It becomes an affirmation of the contention beloved of rulers ancient and modern, Chinese and foreign, that what is good for them is good for everyone and that those for whom it is not good do not count. One need not be a Marxist to find some truth in statements about exploitation and false consciousness, nor need one adhere to liberal utilitarianism to see that the questions that school attempted to answer are being begged, as if they had never been raised.

The critique of the revolutionary society models, of course, implies no positive (or negative) assertions about Chinese politics itself. That an argument which purports to show that a certain country is the People's Republic of Paradise turns out to be invalid does not imply that the country is a living hell for the ordinary man. The point, rather, is that interpretations of Chinese politics that fail to take into account the possibility of divergence of interests between rulers and ruled, or among the rulers, are flawed, and thus the exploration of the possibility of conflict remains a legitimate enterprise.

RADICAL POPULISM

The revolutionary society model does remind us that we are dealing with a revolutionary situation, that things have changed in China, and that a new social order has not been fully consolidated. It also sets out a perhaps romanticized view of the ideology of the rulers of that society. It is possible to take a somewhat more cold-hearted view of that ideology.

A. James Gregor has developed an interesting and controversial argument: ''Where classical Marxism can provide only a tortured and implausible rationale for the totalitarianism of Stalinism, Maoism, or Castroism, the logic of the Fascist argument is its straight-forward justification.''[40] This seems a return to the ''unitotalitarian''[41] view more common twenty years ago than now: ''Both fascism and the variants of Marxism that today receive so much attention constitute species of a single genus: totalitarianism.''[42] Gregor's approach does, I think, help explain much that we would consider bizarre in contemporary radicalism, were we not so used to it, and also helps place the Chinese experience in comparative and historical perspective. While, like all Marxist-Leninists, the Chinese communists dislike revisionism, also like all Marxist-Leninists they favor creative developments; and creative developments in Marxism are necessary mainly where Marx was wrong. Thus, the nation has continued to be a more potent political entity than the class, and the proletariat does not seem to develop spontaneous revolutionary consciousness.[43] Successful Marxists have adjusted to this; but Gregor argues that the Marxist categories hide the implications of these creative developments, whereas the same implications are spelled out in fascist thinking, particularly that of Mussolini and his friends. Much contemporary radicalism, then, can be described as generic fascism. No contemporary radical, of course, would accept that label, and while Gregor advocates that *fascist* be used in a value-free way, the term is now about as value-free as the term *sodomite*. *Radical populism* is perhaps a less offensive label for the phenomenon.

It is simple enough to find similarities between Chinese communism and fascistlike movements elsewhere.[44] Gregor claims that the more important twentieth-century radicals "all acknowledge an indebtedness to a non-Marxist source or sources for the principal constituents of the world-view they ultimately espoused."[45] Mao would seem to be no exception.[46] It is common to hear that fascism stresses *will* while Marxism stresses *reason*, and this is true in a way (although it would seem that for Marx, reason ultimately is the will of the proletariat). But there is a strong voluntaristic strain in Chinese communism,[47] as there is, in a different way, in Stalinism. Nationalism has been identified as a trait of Chinese communism,[48] as has populism—the conception of the people as a "more or less single entity with collectivist social aspirations."[49] This populism allegedly entails hostility to urban values and to bureaucracy,[50] which the more conventional fascists also professed to detest; and, as in more conventional fascism, this populism is not incompatible with elitism.[51] Mao was perhaps not as given as Mussolini to uttering statements contemptuous of ordinary people (it has never really been characteristic of any Chinese elite to regard their fellow men as rabble), but Mao's statement of how "poor and blank" the Chinese people are can be construed as Gregor does: "The Chinese people provide the material out of which the artist builds his masterpiece. . . . Mussolini was fond of the same metaphor."[52] Other attributes of Maoism also seem similar to what is usually called fascism: the cult of the leader, the stress on struggle, the emphasis on spirit and sacrifice, and the occasional glorification of violence.

As noted above, a problem with this line of argument is that *fascism* is too much a term of abuse. But if similarities are seen to exist between what is usually considered fascism and a certain style of thought and action in the People's Republic, and if we fail to see in the People's Republic the radical evil we usually associate with fascism, this might lead us to reevaluate fascism. Gregor notes: "Fascist statements have never been analyzed as such. They are always 'interpreted.' Fascists are never understood to mean what they say. . . ." But there is a more serious problem with this line of analysis. "Fascist regimes, as they have been traditionally identified, have always represented the union of the *fascist movement* with *non-fascist allies*."[53] This means, however, that Gregor's analysis of fascism, like the totalitarian model and the revolutionary society model, cannot provide an adequate description. The concept of generic fascism is useful as a reconstruction of at least part of the ideology of the Chinese regime. It helps us to understand the way elements of the Chinese elite might look at politics and provides a comparative context for understanding the Chinese ideology (and perhaps even the Western theories of revolutionary society). We may also understand from the analysis part of the context in which conflict must take place and some of the things the oppositionists might object to. Yet it remains insufficient simply to look at the ideology; we must also try to get a general picture of the actual political process.

CHINESE POLITICS

It is perhaps possible to find, at least at a very general level, structural regularities in most political behavior,[54] and totalitarian politics no doubt has much in common with other sorts of politics. On a narrower basis, it is possible to identify recurring patterns in communist politics.[55] As this study assumes, politics involves politics: the play of opinions, interests, ambition. An ideology may help determine the rules, but it does not eliminate the game.

The simplest approach to Chinese politics in the decades following 1949, and the approach that would allow the easiest deductions from ideology to practice, is to take what has been called the ''Mao in command'' model.[56] In this view, Chinese politics of the period is largely explained as a reflection of the wishes of Chairman Mao. This has a certain plausibility, since many policies adopted are specifically attributed to him, and I do not think that any policy, at the time it was in effect and not under attack, was explicitly said to have been against the Chairman's wishes. On a deeper level, a study of the data available reveals that many of the major policy initiatives in the People's Republic had been undertaken by Mao himself or, what at one time may have amounted to the same thing, by his erstwhile private secretary, Ch'en Po-ta.[57] A stress on Mao's role can be justified on theoretical as well as practical grounds. Robert Tucker argues that the evidence shows that dictators such as Lenin, Stalin, Mussolini, and Hitler did in fact have control over the movements they led and that the differences among these movements can be explained in large part by the different personalities of these leaders. Leonard Schapiro says the ''totalitarian regime is essentially a leadership regime,'' with the leader always jealous of any person or organization that might challenge his supremacy.[58] This might help explain Mao's hostility to elitism and bureaucracy, his sometimes cavalier treatment of the prime Leninist instrument, the party, and even whole policy movements such as the Cultural Revolution.

The stress on the person of Mao alone, however, fails to account for some apparent facts. Mao complained at times that he had been ignored, that his wishes did not prevail. One can identify, in retrospect, periods in which Mao or other leaders were apparently deadlocked. Mao's name has been used to justify many different policies, including, in the early 1970s, attempts to tone down the cult of the individual that had grown up around him. Mao was often able to implement policies associated with his name only by acting in concert with others, such as Lin Piao. This implies that our picture of Chinese politics must at least allow for interests other than Mao's. A focus on other interests will also help explain policy shifts. Mao may have had a radical vision, but this vision was not always translated into action; and the imputation of radicalism to Mao is often just that—an imputation. It is possible that he changed his mind, of course, but a focus on Mao alone may lead us to ignore what caused him to change his mind. Also, Mao was often unable (and perhaps in some cases unwilling) to eliminate his old colleagues the way Stalin did, and those Mao did eliminate (at least before the second fall of Teng Hsiao-p'ing) were overthrown by a rather heterogeneous coalition. It would seem plausible to hold that Mao did not dominate his movement in precisely the same way that Stalin, say, did his.

Andrew Nathan, a critic of the "Mao in command" approach, prefers to view Chinese politics in terms of a factionalism model. Nathan's abstract model of factional politics helps explain much of the available data on Chinese politics but also has gaps. It explains, for example, the apparent irrelevance of ideological considerations in elite alignments during the Cultural Revolution.[59] It is not clear, however, that all relevant groups in Chinese politics fit Nathan's rather rigorous anthropological description of factions. His construct may be too sophisticated for the data. It is hard to speak of factions without some reliable way of specifying what they are. Nathan generates fifteen propositions descriptive of factional politics in general. But if some of these fail to apply to the Chinese situation it is hard to say whether (1) Nathan is wrong (i.e., factional politics are not as Nathan says they are), or (2) Chinese politics is not factional in Nathan's sense. If the model is taken most rigorously as a description of the laws that Chinese politics follows, then if the postulated rules can be unilaterally violated by a participant, it would seem that the theory implied by the model is falsified. For example, according to Nathan, in a factional system the factions do not try to eliminate each other—this sets a dangerous precedent, and what you do to others may be done to you. But in the early 1960s, he says, Mao acted to eliminate some of the factions.[60] Nathan's theory, then, as applied to China, is wrong. One obvious weakness is that, while correctly showing the irrelevance of ideology to concrete political alliances, it fails to accord any function at all to ideology in that highly ideological system. This does not mean, however, that we must reject the genuine insights of this theory. It seems clear that something like the factionalism model is required to reflect the complexities of Chinese politics, and the sort of reasoning behind the model allows for full considerations of individual interests and ambitions—matters neglected in a focus on Mao alone. Nathan postulates a factional balance of power in China, limiting the scope of conflict and leading to a kind of immobility in the system.[61] While this view is accurate for long periods, factions do from time to time eliminate each other, which is not what the model predicts. It must therefore be reformulated.

A model of the Chinese political process during the period this study treats should embody the insights of the factionalism model, at the same time allowing for the special role of Mao and the importance of totalitarian ideology. We might recall here Gregor's comment that the fascist movements of the 1930s did not become expressed in pristine fascist regimes. Even if we agree that communist politics to a certain extent follows the fascist pattern, we will obviously not find pure fascism in the communist movements either. Robert Tucker makes a distinction between fascist movements dominated by a leader (these include the Soviet Union under Stalin) and the Leninist or Bolshevik movements in which the party is the dominant force.[62] The totalitarian model predicts that the tendency is for a Leninist party to evolve into a leadership party, but we would also expect some—for example, party bureaucrats—to resist this tendency. For a long period—from the early 1940s up to the Cultural Revolution—the CPC was a kind of hybrid, enjoying both a strong party organization and a charismatic leader. This gives rise to what Marxists might call a contradiction, since the interests of those who occupy top positions in the party organization will tend to differ from those of the leader, especially once the movement comes to power.

It is useful in a way to see Chinese politics in the context of what the Maoists call the two lines.[63] Ideologically, the first line stresses revolution, and the second line stresses consolidation; institutionally, the first line is associated with the leader, and the second line with the established bureaucracies. In the terms used above, the first line is fascist, the second Bolshevik. Most of the dualities that crop up in Chinese communist discourse can be fit into the two lines: red and expert, democracy and centralism, truth and discipline, the Thought of Mao and Marxism-Leninism; (on the bad side) dogmatism and revisionism, commandism and tailism, (most generally) left and right. Since it is expedient to give these lines names, *radical* and *moderate* will do. The two lines represent tendencies.[64] They should not necessarily be associated with specific factions, since factions may take different positions at different times and factional alliances may cut across the tendencies. Nor should they even be associated with individuals—Mao, for example, took a moderate line at times, although in the recent past it had usually been in his interest (and perhaps his conviction) to associate himself primarily with the radical tendency. These tendencies define the way in which the political debate in China is carried on, at least among the elite. The coexistence of the two tendencies is explained by the presence of both a great leader and strong institutions, particularly the party.

The actual political struggle takes place in a context defined by these tendencies but does not reflect the tendencies exactly. It is convenient here to look at the lineup of forces in the Cultural Revolution, discounting the Red

Guard groups. On the losing side (initially) are the top men in the full-time party organization, particularly at the Center, allied with dissident members of the People's Liberation Army (PLA). On the winning side we find the leader, his personal entourage (his secretary, his wife, the younger party functionaries affiliated with them), the top leadership of the PLA and the state bureaucracy, and members of the party bureaucracy from the South-Central Region. This alignment suggests we might look for institutional differences of interest as well as possible "clientelistic" ties based on personal relations—while not omitting the presence of conflict within institutions.

In Nathan's system "politicians . . . compete in expressions of fealty to the constitution or leader and rationalize every action and every position in terms of their fealty to it or him."[65] In China the relevant object was the leader, but this generalization was not always strictly true. Here we must bring in again the role of ideology. It is obviously possible for a totalitarian movement to take a supreme leader as its symbol of legitimacy, but this is difficult to justify in Leninist terms. A Leninist revolution is seen as the collective action of the proletariat, with the party as its self-conscious vanguard. In pre-1966 China there were two possible sources of legitimacy: the leader and the proletarian party.

The ideology also generates certain expectations of dynamism and change among those who adhere to it, and dynamism is perhaps better supplied by a leader than by a bureaucracy.[66] The party, of course, is a bureaucracy and over time comes to act as bureaucracies do, with its own routines and its own interests to protect. This tendency was intensified in China after 1958, when the party became, in addition to a policy-making and control organization, increasingly involved in the day-to-day work of government and economic administration. The party machine at the central and provincial levels lost much of its taste for radical social experimentation (the 1958–60 experiment, of course, doing little to enhance this taste). Given the presence of the radical trend, this put the party machine in a vulnerable position. At the same time, however, large organizations with their routines are required for rule. The *typical* pattern of Chinese politics since 1958 has been for the moderate tendency to dictate what is actually done, while the theory is provided by the radical trend.

Here we may look at concrete interests as well as ideology, drawing on insights of the totalitarian model. The bureaucratized party cramps the leader's style, and its vested interests reduce his scope of control. The party bosses do not seem to have considered purging Mao, but in the early 1960s there were not-too-delicate hints that he should retire. From the leader's point of view, if government is reduced to bureaucratic routine, leadership becomes superfluous. It is, then, in the leader's interest to attack the party for its conservatism—or, more generally, to maintain the radical tendency. To overcome the party (in the specific case of China, anyway), the leader requires allies. Since he is not the only one opposed to complete party control (i.e., control by the party bureaucracy, not party members), he can find such allies. The totalitarian party tends to be expansionist and to encroach upon the interests of other bureaucracies (grossly, the state and the army). These, given the ideological background, are not in themselves alternative sources of legitimacy—which means that they are no threat to the leader and, without the leader, no threat to the party. They do, however, have interests to which the leader must concede. Since the bureaucratized party will tend to embody the moderate tendency, it will be attacked on radical grounds. But those who do the attacking constitute a heterogeneous coalition, the long-term interests of all its members not necessarily being expressed by the radical tendency. The policy (as opposed to the power) interests of Chou En-lai, for example, and many of the soldiers in the Maoist coalition were probably identical with those of the party apparatus under Liu Shao-ch'i. This implies that after victory over the party apparatus, the conflict will continue within the victorious coalition.

A high degree of tension is thus built into the structure of Chinese politics, and a certain amount of tension is no doubt a healthy thing for any political system.[67] But most of us most of the time find some appeal in harmony (although harmony and tension, perhaps, need not exclude each other). Just as harmony is not always to be desired, not all tension is healthy. In the Chinese case we are involved in another contradiction. The system is in one sense pluralistic (i.e., in the oligarchical sense in which some critics say the American system is pluralistic, and perhaps more so), but it operates under a totalitarian ideology, with room only for one vision (the specific content of that vision—radical or moderate—varying from time to time). This not only implies a rather extreme incivility of tone in Chinese politics but also means that the various factions are much less secure than they would be under a system to which the abstract factionalism model applied. While different tendencies exist in China, it is not part of the rules of the game that these tendencies tolerate each other should the occasion to do otherwise present itself.

The taming of the party in the Cultural Revolution eliminated that institution, for a time, as a possible alternative source of legitimacy to the leader. The long-term consequences of that attack on the Leninist party remain to be seen. The ideology may have made a few adjustments to the pluralistic structure of power, but the concessions seem grudging and temporary. The increase in incivility even over what it had been before remains a legacy of the Cultural Revolution. In some ways the political process since the Cultural Revolution more nearly resembles Nathan's factionalism model than it did previously, except that the factions seem to remain determined to eliminate each other.

This very general outline, of course, is predicated upon Mao's presence in the system and does not predict what will happen now that he is gone. Also, like Marxism-Leninism, it is not a dogma, but a guide.

3

Chinese Attitudes on Dissent and Opposition

The notion of routinized political opposition as a legitimate activity is largely a product of the European Enlightenment and the rise of liberal democracy, and its full acceptance is confined mainly to the area of its birth. Studies of Chinese political culture would seem to indicate that the typical Chinese response to politics is submission to power as long as that power remains effective.[1] This certainly characterizes much of Chinese political behavior—as much as it characterizes human political behavior generally. But in traditional, republican, and Communist China there has been opposition and dissent of a sort, and in each case this opposition and dissent has had some kind of philosophical or ideological basis. Chinese responses to what are deemed to be abuses of power may be more complex than the easier clichés would lead us to believe.

TRADITIONAL VIEWS OF OPPOSITION AND DISSENT

Traditional Chinese attitudes have, perhaps, little to do directly with the main subject of this study. It is possible to find analogies between traditional and communist attitudes if one seeks them,[2] but these are often superficial or, what may amount to the same thing, reflections of virtually universal attitudes. The political and intellectual discontinuities between the two systems are rather overwhelming. There is at least a marginal value in examining traditional attitudes, however. Despite the great discontinuities, the past in China is still very recent: as a boy Mao Tse-tung wore a pigtail and studied the Books and Classics. The 1973–75 campaign to criticize Lin Piao and Confucius *may* indicate that some traditional attitudes obnoxious to certain of the current rulers retain some influence in society. Also, a focus on the tradition may be a useful antidote to a view overly impressed with the Western origins of institutional opposition, from which it is deduced that what we in the West might find unappealing suits the Chinese just fine. Chinese attitudes toward politics are not exhausted by the currently approved status quo.

There are two ideal images of traditional China. One shows China as the archetypal oriental despotism, with the bureaucratic state enjoying absolute power over its subjects.[3] The other view is that apparently shared by Sun Yat-sen at some point in his career, holding that China is an incipient democracy, requiring only the overthrow of the autocracy to become a model modern republic. As always in presenting two such oversimplified images, the purpose is to criticize them both, although here the despotism image may be closer to the truth than is the democracy. The concept of political freedom was absent from traditional China, as it was from Europe, a few centuries ago. This does not imply an absence of all freedom, since on matters not influencing the distribution and holding of political power the Chinese government was largely content to let the people alone.[4] At the same time China, over the past two millenia, has largely lacked the antidemocratic institution of a hereditary aristocracy, with the unimportant exception of the imperial family; and there was at least some substance to the myth of equality of opportunity in bureaucratic employment.[5] This limited social equality, however, may have strengthened the despotic aspects of the state, since there were no important privileged vested interests autonomous from the state and jealous of their prerogatives.[6] European feudalism, while undemocratic in itself, may have been conducive in some ways to political liberty in Europe. A prime tenet of feudalism, if such a nebulous and artificial concept can be said to have tenets, is that political power is always properly subject to restraint—the barons do not want the king too much on their backs. A feudalism resembling the European one had once existed in China but had been destroyed by the consolidation of the Ch'in and Han dynasties around 200 B.C. and had been largely moribund for the three centuries before that.[7] Confucianism, which was to become China's most important philosophy and the ideology of the centralized bureaucratic state, was in sociological terms a reactionary product of this decaying feudalism, as communist commentators now point out (they, however, call what is here considered feudalism the "slave society"). In China the aristocratic ethical system was "taken up by a great thinker at the moment when it might have been expected to lapse into archaism,"[8] and in the process the system was rationalized and universalized.

Very early in the development of Confucianism—probably, despite what the communists think, with Confucius himself—any idea that aristocrats constituted a special breed was dropped in favor of the idea of human equality, a concept that came to be common to all major classical Chinese schools of thought.[9] The idea of fundamental human equality, based, according to Mencius, on our common nature, did not imply any political egalitarianism. The Confucian good life is a life spent in proper conformity to the proper demands of proper human relationships, and all relationships but one (that among friends) are hierarchical. The hierarchy is not supposed to imply an unconditional and unilateral subordination, but (a reflection perhaps of Confucianism's feudal origin) a system of reciprocal obligations and expectations. "The father should be a father, the son a son. . . ." The connotation and denotation should coincide: each should be everything the name implies. A sassy, disobedient son is not properly a son—but neither is a father who abuses his children properly a father. A king who behaves like a tyrant is not properly a king, any more than a treasonous minister is properly a minister.

Karl Wittfogel stresses the very real authoritarian element in Confucianism: "A son who obeys his father is well prepared to obey his government."[10] This may be true to a point—many Chinese emperors would seem to have agreed, although the communists seem to doubt it. But Wittfogel's comment may miss two important aspects of Confucianism: the greater importance of family relations (i.e., between parents and children, not, as in most of the contemporary world, between husband and wife) over political ones and the evaluation of all relationships by an ethical standard. The *Analects* contains a famous passage in which the Duke of She praises a good subject who was willing to report his sheep-stealing father to the authorities. Confucius replies: "In my country upright men are quite of another sort. A father will screen his son and a son his father—which, incidentally, does involve a sort of uprightness."[11] This "familism" has been held responsible for an alleged lack of public spirit among pre-Liberation Chinese, but it *does* "involve a sort of uprightness." In early Confucianism there is a principled opposition to statism and thus the basis for principled dissent against state power and its exercise.

From a philosophical, if not necessarily from a sociological, point of view, this "familism" is part of the Confucian subordination of expediency to ethics. The family relationship has moral precedence over all others. The ideal of the *chün-tzu*, the gentleman, is the morally autonomous man who does what is right, not what pays. It is perhaps correct to say that in Confucianism is the discovery of the "autonomous personality as the source of order,"[12] although this must not be taken to imply any modern, Western, Promethean individualism, since usually the proper thing for the gentleman to do is to subordinate himself to someone else. But he alone is the judge of the circumstances of this subordination, and the subordination is always subject to moral norms. The virtue of *hsiao,* filial piety, no doubt usually meant, in practice, obedience; but this is not the philosophical meaning of the term. Rather, the child should do what is in the best interests of his parents, whether they approve or not. Similarly, the twin virtue *chung,* loyalty, does not mean unconditional obedience to the ruler, but action in the ruler's interests—including his moral interests.

In Mencius is found the most liberal interpretation of early Confucianism on the problem of the person and the state, the subject and the ruler. Here is developed the famous, but miscalled, right of revolution:

> "Is it permitted for a subject to kill a ruler?"

> [Mencius] said: "One who violates benevolence is a thief; one who violates righteousness is a tyrant. A thief or a tyrant is called a 'common scoundrel.' I have heard that a common scoundrel, Chou, was executed; I have never heard of anyone killing a ruler."[13]

A king who acts as a tyrant loses the name of king and becomes an outlaw and a usurper. Whether one deserves the name of king depends upon whether one has the mandate of heaven, and heaven bestows this mandate to benefit those who are ruled: "Heaven sees as my people see; heaven hears as my people hear."[14] This is obviously not any theory of popular sovereignty. The doctrine of the mandate of heaven is at least remotely similar to the European notion of the divine right of kings, and like the European theory, while not inconsistent with the idea that authority comes from the people, it is inconsistent with the idea that it comes only from them.[15] In each case the ruler is directly responsible to heaven or to God, not to his subjects. Here, however, the theories diverge. The European theory stresses legitimacy, or birth. A European king may burn in hell for his misdeeds, but in the meantime he remains the legitimate king. A Chinese ruler, however, enjoys his mandate conditionally, and it may be withdrawn upon misbehavior.

The realm (*t'ien-hsia*) is not the property of the ruler; it is bestowed by heaven. A father, unable to transfer his rule to his son, may only recommend his son (or anyone else) to heaven; heaven's approval lasts only so long as the ruler is worthy. On the other hand, "heaven does not speak, but shows itself by its acts and deeds."[16] Good government and a docile (but uncoerced) population are signs of heaven's approval. A rebellion is a sign of heavenly discontent, but not in itself of heavenly endorsement of those who rebel. A failed rebellion, while not always evidence that the ruler retains the mandate (a "common scoundrel" may be able to hang on by sheer force for a time), is decisive evidence that the mandate has not passed to the rebels. To say, then, that for Mencius the right of rebellion is simply an illustration of the adage that successful treason is treason no longer, would miss Mencius's point, which is that political power is always subject to moral constraints.

Mencius was, in fact, no zealot for tyrannicide. In one place he holds that the relatives of a wicked ruler should depose him, but ordinary ministers of a bad ruler who will not listen to reason should simply resign. In later orthodox Confucianism the general principle was that a good minister is one who opposes a bad ruler, even to the point of risking death; but it is improper for a minister who has served a ruler to conspire to overthrow him. It was also considered improper for an official who had served under one dynasty to serve under the one which had overthrown it, even if the older dynasty had clearly lost the mandate of heaven: the mandate is heaven's to give and to take, not the minister's.[17]

Confucianism, of course, was not the only philosophy developed in classical China. Taoism, with its rejection of all human institutions and standards in favor of conformity with the cosmic Way, is a radical critique not only of all politics but also of civilization itself. The critique was so radical, however, that Taoism in itself did not provide much of a guide for government and was unsuited to become a political ideology (although individual Taoists did, of course, gain influence in court in later times, and popularized versions of Taoism would occasionally figure in rebel ideologies). In early times, however, the Legalist school was considered to be close to Taoism; and with the Legalists, the Taoist ontology and "anthropology" were given political relevance (Legalism, and successful despotism generally, is perhaps summed up in Lao-tzu's advice to "fill the bellies and empty the minds"). The Legalists took a "naturalistic" view of rule as a matter of power and its skillful exercise; morals are reflections of interests and, from the ruler's point of view, either superfluous or pernicious. Good rule is rule according to rigid and impersonal standards (law—*fa*) and techniques (*shu*), and it both shapes and meets the exigencies of the physical and social environment (*shih*). Unlike the Confucians, the Legalists wished to make the officials simply the tools of the centralized state. But even the Legalists held that criticism of the ruler by the officials is sometimes proper—not so much when the ruler violates moral standards as when the ruler, through sloth or passion, misperceives his interests in consolidating power and thus violates expediency. The minister should tell the ruler the truth, not necessarily what the ruler wants to hear. Loyal words grate upon the ears.[18]

Legalism certainly provided a guide to political action but in its own way was perhaps as unsuited as Taoism to become a proper ideology. If rule is justified only by power, it is justified only so long as power is retained. The state structure of the Chinese empire was organized largely on a Legalist pattern—as a bureaucracy, with bureaucrats appointed by and responsible to the emperor—but it was an adapted form of Confucianism that in fact came to serve as the ideology of this state. Legalism died out as a separate school of thought, but Confucianism became broadened sufficiently to include much of what had been Legalism. A perennial theme in Chinese politics was an argument between central bureaucrats who would use quasi-Legalist themes and Confucian egalitarianism to argue for greater centralized power, while local elites would counter with arguments based on more orthodox Confucianism.[19]

Dynastic Confucianism was an attenuated Confucianism but was not pure decoration or simply pretty words to cover up the fact of autocracy. There was in dynastic Confucianism a glorification of the ruler, a placing of the ruler within an elaborate cosmological scheme:

> Heaven gives birth to the people. They are good by nature but cannot fulfill their potential. Therefore, a king is established, that they may be good: this is heaven's intention. . . . The ancients who invented writing drew three lines and connected them in the middle, calling this word "king" [*wang*—王].

> The three lines are heaven, earth, and man. The line through the middle links them together. Who, if not a king, could link together heaven, earth, and man?[20]

This cosmological doctrine does shore up the position of the ruler, although the mandate still remains conditional on the behavior of the actual ruler. Also, while perhaps strengthening the ruler's position against challenge, it limits his freedom of action. It was inexpedient and difficult for the ruler to behave in an un-Confucian manner or to do anything strange, new, or unusual. Dynastic Confucianism served as a conservative check on absolute power; in sociological terms, it was perhaps more an ideology of the bureaucracy and the literate elite not currently employed in the bureaucracy than an ideology of the emperor.[21]

In bureaucratic empires, it seems, the bureaucracy tends to become a corporate body somewhat autonomous from the king as its members become "aristocratized."[22] Over the past millennium, at least, the Chinese state was strong enough to prevent the bureaucracy from becoming a self-perpetuating elite able to pass large land-holdings to its children. But the bureaucracy did embody an aristocratic ethos, and this ethos, institutionalized in the examination system, gave it a basis for defending its moral and material interests—and perhaps even, from time to time, the common good—against the emperor or the emperor's entourage. While the bureaucracy was in origin a Legalist institution, the bureaucrats were not, in theory, the compliant instruments of the ruler envisioned by the Legalists, nor even the "king's men" of early modern Europe.[23]

Policy was generally made by consultation, not by imperial fiat,[24] and there was thus some room for factional and palace politics among the elite. Traditional Chinese factions (cliques) often seem based more on personal ties than on principle, with a concern more for patronage than for policy. This, however, was not universal, nor are the above categories mutually exclusive. At times factions could even be linked with the rudiments of public opinion, as scholars affiliated with various private academies would seek both to influence the conduct of public policy and also to gain political office for their friends.[25] But this also shows the limitations on competitive politics in traditional China. Opposition to "bad" policies, while always legitimate, was also dangerous (although perhaps no more dangerous than in the court of, say, Henry VIII) and was under no institutional protection. Concerted activity by cliques was subject to suppression by those in power (who might themselves, of course, constitute a clique) and was difficult to legitimize under the prevailing interpretations of Confucianism. In the Ming dynasty, for example, the partisan political activity of the private academies was not defended even by those who engaged in it, even though such activity might have come from the highest motives and was not directed against the ruling house but against the particular bureaucrats (and eunuchs) who held power at court.[26]

A concrete example is useful to show both the scope and the limitations of opposition within the traditional Confucian framework. The example of Hai Jui, which has been made famous in recent years, shows that even in the unusually despotic Ming dynasty a loyal minister could use language toward the emperor that might be thought out of place if used by a drill sergeant toward a recruit, but without carrying the opposition to the point of challenging the emperor's position.[27]

Hai Jui's criticism of the Chia-ch'ing Emperor begins with platitudes. The emperor has an exalted position, but this means his responsibilities are equally exalted. Even a great emperor such as Han Wen Ti was not immune from criticism, and "His Majesty is hardly Han Wen Ti." His Majesty is strong-willed, but he has abused his strong will. He wastes resources on useless public works while the people starve and rebellion spreads. Bad officials have been removed but have been replaced by officials equally bad. His Majesty never comes to court, neglecting not only affairs of state but his wives and children as well. This is a very bad example. He spends his days in hedonistic self-indulgence and dabbling in Taoist mysticism. His Majesty wishes to live long and never die. Well, is there any Taoist sage from any previous dynasty who is alive today? Why, even His Majesty's own teacher in the mystic arts has died! His Majesty claims heaven has presented him with a magic peach. " 'Does heaven speak?' Are we to suppose it has hands, to present peaches to people?" His Majesty listens only to those who cater to his wishes. The corrupt are always willing to do just what His Majesty wants, while honest officials are punished for their honesty. No wonder the officials all imitate the wicked and corrupt. His Majesty should shape up, cut out the useless Taoist mysticism, return to court, and give some thought to the good of the realm, thus remedying his decades of neglect. "Now the high officials hold office by virtue of their flattery, while lesser officials fear punishment and hold their tongues. This minister cannot overcome his indignation and dares death in the hope His Majesty will listen." Hai Jui's criticism is highly moralistic, touching the emperor's private as well as public behavior. In the heavy-handed sarcasm against Taoism there is, perhaps, a defense of the special bureaucratic interest (and the tone of the criticism—the desire of the emperor to have a political check on the corporate influence of the bureaucracy aside—provides some indication of why emperors might sometimes prefer the company of Taoists and the like to that of upright Confucians). While extremely blunt, the criticism is also highly loyal: there is no suggestion that the emperor resign, much less that he be deposed; rather, the demand is that he exercise the functions of his office. The only pressure brought upon the emperor is moral pressure, and the death Hai Jui risks is literal.

Confucian opposition is conservative, limited opposition, giving little support to any sort of revolutionary activity. The communists, taken as a whole, have had an ambiguous attitude toward this sort of elitist opposition in traditional China, and since 1965 the view has been uniformly hostile. The communists have, however, identified what they consider at least an embryonic tradition of revolutionary opposition in the numerous peasant rebellions in Chinese history[28] (and in recent years have, perhaps with greater justification, stressed the revolutionary implications of Legalism). While it is difficult to say exactly what the ideas of traditional rebels were—they were not the ones who wrote the histories—the weight of the evidence would seem to support the old cliché of T. T. Meadows: "Of all nations that have attained a certain degree of civilization, the Chinese are the least revolutionary and most rebellious."[29] The traditional rebellions were not pure class movements, any more than was the communist movement in this century. Peasants were driven into rebellion by intolerable conditions, but the same conditions could drive them into the imperial armies that fought the rebels. It was usually the poorer peasants who suffered most from the breakdown of order, whatever the cause of that breakdown; and the behavior of rebels was similar to that of their enemies—they all acted like bandits. Hsiao Kung-ch'uan may exaggerate in saying that the term *peasant rebellion* may be good propaganda but that "it can hardly withstand objective historical analysis." Even a defender of the thesis of peasant rebellion, however, has to take a certain roundabout approach: "Peasants who shared their common class grievances still articulated their shared experience according to their lineage, ethnic, and religious affinities rather than their class."[30] This might imply that *peasant rebellion* lacks an empirical referent and that common class grievances constitute an a priori construct of the analyst. (This does not, however, imply that the construct is worthless, and the fifth chapter of this study employs a somewhat similar mode of analysis.)

A weakness of the Chinese Marxist view of peasant rebellions is that these rebellions do not seem to have generated any ideology distinct from the general Confucian consensus, broadly construed.[31] A survey of Chinese rebel ideologies by Vincent Shih shows that, while heterodox religion sometimes played a role in the mobilization of revolt, rebel demands were not directed against the Confucian ethos but against those elites who failed to live up to that ethos. The rebels protested corruption, abuse of authority, high taxes, and sometimes unequal distribution of land (the equal distribution of which can be justified by Confucian norms). The rebel outlook "falls in quite neatly with the main outlines of China's tradition."[32] Shih seems to scold the rebels for their failure to put forth new principles, for their lack of imagination; but the idea that man can, without aid of supernatural power, bring about a brand new and perfect society by means of political action would not seem to be much older than the European Enlightenment, and the idea is probably false anyway. *Revolt* may carry millenarian implications, but in European as well as Chinese revolts prior to the French Revolution (or maybe the English revolution), rebels generally adhered to traditional values. Such revolts may even have been reactionary, in the sense that the social forces had passed the tradition by.[33] Even in modern revolutions, revolutionary ideas may be largely confined to those who organize and lead. In twentieth-century China, peasant discontent was largely a consequence of the decay of traditional institutions and was directed against elites who could no longer follow traditional ways. The Communist Party was able to channel this revolt toward revolutionary goals, but such goals were not necessarily shared by the peasants.[34]

The traditional sources of peasant discontent may remain a more important source of opposition to the current regime than the more abstract aspects of the Great Tradition, at least if the Communists fail in their attempt to eliminate the distinctions between the peasant and other ways of life. The evidence also indicates, however, that most peasants most of the time were politically passive. Throughout the Chinese tradition, whether elite or popular, there is a consensus that it is proper, if dangerous, to resist arbitrary and oppressive power, as well as a consensus that it is the duty of those with power to provide conditions for a decent life in which people can live in peace and be happy in their work. At a more sophisticated level there is a critique of power unchecked by moral restraint, although the institutional checks on power were weak.

MODERNIZATION: NATIONALISM AND LIBERALISM

The Chinese tradition was perhaps not conducive to the development of liberal institutions, and when they were adopted in 1912 with the overthrow of the monarchy, it was an exercise in pure formalism. China's experience with such institutions is typical of the run of non-Western states that have attempted to adopt them.[35] An argument might even be made that liberalism construed as unadorned toleration is deficient as a political principle.[36]

As the nineteenth century ground to its close, Chinese thinkers increasingly recognized the material superiority of the West; the modernizers among them came to adopt material superiority as the criterion of political value and began to argue that the material superiority of the West was related to its political institutions. The stress, however, was on the wealth and power of the state (an old Legalist slogan) rather than on the liberty and autonomy of the individual. Yu-sheng Lin argues that the individualism of many thinkers of the May Fourth period (from around 1915 to 1925) was simply a "ground for the legitimization of their iconoclasm" and that "nothing seems more alien to [their] consciousness than Western liberalism."[37] This would seem to be, if anything, even more true of the earlier generation of noniconoclastic liberals, who saw representative institutions as a means of what we now call mobilization—the uniting of the population and the coherent direction of the material and human resources of the state.[38]

It is at least a half-truth to say that liberal ideas in the West originated as a critique of the anachronistic despotisms and functioned to provide a rationale for the capitalist reorganization of society. The Ch'ing dynasty was also an anachronistic despotism, but this does not mean that liberalism in China would perform exactly the same function. We must also consider what Eberhard calls "world time."[39] The problems of China were not precisely those of the West, and Chinese thinkers did not recapitulate in chronological order Western intellectual history but tended to focus upon what they perceived as most up-to-date. By the time Western ideas began to penetrate China, the original Western liberalism was already old-fashioned. To a certain extent it had become associated with nationalism or other forms of collectivism, and a Chinese thinker such as Yen Fu could even discern the collectivist implications of the philosophy of Herbert Spencer. Chinese intellectuals, in any case, had little reason to be enchanted with capitalism as they saw it operate in China, and they perhaps retained some of the Confucian prejudice against a life devoted to getting and spending. K'ang Yu-wei, the last of the major Confucian philosophers, advocated in practical politics a constitutional monarchy with representative institutions, elections, and civil liberties; his ultimate dream, however, was an adaptation, or perversion, of the traditional vision of *Ta-t'ung,* Great Harmony—in K'ang's hands a more than usually unattractive utopia involving the abolition of the family and a totally regulated, collectivized life, with the crematorium next door to the fertilizer plant.[40] K'ang's pupil, Liang Ch'i-ch'ao, perhaps the most sensible of the late-nineteenth-century reformers, also shared this collectivist vision, if not to K'ang's extreme. For Liang, in the "civilized age"—the age to come—"the freedom of the group develops while individual freedom decreases."[41] The conservative reformers at the end of the Ch'ing dynasty may have been too modern for liberalism.

Yen Fu, K'ang Yu-wei, and Liang Ch'i-ch'ao tried to work within the system. A more radical position was taken by the T'ung-meng-hui, which later evolved into the Kuomintang (KMT). Unlike the more conservative reformers, the T'ung-meng-hui preached a racial nationalism directed against the Manchus. While there is some basis for anti-barbarian racism in the Chinese tradition, the T'ung-meng-hui radicals fit in quite well with the global political-intellectual currents around 1900.[42] Unlike earlier opponents of barbarian rule, the radicals desired the overthrow of the monarchical system itself and the establishment of a republic. Given the radical nature of its goals and the autocratic nature of the system it wished to subvert, the group was forced to adopt conspiracy and violence as its means, but these means are not guaranteed to produce liberal results. At the same time, the young intellectuals of the T'ung-meng-hui do not seem to have thought through very rigorously the problem of ends and means. They were

> compelled by the goal they had set for themselves to deal with ideas they had not yet had time to digest, taken from societies whose differences from China

> they had not yet adequately analyzed. . . . They gave relatively little of their attention and energies to problems beyond those directly related to gaining power.[43]

The KMT did not in fact gain power in the Revolution of 1911 but agreed to serve as loyal opposition to General Yuan Shih-k'ai, who, in return for betraying his Manchu masters, was made first president of the Republic of China. Yuan was not inclined to brook opposition of any sort and in short order murdered several of the KMT parliamentary leaders. The party's main leader, Sun Yat-sen, fled to Japan and there reorganized the party. In 1915 a rebellion broke out in Szechwan in reaction to Yuan's attempt to have himself declared emperor, and after Yuan's death in 1916 his former subordinates gradually became enmeshed in a series of military campaigns against each other. Sun Yat-sen moved to Canton in 1921 and, with the help of the Comintern, attempted to set up the KMT on the basis of democratic centralism. At the same time the party began, under Chiang Kai-shek, to develop its own army, thus allowing it to play Chinese politics by the warlord rules.

While democratic centralism may have inhibited the development of democratic traditions within the KMT, it did not turn that party into a Leninist monolith. The party remained divided into factions even after Chiang Kai-shek's rise to power, the purge of the Communists, and the later defection of much of the erstwhile KMT left to the Japanese. Chiang's Northern Expedition of 1927 to 1929 ended open warlord anarchy but did not really lead to the institutionalized rule of the National Government. The various warlords agreed, in effect, to stop fighting, join the KMT, and accept the nominal authority of Nanking; in return, they would be left alone.[44] At its core, the KMT became a diverse coalition of the Chinese elite, divided in interest, opinion, and policy but held together by personal ties of the various leaders to Chiang and by a common desire to retain power and privilege.[45] The ideology of the KMT, always nebulous, became more so. It retained, and still retains, as its goal the welfare-state democratic republicanism of Sun Yat-sen; but Chiang's general political impotence, coupled with his conservative temperament, led him, in the New Life movement of the 1930s, to work to achieve social order—meaning, for him, peace and quiet and obedience. The revolutionary heritage of the KMT was neglected in favor of a renewed stress on Confucian virtues. China, like any other society, has perhaps never had a superfluity of propriety, righteousness, integrity, and sense of shame; but the Confucianism of the 1930s did not fit the mood of much of articulate public opinion, while at the same time the KMT Confucianism was itself bastardized, being treated no longer so much as universal standards of right and wrong but, rather, as a means of consolidating the power of the state.[46]

The formal position of the KMT as China's ruling party, coupled with its practical impotence, put the party in a difficult situation. Its attempts to enforce its control were usually too weak to be effective, but sufficiently capricious to be irritating. China was not strong enough to meet the Japanese in a full-scale war, but Chiang's early passivity in the face of Japanese aggression and his simultaneous extermination campaigns against the Communists alienated the feelings of the highly nationalistic students.[47] The inability of the government to protect the peasants from the Japanese, local big-shots, and its own officials contributed to Communist strength. There was probably no time during its tenure on the mainland that the KMT could safely have conducted competitive elections and granted full civil liberties, but the seemingly eternal tutelage alienated liberal opinion. Chiang's policy after Pearl Harbor of refusing to use his best soldiers against the Japanese, saving them for the civil war to come, alienated his regime's main foreign supporter, the United States. Under happier circumstances the KMT polity might have evolved into a relatively open and competitive democracy, but the circumstances were not happy. The National Government responded to its growing number of critics by increasing use of police-state methods without, however, police-state efficiency.

The main internal political danger to the KMT came from the Communists, but the Communists were dangerous in part because the KMT was unable to sustain much enthusiasm among literate public opinion. Conventional liberalism gained some following in the May Fourth period, this liberalism providing an effective, if boorish, critique of China's "feudal" ideas and institutions. While various forms of radicalism rapidly displaced liberalism among the more creative intelligentsia, liberalism of a sort was perhaps a major component of the political ideas of most Chinese intellectuals prior to 1949.[48] This is particularly true of academic intellectuals, but for that matter many radicals, and the KMT itself, did not abandon all aspects of liberalism.

Despite its broad appeal, liberalism did not—perhaps could not—produce any relevant program for political action. The political irrelevance of conventional liberalism is symbolized by the ideas of its foremost Chinese exponent, Hu Shih, a man whose memory is loathed equally by the Communists and by the right wing of the KMT.[49] Hu Shih was a pragmatist, a student of John Dewey, a man of moderation and reason. He was too rationalistic to feel the profundities of the traditional ethical system, but also too reasonable to have much faith in radical panaceas. In 1919 he argued against his friend, Li Ta-chao—later one of the first leaders of the CPC—that those who would reform society should avoid isms in favor of the study of particular problems. To worry about fundamental solutions leads nowhere; advances must be made on specifics, and gradually. This is excellent pragmatism and in addition seems to have been correct: success in Chinese politics has gone to those able to handle specific problems, not to those blindly addicted to abstract positions. But, as is inevitably noted in this context, it was those who adhered to isms who actually went to work on the problems. There is perhaps no necessary connection between liberalism and pragmatism, but since the decline of natural law theory, pragmatism has become one way of justifying liberalism. It is a psychological, if not philosophical, weakness of pragmatism, however, that it declares that the insolvable problems that have tormented people since they began to think are unworthy of serious consideration. To refuse to discuss problems of fundamental metaphysical outlook may simply mean, sometimes, that one refuses to subject one's outlook to critical examination. Pragmatism in this sense, when translated into a political ideology, becomes a general endorsement of the status quo.[50] Such an ideology may be useful when the consensus on basic values is so complete that it never comes into question or when those who do not share the ruling consensus are effectively suppressed. Even if pragmatism fit conditions in the United States in Hu Shih's Columbia days, it is not clear that it does so any more.[51] It certainly did not fit Chinese conditions in the early part of this century.

Hu Shih failed to appreciate the passions that moved his countrymen. He opposed the war hysteria against Japan,[52] although he served his country loyally and well in that conflict. His hatred for the bulk of what he understood to be the higher tradition of China, his rather uncritical sharing of the scientistic commonplaces of many enlightened Western intellectuals of his generation, and his distaste for the dictatorial obscurantism of the New Life movement led him to espouse the unfortunate slogan "wholesale westernization,"[53] earning for himself among nationalists of all ideologies a reputation as a running dog of imperialism, an American with a Chinese skin.

One who wished to play politics in twentieth-century China had to dirty his hands. Hu Shih chose not to do so; perhaps his refusal had as much to do with temperament as with conviction. In the last quarter of this century, however, it is perhaps time we outgrew any Sartrean admiration for dirty hands. Hu Shih did not fit with his times, but the fault was as much with the times as with him.

The modernization of China did not result in any foundation for institutionalized opposition, but it did politicize educated public opinion and establish a tradition of active dissent. To the extent that educated Chinese remain politically passive, this is as much a result of fear of consequences as it is of conviction. Every Chinese government since 1919, down to the Communists in Peking and the KMT in Taipei, has had to face the (usually deserved) hostility of its student generations. The political impotence of liberalism in pre-Liberation China does not imply that liberal ideas mean nothing to Chinese, nor that such ideas will forever be impotent.

THE COMMUNISTS AND OPPOSITION

Marxism itself, in its earlier European form, was liberal as far as its ideas about political institutions were concerned. Leninism, however, is perhaps inherently totalitarian, even barring the excesses of the Stalinist *grand Guignol*. Lenin seems to have come to his totalitarianism as much by force of circumstances as by deliberate plan. He first conceived his tightly organized, centralized, conspiratorial party as a necessary means for seizing power from a despotism.[54] After seizing power, however, Lenin also found the party useful as an instrument of rule. The Bolsheviks exercised dictatorship over the rest of society in the name of the proletariat and gradually suppressed even dissent within the party against the policies of the leadership.[55]

The CPC received its Leninism full-blown, although it took the party more than two decades to come to resemble in practice what Leninist theory would have it be. In very general terms, the Chinese communist position on opposition is the Leninist one, but there are refinements and disagreements within this broad framework. The Cultural Revolution, in particular, saw major deviations from the Leninist pattern, although these deviations had precedents, particularly in the thought and actions of Mao. It is useful to divide the discussion of attitudes toward opposition into two periods: that before, and that since, the Cultural Revolution.

Pre–Cultural Revolution Attitudes

The CPC attained ideological and organizational cohesion after its move to northern China in 1936, particularly during the Rectification movement of 1942–44. Not coincidentally, this period marks the consolidation of Mao Tse-tung's leading position in the party. The ideology of the CPC prior to the Cultural Revolution was set largely by Mao and his long-time collaborator, the "renegade, traitor, and scab" Liu Shao-ch'i. It is possible (indeed, almost unavoidable) to see basic differences in the approaches of the two men in retrospect, but it is only in retrospect that the differences appear clearly. Mao may conveniently be held to represent the radical trend and Liu the moderate trend, if we remember that this is an oversimplification and that Liu and Mao are people, not ideas. A more concrete oversimplification might be that Liu stressed mainly the problems of party consolidation and cohesion, while Mao had his eyes on the grander problems of society and revolution; for the bulk of the working lives of the two men, their approaches were complementary. While the two can be treated as representing different trends, it must be remembered that the trends are abstractions. Prior to gaining power in the party, Mao most of the time was part of its right wing, and even in his last years he may have been no more a *Maoist* than Marx was a Marxist. Liu could sometimes take highly radical positions, as he apparently did in the early days of the Great Leap Forward. We must particularly not *identify* the moderate trend with Liu Shao-ch'i, since he was hardly the only one to adhere to that trend; as order was restored after the Cultural Revolution, Liuist themes began to reemerge, although the man himself remains execrated. But recognizing the oversimplification for what it is, and putting cautions and equivocations to the side, we may generalize that the Liuist line predominated as the party's general mode of operation prior to 1966 but that, at least since the late 1950s, it has been the Maoist line that has generally set the ideological tone of People's China.

Liu Shao-ch'i's most famous work, *On the cultivation of a Communist Party member* (which used to be better known in English under the title *How to be a good Communist*) was written in 1939 and served for a quarter of a century as the main training guide for party cadres. The book was severely, if often tendentiously, criticized during the Cultural Revolution, although it contains little that is not capable of being given a Maoist interpretation. Its basic theme is the development of what might be called moral proletarianism, a concept the Maoists share. Liu argues that it is ideology, not class background, that determines whether one is really proletarian or not (although workers, of course, can acquire this ideology relatively easily); anyone can acquire this correct ideology through ideological cultivation and submission to organizational discipline.

Liu begins with the standard Marxist conflict theory. Ever since human beings evolved, they have been struggling against nature. In the course of this struggle classes evolved, and in class society there is always class struggle. This struggle produces changes in nature and in society, and those who are engaged in struggle also undergo changes. Communists are "the most advanced revolutionists in contemporary history." But they, like everyone else, are changed by struggle. Through cultivation these changes are properly directed, and communists can steel themselves for the arduous struggle ahead.[56]

Within this general conflict theory, however, Liu seems to reduce opposition to a nonproblem once cultivation has taken hold:

> The Marxist principle is that individual interest is subordinate to party interest; the interest of the part is subordinate to that of the whole; temporary interests are subordinate to long-term interests; national [*min-tsu*] interests are subordinate to world interests.

The interests of the individual are subordinate to those of the party, but "aside from the interest of the liberation of the proletariat, the Communist Party has no interests of its own"; and the proletariat, in turn, achieves full liberation only with the liberation of mankind.[57] Conflict in itself ceases to be problematic, since once the individual properly perceives his interests they turn out to be the same as those of everyone else.

In his work on cultivation Liu admits the necessity for "intraparty struggle,"[58] and he discusses this more fully in 1942. Party members are products of the old society, and the party itself operates in a corrupt environment. If a liberal attitude is taken toward bourgeois influences, the party will become just like the European social democrats. Hence, there is a need for struggle, which should be limited, however, to "differences and oppositions of ideological principle." There should be no unprincipled struggles, such as fights over power, prestige, perquisites, material comforts. These problems should be resolved by organizational routine, through majority vote or orders from above. To conduct an unprincipled struggle (or fail to accept organizational discipline) is itself an error of principle, and one who does so renders himself subject to struggle. The struggle, however, should not be mechanical and extreme (*chi-hsieh kuo-huo*), and the comrades should not be subjected to "struggle meetings." These only humiliate and do not help—although they may be fine for admitted enemies. Also, struggle meetings are too often designed, not to "correct faults in work," but only to "attack certain persons."[59]

While Liu recognizes opposition as a fact, we may say he does not recognize it as a problem. The enemies of the party are the enemies of humanity and thus require conversion, neutralization, or suppression. The party itself is what the schoolmen might call a perfect society, although it does have its troubles from time to time. Corruption comes to the party from the outside, and to avoid this the comrades should cultivate their persons and submit to organizational discipline. Focusing equally on the greatness of the communist ideal and the difficulty of the struggle, members keep a watch on themselves and their fellows. Innerparty struggle is required to correct or prevent a pathological condition, to eliminate influences that hinder the members' molding themselves into a happy band of selfless comrades dedicated to the good of all mankind.

For Liu, as long as the party is functioning properly there would seem to be no need for struggle. Given the identity of the party's interests with those of humanity, he might expect to see less and less conflict within society once the party takes power. Here Mao and Liu fail to agree. Mao's vision is of a universe beset by omnipresent contradictions:

> Marxist philosophy holds: the unity of opposites is the basic law of the universe. This law has universal being, whether in nature, human society, or human thought. It is the contradiction of the unity and struggle of opposites that propels the movement and change of things.[60]

For Liu, the dialectic originates in the struggle between man and nature. For Mao, the dialectic is read back into nature itself. This may lean more toward Engels's philosophy than toward Marx's, and some may believe the notion of "autodynamic matter" makes nonsense of historical materialism. But Mao's view of the world as contradiction leads him to take conflict and opposition more seriously than does Liu. Contradictions continue within a society ruled by the party, and certain contradictions will continue under communism itself. More importantly, the Communist Party generates its own internal contradictions (although there seems to be an equivocation here—at least as long as it exists within a class society).

Mao's most important pronouncement on the problem of opposition is his 1957 speech on the "correct handling of contradictions among the people," which was part of the liberal Hundred Flowers campaign. Encouraged in part by this speech, rightists within the party and society made known some of their reservations about the regime's rule, but the speech was not published until after they had been suppressed. We now have a revised and supplemented version.

Mao distinguishes two types of contradiction. Some are antagonistic, "between the enemy and us," and these are handled by "dictatorship"; others are nonantagonistic, among the "people," and should be handled in a "democratic" fashion. *People—jen-min—*is a flexible term whose content varies with historical conditions. Thus, during the war against Japan, Chiang Kai-shek was a *people*. Currently (i.e., in 1957) the people are those who support socialist construction. During the stage of socialism there will always be contradictions among the people.[61] If these contradictions are not properly handled, they may turn into antagonistic ones. In particular, these contradictions should be brought into the open. "Marxism develops through struggle." Truth is not absolute but is always developing through the struggle between truth and error. "This is the law of the development of truth; naturally, it is also the law of the development of Marxism." Marxism can therefore be criticized: "Marxism is a scientific truth; it does not fear criticism. If Marxism fears criticism, if it can be overthrown by criticism, then Marxism is of no use."[62] Liu Shao-ch'i, of course, agrees that Marxism is a scientific truth, but it is a truth that can be fully grasped only by those who have a "thoroughly proletarian standpoint."[63] Mao, in turn, might usually agree with this. But it is Liu's tendency to shut himself up in the party; Mao, here, seems more inclined to allow the free play of social forces.

Just how free in practice this play was to be the rightists had already discovered. Mao does not, in fact, endorse liberal spontaneity. In the published version, what Mao gives with one hand, in good dialectical fashion he takes away with the other. Contradictions among the people must be handled democratically, but this is a "guided democracy," not a "situation of anarchy." It is fortunate our suppression of counterrevolutionaries has been so thorough; otherwise, we would have had a Hungarian incident on our hands.[64] Criticism of the party, its ideology, and its program is subject to six conditions: it must contribute to national solidarity, socialist construction, the people's democratic dictatorship, the leadership of the Communist Party, democratic centralism, and international solidarity.[65] Mao seems to indulge in a little of what propaganda analysts call projection: "Some capitalist countries tolerate the legal existence of a communist party, but only to the limit that it not threaten the basic interests of the bourgeoisie. Once this limit is crossed, it is no longer tolerated."[66] In China it would seem things are pretty much the same, except, perhaps, the limits are somewhat narrower.

Even ignoring the particular situation—the suppression of the dissent of the Hundred Flowers period—Mao's position is still illiberal. There is no hint of the toleration of routinized opposition to the party. The definition of the people varies with historical circumstances, which means in effect with the convenience of those who stipulate the definition. Contradictions among the people are contradictions between "right and wrong,"[67] which would seem to exclude, at least in principle, conciliation and mutual adjustment. To speak of right and wrong within the context of a relativistic theory of truth—there is no truth, and Marxism is true—would seem to have totalitarian implications for practice.

The occasion for Mao's speech is almost irrelevant to the larger political significance of the ideas elaborated. The Hundred Flowers campaign can be regarded almost as an accident, a policy adopted in certain circumstances, an experiment that turned sour and was abandoned. The broader and more lasting implications of the speech concern the position of the party in Chinese society and the role of dissent within the party. The approaches of Mao and Liu to two different concrete intraparty conflicts make an interesting, if almost too pat, contrast.

In February 1954 Liu denounced the Kao Kang–Jao Shu-shih Anti-Party Clique, although that this was his target was not announced until a year later. "Our party is a strong Marxist-Leninist party," Liu said.

> However, our party still chooses a policy of alliance with the bourgeoisie; petty bourgeois surround us as the swelling sea surrounds the land. Our party is very large, and our Marxist-Leninist education within the party is still insufficient. Some cadres, even high-ranking cadres, do not have sufficient understanding of the importance of intraparty solidarity [*t'uan-chieh*].

The party must be united on the basis of principle, and to disrupt solidarity is a violation of principle. There must be a "merciless struggle" against those who do this deliberately, although those who are willing to reform should be treated leniently. The party should become like a "united and harmonious family, and as firm as a piece of steel."[68]

"Petty bourgeois surround us as the swelling sea surrounds the land." The position of the party in Chinese society was not quite as pathetic as this image implies, but it does give insight into Liu's outlook. Corruption comes to the party from outside—from all those petty bourgeois—and manifests itself in the disruption of party unity.

Mao sees the party generating its own corruption, although within the more general context of class struggle in society. A Maoist view of intraparty struggle was voiced by Chou En-lai at the end of 1964. Chairman Mao teaches us, Chou says, that "socialism is a very long historical stage." All during this period there will be class struggle. "At the same time, in society, in party and state offices, in economic organizations and education offices, new bourgeois elements are continuously being produced—new bourgeois intellectuals and other exploiting elements."[69] At the time, Mao was preparing to purge Liu Shao-ch'i.

An attempt to sort out the political dynamics of the Maoist and Liuist tendencies leads to a series of paradoxes. The Liuist tendency implies the domination of society by a unified party, while the Maoist, stressing contradictions generated by the party itself, would seem to encourage factionalism. The Maoist tendency stresses continuous struggle, the continuous defeat of enemies, with new enemies being constantly and spontaneously generated. It postulates, in short, a kind of pluralism and then works to overcome that pluralism. The Liuist tendency does not recognize pluralism—factionalism—within the party as a natural condition but does allow for a pluralism of a different sort. Thus, provided that the leading role of the party is assured, there seems to be room within the Liuist tendency for what might be called concessions to everyday life. The Maoist tendency focuses on struggle as the means for the constant revolutionization of society, while the Liuist tendency stresses consolidation of the revolution. The Liuist tendency might allow for concessions to particular interests, such as, say, those of peasants, if this makes the peasants easier to rule and helps bring in the grain. In both tendencies there is a demand for party unity, but the demand has a somewhat different flavor in each case. In 1975, spokesmen for the moderate tendency seem to have called for *t'uan-chieh,* which has connotations of solidarity, while the radicals used the word *t'ung-i,* which connotes a centralized, directed unity. The radicals push for victory for the currently correct line, while the moderates stress a kind of noncompetitive, live-and-let-live, although at the same time disciplined, pluralism within the party, with the party guarding itself mainly from threats to its dominant position.

One moderate criticism of radicals is that radicals do not understand reality, and radicals are sometimes willing to agree that, in a sense, this is true. As the student Lin Hsi-ling, a radical critic of the regime, put it in 1957, "To feel dissatisfied with reality, I believe, is a good thing."[70] The Liuist line is an adaptation to realities, although this adaptation can generate its own contradictions. The *People's Daily* complained in 1954:

> We should promote a creative spirit among youth, and overcome the conservative, precedent-following psychology. . . . Thus, we should not only teach youth to learn humbly from the older generation, . . . but must also encourage among youth independent inquiry, independent work, independent activity, daring, creativity. . . . We naturally wish to teach youth modesty and caution, that they might put effort into avoiding mistakes. But we must be aware that if we cause

> youth always to fear making mistakes, they will become ultracautious in their work, simply going through the motions and following rules to the letter, saying only what others have said before, doing only what others tell them to do. It would then be very difficult to raise them to be good workers.[71]

Workers here is not *kung-jen,* workmen, but *kung-tso-che,* meaning cadres, functionaries. The Liuist vision of a party united as a happy family, full of self-effacing, dedicated, daring, and creative paragons, is a chimera. In practice what comes to count is that the work be done, that orders be obeyed. Initiative is fine, unless it disrupts things—and when things are disrupted people are punished (otherwise they would not fear making mistakes). No one may like bureaucratic routine for its own sake, but the party can get along with bureaucratic routine. In 1958 a young party member complained that the party seemed only to want "brainless, barren tools." He was severely slapped down,[72] but some years later the Red Guards were to make the same complaint.

Those whose jobs involve a day-to-day coping with the realities of rule come to acquire an interest in bureaucratic routinization and may come to wish to limit the influence of the zealots who feel this routinization betrays the goals of the revolution. Thus, in the early postrevolution period the campaign against factions among the Bolsheviks was directed mainly against the left.[73] The exclusion of radicals from the center of things makes them particularly prone to engage in factional activities, if they can get away with it. In China, the structural factors outlined in the previous chapter, particularly the continued presence of the leader as a focus of authority alternative to the institutionalized party, made it difficult to suppress the radical tendency, while the realities of the situation made it difficult to convert that tendency into a coherent policy. Given the general predominance of radical ideology, the position of the communist moderates in China became curiously similar to that of the co-opted liberals in Spain: their policies were hard to legitimize, "except on opportunistic grounds."[74]

The party machine encroached upon the interests of other segments of society, and radical Maoist ideology served to provide grounds for articulating the discontent felt toward the party machine. During the Cultural Revolution certain radicals pushed the logic of the Maoist position into what seems a heretical deviation from Leninism, a defense of factionalism within the party.

Post–Cultural Revolution Attitudes

Foreigners were sometimes moved to admire the public spirit of the Chinese people under Mao. The Chinese slogan is *p'o-ssu li-kung*—"smash the selfish [or private] and establish the public." The slogan is of Legalist derivation, and selflessness is certainly a quality the regime attempts to cultivate in its subjects. In the context of Chinese politics, however, accusations of selfishness often seem directed against the radicals. According to Liu Shao-ch'i, selfishness is manifested in lack of organizational discipline, in wanting the party always to do things one's own way.[75] The selfish are those who engage in factional activity against the party leadership—since the party has no special interest of its own, those who dislike its policies must have an ax to grind. Even prior to the Cultural Revolution those associated with the moderate tendency were criticizing the Maoists for their factional selfishness. In 1964 P'eng Chen, then boss of Peking, later the first major victim of the Cultural Revolution, said in a veiled reference to the literary politics of Chiang Ch'ing:

> The People's Republic of China has nearly 700 million people under the leadership of the Communist Party Center and Comrade Mao Tse-tung. Isn't it a good thing that everyone forms a big unity? Some people are not satisfied with this big unity. Only their small group satisfies them.[76]

The moderates usually control the major governing institutions (perhaps control of such institutions breeds moderation), and have an interest in unity—obedience, and no back talk. The radicals have to turn to factional activities and become open to the charge of selfishness.

This theme was employed within the Red Guard movement itself. In the spring of 1967 Mao, his own purposes largely served, and disturbed by the increasingly anarchic situation, ordered the Red Guard units to return to their schools and there submit to military training.[77] This would have put the radical shock-troops under military control at a time when the soldiers were becoming increasingly impatient with radicalism. The radical Chingkangshan group of Tsinghua University, which seems to have been affiliated with the radical headquarters in the Central Cultural Revolution Group, hailed Mao's directive (it could hardly do otherwise), but with much grumbling against any policy of "false, unprincipled alliance": they did not want to make peace with groups less pure than they.[78] Their Red Guard opponents, closer to the army, could then take up Liu Shao-ch'i's old refrain: the Chingkangshan represents a "reactionary thought tide." They "oppose military training, insult the Liberation Army, and raise an adverse current to pluck down the Great Alliance." They claim to be more leftist than anyone else; in fact, they are just more selfish.[79]

Under democratic centralism a minority is supposed to be able to maintain its dissenting views as long as it obeys the majority, but in a Leninist party persistence in opposition is easily represented as vainglorious egoism. The prohibition of factionalism forestalls legitimate concerted opposition and thus, to a large extent, effective opposition. At the same time, however, the notion of a party founded on principle, coupled with the doctrine of contradictions, particularly in its Maoist form, provides the possibility of moving beyond (or back from) Leninism. The Cultural Revolution radicals provided an ideological basis for opposition and dissent within the Communist movement itself.

Here it is necessary to digress in order to make a distinction. The argument is not so much that a defense of factionalism is inherent in the radical position; rather, the practical impotence of radicals, their lack of access to power, may lead them to defend factionalism; their commitment to this stand might not outlast their minority position. It might be hypothesized that *any* group that finds itself in a minority will try to defend factionalism in some way. In 1962, when the moderate policies adopted in the wake of the Great Leap Forward were under attack by Mao, Liu Shao-ch'i is alleged to have said: "To oppose Chairman Mao is just to oppose an individual. . . . We need an opposition faction [*fan-tui p'ai*] both within the party and within the people."[80] The comment about opposing Mao is plausible enough, but the talk of an opposition faction would seem to go against Liu's whole style. If Liu actually said this, it is a reminder that reality is usually more complex than the abstractions we use to describe it. Still, a defense of factionalism does not form part of Liu's general outlook, and we have no evidence that he developed this idea systematically. It should also be noted that the moderate distaste for factional activity does not mean that moderates never engage in it. In fact, denunciations of factionalism are probably a good way to consolidate the position and maintain the discipline of a dominant faction.

Those who overthrew Liu Shao-ch'i violated party procedure, and moderates, who remained in control of much of the local party bureaucracy throughout 1966, were probably safe as long as party procedures were respected. The circumstances required that the radicals provide a justification for the violations of party rules, rules they were going to violate in any case. In late November Chiang Ch'ing told a meeting, "We cannot depart from the class viewpoint in talking about a 'minority' or a 'majority' "[81]—not the kind of argument one controlling a majority would usually choose to stress. The argument was that a correct minority could take action against a mistaken majority.

In June 1967 Lin Chieh, a relatively low-ranking member of the Cultural Revolution Group, presented a full-scale attack on the Leninist concept of democratic centralism. Lin does not say he is attacking Lenin, of course. Instead he quotes Liu Shao-ch'i: "We emphasize organizational obedience; whoever puts conditions on his obedience is wrong; . . . the rule of democratic centralism is that whatever is decided by the majority, the upper level, or the Center, must be obeyed, even if that decision is a wrong one." This, says Lin, is "out and out slavism," a call for "blind obedience." "Centralism must be based on correct opinions. . . . To sacrifice truth, give up principle, surrender to a mistaken majority—this is thoroughgoing opportunism." In June, however, it was no longer sufficient simply to denounce slavism, and the second half of Lin's essay is devoted to an attack on anarchism, a deviation resulting from the radicals' policy. There must be revolutionary discipline, but discipline must be based on truth. Truth is what Chairman Mao says it is.[82]

The slogan of the early part of 1967 was that the "proletarian revolutionary factions" were to "seize power from the capitalist power-holder faction."[83]

The defense of intraparty factionalism, however, remained embryonic. The radical factions soon became embroiled in fights with each other and with the army, which was trying to restore order. After the chaos of the summer of 1967, particularly after the abortive military mutiny in Wuhan, the Center began to reassess the radical position on factionalism. Minor radicals, including Lin Chieh, were purged, and in September Mao issued a pronouncement on factionalism: "Within the working class there is no basis for fierce conflict. Within the working class under the dictatorship of the proletariat, there is even less reason for splitting into two factional groups."[84] Thereafter, somewhat less was heard of proletarian revolutionary factionalism and rather more of petty-bourgeois factionalism. But factionalism as a phenomenon did not die out. Chinese society had been fragmented, at least in the cities, and the power struggle at the Center had not been resolved.

In January 1968, the role of the PLA was modified somewhat. As before, it should "support the leftist faction of the broad masses" but should no longer support any *particular* leftist faction. "There are, temporarily, many different kinds of revolutionary leftist groups; but if they are the political representatives of the majority of the masses and uphold the revolutionary line of Chairman Mao, they must be given firm support."[85] This probably represented a gain for the radicals—a modest recovery of lost positions—but it may also have worked to the advantage of the revolutionary cadres (mainly Chou En-lai's men). The army, in effect, would protect the factions from each other while allowing them to continue to exist. The army seems to have accepted the policy grudgingly. The *Liberation Army Daily* endorsed the policy, but not without murmuring against the "bourgeois and petty-bourgeois nature" of some of the leftists, "which absolutely cannot be supported." "Bourgeois and petty bourgeois factionalism," the paper reminded its readers, "is a reactionary thought-tide."[86]

The Cultural Revolution, as was said at the time, was a complex, tortuous, and sharp struggle. In the spring of 1968 there was a brief reassertion of the desirability of proletarian revolutionary factionalism. Whatever Mao may have thought a half-year earlier, in April 1968 he was quoted to a different effect: "Outside the party there are other parties; within the party there are factions. This is how it has always been." The only place there are no factions is in the desert. Factionalism is not to be condemned as such but is to be subjected to class analysis.[87] This, however, did not come to anything at the time, and in the summer of 1968 the Cultural Revolution finally moved into its Thermidor.

On August 5, the *People's Daily* denounced what it called the theory of many centers:

> The proletarian headquarters headed by Chairman Mao, with Vice Chairman Lin [Piao] as deputy, is the only leading center of the whole party, whole army, whole state, and the broad revolutionary masses. The whole party, army, and

> state can only have this kind of center. . . . The so-called "theory of many centers" is a bourgeois, mountain-topist, individualist theory; it disperses the unity of the revolutionary ranks based on the Thought of Mao Tse-tung and hinders the thorough implementation of the proletarian revolutionary line. If every department or unit wants "me as the center" [*wo wei chung-hsin*], the country will have so many centers that in effect it will have no center at all.[88]

Around this time the Red Guard factions, which had been causing most of the turmoil, were suppressed, and the Red Guards themselves sent to become peasants for the rest of their lives. As the *People's Daily* implied, however, factionalism permeated many organizations. The policy subsequently adopted toward factionalism seems not only non-Leninist but also surprisingly conservative. Factional activities that might threaten the control by the "one Center" were outlawed, and, once again, the factions no longer permitted to fight among themselves. At the same time, the surviving factions were to be represented on the new revolutionary committees, and perhaps within the new party committees as well. The metaphor used in 1969 was of a cup of water filled to the brim: if the cup is tilted just the slightest bit, some water will spill out. The factions should be represented in leading organizations in such a way that no faction could dominate another. This unity should include not only those who joined the Cultural Revolution early but also those who joined late. Some comrades consider this unprincipled harmony, but they are wrong.[89] The radicals had begun by advocating open factional resistance to the party leadership; now their remnants had to settle for a kind of officially sanctioned elitist pluralism, with the power struggle reverting to its normal covert channels.

The rebuilding of the local party organizations in 1970 and 1971 decreased the importance of the army and especially of the organs of mass representation, such as the revolutionary committees. Factionalism persisted at the Center and no doubt at the local level as well, but it was no longer discussed as much. When Lin Piao was killed in 1971, and before his errors of policy were understood—or before it had been decided just what they were to be—he was accused simply of being an ambitious liar who organized an anti-party clique. The official attitude on factionalism seemed to have reverted to Leninism.

In the late summer of 1972, however, for reasons that remain unclear, the radicals, who had been on the defensive even before Lin's purge, were again able to make their views heard. Lin Piao's defection was explained in terms of the Maoist conflict theory: struggle goes on forever; when the old enemies are overthrown, new ones jump up. A year later this line had evolved into something resembling the earlier Cultural Revolution defense of proletarian revolutionary factionalism. On August 10, 1973, the *People's Daily* reprinted a letter first published in the Liaoning papers, dated June 30, from Chang T'ieh-sheng, a young man who had been sent to work on a commune in Liaoning, protesting the reintroduction of college entrance examinations. As part of his protest he had turned in a blank exam. A comment on this allegedly courageous action a few days later introduced a new theme into Chinese politics: "All new-born revolutionary things, as they advance along the road, will meet hindering forces. . . . The opposition to the tide, as taught by Marxism, is opposition to the reactionary, backward tide."[90]

At the Tenth Party Congress, held at the end of August, the theme of opposition to the tide (*fan ch'ao-liu*) was elevated to a Marxist-Leninist principle. Chou En-lai said:

> When mistaken tendencies swell up like a tide of water, we must not fear isolation but dare to oppose the tide. Chairman Mao says: "To oppose the tide is a Marxist-Leninist principle." Chairman Mao has dared to oppose the tide 10 times in intraparty struggles. He is a guide and teacher who dares to uphold the correct line. All of us comrades should learn from Chairman Mao and uphold this principle.[91]

Wang Hung-wen, at that time the bright young man of the radical tendency, delivered the following anticlimactic doxology:

> We must have the revolutionary spirit of daring to oppose the tide. Chairman Mao points out that "To oppose the tide is a Marxist-Leninist principle." . . . A true Communist proceeds from a public spirit [*ch'u i kung hsin*] and does not fear loss of office, does not fear expulsion from the party, does not fear jail, does not fear execution, does not fear divorce, but dares to oppose the tide.[92]

Daring alone is insufficient, however, Wang warns; we must also have the ability to recognize a mistaken tide; some comrades may be misled by crafty men.

Chou En-lai would seem to have been the quintessence of moderation in the context of People's China, so it would seem both radicals and moderates favor opposing the tide. On the other hand, there were probably those who considered Chou somewhat crafty. The slogan was introduced in criticism of college entrance examinations, an institution abhorred by the radicals, which had been abolished during the Cultural Revolution. The tide could also be identified with other practices disliked by the radicals but which had been defended in 1971 and 1972: remuneration according to work, peasant cottage industry, limitations on collectivization, and the like. In 1972 Lin Piao had been criticized for being too far to the left, and the new slogan seems to be a reversal of one of the catchphrases directed by the moderates against Lin: Lin's radicalism "opposed the tide of history"; it "ran against the tide" and thus was doomed to fail.[93] The implication was that Lin's radicalism—Cultural Revolution radicalism generally—was outdated, no longer appropriate for conditions in China. Thus, to oppose the tide would be a rebuttal by the radicals. On a subjective level, Chou's comments seem platitudinous, a pious call to the imitation of Mao. Wang, however, seems to mean it. He calls for defiance of an erring party leadership, a leadership willing to impose severe sanctions—execution, even divorce—on those who do defy it. This would imply factional opposition. As a later essay noted, "Opposition to the tide is always begun by a minority."[94]

This was 1973, however, not 1967. The last article quoted ends with a perfunctory reminder that party discipline must be observed. A pair of soldiers elaborated this theme:

> A small number of comrades also say: To encourage the spirit of opposing the tide will enable some people to criticize the leadership, whether there is proper cause to do so or not. Thus, it will be hard to do leadership work. This way of thinking is also incorrect. To oppose the tide is to oppose mistaken lines, mistaken thought tides; it is not to follow your heart's desire [*sui hsin so yü*] and to oppose without principle or distinction whatever you fancy to oppose.[95]

Doctrinal discussion in 1974 revolved overwhelmingly around the campaign to criticize Lin Piao and Confucius, a campaign that muddied the basic issues much more than it clarified them. Interestingly, however, one of Confucius's grave errors was said to be his "opposition to the tide of history." The slogan "Oppose the tide" did not vanish entirely, but it fell into disuse.

In the spring of 1975 the idea of factional opposition to the party leadership reappeared in indirect form, with attacks, once again, on the "new bourgeois elements" being generated within the party. Chang Ch'un-ch'iao, the boss of Shanghai and perhaps the most intelligent of the radicals, brought up the problem of the wind of communism (*kung-ch'an feng*)—a moderate term for the excessive collectivization of 1958. This wind of communism is no doubt a very bad thing, Chang says, but perhaps not quite so bad as creating rumors that such a wind is about to blow. Also,

> We must now ask the comrades to pay attention to another kind of wind, the "bourgeois" wind. This is the bourgeois life-style indicated by Chairman Mao, whereby "some" [*i pufen*] become bourgeois elements. Among this "some," the bourgeois wind blown by Communist Party members, *especially leading cadres,* is very dangerous to us. . . . Historically, when the slave-owners, landlords, and bourgeoisie first took power, they did some good things for humanity. But these new bourgeois elements are the opposite of their ancestors. . . . They are nothing but "new" garbage.[96]

Once again the ground seems to have been laid for a minority radical defiance of the party leadership. An August 1975 essay shows the moderate reaction to this. The bourgeois life-style is a wicked thing. Its main manifestation (and this Chang does not say) is bourgeois factionalism. The class enemy lurks, waiting to take advantage of unprincipled factional struggles. We need peace and unity (*an-ting t'uan-chieh*) within the party, although, of course, there must also be struggle—especially against those who want to disrupt the party's peace and unity.[97] As Chang points out, everyone uses the same slogans.[98] The two lines persist.

We may perhaps understand somewhat the dilemma of the dialectic of the CPC by viewing it as a party based on principle—on truth—one of those principles being that truth is never known but is always developing. For the moderates, this relativistic theory of truth presents no particular problem. Truth is simply what contributes to the power and cohesion of the party, to the security of its leadership, at any particular time. For the moderates, opposition is no problem—it is simply something that requires suppression. At the same time, the moderates will tolerate a kind of apolitical pluralism that will not challenge their supremacy (e.g., people may wear pretty clothes, peasants can cultivate private plots, perhaps people can read love stories or adventure stories that do not directly preach the glories of the new order). Continued dominance of the moderate tendency could lead to a China ruled by a technocratic, authoritarian oligarchy. The radicals give truth priority over discipline—at least as long as they are not calling the tune—but, refusing to accept the tide of history (the status quo and whatever will preserve it) as the criterion of truth, they seem to lack any kind of objective criterion whatsoever. During the Cultural Revolution they could resort to a kind of *Führerprinzip, truth* meaning "in accord with the Thought of Mao Tse-tung." Unlike heaven, Mao did occasionally speak; but during his last decade his pronouncements tended to be oracular, and now he will speak no more. Also, after the excesses of the cult of Mao in the Cultural Revolution, it was unlikely that the leader principle could ever have been used in the same way again, even by Mao, much less any successor. Taken literally, and in conjunction with the entire party's apparent hostility to any kind of institutionalized opposition, the radical program would seem a recipe for anarchy. The continued coexistence of the two lines did provide ideological flexibility—perhaps too much. A future synthesis of radical willingness to defy power for the sake of truth and the limited moderate toleration of diversity and depoliticization is certainly possible, although by no means guaranteed and perhaps not even likely. As we shall see, certain party intellectuals attempted to develop such a position in the early 1960s. But that attempt failed.

4

The Handling of Opposition

This study is based in part on the premise that we sometimes resent those who rule us. This, admittedly, is a one-sided view. We resent authority, but we also desire the protection authority brings. Particularly after periods of chaos or disruption we long for what President Harding taught us to call normalcy.[1] By 1949 China had passed through more than a generation of disorder, and anyone who could end this disorder could count on a great reservoir of good will. The Communists, as strong opponents of a weak regime, were in the enviable position of being able convincingly to promise something for everyone, while the KMT increasingly seemed to promise nothing for anyone.[2]

The appeal of the Communists was not limited simply to those who immediately benefited from their rule, such as peasants who were given land, or to those who accepted Marxist-Leninist ideology. The case of the historian Wu Han is not typical, since his goodwill toward the Communists was more active than that of most, but it is illustrative. During the war years Wu Han had become increasingly disgusted with the incompetence and corruption of the KMT. He became active in the China Democratic League and helped organize secret meetings to discuss political affairs. In his published writings he showed no desire for a Leninist autocracy to replace that of the KMT but urged instead that the parties end their civil war and compete through ideas and politics. He had the vaguely leftish attitudes common among his generation of liberal intellectuals in China and elsewhere, but in terms of political form he advocated the then unrealistic and perhaps inappropriate model of Western parliamentary democracy. While he wanted the KMT to stop fighting the Communists, he also believed it was wrong for the CPC, or any political party, to have its own private army. Some time around 1947, however, this apparently standard liberal democrat began to act as liaison between the CPC and the student movement in Peking. After the August 18, 1948, anti-American riots, in which the Communists played a role, Wu Han fled Peking, eventually making his way to the liberated areas.[3] Other liberal intellectuals were less active than Wu Han, but many shared his vision of the Communists as an attractive—and viable—alternative to the current situation.

Eras of good feelings, however, do not always last long. Since the Communists were dedicated to the revolutionary transformation of society, they were soon forced to make people do what people would otherwise choose to leave undone. The case of Wu Han is again illustrative: a decade after Liberation he was beginning to express his disenchantment, if not with the regime itself, at least with important aspects of its policies and style.

The theme of this chapter is the handling of opposition—how it is forestalled, controlled, or suppressed. The methods for handling such contradictions, according to Mao, fall under two headings: democracy for the people and dictatorship for the enemy. The stress on democracy is not unique to China: in the Orwellian caricature of the totalitarian regime, after all, the subjects are persuaded to love Big Brother. The Chinese do, however, seem to take more seriously than did, say, Stalin the problem of obtaining genuine, internalized, self-conscious support. The Chinese have certainly used terror since 1949 (although the number of victims is impossible to calculate); more normally they attempt to achieve control through measures that are nonviolent and not purely administrative, although this does not mean that, strictly speaking, they are noncoercive. Older writings tend to stress terror as the essence of a totalitarian regime. But, to pursue this scholastic vein, it is possible that terror was only an accident of the earlier totalitarian attempts:

> The use of massive terror, so long regarded as the distinctive feature of totalitarian government, may well become superfluous under "perfect" totalitarian conditions, in which the mobilization of the masses is carried forward by a symbiosis of propaganda and organization along a new, uniquely totalitarian continuum, to which the conventional concepts of both consent and coercion are equally irrelevant.[4]

DEMOCRATIC PERSUASION

Persuasion, of course, is carried out through *propaganda,* a term that now seems to smack of the era from the 1930s through the early 1950s. Perhaps it seems old-fashioned simply because it is now so common as no longer to invite comment. Even democratic statesmen strive to create images of themselves, and the process would suggest that whatever relation the image may have to reality is irrelevant.[5] Jacques Ellul, in his dour fashion, argues that propaganda is necessary to any modern state. Public opinion is too unformed to be a guide to state action, but the state cannot act without the consent of its subjects. From the point of view of the subject, propaganda provides some orientation in the formless mass society.[6] This is probably true, but so far it is still necessary to make distinctions.

> The propaganda of totalitarian regimes cannot be measured with the yardstick applied to nontotalitarian societies. Clearly one cannot speak of persuasion, as

that concept is commonly understood, where those to be persuaded are *a priori* denied the freedom to hold contrary views.[7]

Propaganda is generally understood as directed toward collectivities. The Chinese, however, have also given much attention to the winning over of the individual person. Where Stalin would solve a problem with a bullet through a skull, the Chinese have worked for conversion. As the late Chairman put it, "Cure the illness, save the man."

Thought Reform

It seems that the idea of thought reform, or *brainwashing,* as the more lurid term would have it, is no longer as odious to us as we once professed to find it.[8] In liberal societies we increasingly accept behavioral modification (or manipulation, as we used to call it) of our children, our insane, and our jailed. Our public and private bureaucracies occasionally flirt with therapy groups, and the concept of democracy held by the early small-group theorists is remarkably close to the Chinese communist concept of democratic persuasion.[9] Traditionalists expect society to conform to universal and valid norms, and the older liberals believed we could make of ourselves pretty much what we want. Now, perhaps, the best most of us can hope for is to adapt to rapidly changing circumstances over which we have no individual control. "Eternity pleased our parents; one inch looks good to us." Perhaps thought reform, like propaganda, is a functional requisite of modern society.

The Chinese communists are not behaviorists in any technical sense and would be insulted by the comparison. They did not get their techniques from B. F. Skinner, or even Pavlov.[10] They developed similar techniques independently, and it is not surprising that they would if these techniques are in fact effective. Also, communists and behaviorists share certain assumptions, such as that of the overwhelming influence of the environment ("existence determines consciousness"), the malleability of human nature, and the role of ideas as adaptive mechanisms or ideology. Unlike behaviorists, communists believe that history moves in a determined direction. With their stress on struggle—a concept the behaviorists tend to ignore—they hold, with Marx, that men make their own history, and for Mao the constraints under which men do this may be less restrictive than for Marx. The idea that we are both products and makers of our history gives rise to what Marxists delight in, a contradiction—and this contradiction provides the rationale for thought reform.

Thus, the philosopher Ai Ssu-ch'i notes some people wonder why, if existence determines consciousness, there is any need for thought reform. The answer is that existence is always changing, and it is mechanistic to hold that consciousness always changes right along with it. While existence determines consciousness, consciousness also has an opposed autonomy (*hsiang-tui tu-li-hsing*) from existence. Therefore, thought reform is required to "cause the thought of the people to be able to develop in accord with the needs of the material conditions."[11] The rejection of the mechanistic approach means that changes in attitude appropriate to changes in the material conditions can be something other than whatever changes in attitude happen to be correlated with the material changes; the dialectic gives a blank charter to those with the power to define what the material conditions need; they may do what they will, while the rest are induced to conform.

The material conditions of the entire society are designed to encourage thought reform or control. The mass communications media are all under official control, and efforts are made to expose the largest possible proportion of the population to them.[12] A close watch is kept on persons, particularly cadres and the educated; while it is unlikely that anyone is ordinarily under constant surveillance, everyone has reason to expect that at any particular time he might be. Deviations by party members or government employees are entered on permanent dossiers,[13] and their old sins may return to haunt them at any time; this, of course, gives them an incentive to behave in the first place. Supervision is exercised most directly through the small groups into which people are enrolled at their places of work. The assignment to a specific group is made from above, and not by individual choice. This has the advantage of exposing people to the pressures for conformity a small group can generate, without encouraging the development of groups sufficiently cohesive to defend their members against outside power.[14] The desire to be a part of some primary group may be a Chinese cultural trait,[15] and the groups may do much to overcome the impersonality inherent in a modernizing, bureaucratic society. Group members in general seem to be genuinely concerned with each others' comfort and well-being. This concern extends, however, only to the limits of what is politically tolerable (if the group is operating properly from the point of view of the regime). The group members are not friends in the older Western or Confucian sense, but comrades. Real friendship is discouraged by the regime because it may interfere with political loyalty and is avoided by subjects because "people are continually supplying information which causes friends to suffer."[16]

The familiar exercises of study and criticism and self-criticism take place within the small groups. Members discuss current problems of line, direction, and policy; they are sometimes encouraged to voice their doubts, that such doubts may be resolved. To this end the group leader may even practice entrapment, voicing mildly unorthodox opinions himself.[17] A member who takes the bait is then "helped" by the rest of the group and may be urged to go to the root of the problem through a self-examination. The process of group dynamics is supposed to bring about a consensus.

> The individual's adherence to his group is ''conscious'' because he is aware of it and recognizes it, but it is ultimately involuntary because he is trapped in a dialectic that leads him unfailingly to his adherence. . . . Each individual helps to form the opinion of the group, but that group helps each individual to discover the correct line. For miraculously it is always the correct line, the anticipated solution, the ''proper'' convictions, which are eventually discovered.[18]

In addition to giving his approval to the current line, the subject is also expected to undertake voluntarily whatever unpleasant tasks need doing. Thus, a middle-school graduate may be expected to volunteer to go to the countryside and become a peasant for the rest of his life. Social pressures are used to induce volunteering, although the pressures become increasingly strong the longer the person remains obstinate. Eventually the person finds he has given his consent to whatever situation he has found himself in; he can know that the alternatives, over the long run, would have been worse.[19]

There are, or at least were, several varieties of thought reform. The most unpleasant was thought struggle, which was directed against admitted enemies of the party. The most rigorous thought reform was that undertaken by party members and would-be members, with the rigor perhaps balanced by the fact that in this case the process was close to being voluntary in the conventional sense (in the sense that any initiation ordeal into a voluntary group is undertaken voluntarily). Thought reform for nonparty intellectuals was more systematic than that for the bulk of the masses, but was supposed to be milder than that for party members. In practice the distinct types could become confused. Those conducting the thought reform might ''fail to distinguish friends from enemies,'' confuse ''petty bourgeois thought'' with unadulterated reaction, or make demands upon noncommunists that would be appropriate only for party members.[20] It is impossible to say how extensive such excesses were, but they were perhaps responsible for the numerous suicides and nervous breakdowns that accompanied the early period of thought reform. In any case, thought reform was not designed as an amusement. The unpleasantness of the process gives the subject an incentive to have his ''thought summary'' accepted, and the secret to whatever success the process has in changing attitudes is probably the virtual impossibility of getting by with mere lip-service and pro forma statements if the thought reform sessions are frequent and intense enough.[21]

Thought reform seems to depend upon the ability of the regime to control the subject's environment, and the greatest such control is perhaps achieved in prisons and labor camps; this advantage, however, may be in part overweighed by the fact that the prison population is no doubt relatively more stiff-necked than the population at large. Prisoners, like everyone else, are organized into small groups, and the supervision through these groups and the prison administration seems sufficiently strict to prevent the development of an inmate subculture.[22]

Unlike the Stalinist labor camps, Chinese labor camps seem to be run by the guards, not the thieves and murderers. This has definite humane advantages; it prevents, for example, the buggering, literal or figurative, of weak prisoners by the strong.[23] The lack of such a subculture, however, may make it more difficult for prisoners to support each other against the authorities (such a subculture would be a necessary, but not a sufficient, condition for this). A former prisoner, Bao Ruo-wang, says, "It is in the prisons and camps that the notions of friendship and personal freedom are most highly developed in China,"[24] but his account does not make obvious what he means by this. The prisoners do help each other out with daily problems; when possible they cover up for each other and, regular informers aside, do not go out of their way to make trouble for their fellows. Bao reports one instance in which prisoners did join to resist the authorities, but these prisoners were ethnic Koreans.[25] Generally, however, if a prisoner does get into trouble his cell-mates, who ordinarily are his good friends, will turn on him: "They had been coerced into struggling me. They didn't have any other choice. It was simply a fact of Chinese life."[26] This was generally understood and does not seem to have resulted in grudges. The description of group activity inside the prisons, however, sounds much like descriptions of group activities on the outside.[27] Bao did not grow to love his jailers, but he respected them for their honesty and rather liked the few who were humane as well. He does claim to have undergone a change of attitude. Af first, he says, he complied with what was demanded of him in order to save his skin, but before leaving the Chinese jails he "was writing those phrases and believing them."

> I had become, if you like, brainwashed. Or was it that I had simply accepted the bargain that my life [at the labor camp] tendered me: Follow the path marked out for you, don't make trouble, and you will be comfortable.[28]

This would seem like a rational adaptation to circumstances rather than a rational conversion, if that distinction is allowed.

It is hard to say anything unambiguous about the efficacy of thought reform in general. It does not always prevent the development of "dangerous thoughts," but it certainly inhibits their expression. If the new man produced by thought reform is supposed to be a totally selfless being dedicated to the party, the people, and the liberation of mankind, thought reform would seem to be self-defeating: the subject is trained to selflessness by the transparent manipulation of rewards and punishments. Still, the process perhaps converts inner selfishness (if we want to call it that) to behavioral selflessness. The operation of cognitive dissonance, if there is any validity to that theory, should tend to move one's actual attitudes toward those one has, in any case, no choice but to express.[29]

It is not clear, however, that thought reform regularly produces much beyond behavioral compliance, and sometimes, as subsequent discussions of oppositional interests and opposition movements will indicate, it does not always produce that. It is impossible to measure statistically the success or failure of thought reform. Martin King Whyte's study of small group activities indicates that in many cases they varied considerably from the abstract model.[30] Until the Cultural Revolution there was a general tendency for the thought-reform process to become more relaxed, even formalistic. Group members would soon learn just what it was appropriate to say in particular circumstances. The study sessions tended to become just one more part of the regular work routine. Repeated criticism and self-criticism may have helped inhibit the abuse of office, but the Red Guard criticisms of high functionaries indicate the ease with which, even in China, power can be translated into privilege. The Red Guards report the existence of factions in the party, many of these based on friends-and-neighbors relations. Dissident party intellectuals in Peking in the early 1960s formed a genuine friendship group, and this group was protected by the party faction that controlled the city of Peking and the central Propaganda Department, partly because some of the intellectuals were themselves members of this faction and partly because the interests of the faction and the intellectuals happened to coincide. Leadership cadres in the small groups were sometimes able to use the group structure to protect themselves from outside criticism. Thus, it is reported that in the Seventh Ministry of Machine Building a subordinate was about to submit a report critical of a functionary in that ministry to higher authority. The functionary told the subordinate: "In that letter aren't you directing the spearhead against me? We have a party meeting today. We ought to fight in the open, not stab in the back. If there is any trouble it's my head that gets chopped off."[31] Even after the Cultural Revolution, and despite the strong official hostility to "particularistic values," whom one knew and to whom one was related sometimes remained important considerations.[32]

Even the leadership might not take its statements about voluntary compliance and conversion completely seriously. In the mid-1950s the party stressed that after an initial period of "'left' deviation" the nationalization of heavy industry had come about peacefully and in part with the voluntary compliance of the capitalists, who had been given a "political education." In 1975, however, Chang Ch'un-ch'iao said nationalization had come about through dictatorship, by sending in the army and the party.[33] Both statements are true: industry was nationalized without widespread bloodshed (unlike land reform), but the capitalists really had no choice but to comply. In 1971 Mao seemed to have been far from sanguine about the prospects for reform of at least the leaders of defeated factions in the party:

> What should we do about these people [Lin Piao and his friends]? There is still the direction of education: "Warning before punishment; cure the illness, save the man." We want to retain this in regard to Lin Piao. . . . There are two futures:

> there is the possibility of change, and there is the possibility of no change. Those who have committed major errors of principle, mistakes of line and direction, who have been leaders, are all hard to change. Historically, did Ch'en Tu-hsiu change? Did Ch'ü Ch'iu-pai, Li Li-san, Lo Chang-lung, Wang Ming, Chang Kuo-t'ao, Kao Kang, Jao Shu-shih, P'eng Te-huai, or Liu Shao-ch'i change? They did not.[34]

Lin's prognosis would not seem to have been too encouraging; he was killed a few days after these words were spoken. Nor, it would appear, did Teng Hsiao-p'ing change. Party leaders, of course, may constitute a special category. Among the general population the "five-black elements," the class enemies, seem to retain their pariah status for their whole lives, and to varying degrees at varying times their disabilities are passed on to their children.

The behavior of the "bourgeois intellectuals" in the Hundred Flowers campaign is evidence that their thought reform had not taken hold as firmly as might have been hoped, and the reluctance analysts detect on the part of the party bureaucracy to endorse that campaign may show that the bureaucrats knew this.[35] Since that campaign there has been less stress on thought reform in the old style. The "rightists" dragged out in that campaign were sent to "labor education" (a milder version of labor reform), and at least in the labor camps since 1957 there has not been much of the depth-psychology approach to thought reform characteristic of the early 1950s.[36]

With the Cultural Revolution some of the old intellectuals (persons whose education and major activity took place prior to Liberation; many of them are not all that old) killed themselves, as had many during the early 1950s and in 1957. In the Chinese tradition suicide is a protest of last resort, and the Communists find the practice exceedingly irritating. Thus, the semiofficial explanation of the suicide of Lao She (Shu Ch'ing-ch'un), perhaps this century's outstanding Chinese humorist, who killed himself after being "struggled" by Red Guards in 1966, is that it was "at best cowardice, at worst a desperate kind of counter-revolutionary gesture."[37] Most of the other old intellectuals simply disappeared for a time and apparently around 1969 were sent (or volunteered to go) to May 7 Cadre Schools, meaning, perhaps, a milder form of labor education. Many of these reemerged around 1972 and seemed eager to give the impression that this time they had really seen the light. Among Chinese intellectuals with an international reputation who reappeared that year, some, such as the anthropologist Fei Hsiao-t'ung and especially the philosopher Feng Yu-lan, had a record of expressing dissent against certain aspects of the regime whenever the circumstances permitted it. In April 1972 Fei was interviewed by some American colleagues. His two and a half years at the Cadre School had, he said, given him a new understanding. All his former work had been bourgeois; there was no need for anyone to read it anymore. "In China today," Fei said, "sociology and anthropology have been repudiated as disciplines.'' Another Chinese anthropologist present at the meeting explained this, using a metaphor of Mao's that might not bear too literal a construction: ''Just as one comes to know the essence of a pear by eating it, so one comes to know society not just by looking at it, but by participating in the struggle to change it.''[38] That same year Feng Yu-lan greeted American friends minus the beard he had cultivated for most of his eight decades of life, his clean face a symbol of the new Feng Yu-lan.

When the 1973 campaign against Confucius began, the older intellectuals were worried. As Feng expressed it: ''In the beginning I was very tense. I thought, Oh hell! [*tsau-le*]. Before the Cultural Revolution I had always revered Confucius. . . . Once again I am to be the target of revolution.''[39] But this time the old intellectuals were given to understand that they would not only be targets of revolution but could themselves join in the revolution as well. Feng therefore prepared what he aptly calls two extremely banal (*p'ing-fan-te-hen*) essays criticizing Confucius and himself. The first carries a patronizing editorial introduction: ''This is a step forward, and is worth welcoming.''[40] As Feng prepared his articles, his ''tense feelings gradually diminished.'' He is now (February 1974) eighty years old; how fortunate he is to have witnessed this revolution, and how kind is the leadership to encourage an old man like him to write.[41]

During the course of this campaign Fei Hsiao-t'ung was interviewed again, together with the writers Wu Wen-ts'ao and Hsieh Ping-hsin, this time by the journalist Howard Chao (Chao Hao-sheng). Fei again explained his change: In the 1930s he had studied under Malinowsky. The trouble with Malinowsky's system is that it contains no contradictions; it is just one thing related to another. ''This was my former way of thinking. That's the way I talked in the 1930s. At that time I thought it was right to speak from such a standpoint. Now I want to change, because I recognize that the world is changing''—for the better, of course. His foreign friends have their doubts: When was he telling the truth—now, or in the past? ''My answer is, those are two periods; both are true.''[42] There is an ambiguity here. If Malinowsky's system is wrong, it was as wrong in the 1930s as it is now. Fei must mean that he was sincere in accepting the system then, and he is sincere now in rejecting it. He does not tell clearly of any intellectual insights that led him to abandon Malinowsky, but he does make not-too-veiled references to political pressure. And it is the role of political pressure in the formation of his opinions, not his attitude on functionalism, that arouses the doubts of his foreign friends.

Fei concludes his interview on a jocular note: ''Now I have only one remaining problem. I'm too fat.'' Yet his musings on the necessity to change with the times are rather melancholy, at least in cold print. ''But I changed. Lin Piao didn't change, and he is dead. That's the difference between us.''[43] In 1957 Fei says he became a rightist; he had not learned from the workers-peasants-soldiers. He was wrong.

> But the *i-lao* [officials of an overthrown dynasty living in retirement under the new one] of old were always *i-lao*. Wang Kuo-wei [a Ch'ing dynasty scholar unable to adapt to the anarchic, corrupt vulgarity of the Republic] jumped into K'unming Lake. We didn't jump. We chopped off our pigtails. But if we remained always the objects of revolution, we would end up like Wang Kuo-wei. We can also make revolution, if only our standpoint changes.[44]

Some foreign observers are gratified that Fei and those like him are finally living up to their "self-chosen responsibilities as conscientious citizens of the People's Republic of China."[45] It is certainly in bad taste to call these persons shameless opportunists, as do some on Taiwan. It may be in equally bad taste, however, to make too much of choice. "But if we remained always the objects of revolution, we would end up like Wang Kuo-wei." "Lin Piao is dead." Fei gives the impression, deliberately, one would think, of adapting under great pressure to circumstances over which he has no control and which he would not have spontaneously chosen. To change is better than to die. Another foreign evaluation of the role of the old intellectuals corresponds somewhat to Fei's remarks about the *i-lao*: "Like the Great Wall and the Ming Tombs he is tolerated, and exhibited, as a cultural relic."[46] This was the situation in the early 1970s.

Participation or Mobilization

Unlike the traditional Chinese state, the current regime works to involve the masses directly in the functioning of the political order. The method used, of course, is the mass line. The Chinese communist concept of participation is not the same as the liberal one. In liberal terms participation means "exerting popular influence on political decisions," but the "Chinese style defines [its] major function . . . as execution of Party policies."[47] Giovanni Sartori questions whether the sort of popular activity that occurs in regimes like the Chinese is properly called participation; it might more accurately be termed mobilization:

> Thus, the advocates of participatory democracy are hardly satisfied by any kind of involvement in politics. To them participation means *self-motion*. And surely the original definite meaning of the term conveys the idea of a free citizen who acts and intervenes—if he so wishes—according to *his* best judgement. So conceived, participation is the very opposite, or very reverse, of mobilization. Mobilization does not convey the idea of individual self-motion, but the idea of a malleable, passive collectivity which is being *put into motion* at the whim of persuasive—and more than persuasive—authorities.[48]

Mobilization is not only a feature of Chinese politics but is common to the totalitarian regimes of this century. Whether we call it participation or mobilization, it functions primarily as an instrument of social control.

There is the impression, however, that in the Maoist version of the mass line there is more than totalitarian mobilization as a means of maintaining control under conditions of great and directed social change. Some believe the Maoist line does not fear spontaneity and implies a genuine trust in the masses. The Maoist, or radical, position on the mass line is in fact different from the moderate position, and just as the radical position can lead to the justification of a kind of opposition within the party, so too can it lead to something like participation in its normal sense, and therefore opposition, more as an unintended consequence than as anything else. Thus, in the early days of the Cultural Revolution, the party, after its fashion, sent work teams into the schools to direct the student movement and see that those the party establishment wanted purged were purged. Mao, however, ordered the withdrawal of work teams, accusing them of exercising bourgeois dictatorship and implementing "white terror."[49] The masses were to make revolution on their own, without the help of the institutionalized party and even against segments of it.

Here as elsewhere we must not exaggerate the differences between the radicals and the moderates. The radical position, in particular, varies with the concrete circumstances. Thus, rather early in the Cultural Revolution Chiang Ch'ing said "that the problem was not with the form of the work teams, but with their direction and policies."[50] That is, they apparently would have been fine, had Mao been controlling them rather than Liu Shao-ch'i. Nevertheless, the differences remain. The moderate view seems to entail a typical Leninist distrust of mass spontaneity. The radical view, which can be best examined in policies toward agriculture and in the Red Guard movement, is ambivalent and perhaps even contradictory—in the literal, not dialectical, sense of that term.

Mao's earliest major political work, his report on the peasant rebellion in Hunan in 1927, praises the revolutionary spontaneity of poor peasants.[51] Thereafter Mao often spoke as if he believed that the masses would spontaneously adopt a revolutionary position. The epitome of this attitude is perhaps his famous 1958 statement on "poor and blank":

> Aside from other characteristics, the most obvious characteristics of the population of China are: one, it is poor; two, it is blank. This seems bad, but is in fact good. The poor can always change their thought. They dare to do; they want revolution. A sheet of blank paper carries no burden, and the most beautiful characters can be written on it, the most beautiful pictures painted.[52]

This is no unrestrained spontaneity: China's third great advantage turns out to be the "leadership of the party," and a blank piece of paper is a rather passive agent that spontaneously would not seem to do anything except decay. There is, however, some connotation of the workers of the world who have nothing to lose but their chains. Because they are blank, the people must be guided. But they are poor and will spontaneously respond to revolution.

Poor people, all else being equal, will in fact probably choose spontaneously to be less poor. But Mao is perhaps in error if he thinks that the poor (who, after all, are not "blank") will automatically accept any policies their rulers decide to set. Those adopted in 1958, when Mao discovered his theory of poor and blank, tended in the short run to increase hardship rather than alleviate it. Throughout 1958, the year of the Great Leap Forward, there was much talk of unleashing the masses, of freeing their energies from the bondage of conservatism. By 1960, however, there was another twist being given to the mass line. The planning bureaucrat, Li Fu-ch'un (a representative of the type of person who had been ignored in 1958) said: Some people in our party become satisfied when things go well

> and do not sincerely listen to the voice of the masses. They think they know it all [*tzu-i-wei-shih*] and are no longer willing to receive criticism from the masses. When problems arise they do not discuss them with the masses or receive supervision by the masses, but think to resolve them by simple administrative methods. These comrades do not understand that the mass line should be implemented both in times of hardship and in times of victory.

Such comrades "squander the position and prestige of the Party."[53] Another writer argued that during the Great Leap "a minority of comrades were not good at learning lessons by summing up experiences." The first secretary of Shansi complained that agricultural production was suffering from the weather, but the way to improve production would be for the cadres to "reform their work styles" and become "closer to the masses."[54] In the dark days of December 1960, as the leadership was beginning to grasp the magnitude of the disaster, a politician who usually associates himself with the radical tendency discovered: theory is not enough; we also need to unite with the masses in order to find out the facts.

> Thus, cadres should discuss all things with the masses and hear the opinions of the masses. No matter what opinions the masses have, they must be heard patiently and sincerely, after which they may be analyzed and treated distinctly.[55]

The word *masses* is being bandied about, but all of these quotations are criticisms of the great mass movement, the Great Leap Forward. The Chinese radicals and their foreign sympathizers often condemn the moderate tendency as bureaucratic and elitist, and the criticism is sufficiently just. It would seem, however, that on the question of agricultural policy the moderates were more in touch with the felt needs of the people. The radicals sometimes admit this, accusing the moderates of empiricism, of pointing out that popular attitudes are sometimes in fact different from what radical theory would have them be.[56] Both versions of the mass line, as applied to peasants, are elitist. The 1958 radical vision is of an elite mobilization of a passive population. The moderate view does not imply that the peasants should have that much to say about agricultural policy, but, rather, that their attitudes are part of the factors that the leadership must take into consideration, part of the objective reality. The moderates are not less elitist, but less voluntaristic.

By 1962 the radicals no longer spoke so confidently of the spontaneous mass inclination to revolution. The Public Report of the Tenth Plenum of the Eighth Central Committee says, "Within society there still exist bourgeois influences among small producers"—that is, among peasants—and these influences must be wiped out.[57] A few months later Mao set in motion a socialist education campaign designed to train peasants to the attitudes radical theory predicts they have.

The Red Guard movement would indicate, however, that Mao had not entirely lost faith in mass spontaneity, and the mobilization of the Red Guards did in fact come to resemble something close to participation, largely because this mobilization (unlike that of the Leap) was not initially under direct political control. The aim of Mao and his allies was to break the power of the party machine, and a mass uprising was the chosen means to this end. On August 8, 1966, the Central Committee, meeting in enlarged session, passed a Resolution on the Great Proletarian Cultural Revolution, decreeing: "Let 'daring' take the lead; unleash the masses."[58]

The Red Guards were mainly high school and university students, persons in a position to see in stark form the discrepancies between what they had been taught about the new society and its mundane realities. The hand of the party had been particularly heavy upon the students, and as a group students are perhaps less sensitive to the consequences of social indiscipline than are other categories. More than the poor they perhaps dare to do, since many of that age are convinced they are immortal. A typical letter to Mao from an alliance of Red Guard groups captures the atmosphere of the period and the movement.

> Venerable Sir [*Nin Lao-jen-chia*]: You have pointed out to us: If there is revisionism at the Center, what should we do? If there is revisionism in China, what should we do?
>
> Our answer is as sharp as nails of steel: Rebel! Rebel! Rebel![59]

The conventional view of the Cultural Revolution is that it was a "movement fundamentally aimed at destroying established bureaucratic authority."[60] This was probably never the fundamental aim of Chou En-lai or even of Lin Piao, but it may have been the objective of many Red Guards and (temporarily) of some of their high-ranking supporters, those who had no ready access to established bureaucratic authority. In January 1967 an alliance mainly of student groups but including some worker groups as well, led by Chang Ch'un-ch'iao, overthrew the old municipal party committee of Shanghai and proclaimed that city a commune like the Paris Commune.

> From now on Shanghai enters a broad new historical period. Party, governmental, financial, and literary authority has been returned to the hands of the proletarian revolutionary faction. The people of Shanghai have been liberated a second time and have become direct masters of their own soil.[61]

This certainly seems a rejection of bureaucratic authority, although it is not clear that the Shanghai Commune would have been able to avoid the propensity to manipulation, repression, or incohesion characteristic of other experiments in direct participatory democracy. The Peking media ignored the Shanghai Commune, however, although they did report the victory of the proletarian revolutionary faction.

The radical attack on bureaucratic authority was limited by the nature of the coalition at the top attempting to direct the Cultural Revolution, but also, perhaps, by the consequences of unrestrained spontaneity. The Red Guards were able to destroy the influence of the party bureaucracy because the army did not hinder their activities against the party. It seems to have been relatively easy to form a Red Guard group and, particularly after the party establishment had been defeated, the movement tended to fragmentation. It had been predicted all along that there would be "differences of opinion among the masses."[62] In fact, there were Red Guard factions formed in all the schools or other units from which they came, and much of the time there was factionalism within the units.[63] As the movement spread, factionalism also grew among workers and functionaries. In January 1967, efforts began to bring some cohesion to the movement through the Revolutionary Great Alliance, composed of "workers, revolutionary students, and revolutionary masses," or, in another version, the "working class, other revolutionary masses, and revolutionary cadres."[64] To replace the political institutions that had been destroyed, the revolutionary masses were to join with the revolutionary cadres and the army to form the triple alliance and establish temporary power organs, the revolutionary committees.[65] This, at least formally, implied that the revolutionary masses would be allowed to participate in policy making directly, although in conjunction with others.

The required alliances, however, were difficult to form. The Red Guards had been told that "to rebel is justified" and were reluctant to submit to authority once again. At the same time, the hostility between factions, sometimes based upon long-standing personal grievances, made them reluctant to join with each other and eager to seek allies among the enemies of their enemies. The local struggles reflected the struggle at the top to the extent that some groups seem to have had connections reaching up to the Central Cultural Revolution Group and others had connections with the local military forces. Sometimes issues of principle were involved, but often the alliances would be based on the logic of the local situation. If your enemies were close to someone who was close to someone who was close to someone who was close to Chiang Ch'ing, your group would attempt to come to terms with the soldiers in the locality. Even where ideological issues seem to have played a role, the struggle came to be conceived in terms of pure power. A spokesman for the Chingkangshan, taking off from a statement of Mao's that the basic problem of revolution is the problem of political power, railed at his enemies:

> Political power is the center, political power is the direction, political power is the root of revolution; in a word, power over all. . . . Some people mock us saying our breasts are full of power, power, power; that we are ambitionists who never think of anything but seizing power. Right! . . . What is wrong with seizing power for the proletariat, for the party?[66]

"Some people" provided the obvious rejoinder: "What they are struggling for is not revolutionary great power, but for individualistic small power. The only thing they are afraid of is that someone will seize their power."[67] The second group here claims to be calling for unity, but clearly it would not mind seizing the Chingkangshan's power. One story of the fight within the Seventh Ministry of Machine Building indicates it grew out of personal hostilities festering since the early 1960s. The two groups involved were the 916 (September 16) Revolutionary Rebels and the New 915 Revolutionary Rebels. The difference in name, if it does anything, exaggerates the difference in principle.[68]

Military intervention had been ordered in January 1967 to restore order—something the army's commander, Lin Piao, had no doubt anticipated when he first encouraged disorder. The actual intervention was taken under the direction of the regional and provincial commanders, who were ordered to support the left. But everyone claimed to be the left. The soldiers were naturally inclined to support the more docile groups; the students, who had tasted both blood and freedom, were not inclined to submit to the army. Matters came to a head in July, when the commander of the Wuhan Military Region apparently broke under the strain of attempting to support the left while at the same time restoring normal order, and suppressed the Red Guards allied with the Central Cultural Revolution Group, ignoring orders from the Center to desist. Wuhan was brought to heel by paratroopers and gunboats under direct Central command, but thereafter the authorities found it expedient to allow the soldiers a freer hand in restoring order.[69]

After the Wuhan incident the Red Guard movement was under restraint; it was brought to an end a year later, when the Cultural Revolution Group finally abandoned its shock-troops. Yao Wen-yuan announced to the Red Guards that they had fulfilled their historical function. The former "revolutionary masses" had turned out to be "petty-bourgeois intellectuals" who should accept reeducation from the working class.[70] In early September the Red Guards held their last hurrah, a final mass rally in Peking. Chou En-lai blandly told the little red generals:

> Young people must respond to the summons of our great leader Chairman Mao: Face the basic level, face the masses, face production; go up to the mountains and down to the farm; go to the factories, to the mines, to the villages: Go labor.[71]

Chiang Ch'ing also spoke, and her remarks are the only hint by a high-ranking radical that the Red Guards might be receiving somewhat shabby treatment. The speech itself is somewhat incoherent ("I only heard about the meeting this morning").

> We do not want to forget the rich contributions established by the revolutionary youth and the little red generals in the early and middle stages of the revolution. . . . Now there are a minority of little red generals who have committed this or that mistake. It is our responsibility to straighten them out. . . . If there are just a few individual units, or some armed struggles—well, that's very funny. Naturally it is a bad thing to depart from the masses and to depart from the masses in the unit—that's not good; we oppose it. But bad things can become good things, if we learn from experience.[72]

While the Red Guard movement did involve genuine participation of a sort, the movement itself was always somewhat artificial. It had been put into motion by an elite in order to destroy another segment of the elite and was closed down when it had served its purpose. The delay in closing it down was mostly a consequence of continued factional maneuverings among the victorious elite. Still, a great upheaval remains a great upheaval, even if it is artificial, and it will have consequences. The Red Guards had been sent to the countryside in 1968, but factionalism was by then endemic, and other factions—say, among workers—could not be treated so cavalierly. The party membership was broadened, and provisions were made for a kind of participation different from totalitarian mobilization. This pattern, characterized in the last chapter as elitist pluralism, does not fit either the moderate or the radical tendency but was a consequence of their interplay.

October 1968 saw a drive to "absorb new proletarian blood" into the party. "Outstanding rebels"—particularly workmen—should be brought into the party. The "mass representatives"—factional chieftains—have "defects," but these can be overcome by education. We must "gradually work for a united, monolithic leadership."[73] It is natural enough that the vanguard of the proletariat should wish to include a fairly substantial number of proletarians, and perhaps Liu Shao-ch'i in his days of running the party had been too negligent of this. But the drive to absorb new blood also seems to have been an effort to co-opt, and put under party discipline, those workers who had managed to establish strong factional followings among their mates. The manner of conducting the recruiting drive shows a desire to achieve factional balance. The comrades should avoid the superstitious belief in elections (*mi-hsin hsüan-chü*): "This also is a form of conservatism." "The decisive factor in determining the nature of a power organ is the line it upholds, the class interest it reflects, not the form by which it is chosen."[74] The party has never really been too superstitious about elections. Part of the point of this warning may have been a response to those Red Guard groups who were calling, as they were being suppressed, for democratic elections. But the avoidance of elections is also a manifestation of the conservative, elitist nature of the new participation. Were elections to be held within units, a dominant faction might have been able to monopolize the leading positions, resulting in continued lack of cooperation or even continued fights. The line called for the factions to coexist. Thus, the new line encouraged participation in one sense by bringing many outside the party into it, but it discouraged participation in another sense by limiting political competition. In 1969 the slogan for this policy was the "cup of water filled to the brim," an endorsement of the status quo at the local or basic levels. This conciliatory policy was not universally popular. In August 1968 the *People's Daily* and *Red Flag* reprinted a protest against the emerging trend from *Workers' Rebel News*, an organ of some Shanghai radicals.

> These bigshots [*t'ou-t'ou*] depart from the workers, the peasants, the warriors, the inhabitants, the majority of the masses. None of the masses are happy; even the people who support their faction are not happy. The masses should rise up and exercise supervision over the bigshots.[75]

The line, however, called for the conciliation of the factional bigshots.[76]

As the party began to reconsolidate itself after 1969, it took over once more the leadership functions until then performed by the revolutionary committees based on the triple alliance. The party did incorporate factional leaders, but there had never been the intention that the party should become a corporatist combination. Rather, the goal had been gradually to restore monolithic leadership. Throughout the early 1970s there seems to have been a decreasing stress on direct class representation. A draft for a new state constitution drawn up in 1970, in addition to the functional revolutionary triple alliance of army, cadres, and masses, speaks of a new triple alliance: "old, middle-aged, and young" cadres.[77] If *old* is in part a synonym for *moderate*, and *young* for *radical*, this would imply an agreement to seek a balance of tendencies rather than any direct mass representation. The final version of this constitution, adopted in 1975, omits the functional combination, and only the "old, middle, and young" remain.[78]

Despite the tendency since the Cultural Revolution to limit mass influence, Richard Pfeffer argues that China has developed institutions that should result in greater mass control over policy, or at least serve to keep policy geared to the needs of the masses. These include open-door rectification, reform of the educational system, the May 7 Cadre Schools, and direct class representation in governing organizations.[79] Educational reform, like the much-publicized rural health programs, may serve the general well-being of the population but would not seem to imply any popular control over policy. Similarly, open-door rectification (the soliciting of criticisms of party members from persons outside the party) and the May 7 Cadre Schools might serve to keep functionaries aware of the problems of ordinary people but again do not imply mass influence on policy. Their main function may be to increase control by the higher levels over the lower levels within the party.

Even direct class participation by itself need not mean much.[80] Since the locus of real decision making is the party, we may perhaps now ignore the mass representation on the revolutionary committees. The central committees "produced by election" in 1969 and 1973 include a substantial proportion of mass representatives, unlike earlier CPC central committees. But the Central Committee of the Communist Party of the Soviet Union has included proletarians for a long time, and the bulk of party and government officials in Russia are of worker or peasant background.[81] Yet this direct class representation does not seem to have made the Soviet regime particularly responsive to popular demands. To the extent that the Chinese and Soviet parties are unresponsive to popular pressure, this is a result of their Leninist organization and ideological goals, not of their social composition.[82]

If there is genuine and routine consultation with those outside the party, combined with a broadening of the base of the party, this *could* lead to greater popular influence over policy. Pfeffer's hypothesis is difficult to test, since descriptions of the decision-making process in the Chinese press are stereotyped and vague. It is clear that consultation does occur, but its significance is not always obvious.

Thus, in 1970 the party secretary of a production brigade in Chekiang visited the famous Tachai Brigade in Shansi and upon returning consulted with his masses on whether the Tachai system should be adopted there. This would mean that remuneration would be made partly according to political reliability rather than simply according to labor and that the basic accounting unit—the unit which divides among itself grain for consumption—would be the production brigade (*sheng-ch'an-tui*) rather than the production team (*sheng-ch'an-hsiao-tui*) that had been the norm for most of China since around 1961. The Tachai system, in effect, is a higher level of collectivization than that represented on most of the communes. The reaction of the masses here was pretty much what one might expect: the poorer teams wanted more collectivization and the richer teams wanted less. The decision was to leave things as they were.[83]

This is somewhat vitiated as an example of grass-roots democracy when we realize that the decision is in fact in accord with a policy apparently decreed by the Center some months earlier. The 1970 draft state constitution had explicitly retained the production team as the accounting unit, and throughout the spring of 1971 the official press was emphasizing the propriety of remuneration according to labor. The decision at the Center, however, could have been a consequence of many such consultations at the local level.

There seems to have been considerable local variation in the organization of agriculture in the early 1970s. This does not necessarily imply democracy in all cases, but it may imply some form of local control. In December 1971 the party moved to bring about more uniformity. An internal document complained that in some cases collectivization had been pushed too far, while in others peasants were eating all they produced and not selling grain to the state. The document sets out some detailed guidelines: the amount of grain that accrues to the commune (rather than to the household) should be gradually increased, but only "after discussion with and approval by the commune members." Grain should be distributed so that everyone receives a basic ration, and the remainder distributed according to labor. "Also, other methods [e.g., Tachai] supported by the majority of the commune members may be implemented." "Presently," however, "we must pay attention to egalitarianism"—that is, discourage it.[84] This perhaps tends to support Pfeffer's hypothesis of popular control of a sort, but the consequences of consultation with the masses seem to be decidedly non-Maoist.

This, I think, is the contradiction within the radical mass line policy: when the masses are allowed to act spontaneously and social discipline is maintained, they do not act in a radical way. The 1975 state constitution repeats the moderate guarantees of the 1970 draft: the team is the basic unit; to each according to his work; the commune members (peasants) may retain some private land. Immediately after the promulgation of the constitution, however, the radical group began a campaign against bourgeois legal rights (*tzu-ch'an-chieh-chi fa-ch'üan*), those constitutional guarantees.[85] Bourgeois rights are a residue of the old society and will vanish under communism. They cannot be eliminated immediately, but they should be considered a defect in our socialist society. They should be limited, not expanded. The practical import of this (if the radicals are able to control policy at all) is perhaps to cut back concessions to the peasants to the minimum allowed by party policy (there is evidence that the amount of land under private cultivation has in some places been greater than that allowed;[86] this, presumably, was to change). The attack on bourgeois rights stressed dictatorship, not consultation, and involved renewed criticisms of peasant spontaneity: ''Socialist thought cannot develop spontaneously among peasants.''[87]

The new style of decision making, as outlined in a report on pig raising in a county in Hunan, may be contrasted with the approved form of earlier years. Pigs are proverbially bourgeois animals and have not taken well to collectivization. Nevertheless, this report says, they should be raised collectively by the communes and the production brigades. Some cadres have been influenced by a theory spread by the class enemy: ''You go broke trying to raise pigs collectively.'' Therefore, the county party committee ''helped the party branch study Chairman Mao's directives on developing pig raising. They deepened their criticism of the revisionist line, criticized capitalist inclinations, and mobilized the masses to expose and criticize the sabotage activities of the class enemy.'' Now 32 percent of the pigs in the county are being raised collectively. In the fight against bourgeois rights, some brigade cadres ''improperly limited family pig raising by commune members and thus influenced [discouraged] the commune members' activism in pig raising.'' The county comrades then stepped in again with more help, although this time they did not look for a class enemy. The proper direction is: ''Actively develop collective pig raising; continue to encourage commune members to raise pigs'' (i.e., privately).[88]

Here, direction comes from above, from the county, which has to help the poor basic level cadres who, when they are not committing one kind of mistake, are committing another. The role of the masses is passive: they are available for mobilization against the class enemy, and they lose interest in pigs when their own are taken away and they have to continue to do the work and bear the expense without receiving the benefit. The masses may also provide the ''class enemy.'' There is no apparent consultation, but there is a recognition of the unpopularity of the approved policy and a willingness to accept some of the limitations on the policy growing from its unpopularity.

The CPC moderates have been willing to allow some popular influence on policy, this influence resulting in an endorsement of the status quo. The radicals have, perhaps, a greater abstract trust in mass spontaneity. But when the population can influence the policies chosen, it does not choose radical policies. When, as in the Cultural Revolution, mass spontaneity is encouraged and most political controls removed, the result is fragmentation. ''Whether or not mass society is a necessary condition for totalitarianism, it would certainly seem to be the case that totalitarianism is a sufficient condition for mass society.''[89] The small groups organized by the regime have not countered this, nor should they have been expected to insofar as they fulfilled their function of enhancing political control. The groups that formed spontaneously in the Cultural Revolution inhibited control by the regime. There is a theory to the effect that the party bosses, like the bulk of the Chinese population, are dependent, uptight types who fear that any relaxation of control will lead to *luan,* chaos. Mao, on the other hand, hung loose.[90] Mao's position, as we have seen, was more ambivalent. But whatever their personality problems might be, if the party bosses do in fact have the attitudes attributed to them, experience would indicate that the bosses are factually correct.

DICTATORSHIP

The regime deals with its enemies through dictatorship. The Chinese communists share the Marxist conception of the state as the executive committee of the ruling class, and their own state as no exception. At its founding the regime proclaimed itself a people's democratic dictatorship, a form that corresponds roughly to the European people's democracies. The 1975 constitution calls China "a socialist state of the dictatorship of the proletariat," although there are still occasional mentions of the people's democratic dictatorship. The essence of the idea of dictatorship seems to be arbitrary rule; to paraphrase the proponents of a different kind of dictatorship, the class enemy has no rights the proletariat is bound to respect. In the introduction to this chapter it is suggested that in the totalitarian context it is not always useful to make too fine a distinction between coercive and noncoercive methods of social control. Still, it is useful to examine under the rubric of dictatorship those methods that involve physical violence against persons, the threat of violence, or the direct use of coercive institutions such as courts, police, and jails.

Revolutionary dictatorship is often associated with terror, the "arbitrary use, by organs of political authority, of severe coercion against persons or groups, the credible threat of such use, or the arbitrary extermination of such individuals and groups."[91] If terror is identified with its most flagrant form, mass killing, the regime was most openly terroristic in its earlier period, during land reform, when landlords and counterrevolutionaries were exterminated after trials by people's tribunals.[92] The later collectivization campaigns, however, were carried out without the large-scale extermination of rich peasants. Some Chinese legal officials told a German reporter in 1974 that extremely few criminals are sentenced to death[93] and in relative terms this may well be true. Following the crackdown on the Hundred Flowers campaign, only three executions were announced, those of the leaders of a student riot in Wuhan.[94] In early 1968 there were reports of televised mass trials and executions in certain parts of China, apparently of undisciplined leftists.[95] According to the reports, however, only a few of those convicted at the trials were executed, the others receiving prison or labor-camp sentences. In addition to executions, there are certainly some casualties resulting from mistreatment by political authorities (i.e., from torture), and the fighting during the Cultural Revolution resulted in numerous deaths, although it is impossible to say how many.

Even if in relative terms few are executed, in absolute terms the number killed by the regime seems to be enormous. In 1957 student protesters claimed 770,000 persons had been killed since Liberation, of whom 720,000 (the population of a small nation) "were executed on the basis of false charges."[96] This century's bloodletting encourages a *Guiness Book of Records* approach to atrocities, so we might as well turn to that source itself. *Guiness* accords China its prize for the greatest mass killings, quoting a figure from Radio Moscow of April 7, 1969, of 26,300,000 killed between 1949 and 1965. Po I-po, a former functionary purged in the Cultural Revolution, is cited as saying two million "bandits" were executed from 1950 through 1953. A Taiwan estimate is given as "at least 39,940,000" from 1949 to 1969, but excluding those killed in the Cultural Revolution. The report by Richard Walker to the U.S. Senate Judiciary Committee in 1971 estimates 32.25–61.7 million killed.[97]

As Walker says in his report, however, all estimates are "rough guesses at best,"[98] and in fact there is no evidence to support any number given. It is equally difficult to estimate the number jailed. In 1958 Lo Jui-ch'ing, then minister of public security, gave some figures for the great *su-fan,* purge of counterrevolutionaries, campaign of June 1955 to October 1957. During this period he says his people captured 100,000 "reactionary counterrevolutionaries and other bad elements," plus 65,000 "ordinary counterrevolutionaries and criminals." In addition, he discovered 250,000 persons with "political problems." These numbers may or may not include the "very small number of good people" Lo says were arrested by mistake.[99] If we take Chou En-lai's 1957 estimate that since 1949, 16 percent of arrested counterrevolutionaries were executed,[100] this would put the *su-fan* death toll between 16,000 and 26,400 persons. There is no reason to think this is a legitimate extrapolation, however, since Chou says most executions took place in the early years; and there is no reason to extrapolate from the *su-fan* to other periods. Lo's estimates of the number arrested may, however, be rather low. One report says that in 1954, 11 percent of those arrested in a single county in Hunan were recidivist labor criminals; the 11 percent amounted to 95 persons.[101] This means that about 863 persons were arrested in a single county in what was not a very harsh year. Still, there is no reliable way of estimating even the order of magnitude of those either arrested or killed.

Our bloodlust sated, we might examine terror not as simply killing, but as the arbitrary use of political violence. In this sense the whole political-criminal process in China might be considered terrorist, since there is no rule of law, although we must then disassociate the term *terror* from its connotation of people going around quivering with fright. It is possible to argue, of course, that there was no real rule of law in traditional China either, and that was not, on the whole, a terrorist system. In traditional China the scope of political power was limited by *li*, ritual (or, to stretch a point, natural law); and while some, including dissidents on the Chinese mainland, find similarities between the Confucian *li* and the Maoist *ethos*, Maoism obviously does nothing to limit the scope of political power. In fact, although Chinese rulers traditionally disliked a rigid rule of law, each dynasty did have its detailed law codes. A form of due process operated, although it was not the Western form. Thus, there could be no conviction without a confession, and to this end some forms of judicial torture were permitted. Also, if a bad act did not happen to be covered by a law, another law could be applied analogously.[102]

The KMT wanted to set up a Western-like system of law, and in the mid-1950s the Communists were moving toward the establishment of socialist legality. In 1954 the late Tung Pi-wu, the prime champion of this trend, told the National People's Congress that since the People's Republic now had a constitution (its first was adopted that year), that constitution should be observed. Previously, because of the need to suppress counterrevolutionaries, it had been inexpedient to have a detailed system of law. But "hereafter it is not only possible but also necessary gradually to stipulate a relatively complete code of laws, in order effectively to guarantee state construction and to protect the democratic rights of the people."[103] Within a year, however, with the onset of the *su-fan* campaign, the concern switched to the "digging out of hidden counterrevolutionaries."[104] In the wake of the Hundred Flowers campaign, in which a prime demand had been that the party obey the constitution, party control was reasserted over the courts and all other legal institutions:

> To support and implement the leadership function of the party is the responsibility of the personnel of the state organs, especially the responsibility of party members. All state organs must have a party organization and must have party members participating in leadership functions. . . . But the rightist elements in the party are completely opposed to this. They seek to depart from party leadership and are scared the party will "interfere" with their work. . . .[105]

Lo Jui-ch'ing refuted those who think it a violation of the constitution for the party to interfere in the legal process: the party is simply carrying out the constitution.[106]

The courts are guided by "party policy and the law of the state." There has been no public codification of law, but there are individual regulations. "If the case is not covered by one of the special regulations, we deal with it according to the policy of the party." The absence of a complex code of laws has one happy advantage, Chinese legal officials say: there is no need for defense attorneys. The system "disappeared naturally," since no one ever wanted a lawyer. Defense attorneys may not be the only legal institution that has atrophied. Victor Li reports that in at least one area both the courts and the procuracy are inactive, and the Public Security Bureau—the police—handles cases all by itself.[107]

The usual penalty for running seriously afoul of the rulers is some form of forced labor. Labor reform, the most severe variety, is supposed to be imposed by a court. There is a right of appeal, but according to a former prisoner:

> an appeal of a sentence means the prisoner is not repentant for his crimes, and has not accepted the government leniency. Ipso facto, it is proof he has not learned his lesson. An appeal, therefore, is a demand for further punishment.[108]

Labor reform is for a set period of time. According to Lo Jui-ch'ing, a provision was added to the statute on labor reform by popular prisoner demand: "Any prisoner may voluntarily remain at his work with his team" after his term expires. Bao Ruo-wang says that it is virtually universal for released prisoners to remain in the camps, as it is almost impossible for them to find employment outside. They are treated like ordinary prisoners, except for being given a salary and allowed periods of home leave. The practice is not completely universal, however, as Whyte has interviewed a former labor-reform criminal who was released at the end of his term; he was, however, thereafter kept under supervision in his home area.[109]

Labor education, a less severe sanction than labor reform, was introduced in 1957 to take care of the rightists who had exposed themselves in the Hundred Flowers movement. The decision to send a person to labor education is not judicial but administrative, imposed by the person's work unit or by the police.[110] Originally there was no set period for labor education—one remained for as long as it took to improve one's attitude. In 1961, however, fixed sentences ranging from six months to three years were introduced.[111] Bao Ruo-wang claims that consistent failure by those undergoing labor education to meet work quotas can mean a change in the sentence to labor reform.[112]

There are also "voluntary" forms of forced labor in China that, while supposedly not punitive, may be regarded as such by some who undergo them. One of Lin Piao's alleged grievances against the Maoist system was that the sending of educated youths to the countryside had "become a type of labor reform."[113] The May 7 Cadre Schools, when they were first introduced, seem to have been similar to labor education; but now all cadres are supposed to pass through them, and the process may be becoming a kind of routinized sabbatical.[114]

From the very little that is known about Chinese jails and labor camps, there seems to be hardly any of the gratuitous brutality that characterized the Stalinist camps (what brutality there is, is calculated). Prisoners are not normally beaten but may be deprived of food to induce confession. Bao Ruo-wang says that labor camp inmates are very poorly fed; his experience, however, includes the years 1959–62, when very few Chinese even on the outside were well fed.[115] Exiles in Hong Kong report that in the campaigns against the class enemy in the countryside persons are often tortured or otherwise grossly abused, with death sometimes resulting from the mistreatment. This is corroborated by official documents, and officially these practices are condemned.[116] Red Guards arrested in the summer of 1966 as counterrevolutionaries, when Liu Shao-ch'i was still in control of the Cultural Revolution, report being beaten by the police.[117]

These do not exhaust the methods of dictatorship. Most class enemies are neither jailed nor killed but remain available as scapegoats, under supervision in their home areas. In concluding and in passing, we might also mention some unofficial forms of dictatorship. An official at a Peking hospital claims he criticized Liu Shao-ch'i in 1964, that is, well before it was the fashion to do so. He was fired from his job and told to report to work in the Shensi countryside. When he refused to go, he was declared insane and shut up in an asylum. He attempted a hunger strike but was fed through a hose.[118] Around the same time, Red Guards claim that Ai Ssu-ch'i, whom we met earlier in this chapter, was the victim of a medical murder instigated by his enemies in the Propaganda Department.[119] T'an Fu-jen, the boss of the Yunnan province after the Cultural Revolution, may have been murdered in 1970.[120] Lin Piao *may* have been murdered the following year.

IMPLICATIONS AND PROSPECTS

Chalmers Johnson, writing soon after the beginning of the Cultural Revolution, argued that prior to coming to power the CPC had to meet the genuinely felt needs of the population but that in recent years it has turned to defining those needs and imposing its chosen line. He hypothesizes, "Mao must either replace the mass line with policies of coercion or abandon his Communist vision in favor of some form of 'modern revisionism.'"[121] That it is still difficult to say whether this prediction has merit is in part because the terms used are vague, but mainly because the policies themselves are vague and shifting. It is possible to see, however, a general tendency away from democratic persuasion and toward dictatorship since 1962 or so.

After the abandonment of the capitalist road in 1962, the party line has generally stressed the economic interests of the population less than their duty in the task of building socialism—although after the death of Lin Piao there was a partial return to talk of the welfare advantages of socialism. Before 1962, even the sacrifices of the Great Leap Forward were justified as short-term necessities for a glorious future. In 1963, however, the emulation of Lei Feng, a dead soldier whose every thought, word, and deed was devoted to selfless service to Mao and the people, was introduced.[122] According to Tung Chi-ping, a defector who was a student at the time, "the promise of great prosperity just around the corner aroused only bitterness and resentment. . . . Then, the only possible approach in propaganda was to . . . make us accept our suffering cheerfully." Tung, of course, is hardly in a position to know the reasoning behind the campaign, but he was in a position to testify to its effects: "No one, not even the most backward youngster, believed in Lei Feng. He became the butt of innumerable jokes. Invariably the idea of these jokes was to exhort someone to emulate Lei Feng by doing something for one's selfish benefit."[123] We cannot know how widespread this attitude was. The point remains, however, that the people were no longer being offered the carrot; and to the extent that they remained uninspired by visions of carrots for others, all that remained was the stick.

The Cultural Revolution was a highly violent and coercive movement. The ideological line since 1972, particularly that associated with the radical tendency, also has a coercive ring. Lin Piao had allegedly complained of the lack of freedom in China. In February 1972, *Red Flag* reminded its readers that proletarian dictatorship is, after all, dictatorship. "All political power is the dictatorship [*chüan-cheng*] or so-called autocracy [*tu-ts'ai*] of a given class." Toward enemies there is "suppression and violence, not any 'kindness and mercy.'"[124] The campaign against Confucius from 1973 to 1975 hailed the progressive nature of China's foremost tyrant, the First Ch'in Emperor, praising not only his unification of China but his tyranny itself. The mainstream of this campaign is probably an argument for the moderate trend, but some of the praise for Ch'in's dictatorship would seem to come from the radicals. The 1975 campaign against bourgeois rights and the concomitant stress on dictatorship may bear the promise of more coercion.

Since the Cultural Revolution there has been an increase in the representation of the more coercive institutions on the ruling organizations, as well as increased representation of the masses. Soldiers constituted a very high proportion of the Central Committee elected in 1969.[125] The fall of Lin Piao may have reduced the influence of the military but may also have increased the influence of the police system, which, since the Cultural Revolution (and until October 1976), seems to have been allied with the radicals.[126] In early 1976 the police boss, Hua Kuo-feng, became premier of the State Council, and party chairman later that year.

It is not clear, however, that this stress on coercion, if that is what it is, represents a secular trend or simply a reaction to increasing social disorder. Military intervention was required to suppress the Cultural Revolution. In the fall of 1973 a new coercive instrument was introduced, the urban militia. This would work "under the monolithic leadership of the party" and "exercise full-scale dictatorship over the class enemy." "Their ears are sharp, their eyes are bright; they dare to struggle, are skilled at struggle. They firmly implement the party's policies."[127] The urban militia may represent an attempt by the radicals in local party office to form for themselves an agency of coercion independent of the army. The desire for such an agency is not gratuitous, however, or merely a reflection of ambition. The militia was formed "at a time when the rusticated youths [who had been returning to the cities in large numbers] were posing increasing problems of law and order in the cities and the PLA's role in urban politics was being phased out in the developing anti–Lin Piao campaign."[128] Of course, increased social disorder itself may be a symptom of the increasing ineffectiveness of democratic persuasion. If social disorder increases, we should expect the regime to become increasingly coercive. An alternative—although a risky one—might be liberalization, with the regime still maintaining a firm hold over the instruments of violence.

5

Oppositional Interests

This chapter examines some possible sources of opposition to and within the regime in China, opposition that may vary in intensity from specific to integral. The concentration is upon occupational or other objectively defined interests, rather than on opinion groups,[1] which are discussed in the next chapter. To the extent that the regime succeeds in the Marxist goal of the elimination of distinctions based upon the division of labor, discussion of this sort may become futile. In recent years, however, in reaction to an oversimplified version of the totalitarian model, students have come to recognize that interests persist in a society like China's, even if their expression is blocked; and new interests develop as the regime becomes consolidated.[2] Mao's theory of contradictions among the people is itself a partial legitimization of the persistence of distinct interests.

Chinese politics, however, can hardly be discussed in terms of interest-group politics, if only because interest groups as such as not allowed to form. It is possible to consider Chinese politics in terms of certain institutional interests, although, as the discussion below—particularly of the army—should show, the larger abstractions break down upon closer examination. Also, much potential opposition to the regime may have no institutional expression whatsoever: it is partly to this end that the regime is structured as it is.

Instead of examining the operation of actual interest groups, we must try to define what David Truman calls potential groups: interests that may exist "whether or not [they are] found at the moment . . . as characteristic of a particular organized group."[3] It is easy enough to identify potential interests in the abstract. The problem is that not all conceivable potential interests are necessarily relevant to anything.[4] The Marxist problem of consciousness and false consciousness might be discussed in terms of potential interests. It is plausible to argue that all workers share overriding common interests, and that if they identify more with their bosses or their nations than with other workers they somehow misperceive their true interests. While such ideas are relevant to politics construed as a branch of moral philosophy, they are not directly relevant to politics as an empirical study. It is easy to think of reasons why peasants might be unhappy with the current regime in China, or with any other regime anywhere.

But there is no guarantee that peasants will perceive their interests as an outside observer might, and certainly no ground to hold a priori that the observer's perception of peasants' interests is more accurate than their own.

In a discussion of potential sources of discontent, then, it is desirable to show that at least in some cases this discontent is also actual. Here there are grave problems of evidence. There is no valid or reliable way to sample Chinese opinion. Political discussions are conducted in tortuous, indirect, symbolic language. Much evidence of discontent is based upon rumor. Information from refugees may be suspect, as refugees have axes to grind and behavior to justify. The Communist press does not dwell much on discontent of a specific nature, except to say that the abuses identified are already being corrected. When unhappiness with policies is mentioned, it is usually attributed to class enemies—and in some cases it is at least possible that only the class enemies are unhappy. Assuming we can get reliable information, we must also be cautious in assessing its meaning: few people are simply peasants, or simply anything else; what bothers a man as a peasant may please him as a patriot. Until China becomes a much more open society than it now is it will be impossible to form a reliable estimate of the nature or extent of potential oppositional interests. In the meantime we can only present what evidence there is and form hypotheses.[5]

THE RULED

Black Elements

The black elements, *hei-lei fen-tzu,* are the pariahs of the new society. They may constitute about 5 percent of the general population (that is, the regime routinely claims it represents the interests of 95 percent of the population), or perhaps a little more. The black elements usually include landlords, rich peasants, counterrevolutionaries, "bad elements," and rightists. The landlords are those who had leased land to tenants prior to land reform. Rich peasants did not lease land but did employ (i.e., exploit) labor to work their own land and did not labor themselves. Counterrevolutionaries include those who had actively opposed the Communists prior to Liberation—minus those who changed sides in time—and persons who have actively resisted the regime since. Bad elements are criminals, rowdies, bums, and the like—in effect, bad elements. The rightist category was added in 1957 to embrace those who had shown themselves unhappy with the regime during the Hundred Flowers; in general they are those whose discontent has not led to overt acts of defiance, other than speech. For some reason, in many 1975 discussions rightists were not specifically mentioned in the list of the damned; the category was perhaps in the process of being replaced by a new one, "new bourgeois elements," to encompass, in particular, party members who had fallen out of favor—specifically, for rightist errors (*rightists* did return in 1976, however). The bourgeoisie as such, while not a favored class and also the source of all erroneous ideas and all outside corruption, is not included among the black elements and formed, in fact, a part of the people's democratic dictatorship. But many a former bourgeois falls under the classification of counterrevolutionary or rightist.

Landlord and *rich peasant* are supposedly economic classifications, although the terms have not reflected the economic realities for almost a generation. The other classifications are based upon political criteria. From time to time there are purgings of class ranks, in which additional persons may be classified as enemies. Class enemies are deprived of certain rights and privileges enjoyed by ordinary citizens (such as free or cheap medical care), are kept under supervision (if not imprisoned), and are expected to try to reform themselves. Few are sufficiently successful in this (in theory) to remove themselves from suspicion. The class-enemy status is not technically hereditary, and the children of class enemies are urged to draw a line of demarcation with their families; in practice the status is often handed from parents to children.

When the regime speaks of class struggle, the struggle is ostensibly against these class enemies. The black elements are perhaps those with the least to lose from an overthrow of the regime, and many of those so classified, along with their children, may have a deep hatred of the regime—possibly more, despite Machiavelli, for the murder of their fathers than for the theft of their patrimony. In 1957 the son of a landlord incautiously showed his diary to a "friend," and excerpts were printed in the *People's Daily*.

> I know this slave-labor China cannot last long. . . . Naturally I am now regarded as extremely "reactionary": fight! fight! fight! . . .
>
> Tomorrow is the birthday of the "party." I hate that birthday, since it marks the enslavement of China. All of Communist China is darkness, inequality. I hate the Communist Party, I hate the Chinese system. I wish to overthrow that system. . . . If I become a writer, I will direct my works against the slave system. Naturally, this might lead to bloodshed. I will spend the last drop of my blood attacking them. . . .
>
> I received a letter from my family and I cried. The family's hardships are too great to utter. They often eat unripe pumpkins. . . . Hateful. They don't even have rice to eat. But I know who causes the people to suffer in this way. . . .
>
> If people won't respect me I'll answer them with a whip. I must not lose my self-respect.

The paper gloats: "Just as he himself wrote on December 12 of last year in his diary, 'A diary is easily discovered. Therefore, . . . I must try to say less but store it in my heart!'''[6] Other class enemies have apparently used more than secret writings to manifest their opposition. When the first commune, *Wei-hsing* (Sputnik), was formed in Honan in 1958, it is said that one former landlord poisoned a fish pond and another stole sixty *chin* of corn; a ''bad element'' chopped down 200 trees.[7] In 1962 the KMT conducted a number of raids against the Fukien coast, and the local party said that this did much to cheer the black elements there.[8]

Not everything said about the activity of the class enemy is entirely credible. Any class enemy who actually goes around spreading the ''theories'' attributed to him (e.g., ''You go broke raising pigs collectively'') would seem to be either too audacious or too stupid to live. One would expect that those classified as enemies would ordinarily be abnormally cautious, avoiding anything that could give offense. According to a black-element exile in Hong Kong, ''The children of the five black elements have strong anticommunist thoughts, but being restricted by a lack of unified organization, united leadership, a struggle program, outside help, and so forth, no one dares express this.''[9] In many cases, perhaps, it is not a class enemy who expresses complaints; rather, those who voice complaints come to be termed class enemies.

Far from posing any threat to the regime, the class enemy may perform a useful role within it. We often hear such things as, ''To combat the natural disaster, it was first imperative to wage struggle against the class enemy.'' A 1971 report tells of such a struggle. When the class ranks were being purged in a village in 1968,

> there was a man of landlord status called Chiang Jui-lu. He had gone away for a long time and did not return to the village until 1948. After the agrarian reform in the winter of 1950, he took part in production under the surveillance of the masses. This man seemed to be quite honest and quite enthusiastic in his labor, and he never quarreled with anybody. . . . Sometimes he showed minor kindnesses by distributing medicine among the masses.

When the purge began, the local party committee reviewed his background. As the story goes, he then sent away a leather suitcase. This was intercepted and found to contain documentary evidence that he ''had served as a reactionary official for around 20 years and was a historical counterrevolutionary [a major in the National Army] who had perpetrated a heap of criminal acts. He was actually a dog that did not bark but could bite the people.'' The brigade party branch then had the masses ransack the man's house. On the third try they came up with some ''bayonettes and ammunition.''[10]

It is obviously impossible to say, but the whole thing sounds phony. It is unlikely that the man's background was really unknown. It is unlikely that he would have kept incriminating evidence around for so long (did he perhaps expect that when Chiang Kai-shek came back he would ask him for his credentials?) and then try to dispose of it in such an obvious manner at such a convenient time. The documentary evidence, along with the weapons, was probably planted. It is unlikely that anyone really regarded this poor man as a threat. He was available as a target for hostility that might otherwise be directed against the party; his elimination got rid of someone perhaps more popular than the party functionaries in the neighborhood; his exposure could *encourager les autres,* remind the people the party means business; and he could be offered by the local branch to the higher levels in order to display their vigilance.

Perhaps not all class enemies are quite this innocuous. The KMT claims to have information on the activities of numerous organized anticommunist and anti-Mao groups on the mainland and from time to time reports with satisfaction how these burn and loot and kill.[11] This is an aspect of life the regime prefers not to publicize, and it is difficult to know how reliable the Nationalist allegations are. The Communists are not completely silent on this, however, and banditry (which now, as in the past, can have political implications) may remain at least a minor problem, particularly in times of more general turmoil. Thus, in 1967 a "handful of class enemies" came and set up a gambling game in the brigade from which poor Chiang Jui-lu was later purged. "They actually belonged to a small group engaged in corruption, theft, and speculation."

> Later, these bad people hid themselves in a small valley on the border of Chekiang and Kiangsi, and they thought it was safe there. When the masses of Chekiang province went to arrest them, it took them half a minute to run over to the Kiangsi side, where they claimed to belong to Kiangsi. When the masses of Kiangsi came to arrest them, it took them half a minute to run over to the Chekiang side, where they claimed to belong to Chekiang.[12]

This border-hopping is a time-honored habit of Chinese bandits, practiced most notably in this century by Mao Tse-tung when he first climbed Chingkangshan. The lackadaisical attitude of the authorities implied in the above account is testimony to the chaotic conditions of 1967.

Some areas of the Chinese countryside may have remained unsafe into the 1970s. One report tells of a sent-down youth on mountain patrol who came across a bad scoundrel (*huai chia-huo*) cutting down trees. There was a fight, and the youth was wounded by the ax. Finally help came, and the scoundrel was arrested. He was discovered, "after investigation, to be a class enemy." The editorial comment by the *People's Daily* is interesting: "That youth is very brave. But in arranging forest patrol, the rural basic-level party organizations must pay attention to safety and not let educated youths undertake this duty alone."[13]

Bandits and criminals, political or otherwise, pose a threat to public order—unlike landlords, rich peasants, or run-of-the-mill rightists—but probably no real threat to the regime. As a generation comes and a generation passes away it might be expected that the original enemy classifications will come to lose whatever meaning they now retain. The old totalitarian model, in some versions, holds that a totalitarian regime requires enemies. In 1975 renewed stress was put on a theme that had been developed since 1962: "As long as overthrown classes exist, there can still appear within the party (and in society) representatives of the bourgeoisie who hope for a restoration and conduct restorationist activities."[14] These new bourgeois elements, presumably, will generate others like themselves—reactionary successors for the revolutionary successors to crush. The old landlords will soon all be dead; but without a major change, it will be a long time before China suffers from a dearth of class enemies.

Peasants

Balancing the black elements are the supposedly favored classes, the "five-red categories," which include a much larger number of people: workers, poor peasants, lower-middle peasants, soldiers, cadres, and the dependents of revolutionary martyrs. (Middle peasants—former independent entrepreneurs, professional people, and the like—occupy a sort of limbo position.) C. S. Chen argues that the poor and lower-middle peasants "have now replaced the landed interests as the most powerful class in the countryside."[15] His evidence is that in the area for which he had data the bulk of the rural cadres are recruited from these classes. This may imply a certain amount of power for those who become cadres, but it does not imply that peasants have power as a class. Most peasants have probably benefited in some ways from the regime—from the general restoration of order if from nothing else. Especially since the Cultural Revolution there have been efforts to improve peasant health care and to spread literacy in the countryside. In the early years the regime followed the example of the Soviet Union and concentrated upon the development of heavy industry. Since the late 1950s, however, there has been a general recognition of the primary economic importance of agriculture. Despite this, and despite the role of the peasantry in the Communist revolution, the regime is not prepared to pour large amounts of money into the countryside. Rural development is supposed to follow the example of the Tachai Brigade in Shansi, which stresses self-reliance (*tzu-li keng-sheng*). Also, peasant interests seem to be neglected when they conflict with other interests. This is brought out in a 1975 story, an idealized account of rural life designed to show educated youths how glorious it is to be a peasant. The report describes a contradiction between workers and peasants:

> Last year, because of negligence, effluent from the Red Hsiang River Machine Factory leaked into the . . . brigade's fish pond, poisoning more than 20,000 fish. The factory decided to pay $400 in compensation. The rural comrades pointed out:

> If the factory compensates us, it will use the state's money. It is better that we suffer this collective loss and not cause a loss to the state. The brigade party secretary said: "What compensation? You didn't do it on purpose. The factory's waste poisoned our fish, but it also fertilizes our fields." This incident was a very big lesson for the factory leadership. If this kind of contradiction between ownership by the whole people [the factory] and collective ownership [the fish pond] is not handled by putting politics in command, but simply through the use of money, it will be difficult to resolve well.[16]

This is one of the many instances where one suspects the whole story has not been told. It is possible that the rural comrades were shaming the factory for what seems like a rather mean offer (about U.S.$212). It is probably significant, in any case, that this report, departing from the usual custom, does not have poor and lower-middle peasants chiming in with homey approval of the party for being so generous with their fish.

It is fairly safe to say that in general terms the regime's rural policies help some peasants and hurt others. It is sometimes argued that peasants are wedded to private land ownership, and probably few peasants were pleased to lose to collectivization what they had gained a few years earlier in land reform. This, however, would probably not be a cause for long-term resentment if collectivization resulted in an improved standard of living. Some peasants—those with poor land or those who are not very good farmers—probably benefited immediately from land collectivization, in 1955 if not in 1958. More general resentment may, in ordinary times, be directed against those policies not directly related to narrowly economic livelihood, particularly toward the regime's family policy, which, in the abstract, cuts into the core of the peasant way of life. The regime's basic attitude has been consistent.

> To whom do children belong? Each class has its own understanding. [In feudal times children were supposed to bring wealth and fame to the family.] The bourgeoisie treats the younger generation as a commodity and substitutes money for so-called feelings, in order to satisfy their own selfish ends. In sum, they treat their children as private property, spoiling them when they are happy and cursing them when they are angry. . . . But in the eyes of the proletariat, children do not belong to the parents personally but should belong to the class, to the party.[17]

This attitude would seem as crass as anything attributed to the bourgeoisie and in any case is not the traditional attitude of the Chinese peasant.

Resistance to the family-reform law of the early 1950s was widespread in rural areas, particularly among men and mothers-in-law, and there are reports of the murder of numerous activist females.[18] Women's liberation for the peasant came to mean primarily that his wife would have to go to work in the fields; after collectivization, when family income came to depend upon work points, this became for many an economic necessity. In 1956 the *People's Daily* expressed shock that women doing heavy work were suffering injuries and miscarriages and that children were neglected because mothers were in the fields.[19] The nurseries on the communes may have helped ameliorate the problem of child neglect.

Despite the consistency of the regime's basic view of family life, it is perhaps in this area that the regime has been most willing to make pragmatic concessions to peasant views. (It is also probable that in their hearts many high-ranking Communists do not share the official position.) In the summer of 1958 it seemed that the regime had set out to implement the Platonic ideal of a nation of bastards raised in bureaux; but in December the party said it only wanted to destroy the feudal family system, which does not even exist any more under capitalism.[20] In 1959 participation in the public mess halls, the most obnoxious aspect of communal living, was made truly voluntary,[21] although the decision was not widely publicized and does not seem to have become universal until around 1961. A 1973 report scolded local party branches for their reluctance to cultivate female cadres. Part of this reluctance involved simple misogyny: "Some leading cadres say, 'Young women are frivolous and old women dither around and do not make any effort; they are not worth cultivating.'" The main reason was that if a girl had been trained in her own brigade, that brigade would lose her services if she married outside the village: she would, in the traditional manner, go live with her husband's parents. The author of the report accepts this but reminds the comrades that cadres serve the people as a whole, not any particular unit. The local cadres also complain that married women have housework and children and neglect their organizational duties. Here the author can only offer the timid suggestion that husbands of cadres help out around the house from time to time.[22] Among nonagricultural, or educated, cadres, it is not uncommon for husbands and wives to be assigned to work hundreds of miles apart from each other. In the countryside, however, the regime seems reluctant even to push matrilocal marriage, a practice for which there is some traditional precedent.

Traditional peasant attitudes on the family are no doubt good and valid in their own right as conducive to human happiness, although, like any other good, they are liable to abuse. Part of the reason for the persistence of tradition, however, is that it continues to be economically reinforced. China is not a welfare state, and it is expected that children will support their aged parents (making it expedient that the peasant have sons and that they be grown before he is too old—thus hindering the regime's policies on late marriage and birth control). The household still retains important economic functions, particularly in the production of handicrafts and the cultivation of cash-earning private plots. The need for a large agricultural force, combined with the greater attractiveness of life in the cities, means there must be strong official limitations on migration; children of peasants, then, continue to live with or near their parents.[23]

The regime, of course, is not prepared to tolerate the existence of the extended family as a source of authority alternative to itself, and the influence of the clan organizations, once especially strong in the south, has been reduced, if not eliminated entirely. Identification with the clan, however, does not seem to have given way completely to identification with the class. With the disruption of political control in the Cultural Revolution there seems to have been a modest clan revival.[24] It is difficult to say, however, what significance this may have; it is unlikely that, in the absence of complete chaos, the clans will regain anything approaching their former authority.

The land-reform program wiped out the economic basis for clan authority, as well as the economic basis of all nonparty local authority. The original policy was probably quite popular among those peasants who had little or no land, although it is impossible to determine the popularity of the killing that went along with land redistribution. Unlike in Russia, but like in East Europe, land was collectivized (a few years after it had been redistributed) without widespread killing, although collectivization met with opposition both from peasants and from basic-level cadres who had received land themselves a few years earlier.[25] While the regime stressed the mass line in its collectivization efforts, dictatorship was not entirely absent. The cooperatives were formed during the great *su-fan*, purge of counterrevolutionaries, campaign of 1955, and communization in 1958 followed upon an extensive antirightist and antilocalist campaign. There may even have been some temporarily effective resistance to the formation of communes. The big drive to establish communes took place in 1958, but years later a report from a brigade in Chekiang mentioned in an off-hand way that the brigade was not ''consolidated'' until 1959, and then with the ''help'' of ''PLA kinsmen'' (in context, the term does not imply a blood relationship).[26] P'eng Te-huai, a Politburo member and minister of defense until 1959, ''in 1958 . . . went to Hunan to make an investigation.''

> Returning to Peking, he said that his folks [*chia-jen*] had not a single cooking pan at home and found inconvenience in preparing meals because the pans were used as scrap in the large-scale refining of steel. He was dissatisfied with the mass movement. He grumbled and sighed.[27]

The confiscation of cooking implements for scrap was one way of inducing peasants to use the mess halls.

Although the regime does not justify its policy in these terms, the collectivization of agriculture should enhance political control over the peasants and make it easier to extract from them their surplus production. Collectivization also, however, seems to limit the amount produced; and in the past, when the regime has been concerned with its food supply, it has eased collectivization policies. According to one line of argument:

> China's agriculture was, until recently, at a highly advanced stage within the framework of ''traditional agriculture,'' i.e., all the components of the productive

> structure were combined in such a way as to attain a balance at a very high output level under the constraints of resources supplied from within the farm sector. Hence, the attempts to increase output by altering some components was likely to disrupt the balance and lead to a decrease in output unless agriculture was supported by resources from the modern non-farm sector.[28]

At the same time, "during the entire period from 1952 to 1965 there had been no observable technical progress or modernization in the agriculture of mainland China."[29]

These conclusions may be based upon faulty economic theory; the Chinese radicals would certainly argue that they are. Even within the party, however, there have always been those who have doubted the wisdom of collectivization in the absence of mechanization (although mechanization, of course, need not imply collectivization), and the problem of land ownership remains a very touchy one. The peasants themselves attributed the "temporary economic difficulties" of 1959–1961 to the policies of the Great Leap Forward. Ch'en Yun, at that time officially the seventh-ranking person on the Central Committee, inspected a commune near Shanghai in 1961 and reported, "The explanation to the effect that the policies formulated at the higher levels are completely correct, and that individual cadres in some localities have erred in their execution, is obviously difficult to satisfy the peasants." Ch'en quoted peasants as saying such things as, "Those who suffered at the hands of Chiang Kai-shek had cooked rice for their meals. Those who live in the blessed days of Chairman Mao have only congee." "The Communist Party's policies are all good, but none of them are workable."[30] A spokesman of the P'eng Chen faction within the party told a writers' conference in 1962: "There is a contradiction between the socialist ideological leadership and the actual needs of the peasants," and this contradiction has rendered that between socialism and capitalism secondary.[31]

All land was collectivized in the first days of the 1958 Leap, but after a few months the peasants were again permitted private plots. These are devoted mainly to the growing of vegetables, which are a source of cash income and provide a greater return than grain, whose price is controlled. Grain and commercial crops are grown on the collective land. About half the quota production is taken by the state as taxes or through compulsory purchase. An additional 10 percent or so goes for seed, feed, reserves, administrative funds, and welfare funds. The remainder is distributed to households by either the team or the brigade, depending upon which is the accounting unit on the particular commune. Each person receives a basic ration, and what is left over is divided according to the number of work points earned.[32] There are two methods for computing work points. In each case, points are earned for each day's work. One system is based upon ability to labor. Not all labor has the same value, and a strong, skilled farmer may be allowed fifteen points, say, for a day's work, while his wife would earn ten, and his young son, five. In the Tachai system, work-point assignments are not based on ability to labor but on political attitude (*cheng-chih piao-hsien*). Neither system satisfies everyone. A former sent-down youth reports that on the commune where he worked the first system "undeniably stimulated greatly the peasants' production activism but also tended to make the peasants pay attention to the rate of work, not the quality." Also, the system encouraged inequality. Later, the Tachai system was adopted. The brigade became the accounting unit, and work points were assigned by political criteria. The cadres all had themselves placed in the highest category. "Otherwise, why be a cadre?" Under the new system, an adolescent girl who knew the right things to say could find herself earning more than a stout yeoman.[33] The Tachai system is favored by the radical trend, as it represents a higher degree of collectivization and supposedly encourages communal attitudes and discourages the lusting after material incentives. But as the system in effect amounts to "giving people material incentives for putting politics in command over economics," it may be as apt to breed glib hypocrisy. It is certainly possible that "a system distributing material benefits according to vaguely defined criteria of political loyalty carries the seeds of corruption within itself, and no such system can hope to retain the good will even of its beneficiaries for long."[34] This, however, remains to be seen.

Information on active peasant resistance to regime policies is rather spotty. When compulsory grain sales were introduced in 1954 there were reports of peasants withholding grain, a manifestation of "individual selfishness," it was said.[35] Reports from 1955 tell of extensive unrest in the Yangtze valley region, the work, naturally, of the class enemy.[36] According to an exile report, for which I have seen no corroborating evidence:

> As early as 1960 the peasants of Kuang-shan county in Honan organized a guerrilla force of more than 2,000 people. . . . They broke open the Maoist graineries and distributed food to the starving peasants. . . . Within three months that guerrilla force had grown to more than 10,000 strong.

The Maoists put a "blockade on all news and sent in large numbers of infantry, airplanes, tanks, and special agents, conducting an extermination campaign for more than two years."[37] According to the *Work Bulletin,* the militia in some areas (around 1959 and 1960) would burn, pillage, and rape, "seriously wrecking party policy and violating the law of the land. These are startling conditions."[38]

> Now the U.S. and Chiang Kai-shek are giving attention to our people's militia and expect to send counterrevolutionaries into the ranks of the people's militia to seize control; they think to start some kind of "guerrilla warfare." We should arouse sufficient vigilance.[39]

It is possible that the United States and Chiang were behind some of this, but much of the disorder in the militia may have been small, spontaneous peasant rebellions. According to T'an Fu-jen, the military boss of Yunnan, in 1967

> the counterrevolutionary line [is spread] very broadly and deeply in the countryside, and it has not been purged. The [black elements] who have not been reformed and counterrevolutionary elements still undertake covert activities, set fires, lead extravagant lives, attacking the proletariat.[40]

During the Cultural Revolution, peasants in some areas, sometimes with the encouragement of local cadres, would invade the towns and fight Red Guards. That period also provided many opportunities for passive resistance ("leading extravagant lives"). In 1970 the Military Control and Revolutionary Committee of Pao-an county, Kwangtung, issued an order forbidding black-market speculation in rationed commodities (rice, wheat, beans, corn, peanuts, lumber, and cotton). Also, "it is not permitted to abandon agriculture for commerce or for itinerant peddling."[41]

According to conventional economic theory, the socialist transformation of the countryside in the absence of technical modernization should tend to restrict output. In times of trouble the moderate policy of making concessions to existing peasant interests has been adopted. By 1975, however, the regime—largely, it seemed, with the support of the moderate tendency—claimed to be committed to the policy of gradually intensifying collectivization while at the same time achieving basic mechanization of the countryside by 1980.[42] The process was apparently not to involve much grass-roots consultation, since the main responsibility for implementing the program was given to the county party committees, not to the basic-level organizations. The structural reform of agriculture, if successful, may make collectivization more palatable, if only by eliminating peasant interests as such, turning the peasantry into a rural proletariat. If the way of life in the countryside changes radically, many of the interests discussed here may cease to be relevant. On the other hand, this is hardly the first radical change the regime has promised since 1949.

Workers

The CPC is the "vanguard of the proletariat," and while the party had few direct relationships with the working class prior to the conquest of the cities in 1948 and 1949, its relations with workers since then have perhaps been less complex than those with peasants. The conventional and probably correct foreign view is well stated by Paul Harper:

> To what extent the workers believe themselves to be "masters of the state" is irrelevant; the workers as a whole have tendered solid support to the CCP as the

> leading body of the Chinese polity. There is no evidence of disaffection from the party by a significant part of the industrial workers even during times of deepest disturbance. . . . Generally speaking, the Maoist revolutionary visions and ideology have been rejected by the workers, but the ties to the object of Maoist attack, the party and the industrial bureaucracy, remained firm.[43]

These ties—to the moderate, but not to the radical tendency—are perhaps a tribute to efficient organization as well as worker sentiment. The regimes of Hungary, Poland, and East Germany have been threatened by joint attacks upon them by workers and students. Such a coalition has not formed in China (at least before 1976). In 1957 there was considerable unrest among workers in China, but this was not linked concretely to the concurrent student unrest, and the Communist press reports that workers even helped suppress student riots.[44] Workers perhaps realize that if unrest becomes too severe they will not be paid; also, contrary to Marx, but not Lenin, workers in general do not seem to be given to rebellion if conditions are at all tolerable. The conditions of Chinese workmen have been generally tolerable.

The workers' state, however, is not the workers' paradise; and while Chinese workers may be docile, they also have potential sources of grievance. During the campaign to socialize industry in 1956 the *People's Daily* noted:

> There are still some employees of private firms who, because in their firms wages and benefits are high or because they have become accustomed to a free and easy life, fear a drop in wages and benefits after the implementation of joint public-private management, or fear the severity of labor discipline, and so forth. These employees mainly lack the collectivist thought of the working class. They can see only the teeny advantage before their own eyes and are not able to see the collective and long-term advantage of the working class.[45]

For many workers, particularly those in the smaller enterprises where paternalistic relations still held, the transition to public ownership meant more work for less pay. There would probably be little support for the return of large industries to private ownership—the question would not even arise. Workers sometimes object, however, to the regime's policy of holding down the wage rate. The rationale for this policy was explained in 1955: The increase in the wage rate should be less than the increase in productivity. This aids capital accumulation, holds down inflation (in 1955, a problem left over from the Nationalist period), and "guarantees a balanced supply of commercial commodities," meaning that it holds down the demand for consumption goods. Also, it is necessary to increase agricultural production. This means that rural consumption will lag behind the increases in rural productivity, while the rate of increase in the modern sector will naturally be much greater than that in the agricultural sector. If urban wage rates rise too steeply, peasants will be attracted away from the farms, hindering the growth of agriculture. Still, workers are entitled to a higher income than peasants, since they are more productive.[46]

The policy sounds a little like what Marx used to call exploitation, but the reasoning behind it is plausible. Most people are probably willing to make reasonable sacrifices for the common good, especially if the cost of the sacrifice is less than the cost of attempting to avoid it. As Harper notes, however, while low wages may be tolerated, workers seem less tolerant of Maoist programs to eliminate pay differentials and material incentives or programs that would make pay independent of skill, experience, or effort. During the Cultural Revolution, workers were notoriously hostile to the radical Red Guards and in most areas supported the party establishment. The radicals attributed worker support for their enemies to "economism." A Center document of January 1967 accuses the "power-holders on the capitalist road" of using "all kinds of economic methods in the hope of tempting some masses toward the heterodox economist road, so that disregarding the interests of the state, the collective, and the long term, they will simply pursue private advantage."[47] At the time, *economism* often simply meant the handing out of bribes, but in general Chinese communist discourse it refers to policies aimed at raising the standard of living of workers by fixing wages to have some correspondence to the worker's productivity. It is likely that, all things considered, workers felt they would get a better deal from the bureaucracy than from the radicals.

It is sometimes argued that utopian policies such as those attributed to Mao are bound to fail because they are too idealistic, because human nature is so unredeemably selfish. This, however, may not be the real issue. After a visit to the Shenyang Transformer Factory in 1972, in which policies similar to those prior to the Cultural Revolution had been reintroduced, a member of the Committee of Concerned Asian Scholars' Second Friendship Delegation to China had some thoughts on pay differentials:

> My feeling on this discussion, although intuitive and vague, is that "material incentives" as usually considered in our terminology is not so much the issue here; rather, there is a quality of equity or rightness about the payment system that would be brought into question if there was no differentiation of rewards.[48]

This may be exactly the point—and one that would hold for peasants as well as workers. Much of the moral appeal of Marxism, after all, revolves around its defense of the proposition that the laborer is worthy of his hire.

While the workers may be more comfortable with the moderate tendency than with the radical, this need not imply perfect contentment. They would probably prefer that their wages be higher and may at times object to the severity of labor discipline and to the sometimes casual attitude of the authorities toward work safety. The interests of the state and the collective take precedence over those of the individual, and sometimes the individual feels his interests are neglected entirely. The trade unions are supposed to protect workers' interests but are also supposed to persuade the workers to restrain their short-term interests and support the policies of the party and the state. Prior to the Cultural Revolution (after which the situation may have become more complex) the trade unions tended to act as simply another bureaucracy devoted to extracting the greatest amount of labor from the person. As Lai Jo-yü, then head of the Trade Union Federation, put it in 1956: "After the working class has gained political power, its most basic duty is earnestly to develop production, unceasingly to raise socialist productivity." The labor unions must still protect workers' interests. "The problem is not whether to protect the interests of the employed masses, but how to protect them." This was easy before Liberation but has become more complex since. The workers, for example, are the leading class, but each individual worker is led. While "in our country the state interest and the workers' interest are the same," the state interest may conflict with that of individuals. Well, then, what do we do? "We must educate the working masses correctly to recognize the state interest and also organize the working masses to protect their own interests; in this way we can effectively unite with the masses."[49] In effect, however, when there is conflict the individual interest gives way. A few months later, after a series of small wildcat strikes, Lai said that the unions should recognize whatever justice there may be in the complaints of the masses, but the policy of a hundred flowers blooming is not appropriate for workers. Anyway, the trade union is not merely a mass organization and "may not give in to unreasonable demands from the workers."[50]

During the Hundred Flowers movement there were complaints of trade-union indifference to worker welfare. This contradiction is explored in a short story published around that time, a work that "maliciously opposed the old worker who serves the masses and the masses who love and support him to the Communist Party and the trade union organization, describing the party and state leadership of the factory as lazy, bureaucratic, contemptible personages."[51] The story is "Reelection" (*Kai-hsuan*) by a young writer, Li Kuo-wen. It appeared in the July 1957 issue of *People's Literature,* when the time for blooming and contending was well past. The editors showed courage in publishing the story when they did, and a few months later they were made to crawl for it. The story is fiction and thus proves nothing, but it may give the flavor of some aspects of the life of Chinese workmen that are usually neglected by the official media.

As a literary work the story may be a bit too pat, even for satire. The hero's name is "old Hao," a Communist union organizer for forty years. *Hao* is pronounced in the same way as the word for "good," and the masses often call him "old Good." Old Good is very, very good, and everyone else is horrid. The conflict in the story is an intergenerational one as well as one between the bureaucracy and the individual. The new men have come up, and old Hao is uncomfortable with them and their jargon. The union chairman always wants his underlings to write up stories about model workers so he can make a good report to the Center, and for *model* or *example* he uses the now common term *yang-pan,* template. "Who knows where that ass-hole term comes from?" old Hao says. The chairman is a young whippersnapper, combining the faults of the bureaucrat with those of youth. "How could (old Hao) feel so soft, so old, so cowardly before this man who was even younger than his son? Old Hao's courage was not broken all at once. Although old Hao was a union cadre, for the past few years there had been a wind blowing through the trade union, and it could possibly blow this old fellow down."[52] Other stories at the time depict old cadres as having become corrupted by the easy life after Liberation and quashing the idealism of the young.[53] In this story, however, the youngsters are thoroughly bureaucratized, and they snicker at old Hao's lack of culture.

While old Hao consoles widows and tries to get materials to repair the roof of the old workers' home before the rains come, everyone else plays bureaucratic games. The union chairman is concerned only with turning in a good report. The factory management cares only about production. Old Hao had once been union chairman himself, but because of his inability to cope with party jargon he had been accused of "errors of political principle" and demoted to vice-chairman. He does not care about his position, however, but only wants to be of service. He asks his section chief for material to repair the roof and is told, "OK, you are a trade union cadre. Don't you know what planning is? The plan is the law, and even the factory can't violate it. If they can't stand a little rain leaking in, how did they ever get along before Liberation?"[54]

Under old Hao's direction the union had built a small bean-curd mill near the factory so the workers could have lunch without going home or bothering their wives in the morning. The union, the youth league branch, and the management (Li perhaps refrains out of caution from including the party branch) all sent in reports taking credit for this, naturally without mentioning old Hao. But then "the wind of opposition to trade-union economist tendencies blew in from thousands of miles away, and by the time the wind had passed through, that little mill had collapsed under the storm."[55] Old Hao is blamed for having built the mill and forced to make a self-examination. He is also demoted to simple committee member. He busies himself clearing a vacant lot where the former factory owner had planned to build his house, to make a park where the children of the workmen could play without the danger of being run over. The union thinks a recreation area is a good idea—for cadres, if not for children. It decides, however, to locate it miles away, up in the mountains. Old Hao's protest is met with: "This is the decision of the organization. You support it."[56] As he had warned, the area chosen is inconvenient to reach, the local peasants do not want people swimming in the water, and at night there are so many wolves around that only former soldiers dare go there. Then the "wind against extravagant life-styles'' begins to blow, and old Hao is blamed for having thought up the idea of a recreation area in the first place. At union election time, his name is omitted from the list of candidates. The workers rebel at this (is this realistic?). The chairman tries to stall them, protesting it is too late to draw up new ballots. But the workers write in old Hao's name, and he receives more votes than any other candidate. The excitement is too much for him, though, and he dies as the election is being held.

Radicals might consider old Hao an overly paternalistic figure, especially since he does not accompany his good deeds with paeans to the party, the Chairman, and his own selflessness. But in its attack on oppressive bureaucracy the story could show an area where workers and radicals might agree. As noted before, with perhaps the partial exception of Shanghai the radicals did not have worker support in the early days of the Cultural Revolution, despite the radical attack on bureaucratic arrogance and unreasonable regulations. In the course of the Cultural Revolution, however, factories, like many other institutions in China, became factionalized as the old system decayed. Abandoning the Red Guards in 1968, the radicals tried to make friends with the workers. The Red Guards were told to learn from the workers: ''The entire process of the Great Proletarian Cultural Revolution was solely and entirely led by the working class. Our party is the vanguard of the proletariat.''[57] Taken literally, the first sentence quoted is a lie; it must be understood in the context of the second. It is hard to determine what the new policy meant for the ordinary workers. Those appointed to the ''worker propaganda teams'' may have gained some status, as did, at least temporarily, the factional leaders. Lai Jo-yü's dictum still held, however: the workers may be the leading class, but the individual worker is led. In the Shenyang Transformer Factory in 1972 the management and technicians were no longer arrogant—or so it was said (and if they ever had been)—but they did continue to run the factory. The key positions were held by soldiers, although the soldiers claimed to obey party leadership.[58] (This was probably not too hard, since it is reasonable to guess that the soldiers also dominated the party committee.) While the radicals probably did not control the management of most factories during the return to ''normalcy'' of the early 1970s, however, the reconstruction of the trade unions in 1973 took place under radical auspices,[59] and later the urban militia was formed around the trade unions. This probably encouraged the persistence of factionalism within the factories.

The usual method of labor protest is, of course, the strike. In his speech on contradictions among the people Mao mentioned, without giving details, small strikes in 1956 and early 1957. The occasion for the strikes, Mao said, was dissatisfaction with material conditions, but the basic cause was bureaucratism coupled with inferior political education for workers. Also, criminals sometimes lead the masses to make unreasonable demands. During the Cultural Revolution there were work stoppages and sometimes even pitched battles. Labor unrest broke out again from 1973 to 1975 in wide areas of China, although information on this is very sketchy. In early 1974 Wang Hung-wen mentioned vaguely the problems of twelve factories in Szechwan; one plant had been in a state of chaos for eight years (since the beginning of the Cultural Revolution). But now the correct line had been implemented and the problems were resolved.[60] At the end of October of that year there was a brief notice in the *People's Daily* to the effect that soldiers were doing a fine job in setting examples in manual labor by loading trains in Inner Mongolia. Around the same time came a spate of reports from the provincial media on military work in transportation from Kiangsi, Kiangsu, Kansu, and Honan. Szechwan, meanwhile, despite the efforts of Wang Hung-wen, continued to be plagued by bourgeois factionalism. It is a reasonable interpretation that the country was then undergoing a strike by transportation workers.[61] Meanwhile, "People coming from the Mainland have reported a prolonged strike by workers at the Wuhan Steelworks."[62] In July 1975 soldiers were sent to factories in Hangchow to "support production" and suppress labor unrest there, and other reports claim sabotage by railway workers in Yunnan.[63] A *People's Daily* report from Tsingtao, Shantung, gives no real details, but says that in factories in that city, "Formerly, because of bourgeois factionalism, there was lack of solidarity among the cadres and among the masses." The report praises the cadres for "daring to uphold the new revolutionary things,"[64] which means, one fears, that they defended low wage rates and the radical line generally against worker resistance.

The 1975 state constitution gives workers the right to strike. This was not, as might be thought, a reaction to the current situation, since the same clause is included in the 1970 draft. The commentary on this right is terse and enigmatic: "The constitution stipulates that the popular masses have the rights of big contending, big blooming, big debates, and big-character posters. At the suggestion of Chairman Mao, the freedom of citizens to strike was also added."[65] The "big contending" and so forth are of no moment. The explicit attribution of the right to strike to Mao, in addition to its factual content, may have been a way of forestalling overreactions by local authorities to the strikes; it may also be a subtle way of expressing that this is a stupid thing to have in the constitution, but since the Chairman wanted it, what could we do? He can take the credit—and the blame. The right to strike, like the other constitutional rights, is perhaps not very meaningful. It is no doubt one of those bourgeois rights doomed to extinction. This is certainly true if the motivation behind the strikes is desire for better material conditions.[66]

One can only speculate concerning what does motivate the strikes. Workers had not received pay increases for several years prior to the strikes of the 1970s, and any resentment of this was perhaps not appeased by the 1975 radical drive against bourgeois rights and material incentives. The attribution of the strikes to bourgeois factionalism seems like a slap at the radicals, although in 1975 the high-ranking radicals had no desire for overt disorder. If factory management is largely dominated by the moderate tendency and the radicals control the labor unions, the ordinary worker may be caught in the middle and resentful of the imposition of discipline by either or both. The factional ties formed in the Cultural Revolution probably survive in many places. While the army was still in the factories these sources of potential discontent could be covered up, but following the death of Lin Piao the soldiers were gradually withdrawn.

Strikes indicate opposition but need not indicate anything beyond specific opposition. Between the regime and the peasants there is probably latent fundamental opposition, the relief of which would require either a change in the peasant way of life or a change in the basic policies of the regime. The workers, like the party, are part of the modern sector of Chinese society, and perhaps no such fundamental conflict exists between them. Workers may even prefer the public ownership of the means of production, although, since in any case the workers remain *led*, the ownership system is perhaps more likely to be in the long term a matter of indifference to them. Chinese workers have been on the whole a conservative force since 1949, and there would seem to be no reason why their narrower demands—a fair day's pay for a fair day's work, and the like—cannot be satisfied under the current regime, or any other.

Educated Youth

In the abstract it is a bit curious to assign even a potential interest to youth, since youth is a notoriously transitory stage and those who are young are usually something else besides—workers, peasants, students, thieves, unemployed, and so forth. Still, youth as an active political interest is a fact of this century, in China and elsewhere. The focus here on educated youth—in China, children who have received at least a lower-middle school (ninth grade) education—is not a reflection of snobbishness; rather, this category has been an explicit object of policy for both the KMT and the CPC. It is these educated youths, *chih-shih ch'ing-nien,* who are considered the main component of the revolutionary successors, *ko-ming chieh-pan-jen,* literally, the "revolutionary next shift." "Proles and animals are free," and compared with workers and peasants, students and educated persons generally are part of the categories (which also include class enemies and functionaries) under the closest supervision by the regime.

It is appropriate at least to mention, however, a more general problem—that of juvenile delinquency. Any resistance youth puts up against the party will probably take delinquent forms, especially since the regime puts a broad construction on what behavior constitutes delinquency. Also, even ostensibly apolitical delinquency is often politicized by the regime, and perhaps justly so, since certain forms of delinquent behavior—living by one's wits, opting out of the official small group and bureaucratic nexus—constitute a type of passive resistance. Surprisingly, there is something of a tradition of juvenile delinquency in China. Juvenile gangs were sometimes found in Chinese villages more than a thousand years ago. In addition to engaging in general rowdyism, such gangs also made up the fodder of clan feuds, fighting their fathers' wars. If expelled from the villages the gangs would sometimes take to the mountains to become bandits.[67] Given the large-scale social dislocation of this century and the weakening of the traditional family system, especially in the cities, it is not surprising that juvenile gangs should form.[68] In 1954 the *People's Daily* complained of young louts "in all the big cities" who spent their time stealing, gambling, seducing and insulting women, buying pornography, and frequenting "low-life amusement places." In some places these children formed large, organized criminal gangs.[69] While not much publicized, and probably most of the time not very serious, the problem of *she-hui ch'ing nien* (social youth) and *Ah Fei* (roughly, punks) has remained and may have intensified since the Cultural Revolution. Much of Red Guard behavior was a kind of officially sanctioned delinquency, and the Red Guard factions became increasingly like gangs—somewhat like Western street gangs, but perhaps more like the traditional Chinese bands of sworn brothers. Since the suppression of the Red Guards many youths have apparently returned illegally to the cities, where, since they cannot get ration cards, many have turned to crime. Others may have taken to the mountains in the traditional fashion. This last, however, is speculation.

Most children, of course, are not delinquent; an increasing proportion of them, especially in their younger years, are students. Prior to the Cultural Revolution, the school system, patterned after that of the Soviet Union, was extremely rigorous. Children from the "red" classes were given a certain preference in the system, but those from other categories were generally better prepared by family background for academic work. Foreigners generally hold that the radicals dislike the old system for its perpetuation of class distinctions; the graver problem, however, was that it tended to favor those classes not favored by the regime. Part of the Cultural Revolution reforms included the shortening of the period of study, the simplification of the curriculum, and the elimination of examinations (such policies had also been flirted with during the Great Leap Forward). On this subject Mao has uttered some of his more entertaining thoughts:

> Our present method of conducting examinations is a method for dealing with the enemy, not dealing with the people. It is a method of surprise attack, asking oblique and strange questions. . . . I am in favour of publishing the questions in advance and letting the students study and answer them with the aid of books. . . . At examinations whispering into each others' ears and taking other people's places ought to be allowed. If your answer is good and I copy it, then mine should be counted as good. . . . Let's give it a try.[70]

It has been pointed out that some of the Maoist reforms are similar to those proposed in the United States[71] (e.g., open-book exams; not, so far as I know, the condoning of cheating—although it is not always easy to know when Mao is serious), where a similar curious form of the egalitarian drive exists; and the radical system, while not conducive to academic excellence, may fit the needs of a poor and growing country better than the more orthodox system does. It has been, however, a matter of controversy within the elite whether the radical reforms do in fact fit the needs of the country. In the early 1970s, entrance examinations were again held by universities; this policy came under attack in 1973. At the end of 1975, apparently as part of the preparation for the radical offensive that was to follow the death of Chou En-lai, there were attacks on the "strange talk and bizarre theories" of "revisionists" who held that the educational reforms were producing ignoramuses. The revisionists said the "worker-peasant-soldier" students (persons selected for political reliability, not academic competence) should be "voided like diarrhea."[72]

Under the old system the students had to work hard. Under both systems they are under strict party supervision, exercised both by the party committee within the school and by the Youth League branch. The epitome of the conventional party attitude toward students is well captured in a 1960 article. Youths should be the docile tools (*shun-fu kung-chü*) of the party, owing the party unconditional obedience:

> Not talking about conditions in work means you must unconditionally follow the needs of the party, the needs of work. If something benefits the party or the communist enterprise, we will do it. Where the party tells us to go, there we will go; what the party wants us to do, that we will do.[73]

The phrase *docile tools* was used extensively in the party's discourse with youth in the early 1960s[74] and became for the Red Guards the symbol of the party's bureaucratic tyranny. The phrase originated with the Liu Shao-ch'i line and is no longer used, except pejoratively; but the content of the demands has perhaps not changed much.

Students spend much time in political study. Since 1957 part of political study includes spending time in productive labor, in order that students overcome their intellectual snobbishness and develop the outlook of the laboring people. In some cases the practice may go further than this. One thinks in particular of the party fetish about nightsoil—human excrement used as fertilizer. At its most harmless this theme is directed against certain natural but still unattractive attitudes among city-bred youth:

> When they were still students they would go singing happily down the asphalt road in the morning or evening. Suddenly they would see a peasant hauling a pail of nightsoil, his body covered with sweat. . . . They would hold their noses and

> turn away their faces, feeling disgusted. But after going down to the farm, the youths themselves made the acquaintance of nightsoil. As they collected fertilizer together with the peasants, spread the manure, and watered the ground, their thoughts and feelings also changed.[75]

It is probably reasonable enough to demand that students learn what others have to undergo in order that students be fed. Sometimes, however, this hauling of nightsoil becomes almost a sacrament, a kind of scatological transubstantiation, as in this free-verse poem attributed to an educated youth: "In hauling nightsoil with you, what is carried is not feces, but bourgeois thought. What is brought back is not filthy clothes and socks, but the highest-quality thought of the proletariat."[76]

The nightsoil cult is one aspect of a more general party line that seems to run counter to what might be called the idealism and spontaneity of youth, feelings which those who have outgrown that stage may find difficult to take seriously but which seem serious enough to those who have them. Conceivably the liberation of mankind and the building of communism are ideals that can capture the imagination of youth, but it is possible that these ideals may be more genuinely appealing to children in countries not ruled by a communist party. The party, with its distrust of spontaneity, tends to stifle any kind of idealism not directly instrumental to its purposes, any manifestation of "bourgeois individualism" in which the person thinks to make a contribution his way, rather than the party's way. On the eve of the Cultural Revolution a young girl, Ch'un-mei (Spring Plum—probably her given name) had been so incautious as to praise publicly a movie then being criticized for advocating love for all people, contradicting the Chairman's dictum that love transcending class is impossible. After some to-do, Ch'un-mei wrote a confession. When she had been a primary-school teacher, she said, she had not been interested in her work. She "had not established the thought of serving the people, so [she] always thought that the salary of a primary-school teacher was too low and that there was no future in it." Later she was transferred to what she calls an even more brainless position as a clerk in a tax collection office in Peking. The leader (i.e., the party) and the comrades tried to help her, but her attitude remained bad. She lost all interest in work and found her pleasure in reading and going to the movies.

Perhaps she did have a bad attitude, but since this is a self-criticism she is bound to put the worst (the party's) construction on her behavior. For some, the low salary of a primary-school teacher may be outweighed by the importance of the work, although this is a matter of temperament. Tools, however, are not supposed to have temperament. Probably few would consider tax collecting a very romantic way of serving the people. Ch'un-mei does not show herself to be callous, or lacking in generous feelings—if she were, she would not have gotten into trouble.

> I wanted in real life to live according to the "high ideals" of [the hero of the movie]. If someone lacked clothes, I would send some (even if I myself did not have enough); if someone was brokenhearted over disappointed love, I would suffer along with her, to the point of being unable to eat. . . . In life, I thought that to revolutionize meant to render life dull and tasteless. I never thought about there being class struggle in life.[77]

The party demands idealism and enthusiasm, but only for the objects of which it approves; and those objects are often at best dull and tasteless (nightsoil is not the best). Enthusiasm for anything else is often regarded as evidence of a low political standard. The consequence in many cases may be to produce apathy and cynicism, and occasionally hostility.

During the early 1960s the regime became increasingly concerned with the attitude of the nation's youth. There is one famous instance of outright integral defiance of the regime. The last issue (number 24) of *China Youth* for 1964 carried on its back cover a reproduction of an oil painting by a young artist, Li Tse-hao, entitled "You pursue, I overtake" (*Ni chui wo kan*). The picture (see p. 102) shows two groups of smiling children carrying bundles of wheat across a field, led by a man in a cadre hat whose face is hidden. In the far background are two villages. One village has three red flags, one of which has fallen to the ground (the three red flags: the general line, the Great Leap Forward, the people's communes). The picture is mildly disturbing even at first glance (if I am not misled by knowing what I am supposed to see), partly because of the unnatural gaiety of the children (but this, perhaps, is revolutionary realism), but mostly because the standing wheat and the children's clothes are being blown by the wind in opposite directions. When closely examined, skulls and a dagger may be seen among the standing wheat, and the wheat on the ground forms the picture of a prone Stalin (others say it is Marx or Lenin) over whom the children are treading. There is also said to be a figure of Mao among the wheat (I think I see this, but I am not sure). Stalks of wheat form the characters: *Sha-ssu Kung-ch'an-tang Chiang chieh-shih wan sui,* "Kill the Communists, long live Chiang Kai-shek."

This issue of *China Youth* was withdrawn after the irregularity was belatedly discovered; nothing else seems to be known of the matter. This was probably an isolated act, but discontent of a milder sort seems to have been endemic among the youth of the period. The main manifestation was apolitical apathy and for some a kind of Uncle Tom stepping and fetching for the benefit of the authorities:

> When I had finished my report she [the Youth League secretary] complimented me in the way one might flatter a spastic five-year-old who had managed to put on his own shoes. I responded with a moronic show of modesty and pleasure; I hung my head, shuffled my feet, and made incoherent sounds of embarrassment.[78]

Ni chui wo kan ["You pursue, I overtake"] by Li Tse-hao
Oil painting reproduced on the back cover of *Chung-kuo ch'ing-nien* [*China Youth*], no. 24 (1964).

Throughout the 1960s students were presented with a series of military models for emulation, beginning with Lei Feng. There was also an effort to beef up the Communist Youth League.[79] In late 1964 Mao told Edgar Snow of his worries over the future of the youth of China.[80]

This general malaise among students forms the background to the Red Guard movement. The Cultural Revolution cannot be regarded as a spontaneous rebellion by youth—the children were deliberately mobilized. But their discontent provided the conditions that allowed the mobilization, just as the mobilization permitted the discontent to be channeled against segments of the party bureaucracy rather than against the regime itself. Some are wary of counting the Red Guard movement as opposition at all: the students "accepted the legitimacy of central institutions and strove to act as they thought they should."[81] With some at least partial exceptions, discussed in the next chapter, Red Guard criticisms were not integral and are for the most part utterly lacking in any theoretical depth. But the affirmation of rebellion and the distaste for bureaucracy and authority show, I think, an opposition to much of the predominant political atmosphere in China since Liberation, coupled with a hope that the promise of Liberation might possibly be realized.

As noted before, the Red Guard movement rapidly became factionalized.[82] For some groups in the beginning an important line of cleavage was between those from red backgrounds and those from non-red backgrounds, with the reds attempting to exclude non-reds. Parris Chang hypothesizes that the former were the more conservative (many of them being the children of cadres, and their parents under attack), whereas "most of the militant and anti-Establishment Red Guard groups came from the politically less favored or economically underprivileged strata of society."[83] (It also seems that at least at the beginning the red groups behaved with greater brutality than did the non-reds.) Chang's hypothesis makes sense, although it does not seem to be universally valid. The Capital Corps Red Guards, a Peking Group that seems conservative in its stress on unity, leniency for erring comrades, and limitations on the struggle,[84] accused its enemies of preaching the theory of naturally red (*tzu-lai hung*)—that only those of red background could be revolutionary.[85] It may be hopeless, however, to try to sort out the Red Guards according to ideological conviction; in theoretical matters most say the same things.

Factional battles seem to have been based less on ideology than on the different affiliations each group had throughout the political system, and these affiliations could shift. With whom a group would ally itself often depended on the local situation and the alignments of its rivals. Some groups are accused of having broken with higher politics altogether in order to act on their own.[86] The factional fights were perhaps mostly a consequence of the existence of factions themselves, as the groups took on a gang character. The factions became what the officially sponsored small groups could not be, a source of support and a focus of loyalty.[87] The social historian Sa Meng-wu distinguishes two ethical systems in traditional China. One is the system of the gentry, stressing loyalty to family and superiors. The other is the system of what Sa calls the *liu-mang*, gangsters, based on ties of blood-brotherhood. This is the ethical system idealized in the traditional novel *Water margin,* stressing loyalty to friends, mutual support, and indebtedness to friends arising from grace (*en*), or, as we might say, favors.[88] In their regard for the honor of the faction, the Red Guards may represent a revival of the ethos of the *lü-lin hao-han,* the good fellows of the greenwood. Something similar to this sort of gangster ethics will probably develop wherever both security and social restraint are lacking. The ties formed are strong. I am told that in Hong Kong refugee Red Guards continue their factional battles; the old political pretexts are gone, but there are still scores to settle, brothers to avenge. These ties probably also persist in China proper, where many of the good fellows have literally been sent to the greenwood. This sounds romantic, but it should not be idealized. The experience of the Red Guard movement may have left many young Chinese with a viciousness of mind that does not bode well for the future of the country.[89]

The massive sending of students up to the mountain and down to the farm (*shang-shan hsia-hsiang*) was resumed in 1968 on a larger scale than before. Unlike the earlier sending-down movements, the children were told they would become peasants for the rest of their lives. At the time this was a way of suppressing the Red Guard movement. Subsequently it has become a way of avoiding unemployment among the urban educated (China, like many poor countries, educates more persons than the economy can absorb), although the policy is not publicly justified in these terms. The policy is also supposed to help eliminate the distinction between city and countryside, thus reversing the massive brain drain into the cities that has plagued China this century. Much of the rustication movement is perhaps in the public interest, although even if it were entirely so there would still be those who resent it. The 1968 cohort, in particular, may have the feeling of having been had; that the sending-down is not truly voluntary may also create resentments. The regime has made no effort to hide the hardship, discomfort, and even danger of life in the countryside.[90] At the same time, there is evidence that the youths are not always welcomed by the local population. Part of the reason is not hard to guess:

> During the Great Proletarian Cultural Revolution movement the little generals of the Red Guard broke the barriers, taking the lead in sweeping away the four olds of the landlord bourgeoisie, fiercely attacking the ideology of the exploiting class. A new socialist style developed.[91]

Concretely, the little generals broke open graves, desecrated temples, smashed family altars, and beat up and humiliated persons with old-fashioned views.

Another hindrance to peasant hospitality is that when the city babies came to the farm, in the past at least they had to be fed at peasant expense, and the state did not compensate for the influx of people ignorant of farming by reducing the grain levies.[92] There also seems to be a surprisingly great social distance between the peasants and the students. A girl sent to a commune in Hupei waxes enthusiastic about the life: "In the villages there is knowledge so vast that it can never be studied, work so great it can never be finished. I love being in the village and am determined to put in roots and make revolution all my life. A year after arriving, I set up a household here and married a common peasant." When she did this she was attacked by those of the same educational status as herself as shameless. "Could it be," she asks, "that a college student does well only if she marries a worker or a cadre, but it is shameful to marry a peasant?"[93]

As a kind of converse to this last point, it seems that educated girls sent to communes are sometimes subject to sexual abuse by the local functionaries—not so much forcible rape as the extortion of sexual favors by the use of superior position. The problem is hardly new in China (or anywhere else), as this morally obtuse passage from 1954 indicates:

> Some organization cadres in Szechwan often seek out [female] middle school students to come dance at the organization. During the dances they talk of love [*t'an lien-ai*—somewhat less romantic than the literal translation suggests] to the students. Obviously, . . . middle school students are very young and naïve in every way. They should at this time be concentrating entirely on their studies. If people are always seeking them out to dance and making love [*kao lien-ai*] to them, this will have no good influence on them.[94]

I have not seen any publicity in the open media on similar problems on the communes, although at times there may be a few hints.[95] In August 1973, however, a list was posted in Tientsin of twenty-nine gangsters who had raped young girls sent down to the farm (*liu-mang ch'iang-chien hsia-hsiang nü ch'ing-nien*) and who had been executed or sentenced to long terms.[96] There are a few common peasants on the list, but most of the offenders are doctors or other cadres, and their crime is not rape in the usual sense but a kind of coercive seduction. The list appeared at a time when the public media were urging better treatment for the rusticated youths, and the length of the list (which takes its victims from a small geographic area), coupled with the severity of the punishment and the fact that some of the seducers had careers going back a decade or more, would indicate a crackdown directed against a serious problem.

Lin Piao, or more accurately, his son Lin Li-kuo, is said to have said that the rustication movement had become like labor reform. In 1973 there were moves to improve the treatment of educated youth. After all, it was said, they are part of the masses, products of New China. They should be trusted, and more care should be taken for their material comfort.[97] That year a program was begun whereby each winter a portion of the rusticated youths would be given home leave. The regime seemed concerned that they not enjoy themselves too much while at home. They must not just eat and fool around; neighborhood and factory organizations must "actively organize them into all kinds of beneficial activities, implement thought education toward them . . ." Also, the comrades must see that the youths let pass no opportunity to talk of how much they like the countryside.[98] There were also apparently moves at that time to relieve peasant households of the burden of feeding the rusticated youths.

According to the media, the main complaint of rusticated youths is that they have no future. The party, perhaps to remedy this, seems to have adopted a policy of recruiting them into the party, and these may constitute a substantial proportion of the next generation of rural leadership.[99] At the same time, however, this may help block upward mobility for peasants and perpetuate the caste system the radicals allegedly want to eliminate. Given the social distance that seems to prevail between the educated outsiders, or even educated natives, and the local population, this may lead to a more bureaucratic work style, to a leadership more divorced from the masses. An advantage, from the party's point of view, is that educated youths recruited into the party may not be as closely tied in to the complex networks of personal relationships within Chinese villages as are the older local cadres and will probably be more willing to carry through policies calling for greater collectivization than will cadres recruited directly from among the poor and lower-middle peasants, whose wives, in any case, nag them to spend more time working their private plots. One story tells that a twenty-one-year-old female brigade party branch secretary was so upset when material incentives were reintroduced that she became sick, and the comrades had to explain to her that revolution is not smooth sailing all the way.[100]

Some may not consider the job of basic-level rural cadre to have that much future anyway, and there will probably long be a condition of many monks and little gruel. The most obvious sign of youthful discontent with the rustication program has been the exodus of large numbers of sent-down youth from southern China into Hong Kong from 1969 to 1975, when the English became more strict about admitting refugees into that overcrowded colony. These youths found life sufficiently intolerable to risk death to escape, and it is likely that those who die in the attempt or are captured greatly outnumber those who make it. Once in Hong Kong their troubles are far from over. Work is hard to come by, and they face loneliness, indifference, and even hostility from the older inhabitants. To the people of Hong Kong "we are a mob of stupid pigs who only know how to eat and don't know how to work." "On this small colonial island, there are very few who are able to understand us. . . . Our concepts are not theirs."[101] Many become criminals. Inside China proper other youths return surreptitiously to the cities, swelling the ranks of "social youth."

In the Balkans prior to the Second World War the most notoriously revolutionary segment of society was the village schoolteachers. In China, educated youth are in a similar position; many have exactly that job. They are not living in the comfort they had been brought up to expect and are educated beyond the ability of the country to put their education to use. They are also exposed to that part of Chinese society that suffers the greatest material privation. They will probably be inclined to support the policies of the elite radicals, for both idealistic and opportunistic reasons (the radicals, for example, are more likely to create vacancies in officialdom above the basic level). If the policies prove unsuccessful, or they feel unappreciated, their alienation could increase.

In the spring of 1976 wall posters were up again, capitalist roaders were being attacked again, and the tradition of the Red Guard was being recalled. It was difficult for an outsider to believe that anyone in a position of authority in China was eager to see an exact repetition of 1966–69. The worker-peasant-soldier students in the schools are probably more tractable than those of 1966, if at least as bloody-minded. The Cultural Revolution itself was an *ersatz* revolution; in early 1976 China seemed to be preparing for an *ersatz Ersatz*. But if the Center does not hold, it may once again be in the power of those in the schools and those in the villages to throw China into anarchy.

Writers and Intellectuals

Perhaps the most prominent dissent in People's China has been that by intellectuals and creative writers; and literary dissent, particularly for the 1950s, has been the subject of several excellent studies.[102] Dissent from creative intellectuals is no marvel, of course, since they are apt to be more articulate than the ordinary person. A distinction might be made between literary dissent, meaning dissent from the dominant literary doctrine—that is, the defense by writers of their own special interest—and dissent through the means of literature. Without such a distinction, literary dissent would include virtually all forms of dissent, especially if essays and the like are counted as literature. Thus, Li Kuo-wen's story about the trade union would be taken here as dissent by means of literature, but not strictly as literary dissent. This distinction, while necessary, is often hard to maintain in practice, since one of the functions of the official doctrine seems to be to make it impossible to express ideas disagreeable to whoever currently dominates the leadership.

As in the Soviet Union, the Chinese literary doctrine not only entails censorship of what a writer says but also "dictates what he will have to say."[103] The literary line is based upon Mao Tse-tung's speech at the Yenan Forum on Literature and Art in May 1942: literature, like everything else, has a class character; our literature should "serve the broad masses of the people." While our literature should have artistic quality, political criteria should have precedence over artistic criteria in evaluating literary merit. In fact, a work that is good art but bad politics is much worse than a shoddy work expressing similar ideas. Writers and artists should remold their thoughts, so the people will accept them.[104] As in the Soviet Union, the approved style was once called socialist realism (now it is called revolutionary realism) although the Chinese wish to combine this with revolutionary romanticism.[105]

The poet's Yenan pronouncements are rather vague, and for a fuller understanding we must turn to the commentators. The commentator of choice is Yao Wen-yuan. He has been in the forefront of virtually all the attacks on literary figures since the early 1950s (among writers he used to enjoy the nickname *kun*, which means stick, but is perhaps better translated by the similar-sounding word *goon*), and since 1969 he has been a member of the Politburo. His ideas are both orthodox and influential, and since he is relatively young his influence may continue to be felt.*

Yao's literary theory is predicated on relativism and the political function of literature:

> People always evaluate their behavior by the standard of personal advantage. Therefore, if people are divided into all sorts of social classes in a class society with private ownership, the concepts of good and evil, right and wrong, will carry a class nature.[106]

China is still a class society, and our literature should therefore reflect the morality of the proletariat. All themes, including the "problem of love," which is a "political problem," should be treated according to correct political standards. Yao goes into a blue-nosed frenzy over a poem in which the speaker imagines his bride-to-be taking a bath. There is no place for this sort of thing in a life of labor and struggle.[107]

Yao, obviously, opposes the literary orientation he calls humanism. As Morgan, among others, has conclusively demonstrated, "Abstract, class-transcending, unchanging man exists only in the brains of idealists, and does not exist in real life." Most of his ire, however, is directed against what he thinks is the opposite form of revisionism—realism, construed as writing the truth (*hsieh chen-shih*). His ire is perhaps well placed, since realism is the style favored by the harder leftist writers, writers able to argue with the regime on its own terms. Realism is also pernicious since it sounds a little like socialist realism. The two concepts, of course, are not at all the same. "Different world views and different modes of thought produce different perceptions of reality. . . . In history there is just concrete, developing realism, no abstract, eternally unchanging realism." "If a writer lacks the ability to recognize the mainstream and grasps only 'writing the truth,' it may be possible to produce writings opposed to the basic nature and

*Note of October 1976: A bad guess. Yao always voiced the currently orthodox line, however, and it therefore remains useful to examine his views.

mainstream of today's life."[108] For example, a writer might describe some people who are not happy with socialism. As a matter of fact, rightists and revisionists always have a political motive for their defense of writing the truth: they wish to satirize socialism. In a generous moment Yao allows that it might be all right to mention defects, as long as the defects are not attributed to the policy of the party.[109]

Socialist or revolutionary realism would seem to mean that writers are realistically to describe things as the regime really wishes they were; revolutionary romanticism permits them to make this idealized reality a little more glamorous than it really would be. Especially since the Cultural Revolution the official taste has been for works in which the characters go around saying such things as: "'Chairman Mao and the party Center always place firm confidence in us at the key moment, setting the course and defeating all kinds of difficulties. . . .' 'Old Ch'en, you are right. With the clear and heroic leadership of Chairman Mao and the party Center, we shall this year fight to the end a battle for emancipation. . . .'"[110]

Whatever the validity of statements about class-transcending realism and the like, this doctrine, imposed by political power, can only run counter to the interests of any creative writer. Chinese writers since 1949 have largely accepted socialist or revolutionary realism (those who reject it are not published, and those who circulate manuscripts privately are punished), but they prefer to define it for themselves. The party enjoyed much support among writers prior to Liberation, and most creative writers since the May Fourth movement have been leftists in one way or another.[111] This does not mean, however, that even before Liberation they were reconciled to the literary dictatorship of the party. The Marxism of the Chinese writers tended to derive not, say, from an intellectual appreciation of the "Theses on Feuerbach" but was often a manifestation of romantic individualism[112] (revolution is new, noisy, exciting; it allows one to strike postures . . .), and obviously the party had to disabuse these writers. There is perhaps some justice in Yao Wen-yuan's comment that all the heroines of the stories by the party writer Ting Ling are nothing but the precious, ultrasensitive Miss Sophia of her first story (Ting Ling herself), dressed up in different costumes (and carrying a party card).[113] The party made no pretense of favoring creative independence. Part of Mao's point in his Yenan speech was that while realistic—that is, unflattering—descriptions of life in KMT areas are fine, one takes a different approach in dealing with the liberated areas.

After Liberation it seems that most writers shared a common interest in attempting to loosen up the rigid literary doctrine, but they rarely if ever presented a common front against the regime. The writers were divided into little cliques and friendship groups, these groups often as hostile to each other as they were to officialdom and willing to use officialdom against one another.[114] The fallacy of this last strategy was that officialdom was much better at using people than were the writers. The theme of the earlier post-Liberation literary politics was the effort by Chou Yang, the deputy director of the Propaganda Department in charge of dealing with literature, to gain organizational control of all journals and writers. He was hindered from doing so rapidly because his opponents also had long histories of party membership and impressive reputations. Chou was eventually able to bring his enemies down on charges of heresy, and these charges usually have some foundation because of the common interest of the writers in more creative freedom. After he had gained control, Chou, in the fashion of the moderate tendency of which he formed a part, was apparently willing to loosen up, and when he fell in 1966 it was ostensibly because he was too liberal.[115]

Literary purges had been going on since Yenan. The first really major one after Liberation was of a relatively minor figure, Hu Feng. He had been a fellow traveler since the early 1930s but was not close to either the party bureaucracy or the more influential literary cliques. Like other writers, he fancied himself the successor to China's foremost satirist of this century, Lu Hsun, and he continued Lu Hsun's feud with Chou Yang. Hu's hostility to Chou dates to 1944 or earlier.[116] Hu also adopted Lu Hsun's literary mannerisms, with a nasty word for everyone. He had his friends, but he was not widely liked.

After Liberation the bureaucracy put pressure on Hu Feng's friends, and one of them, Shu Wu, was induced to publish a self-criticism in the summer of 1952. He did not mention Hu Feng by name but spoke of "certain literary workers" who had said that Mao's Yenan speech was "nothing but the ABC of Marxism." Shu's exercise was originally published in the Wuhan paper. When it was republished in the *People's Daily* the editor added a note: the old essay Shu is now doing penance for was first published in 1944 in a journal edited by a "small clique headed by Hu Feng." This performance earned for Shu Wu the nickname Wu Ch'ih (Shameless) from Hu Feng.[117]

In January 1953 Lin Mo-han, one of Chou Yang's henchmen, wrote that Hu Feng's "literary thought" was "anti-Marxist," as was that of his "small clique" generally. After the publication of Shu Wu's self-criticism, meetings had been held with Hu Feng, but "while he has begun a self-examination on specifics, on the basic point he has not recognized his mistaken viewpoints." He treats revolutionary theory as "icy-cold dogma." He thinks that all Chinese literature prior to the May Fourth movement is worthless.[118] At that time the official position was that there is much worth in China's heritage—a position usually identified with the moderate tendency.

After a few other attacks, the affair went beneath the surface, although Hu Feng continued to attend meetings. In July 1954 Hu submitted a letter of opinion to the party Center defending his position. Kuo Mo-jo, the doyen of Chinese leftist letters, later summed up the official view of Hu Feng's argument: Hu urges (1) that writers need not have a communist world view, (2) that writers need not unite with the workers and peasants, (3) that writers do not need thought reform, (4) that writers need not use national forms (the stylistic devices of traditional popular literature), and (5) that writings need not serve the current political situation. The demands of the party to the contrary are "five knives" directed against the heads of writers. Precisely, says Kuo: they are weapons of the party against its enemies.[119]

Kuo's summary is accurate enough, although he does not present Hu's expressed opinions, but rather, the implications of Hu's opinions should they be consistently carried through. Hu's extremely long letter is hardly the exercise in integral opposition Kuo makes it out to be. Hu instead argues against what he feels is a crude and mechanical imposition of the party line, and he makes his own position out to be orthodox, citing extensively the works of Mao and of this century's other great literary critic, Comrade Stalin (Stalin, it turns out, is the source of the phrase, "Write the truth"). Hu had always been a politically involved writer, and he certainly does not argue for art for art's sake or for political indifference: "Our realism is a fighting realism guided by a political program."[120] Lin Mo-han and his friends, however, want to subordinate literature to dogma, with Marxism replacing literature—and this is un-Marxist and in opposition to Chairman Mao. The comrades oppose something they call objectivism.

> [They] will just not recognize its nature, and think that to oppose "objectivism" is to oppose objectivity. This is because they have only an a priori, flawless, correct, icy-cold "world view," and do not want writers to work from the spirit of practice among the joys and sorrows of the masses, under the guidance of a political program.

We must take a realistic attitude and adhere to practice. Of course, disagreements will arise.

> So, then, how do we distinguish good and bad? Some people affirm things that may not be good, and others deny things that may not be bad. What should the leadership grasp—where should it stand? This is really a problem, a big problem. But it can be resolved only by practice, only in the process of struggle.

There is a need for constant criticism and argument, not "commandism."[121]

Hu Feng quotes extensively from Mao's Yenan speech, but this is not entirely in good faith. Privately he was more frank, as in a letter written in "195X":

> This little pamphlet that has now become such a totem [*t'u-t'eng*] is the most difficult problem. The problem is not necessarily the great influence of the pamphlet itself, but the crude way it is used by malevolent incompetents. . . . These "critics" are all power-holders, and no one dares to speak. . . .[122]

Hu Feng's protest, both to the party and to his friends, was not overtly directed against the official doctrine, but against the way the doctrine was being applied by the literary bureaucracy. The party leadership, however, chose to put on his opinions, and to exaggerate a heterodox construction. By sending his letter to the party Center Hu had apparently raised the argument from a literary squabble to a political question. Why the party chose to react as it did is unclear. Hu's opinions are innocuous enough in themselves but may have been seen as the thin edge of the wedge. By appealing directly to the Center, Hu may have caused Chou Yang a loss of face, something the party did not then allow for its high functionaries; and the letter in fact amounts to an attack on Chou Yang, references to Lin Mo-han fooling no one.

The party's immediate reaction was to give Hu Feng enough rope, and Hu was eager to grasp it. Some young Marxist scholars had developed a new approach to the traditional novel *Dream of the red chamber* (*Hung lou meng*), and the *Literary Gazette* had published some pieces by older scholars refuting the new interpretation. By the fall of 1954 Chou Yang was using this as his pretext in a campaign against the editor of the *Literary Gazette,* Feng Hsueh-feng, a much bigger shot in communist letters than Hu Feng. Feng, as part of the literary apparatus, had been one of Hu Feng's early enemies, and Hu took advantage of this split among those opposed to him, joining in the rectification of *Literary Gazette*. Hu criticized Feng for printing the works of bourgeois scholars, disciples of the reactionary Hu Shih, while at the same time persecuting good revolutionary writers, such as Hu Feng's friend Ah Lung. Feng has not only "surrendered" to the Hu Shih faction but is also guilty of "vulgar sociology" (i.e., vulgar Marxism). Feng holds, for example, that in any story describing the post-Liberation period, it is impermissible to show a backward worker. Comrade Chou Yang has corrected one instance of this kind of excess but has ignored all the others. Vulgar sociology "does not proceed from reality, does not depend on principle to lead to an understanding of reality, but instead substitutes principle for reality . . . using Marxist phrases to evaluate literary works." Feng Hsueh-feng enjoys rectifying others but never thinks of rectifying himself.[123]

A few weeks later Chou Yang responded to Hu's speech. He is gratified that "Mr. Hu Feng" is finally joining in the criticism of Hu Shih's idealism and that he now places a higher value on traditional literature (the *Dream of the red chamber*) than he used to—although it is still not high enough. Given his own vulgar view of the national heritage, Hu Feng is hardly one to talk of vulgar sociology. Also, it is wrong for Hu Feng to accuse the *Literary Gazette* of formalism (a reference to Hu's criticism of the Marxist phrases). Hu Feng, in fact, has an "aristocratic bias"; he is a snob.[124]

This is mildly nasty, but still mild. At the turn of the year the campaign really began. Hu Feng was not only accused of the same old literary errors, but now article after article accused him of being a counterrevolutionary who had organized an antiparty clique in the pay of the United States and Chiang Kai-shek. In May Hu published his self-criticism, written in January, a long, dry, formalistic recitation of his literary, but not political, crimes.[125] An editorial note says: "We will not continue to allow Hu Feng to use our newspaper to cheat our readers." The same day the *People's Daily* published excerpts from Hu Feng's letters to Shu Wu, written before the two fell out, and warned Hu's other friends that they had also better come across with the letters they had received from him. In July Hu was arrested and disappeared.

Hu's letters show him to be more outspoken in private than he was in public, particularly in his contempt for the literary bureaucracy. They do not show that he opposed the revolution, or organized a clique, or that he himself had any political ambitions whatsoever. The piling of the political accusations on top of the literary ones in 1955 seems a grotesque overreaction. In 1955 the party was in a general state of hysteria; this was the year of the great *su-fan*. The Hu Feng incident, however, would seem to be more a prelude to, and possibly a cause of, this hysteria, than a consequence of it. The purge of Hu Feng is perhaps *the* paradigmatic literary purge in contemporary China—which is why so much space has been given to it here—and the regime probably deliberately made it so. The likely motive for the overreaction was to use Hu as an example, to "cut off a head to frighten the crowd." After Hu's purge, Chou Yang would have much less trouble eliminating rivals with considerably more prestige than Hu, such as Feng Hsueh-feng. To be a trifle melodramatic, Chou had also dug his own grave.

It is interesting to try to place Hu Feng into the moderate-radical dichotomy used in this study, although the attempt may be anachronistic, since the two tendencies had probably not solidified at that time. Still, much of what Hu said was later to be said by the radicals, although the radicals lack his breadth and tolerance. One of Hu's critics said his poetry was sycophantic: he "distorts the image of Comrade Mao Tse-tung, describing him as a god separated from the masses and enveloped in the highest clouds. . . .[126] Hu was neither then nor later the only one to do this. It is perhaps most accurate to say that radicalism, as the term is used here, had not yet emerged as a separate tendency in Chinese communism, but that the purge of Hu Feng was part of the consolidation of the power of those who were to come to represent the moderate tendency. It must be said, however, that the radicals have made no moves to rehabilitate Hu Feng.

If Hu Feng is still alive, and if he is a bitter man, he has had the satisfaction of having seen the fall of almost all his enemies except Kuo Mo-jo, a veritable *pu-tao-weng*, a weeble who wobbles but doesn't fall down, and Yao Wen-yuan,* who seems to have made his bones on Hu.[127] Feng Hsueh-feng's turn came in 1957, when he also was accused of having formed an antiparty clique, along with the writers Ting Ling and Ch'en Ch'i-hsia. In this case the accusation of

*October 1976: Apparently Yao as well.

factionalism may have more foundation than in the case of Hu Feng, although the clique was antiparty only in that it wanted to retain a certain independence from the Propaganda Department. The substantive charges may have less foundation: "Especially since the Hungarian incident of last year, they used the opportunity of the international anticommunist tide and this year's domestic attacks by rightists on the party, and once again struck out at the party."[128] In fact, in late 1956 and early 1957 *Literary Gazette* had published some timid columns urging less control of creative activity—a position in accord with the party line of the time. Feng's literary errors were said to be exactly the same as Hu Feng's, except Feng was better at using Marxist phrases.[129]

In the early 1960s, following the collapse of the Great Leap Forward, pressures on writers were relaxed. Chou Yang's people, perhaps motivated in part by considerations of the factional struggle, now in effect came over to Hu Feng's point of view, urging writers to write the truth. Insufficient attention has been paid to the defects of the new society, and these cannot be corrected unless they are understood. Writers should show life realistically. Merle Goldman argues that this "1961–1962 relaxation repudiates the theory that a Communist regime invariably is in opposition to the intellectuals."[130] This seems a valid point if "invariably" is taken strictly enough. The writers were obviously allied with one part of the regime and in opposition to another part of it. It is unclear whether there could ever be perfect concord between creative intellectuals and those who claim the authority to dictate what they should say.

The call for more realism was mainly a call for dissent through literature rather than for literary dissent, although Chou Yang was apparently willing to unbend the doctrine a little bit. One of his long-time associates, Shao Ch'üan-lin, argued in 1962 that writers should pay attention to middle characters, characters who combine the good and the bad, progress and backwardness. This would allow a more subtle treatment of contradictions, which "are often concentrated in middle characters."[131] After 1962, however, the radicals gradually won the authority to set the literary line, and in 1964 Shao's views were condemned as a denial of the proletarian point of view in literature. The radicals like their heroes good, their villains bad, and neither very complicated.[132]

Between 1963 and 1965 the intellectuals, perhaps because they had the support of the apparatus, were apparently able to continue certain indirect, sniping attacks on the radicals. Given the nature of the political system it is impossible to be dogmatic about this, but much of what was written in the early 1960s seems to have a satirical import. In May 1963 Mao had said, "Generally speaking, what succeeds is correct, what fails is mistaken." That same month the *People's Daily* published an attack on pragmatism, a philosophy which asserts that "truth is nothing but the expedient method."[133] In 1964 the *People's Daily* took note of Shakespeare's coming 400th birthday and how this was being commercialized in the West. The capitalists hope to make a lot of money out of Shakespeare. Unfortunately, the current notion of high culture in the West is the twist.

Therefore, the capitalists must vulgarize Shakespeare. In a 1960 London performance of *Henry V* "not only did the old-time warriors wear modern uniforms, but also called out [modern] orders." As Shakespeare would have said, "Hence, pack! There's gold; you came for gold, ye slaves."[134] The criticism seems well taken but perhaps not of great intrinsic interest to most Chinese—unless this is in fact a reference to the modern revolutionary operas Chiang Ch'ing was developing at that time—modern-dress vulgarizations, aficionados say, of the traditional Peking opera. The same issue of the *People's Daily* carries a more scholarly article, a critique of the new conservative movement in the United States. The new conservatives get most of their stuff from Burke, but they are also influenced by the "reactionary theories of Plato and Thomas Aquinas" and have "eclectically absorbed much other ideological garbage." They carry their superstitious theism over into their social theories, stressing spirit first, *ching-shen ti-i*. They forget: "Myth in the end is only myth, and reality is always reality. Where there is oppression there must be revolution. . . ."[135] "Spirit first" is the idiom more of Lin Piao than of Burke, and this is perhaps an attack upon radical voluntarism.

These attacks (if that is what they are) came to an end with the Great Simplification of the Cultural Revolution, and the literary doctrine that has held since then makes even Chou Yang or the 1957 Yao Wen-yuan look like aesthetes. The surprising thing is that even in these conditions it remains possible (we are told) to express dissent by literary means. In February 1974 the new, revolutionary Shansi opera, "Three times up peach peak" (*San shang t'ao feng*) was attacked. In the play, one brigade swindles another (Peach Peak brigade), selling it a sick horse. A conscientious party secretary from the first brigade discovers this and goes to Peach Peak three times to return the money; finally everything is straightened out. It turns out that this is a revision of a 1965 play, "Three times down to peach garden," written to glorify the experience of Liu Shao-ch'i's wife in rectifying things in the Peach Garden brigade in Honan. To make sure the audience would get the point, the original play had a female county head named Wang (Madame Liu was named Wang Kuang-mei). In the new version, Miss Wang is dropped, *garden* is changed to *peak*, and the setting is changed from 1965 to 1959. It might be thought that the new version was an attempt to eliminate the objectionable features, but the change in date only makes the play more pernicious: in 1959 the rightists were all comparing the Great Leap to a sick horse. The play is an attack on Chairman Mao's proletarian revolutionary line.[136] No script of this play is available outside China, so it is difficult to determine whether it really has the kind of oppositional content ascribed to it; in other cases since the Cultural Revolution, attacks on literary works have a distinctly phony ring.[137]

Writers from Hu Feng to Shao Ch'üan-lin, in appealing for greater freedom, have cast their arguments in the regime's terms. While they perhaps had little choice in the matter, such tactics are probably self-defeating. The regime's policies as well, however, may be self-defeating—if not in terms of naked political control, then in terms of encouraging literature of genuine persuasiveness and artistic merit. Since 1958, and especially since the Cultural Revolution, there has been an effort to cultivate proletarian writers. In 1975, however, it was said that workmen turned writers are as eager to acquire the good life as anyone else. "Since existence determines consciousness, their standpoint and views must necessarily change."[138] Perhaps it requires a certain amount of misanthropy to become too upset by this. More importantly, the regime seems to realize that what it likes is not necessarily liked by the workers, peasants, and soldiers the literature is supposed to serve. It is impossible to measure current Chinese taste (if only because reading habits depend upon what is available), and most of the time publication figures will not do (since the regime publishes what it likes). The figures for 1962, however, which was the time of the capitalist road and, presumably, a concern for profit, may provide clues. The radicals argue the revisionists were then poisoning the people with trash, but it was trash people were willing to buy; and there was still a wide range of choice in books. Among the works published by the People's Literature Publishing Company that year, those printed in greatest numbers were three traditional novels: *Water margin* (822,000 copies), *Romance of the three kingdoms* (648,000 copies), and *Monkey* (*Hsi yu chi*) (622,000 copies). The ranking corresponds with the usual impressions of the popular esteem with which these works have been held over the centuries, although in terms of literary merit *Dream of the red chamber* (88,000 copies) should probably come first. Rather surprisingly, 40,000 copies of *Lao ts'an yu chi,* a charming but rather decadent little novel of the late Ch'ing period, were printed. The most widely printed contemporary work was *February, early spring* (138,000 copies), the source of the movie poor Ch'un-mei liked so much. The company also printed 10,000 copies of *Chairman Mao on literature and art.*[139]

The regime is worried that "works which lack depth never move people, are uninteresting, and thus have no great educational function." Yet the works it likes apparently lack depth and are characterized by simplicity and rigidity.[140] According to rumor, in 1973 Chiang Ch'ing told her writers to read certain Western classics, including the *Count of Monte Cristo* and *Crime and Punishment,* in order to improve their styles.[141] Around the same time the general public was given access to works not sanctioned by the regime, although indirectly. In January 1974 the radical Shanghai journal *Study and Criticism* attacked *Jonathan Livingston Seagull,* popular then on Taiwan as well as in the United States. The novel, with its mystical concepts, is a reflection of the crisis of monopoly capitalism in the 1970s, when all the glory has turned to dross. Its subjective idealism meets the needs of the reactionary class. To make his point, the author of the article appends a translation of extended passages from the novel.[142] The campaign against Confucius has probably served in part to familiarize an ignorant generation with the ideas of that philosopher. During the campaign the *Analects* was reissued, although, of course, with the proper annotations to show what a wicked fellow Confucius really was. When *Water margin* was attacked in late 1975, the various traditional editions of the novel were also reissued, again with the appropriate introductions and notes. The words of Master K'ung and the deeds of the noble bandits of Liang-shan-po have held meaning for people throughout the centuries and, despite the notes, will probably continue to do so. There will no doubt continue to be Chinese who discover in their literary heritage—and maybe even in that silly seagull—some truths not covered by the program of the present regime.

The Cloak of Religion

The Communists, of course, are atheists, and they take their atheism with a seriousness one would not expect from a study of the Chinese tradition, a tradition in which the question of theism and atheism, as such, had rarely figured as a major problem and in which organized religion had seldom been a competitor in the political realm. The Communist attitude might be seen as a continuation of the Confucian elite's scorn for superstition (cf. Hai Jui), although the Communists are more vehement than most Confucians ever intended to be. It is probably more accurate to see the party's atheism as a reflection of its modernity. In the last decade of the nineteenth century Protestant missionaries began to promote modern, Western education, both as a way of attracting young Chinese not otherwise attracted by Christian dogma and also out of a sense that China must become civilized, that is, Victorian.[143] Young Chinese were eager enough for modern education, and many of them accepted the Protestant critique of traditional society. Modernism is not completely compatible with Christianity, however, and a generation of educated Chinese grew up to look with equal contempt upon the superstitions of all old societies, both their own and those of the West. This attitude was hardly confined to Marxists: Hu Shih was as much an atheist as Chairman Mao—perhaps even a more cocksure one.

Since religion is superstition, a product of backward social conditions, the Communists expect that it will die out naturally. No more than Nero or Domitian do they engage in religious persecution as such; they only guard against "counterrevolutionary activities carried out under the cloak of religion." The regime also deprives religious groups of organizational and economic autonomy, but in this respect religious groups are treated no differently from any other. The constitution of the People's Republic guarantees freedom of religion. The 1954 constitution says, "Citizens of the People's Republic of China enjoy freedom of religious belief." The 1975 constitution says they "enjoy freedom to believe in religion and freedom not to believe in religion and to propagate atheism."[144]

The 1975 change is puzzling. Freedom of belief entails freedom of disbelief, and the Communists did not suddenly hit on this constitutional truism in 1970, when the current document was drafted. Lu Ting-i explained in 1956 that freedom of religion means there should be no atheist propaganda in churches, temples, and the like and no religious propaganda anywhere else.[145] The new explicit freedom to propagate atheism may mean there is no legally guaranteed freedom to propagate religion at all now, and perhaps the comrades need no longer be so squeamish about churches and temples (not that they always were before).

Holmes Welch finds an "inverse correlation between political movements and Buddhist activity," and this relationship holds for other religious activity as well. In the relatively relaxed years of 1961 and 1962, for example, one commune in Lien-chiang county, Fukien, built three new temples and repaired eleven old ones. "Many cadre members do not dare to take any action against superstitious conduct, and have led the way in participating in superstition, crying 'Freedom of belief' and 'Superstition is the demand of the masses.'"[146] In general, however, it is fair enough to say that religious activity is discouraged.

Because of the imperialist—and to a large degree, specifically American—origins of contemporary Christianity in China, it was to be expected that Christian churches would have a hard time. Christianity was condemned as a form of cultural imperialism.[147] In 1950 Chinese Protestants implemented the "three-selfs patriotic movement," cutting all ties with foreign churches. Foreign missionaries, both Catholic and Protestant, were gradually expelled from China, some after serving prison terms. All separate Protestant denominations were dissolved, presumably for the administrative convenience of the regime, although a Canadian divine who reports this calls it a liberation from sectarian controversy.[148] Even Chinese Protestants who cooperated with the regime did not have an easy time. Wu Yao-tsung, the head of the Chinese YMCA, was able to unburden himself a bit during the Hundred Flowers movement. He thanked the regime for its favors to religion; for example, the government had helped repair some churches. "Especially worth pointing out is that the government helped expose certain counterrevolutionary groups using the cloak of religion." There is a dark side, however. Urban churches operate relatively normally, but many rural churches shut down during land reform have not been permitted to reopen. Bibles and hymnals have been confiscated and not returned. Since the *su-fan* campaign of 1955 many believers are intimidated and afraid to go to church. Wu also protests the vulgarity of some of the atheist propaganda. Of course, the imperialists lie when they say all ministers in China have been jailed or shot, but the government should do more to protect religious freedom.[149]

The situation has not improved since 1957, and it is likely that for the time being organized Protestantism is dead in China. A Canadian cleric traveling in China in 1975 was told by a Chinese minister in Nanking that "Christian groups are de-institutionalized and de-religionized in their practices" (the terms, it might be noted, sound more like Western liberal Christian jargon than like that of the regime). In Shanghai he learned that "since the Cultural Revolution no churches have been open for Christian meetings." "Shanghai has no general meetings of Christians or home meetings which might look like a community apart. At this point they are seeking to become fully a part of China. Christians do not want to seem separated from their fellow Chinese."[150] The more power to them, the pious doctor feels. The evaluation of this as the death of Protestantism is, of course, a matter of interpretation; the author of this traveler's tale claims to show how Christianity thrives in China. It seems likely that there are groups that gather for prayer in private without the sanction of the regime or its surviving clergy, but there is no evidence for this.

The Catholic church presented a more difficult problem than did the Protestant denominations, partly, perhaps, because it is better organized and partly because that church is, by its nature, transnational. The first major campaign against Catholics began in 1951, with the expulsion of foreign priests and nuns and the resurrection of the old gentry tales of how nuns murder orphans.[151] The regime did not attack the Church directly but concentrated instead upon its militant youth organization, the Legion of Mary, an "international fascist organization inside the Catholic Church." From the way the legion is described, it is no wonder the regime should oppose it: it sounds rather like the Communist Party. In order to combat the "influence of an atheist age," it demands unlimited obedience and discipline from its members. The organization was said to engage in sabotage activities and murder, but no evidence is given; more concretely, the members listened to the Voice of America and attempted to persuade patriotic youths to be less patriotic.[152]

As with the Protestant churches, most Catholic churches in the cities continued to operate fairly normally in the early 1950s, but again as with the Protestants, many in the countryside did not. According to Lo Jui-ch'ing, rural Catholics sometimes put up active resistance:

> Counterrevolutionary elements in religious bodies, under the cloak of religion, have plotted to undertake and develop secret counterrevolutionary organizations. In May 1953 and April 1954 [two districts] in Hopei smashed two secret organizations that undertook rebellious activities in the name of Catholicism. In all, 110 some caves, secret rooms, and holes in walls were discovered, the largest cave being able to hold more than 100 people.[153]

Lo does not say what the counterrevolutionaries did in their caves and holes. Perhaps they hid priests and heard Mass.

Some members of the Catholic hierarchy put up stiffer resistance to the policies of the regime than did most of the Protestant clergy. The most intransigent was Kung P'in-mei, bishop of Shanghai. In 1952 Kung forbade Catholics to join the party, the Youth League, or the Pioneers; to sign petitions for the expulsion of the papal nuncio; or to bring accusations against priests. In 1953 he refused an invitation to sit among the guests of honor at the National Day celebration in Shanghai, saying that since the party had imprisoned his priests he would not help it with its propaganda.[154] In September 1955 Kung himself was arrested, along with fourteen of his priests, and accused of counterrevolution. He had said publicly that the new China was a "black, dark world" ruled by "devils." He allegedly detained by force a nun who wished to leave the convent. He tried to sabotage land reform, forbidding the faithful to accuse landlords at mass meetings or to share in the spoils—if they could not safely refuse the land given them, they should be prepared to return it and not sell it without the landlord's permission (as Kung was being arrested the regime was collectivizing the land it had distributed a few years earlier). He sent money to landlords whose property had been expropriated, and he had taken care of the wives and children of counterrevolutionaries; and all the while he listened to the Voice of America. He plotted against the regime. One of his clique allegedly said that Hu Feng had been too open in his opposition; we must be more careful. "But all of these activities are in no way at all able to hinder the advance of the task of the revolution of the people of our country."[155] Obviously; but it would be naïve to ask why, in that case, he was arrested. Bishop Kung was not tried until 1961, when he was sentenced to life imprisonment. The Communists encouraged stories to the effect that he had admitted his errors, but if this is true it is likely that his confession would have been made public, and perhaps the man himself released.[156]

In the early 1950s the regime had attempted to gain control of the church through a Reform Society (*ko-hsin-hui*), but this was abandoned, allegedly because the laxness and immorality of the members alienated the faithful.[157] In 1957, after a long meeting of bishops, priests, and laymen who had previously cooperated with the regime, the regime formed a Catholic Patriotic Association. According to a source who claims to have spoken with some who attended this meeting, spokesmen for the regime had urged a complete break with the Vatican, with the self-selection and self-consecration (*tzu-hsuan tzu-sheng*) of bishops, following the model of the eastern European peace priests. All the bishops attending, however, said they would never consecrate any bishop not appointed by the pope.[158] In the final communiqué of the meeting the sphere of autonomy claimed was more modest: the association "breaks all political and economic relations with the Vatican, and firmly opposes the use of religion by the Vatican curia to interfere in our country's internal politics." P'i Shu-shih, the archbishop of Shenyang, who presided over the meeting, added a subtlety, opposing all unreasonable interference by the Vatican.[159] The religious authority of the Vatican was still recognized; the problem here for both sides, perhaps, is that politics is not entirely divorced from questions of faith and morals.

This meeting took place during the 1957 antirightist campaign, in the midst of much talk of rightists in the Catholic church. The pressure by the regime continued unabated into 1958. The full rupture with the Vatican came that year, when two bishops not appointed by the pope were consecrated in Wuhan. In 1959 P'i Shu-shih did what he allegedly swore he would never do and consecrated an unauthorized bishop in Peking.[160] The churches in China were closed during the Cultural Revolution and seem to have remained closed, except for one in Peking, which serves the convenience of the foreign diplomatic corps and the edification of foreign visitors.

The motives behind the active persecution have, of course, been political. Bishop Kung, some might say, was asking for martyrdom and got less than was coming to him. The uncompromising anticommunism of the Vatican in the 1950s was little immediate help to the faithful in Communist countries, and many American churches that had sponsored China missions may have been overly impressed with the Methodist rule of Chiang Kai-shek. The church must, of course, denounce anything that hinders salvation or violates natural law. The church may also have the duty to defend its own legitimate rights, and whatever these rights may be it can hardly allow their unilateral definition by the state. But it is probably inexpedient as well as un-Christian for the church to fall into partisanship, into unconditional commitment for or against a specific political group in competition with other political groups.

The Western ecclesiastical bureaucracies have changed since the 1950s, perhaps realizing that the powers that be in China are as much ordained by God as are those anywhere else. It is not clear, however, that the change in policy implies any growth in wisdom. Christian discussions on China in the 1970s seem partisan in favor of the regime and against their own martyrs; they are conducted in a tone of syrupy fatuity that might seem Swiftian, did not those who undertake them seem so humorless. It remains to be seen whether this kind of partisanship is any favor to the remnant in China. The new attitude may at least not create gratuitous difficulties.

The Chinese Christians who had cooperated with the regime no doubt approved of much of the regime's program; it would be foolish to argue, however, that, despite the regime's talk of a common political front among those of different views of the universe, Chinese Christians have never had to choose between obedience and conscience. The concessions made have been justified as necessary in order to keep the faith alive at all. After the capitulation of the Catholic church in 1957 and 1958, for example, Catholics were able to enjoy another seven years or so of fairly normal worship.[161] The regime apparently did not even molest members of the nonjuring clergy who did not go out of their way to make themselves obnoxious to it. The cooperating clergy were bargaining with the tiger for his hide, however, and in retrospect and from a purely wordly point of view the way taken by Wu Yao-tsung or P'i Shu-shih does not seem to have proved any more expedient than that of Kung P'in-mei.

This discussion has followed the regime's stress on the foreign ties of organized Christianity. It does not appear, however, that Christians have been treated any worse than the devotees of more long-established religions. The foreign ties of Buddhism actually helped that religion for a while, serving the regime's relations with Buddhist countries in Southeast Asia (countries that were not, of course, any threat to China—unlike the erstwhile Christian countries). The Taoist clergy did not share this transnational advantage and was treated much more brusquely, despite the Communists' occasional limited admiration for Taoism as a philosophy. Taoism also met trouble because Taoist elements form much of the ritual of the various secret societies. These were not tolerated because they are tightly organized groups autonomous from the regime and also because they have a custom of engaging in criminal activities. When Lo Jui-ch'ing expressed concern about "counterrevolutionary groups using the cloak of religion" he was referring more to the traditional secret societies than to Catholics. The party and the societies had sometimes cooperated prior to 1949, but upon Liberation the party judged that they had fulfilled their historical function. The party, through the trade unions, conducted a protracted struggle against secret societies in Tientsin (and perhaps other cities as well) for the allegiance of the workers.[162] Lo Jui-ch'ing in 1955 mentioned the smashing of a branch of the *i-kuan-tao* in Shensi; unlike the Catholics, these sectarians were said to have amassed rifles, ammunition, and KMT flags. That same year there were said to be five thousand chieftains of the *hui tao men* active in Shao-hsing, Chekiang. They "spread rumors and reactionary slogans" and threatened members of the militia.[163] The secret societies had opposed the Ch'ing and later the warlords. In alliance with the Communists and with dissident warlords (and perhaps with American intelligence organizations)[164] they had opposed Chiang Kai-shek. Their remnants continue their tradition of dissent, it appears, and now, in alliance with the KMT, oppose the Communists.

The regime has treated the secret societies in the way a similar regime in the United States might be expected to treat the Mafia. But religious organizations, including the Buddhist and Taoist clergy, posing less of a threat to social order, have not been spared either. Since Liberation the regime has conducted a vacillating campaign against the religious organizations, culminating in the closing of temples and monasteries during the Cultural Revolution. The Buddhist Sangha has sometimes been shown respect, but in general the modern hostility to superstition is reinforced among the cadres by the traditional stereotype of monks as fat, lazy fellows who live off others' sweat and are given to seducing credulous women—the same stereotype of monasticism as in the West, and in each case probably containing about the same amount of truth. Many monasteries owned large amounts of land, and these, of course, were expropriated during land reform. According to a refugee monk who was a novice at the time, he and his fellows were told that "exploitation was a serious crime, but if the youngsters would confess to it and then join in accusing their elders at a public meeting, they would be given immunity. If not, they would be shot.'' There was pressure on monks to find regular work, and even if this did not always mean their leaving the monastery, it did leave them little time for cultivating the Way. Until the Cultural Revolution many monasteries continued to function, although without their prior economic independence, and ordinations continued to be held. Chinese Buddhism also served the regime in its people-to-people relations with countries with large Buddhist populations.[165]

The Sangha was not without men made of the same stuff as Kung P'in-mei. The most notorious example, perhaps, is Pen-huan, a ''traitor and a gangster,'' the abbot of Nan-hua Ssu, an important monastery in Kwangtung. The regime is unwilling to admit that any political opponent is other than a moral abomination. Thus we are told that Pen-huan collaborated with the Japanese (it had been Buddhist practice in this century to attempt not to antagonize any secular authority). He is ''an enemy of the people; he used his religious position to engage in smuggling, black-marketeering, selling of stolen grain, selling of gold, and other illegal activities.'' For years he ''insulted'' the regime's policy on religion and ''spread rumors.'' He said the government prevented ordinations—an outright lie, since he himself ordained fifty disciples. The matter cannot be this simple, however, since he also conducted ''secret ordinations.'' It is likely that in fact Pen-huan protested limitations placed on ordinations. He hated land reform, he criticized the cooperatives, and he did not want monks to participate in labor. ''When the KMT ruled, there was no need to labor,'' he said. He permitted counterrevolutionaries to become monks; why, he even ordained a released labor-reform criminal. He forbade disciples to read new books or newspapers. He dallied with nuns.

> In June, 1954, on the feast of the Six Ancestors [*liu-tsu*] many people came to Nan-Hua Ssu to worship the Buddha. The public security organs, in order to preserve public order, talked with Pen-huan and others and demanded they help in doing good security work and register the names and addresses of the visitors. But later Pen-huan said openly and maliciously to the monks that this is harassment by the People's Government and that the freedom of belief is a fake. . . .
>
> The People's Government urged in good faith that Pen-huan not turn Nan-Hua Ssu into a special place for bad people. But Pen-huan took a completely antagonistic attitude.[166]

In 1958 the People's Government vindicated freedom of belief by arresting Pen-huan. It is impossible to judge the accuracy of the reports of his more nefarious doings, but it was not any dallying with nuns or selling of gold that got him jailed. He refused to act as a policeman (and the registering of pilgrims would seem in fact to be a form of harassment), gave refuge to persons who had nowhere else to go, and attempted to preserve monastic life and discipline.

During the Cultural Revolution places of worship were closed and were exposed to vandalism by Red Guards, although places containing articles of artistic or historical value were protected.[167] Since the Cultural Revolution a few temples have reopened, virtually as museums with the surviving monks as living exhibits. During the early 1970s the pattern of official toleration and support had returned to the pre-Cultural Revolution norm, although on a much smaller scale, with the few old monks and laymen fewer and older.[168]

The most troublesome religious group seems to have been the Moslems. Unlike serious Chinese Buddhists, Moslems are not pacifists. Also, Islam, unlike Buddhism, is a strong, exclusivist theism, and Chinese Moslems (*Hui*) constitute a distinct subculture, a quasi-ethnic distinction reinforcing the religious one.[169] While the Hui are linguistically and (by now) ethnically identical with their neighbors, they have a tradition of local self-government and are cut off by custom from the bulk of the Chinese population. Chinese Moslems rebelled against the Ch'ing in the 1870s, and while this rebellion was suppressed, the Moslems were largely able to go their own way during the interregnum of 1911–49. They are sufficiently distinct as a people to justify their classification as a separate nationality group. Hui are found in many parts of China, including Taiwan, but are concentrated in the northwest of China proper. Ninghsia is a province-sized Hui autonomous region.

The most troublesome of the Moslems seems to have been a leader in Ninghsia, Ma Chen-wu—another moral moron, naturally. This specimen used the Koran and his "obscene prestige as an imam" to acquire "vast feudal power and feudal influence." He ruled with an iron hand. Until the Communist victory he cooperated with the "reactionary KMT." "There was no evil he would not do." In 1949 he poisoned "his own son." Even if he was as unappetizing as the regime portrays him, his obscene prestige must have been enormous. In May 1950 and April 1952 his supporters led rebellions against the regime. Despite this, "our party and government arranged politically that he should have a position," hoping he might reform himself. Ma continued his "counterrevolutionary activities under the cloak of religion" and in 1958 had another try. That year there were two rebellions in his name. The rebels formed an "Islamic Democratic Party" and proclaimed a "Hui Republic," attempting to gain control of Ninghsia.[170] That Ma should have been tolerated through a series of armed rebellions is probably testimony more to the cohesiveness of the local Moslem community and Ma's position in it than to the sloth, incompetence, or amiability of the regime.

Even in the 1970s there is evidence of local instability among Moslems. According to a 1975 report,

> Minority people, mostly of Hui nationality, were reported to have staged a demonstration recently in Yunnan province against a drive to step up the proletarian dic-

> tatorship movement. The main objection was said to be the call to give up their observance of Friday as a religious holiday. Many arrests were reported.[171]

Most Chinese religion involves folk religion, an amalgam of ancestor veneration and Buddhist and Taoist practices. This also has remarkable staying-power and, while hardly as militant as Islam, will probably be as hard to eradicate. George Kerr, a critic of the Taiwan regime, comments on popular religion in that province:

> Costly traditional religious practices long banned by the Japanese were resumed. These had often led families to bankrupt themselves by providing ostentatious display for weddings, divination rites, and costly funerals. Upon these expenditures the Japanese had placed limits which the older generation resented, but the younger generation—say those born after 1900—had received them as an economic benefit. They were sorry to see them lifted. On the contrary the newcomers [the KMT] encouraged a return to traditional rites and ceremonies as a sign of "reassimilation" to China proper. It was all very colorful and quaint . . . but it represented a marked retrogression, a return to 19th century Chinese standards.[172]

There is more to this than the interesting paradox of a proponent of American-style democracy in Taiwan advocating the political suppression of worship. It has been a generation since the events described, but the practices continue unabated; and whatever may have been the case then, the KMT no longer enthuses over such ceremonies. The attitudes of Kerr, the Japanese, the KMT, and the CPC are almost identical: religion is not a fit thing to spend money on. (The Communists, of course, are also irritated by the superstition itself, the attitude of peasants that what the regime calls the "old man in the sky" has something to do with their lives.) It is a mark of modernity to be a bit upset by the spending of money that might otherwise go for medicine or tanks or portraits of rulers on lazy monks and fancy food, but this attitude may ignore a whole side of human nature (the spiritual aspect of religion aside)—our desire for play, for gaiety and color.[173] The Communists have usually discouraged popular religious practices, particularly since the Cultural Revolution. During that movement the Red Guards were given license to smash the "four olds," including the superstitious practices of the population, and the regime has little sympathy with families who go into debt because of ceremonial expenses: this, no doubt, is the work of the class enemy.[174] Since the Cultural Revolution the regime has celebrated the lunar new year (what it calls the spring festival) with advice to the people to be frugal. One such article notes, however, that despite the best efforts of the Red Guards, the old practices keep creeping back in.[175]

Above we put the spiritual aspect of religion to the side, which is obviously illegitimate. Perhaps the spiritual needs of the Chinese people will eventually be met by the worship of the state or the party or the chairman (late or otherwise) of the party's Central Committee. The cult of Mao, particularly from 1958 until around 1971, bears many of the marks of a religion,[176] and some Western scholars find that cult an excellent "civil religion,"[177] the sort of thing that, if it did not exist, Voltaire would have to invent. It is hard to see, however, how any serious Marxist, supposedly opposed to all mystification, could view this other than with distaste; and the cult of Mao, particularly in its extreme forms, was never without its transparent element of opportunism. In any case, "The notion that man is on his way to become a dialectical materialist seems . . . harder and harder to maintain. Wherever he is free to choose his own way, this is not the way he usually chooses."[178]

Local Interests

China is a large country, and while it forms a cultural unit when compared with other countries, there are wide differences of customs and habits within it. The traditional Chinese state was highly centralized whenever it had the power to be so; much of the work of maintaining local order, however, was carried out by local people. This century's interregnum encouraged the downward transfer of power in much of China. Ordinary Chinese have generally known the difference between a Chinese and a barbarian, but it is only recently that this has become a matter of national identification; and even so, local attachments remain. According to a letter from a soldier to the *People's Daily* in 1975:

> Not long ago I returned to my home in northern Kiangsu to visit my relatives and discovered there were problems in some of the schools concerning the promotion of the common language. Some teachers talked like this: "We are natives of this place; we grew up here. Why should we learn a foreign [*wai-ti*] language?" Some students said: "Rural students should remain true to the countryside. Why study to become half local and half foreign and not truly either? [*Na neng hsueh-te t'u-pu-t'u, yang-pu-yang-te*]." Because of these ways of thinking the common language has not been promoted very well.

In fact, the soldier himself, a lower-middle school graduate, was unable to speak Mandarin when he joined the army.[179] What seems most surprising is that things pertaining to other parts of China are here called *yang*, foreign—literally, ocean. Foreigners, particularly Westerners, are popularly called *yang-jen*, ocean people, a term that has always seemed to me, as one, to be mildly derogatory.

This discussion of local interests deals only with cadres, and thus it might be thought that it should be more properly put with the interests of the rulers. Accusations of localism by the regime, however, seem to imply some kind of unwholesome relationship between cadres native to the place at which they work and the local population—that the cadres are, in effect, representing some popular interest that ought not to be represented. Localism (since Liberation) is considered a form of rightism, and the major campaign against localism was part of the antirightist campaign that followed the Hundred Flowers. Native cadres do not seem to err by pressing for policies more radical than the Center is currently inclined to follow. Thus, the 1955 localists in Chekiang used as their pretext for asserting power the excessive speed of land collectivization, indicating they would have gone more slowly.[180] Ezra Vogel holds that the localists oppose radical policies because they have friends and relatives among the rich peasants.[181] This is probably part of the story: as the KMT learned on Taiwan, it is easier to redistribute someone else's land than one's own. More generally, radical policies are disruptive and disturbing and in many ways unpopular and would therefore be resented by those with personal ties to the local population—by the man who must answer to his mother as well as the county secretary.

During the 1950s the party encouraged what it called the localization of cadres, the appointment to official position of persons native to the locality in which they serve. After the behavior of the native cadres in the cooperative movement in 1955 and the Hundred Flowers movement of 1957, however, there was a change of emphasis. In a report summing up the purge following the Hundred Flowers, Ten Hsiao-p'ing, then head of the Central Secretariat, said that while all in all localization is a good thing, the highest principle is the communization of cadres.[182] Chiang Hua, then first secretary of Chekiang, whose purge of his province was regarded as a model, elaborated:

> Formerly the party brought up the slogan of the "localization of cadres." The main spirit of this was that cadres should establish intimate relations with the masses of the locality. The conditions are advantageous for cadres from the locality to establish intimate relations with the masses there. But after a certain period of effort cadres from outside can also establish intimate relations with the masses, and this also is localization. Thus, we absolutely cannot permit the use of the slogan "localization of cadres" to develop into localism. We absolutely cannot permit persons with ulterior motives to estrange relations between outside and local cadres and undertake sectarian activities. Some people proclaim themselves "representatives of the local cadres"; some claim there must be some local people among the secretaries of party committees at all levels. This is completely mistaken.[183]

The problem of localism was perhaps most severe in Kwangtung province, which is linguistically and in many ways culturally a distinct area. Prior to Liberation there had been a strong locally organized Communist guerrilla movement in that province, largely cut off from the rest of the party. While it took Lin Piao's army to liberate the province, the local leaders were not happy to see the major positions occupied by outsiders. A campaign against localism had been going on since 1952 and culminated in the disciplining in 1958 of the two major local leaders, members of the party's Central Committee, Ku Ta-ts'un and

Feng Pai-chü. Feng was alleged to have had a theory: "Command by cadres sent south violates Marxist principles."[184] In other areas native cadres apparently did not elevate localism to a Marxist principle, but even their more moderate demands were rejected. Local cadres cannot demand as a right, for example, that they hold positions in leading organizations. This does not mean that local leaders are systematically excluded from positions of authority; it may mean that any who have prestige deriving from sources other than their official position are regarded with distrust.

During and after the Cultural Revolution localism was one of the many isms resulting from the fragmentation of that movement. In Kwangtung, after the purge of T'ao Chu, the former boss of that province, Feng Pai-chü's people apparently thought the time for their vindication and revenge had come. They were proved wrong. Some of the post–Cultural Revolution practices may tend to encourage some kind of localism. These would include the institutions of local control that Pfeffer talks about, if those institutions ever attain any real influence. The policy of self-reliance, which in itself encourages what Audrey Donnithorne calls a cellular economy, might also nourish localism.[185]

A more pernicious form of localism might be the growth of regional militarism, a symptom of a decaying dynasty. An exaggerated present example of regional militarism might be the position of Taiwan since 1949. A military commander who claims autonomy, however, need not always be claiming to act as a representative of the population of the area his troops are stationed in, and this problem is better discussed later, in the section "The Army."

THE RULERS

In this study the regime has often been treated as if it were some kind of willful, reasoning entity given to making difficult demands upon people. Clearly this is a matter of convenience. The regime itself is divided in many ways (along factional lines, perhaps; between radicals and moderates), and some members of the regime have interests running counter to those of other members. This section discusses some of those interests at a rather high level of generality—the interests of bureaucrats as opposed to the interests of those who would control them. Specific sectoral interests (those of bureaucrats working in agriculture as opposed to those working in industry, say) are not discussed as such, since, given the bureaucratic mode of Chinese politics, this could become simply a study of Chinese politics rather than of opposition. One specific sectoral interest, that of the army, is discussed in detail, however, because of its special position within the regime.

Bureaucratic Interests

I am His Highness's dog at Kew.
Pray tell me, Sir, whose dog are you?

These lines of Pope's may help focus the discussion of bureaucratic interests on the problem of control: just whose dog will the bureaucrat be? A bureaucracy is ideally an instrument for carrying out policies decided by the political authority, and there will be competition to gain control of that instrument. Bureaucrats may also desire to be in some sense their own dogs, to free themselves from at least some kinds of control and to pursue their own interests. The Chinese radicals have expressed the perennial leftist fear of the bureaucracy as a new class, able to impose its revisionist will on society and to kill the revolution. Like other bureaucracies, the Chinese has a tendency to try to close itself off and to try to do things its own way:

> In 1962 Chairman Mao pointed out both orally and in writing, in a serious manner: "The Central Organization Department has not made reports to the Center, to the point that the comrades at the Center know nothing about the activities of the Organization Department. It has locked itself in and become an independent kingdom." An Tzu-wen [the head of the Organization Department] nourished hatred in his heart for this criticism, and said this kind of nonsense: "Chairman Mao does not understand the situation of the Central Organization Department"; he did not transmit [Mao's directives]. P'eng Chen jumped up and took responsibility for An Tzu-wen.[186]

A preliminary approach to the problem of bureaucracy in China might be through the writings of the Legalists, which tacitly formed the basis for the old bureaucratic state. In recent years the Communists have also expressed great admiration for the Legalists. Legalist administrative theory, which focuses on the problem of control, is closer to the Chinese tradition than is that of, say, Max Weber, and it is also more political; at the same time, Legalist theories are not inconsistent with those of Weber. The various Legalist tenets may give some clues concerning Chinese perception of bureaucratic behavior, and perhaps even concerning that behavior itself.

The major Legalist thinker, Master Han Fei, posits a basic difference of interests between the ruler and the minister. "Superior and inferior fight one hundred battles a day." The ruler wishes to appoint to office men of merit and ability, that they may efficiently carry out his will. The minister wishes to gain office without showing any merit, and he has no abstract desire to please the ruler; instead, he wishes to reap the benefits of office.[187] Through law and technique the ruler can make these interests coincide, by rewarding competence and punishing incompetence, the only measure of competence being performance. Both ruler and minister are motivated by consideration of their own advantage, but the political interests of the ruler correspond with those of the state. Those of the officials do not, and if officials grow too powerful this means the ruin of the state.[188] To counter the officials' lust for power and to prevent them from forming cliques, there must be a clear division of responsibilities, fixed by law.[189] The ruler must remain aloof, listening to everyone and trusting no one: "Misfortune comes to the lord of men through his faith in men, since if he trusts men he will be controlled by men."[190] Ministers always try to outguess the ruler, toadying to his desires, telling him what they think he wants to hear.[191] Therefore, the ruler should show no bias, neither toward persons nor toward policy.

This is a caricature, and a mean-minded one at that; but like any good caricature, it brings out in exaggerated form some real features of its subject. Given the bureaucratic nature of the current Chinese regime, the Legalist model may be an aid to understanding. This model, however, neglects the revolutionary nature of the current regime. The Legalist state is an automatic state, grinding along under its own momentum, the only function of the political authority being to reward or punish according to law. This kind of state prevents the bureaucrat from translating his public position into private privilege, but otherwise it would suit the (abstract) bureaucrat just fine. It might not suit those usually cut off from bureaucratic power or those desiring dynamic leadership—in China, those of the radical tendency. Here, however, the Legalist model is perhaps still useful normatively: it allows us to examine the consequences of deviations from that model.

In discussing bureaucratic interests in China it is helpful to focus on three contradictions, to use the accepted term: that between the party and the state bureaucracies, which was important in the late 1950s but less so afterward; that between the organized bureaucracy and the leader; and the general contradiction between superiors and subordinates, stressing particularly the methods whereby bureaucrats seek to make their lives and jobs easier, attempting to decrease the demands made upon them.

Discussions of Soviet politics sometimes make much of the distinction between the party and state bureaucracies, with, say, the technocrats in the state bureaucracy (the experts) chafing at control by ignorant professional reds in the party. In China a similar distinction could once have been made and may become relevant again. In China as in the Soviet Union all important positions have been held by party members (although in China the formally most important position in a state organization may be held by a figurehead democratic personage). It is useful, however, to distinguish those party members working primarily at state functions within state institutions from those working within the party bureaucracy proper, charged with maintaining party routine and supervising the execution of policy. During the 1950s the party-state distinction somewhat paralleled that of red and expert, or, more generally, radical and moderate. More precisely, while we cannot say the party was always uniformly radical, the state machine, headed until his death by Chou En-lai, has been rather consistently moderate.

A conventional view, expounded with skill and at great length by Barry Richman, is that the ideology of the reds (or super-reds) stands in the way of China's achieving technological and managerial rationality and thus limits the development of the Chinese economy.[192] It is a matter of controversy whether the radical ideology does hinder China's development that much; the important point, however, is that the moderates seem to share Richman's view. The despised experts of the 1950s were employed by state agencies, and the Communists controlling those agencies argued the interests of the experts. Thus, after the Hundred Flowers in 1957, Nieh Jung-chen, head of the Science and Technology Commission, was at pains to explain away the scientists' lack of ardor for socialism: they are not bad people but have been *misled* by rightists.[193] The state required the services of experts, and the comrades in the state were therefore inclined to listen to the experts.

The critics of the Hundred Flowers period were, in a way, very pro-state. They demanded that the constitution be observed, that the courts judge according to law, that those in nominal authority exercise real authority—in short, the abolition of the party-state and of extralegal intervention in the workings of the state by the party. This provided the opportunity for a counterattack upon the state by the party apparatus. The strong assertion of the primacy of the party set the stage for the Great Leap Forward. The 1958 slogan "Politics takes command" captures the voluntarism of that movement, asserting both the primacy of political or ideological considerations over those of technical rationality and the primacy of the party over the champion of technical rationality, the state. The decision to make the Leap was probably Mao's, but the party bureaucracy endorsed it. Liu Shao-ch'i, whose disciples controlled the central party machine, delivered the major address initiating the Leap.[194] Liu may have become rapidly disillusioned with the Leap, but there have been no convincing accusations that he opposed it in 1958, accusations that, if at all plausible, would have been made. The Leap received particularly strong endorsement from the provincial party secretaries.[195] They were not necessarily fired by radical idealism: a major policy of the Leap was the decentralization of the state bureaucracies, together with the expanding of the scope of party activities. From the point of view of the party-state conflict, even the more utopian pronouncements of the Leap acquire a mundane significance. Thus, there was talk at the time of the withering away of the state. The inequities of capitalism are being rapidly eliminated, and "the duty of the state will be only to oppose the external aggression of the enemy; domestically it is already beginning to lose its functions."[196] In a way, this was literally true: at the basic level state functions were being taken over by the commune, or, in effect, by the party. (Soldiers, it might be noted, need not fear for their jobs.)

This enlarging of the scope of the party, however good an idea it may have seemed to the apparatchiks at the time, contributed in the long run to the weakening of the party machine. The party may have taken over state functions, but the same functions had to be performed; this meant a kind of merger of party and state, leading, as Legalist theory would predict, to a lack of cohesion within the bureaucracy. The minister of finance, Li Hsien-nien, explained in early 1959 that state workers will in fact continue to do their old work, but simply as part of the commune. "The people's communes are under the leadership of the party," which means that of the party members, including those who do state work, who are on the commune.[197] After 1958, except perhaps at the very top, it no longer seems useful to make too sharp a distinction between party and state. The Chinese bureaucracy came to be divided into various functional systems (agriculture, culture and education, industry and communications, police work, and the like).[198] Each system was under party control—control by the party members within that system, through the party organizations of the system. Often, the person in a party position would hold a corresponding position in the state. Li Hsien-nien, for example, was a member of the Politburo and of the Central Secretariat (party); a vice premier of the State Council and minister of finance and trade (state); vice-director of the Central Committee Economics and Finance Department (party), and vice-chairman, State Planning Commission. It would seem party control in that system would mean Li's control of himself. Instead of being generalist reds supervising the execution of policy, the party bureaucrats were caught up in the execution itself.[199] At the provincial level the first secretaries seem to have become the effective rulers of their provinces. In 1961, in order to strengthen central control, the party established regional bureaus embracing several provinces each. These had no equivalent at the state level: apparently that would have been superfluous. By the early 1960s the party had become everything, which meant, in good Taoist fashion, that it had become nothing. Instead of a cohesive group able to dominate other interests, the party had become the arena for all interests that divided the Chinese elite.

Throughout the 1960s, even prior to the Cultural Revolution, there was a general deterioration of party organizational life. The Ninth Party Congress should have been held in 1961; it was not held until 1969. There were supposed to be two Central Committee plenary meetings a year; no plenum at all was held between the fall of 1962 and the fall of 1966. Instead, the leadership tended to call irregular work conferences, whose membership could vary with the convenience of those convening them.[200] To argue in new left fashion, this was so in part because it suited powerful interests that it be so.

These interests included Mao but also what we should call, after this analysis, not state bureaucrats but bureaucrats performing state functions. The tendencies, we must remember, set the parameters of the official political discourse in China, but these tendencies do not directly govern political alliances. The entanglement of the party in the routine of ruling, particularly at the provincial level, combined with the unhappy consequences of the Great Leap, had tended to conservatize the party bureaucracy; by 1965 the major leaders of that institution—Liu Shao-ch'i, P'eng Chen, perhaps Teng Hsiao-p'ing—had become as committed to moderation as Chou En-lai. This did not mean, however, that they could form a common front with Chou, or, rather, as it turned out, that Chou would form a common front with them. In Communist countries, particularly in transitional periods, it is common for the party apparatus to dominate the system. The Chinese apparatus could not do this by 1965. As the embodiment of Marxism-Leninism, the apparatus was still a potential danger to Chou, however. He therefore cast his lot with Mao, the Great Leader, who represented the alternative source of legitimacy. The Maoist coalition of 1966 was an ideologically heterogeneous ("unprincipled") one: Mao and the free-floating radicals surrounding him and his wife—in traditional terms, the inner court—together with most of the high-ranking state bureaucracy and most of the army. The leadership of the army took the radical line, but the provincial military commands mostly did not. The targets of this coalition, aside from the military opponents of Lin Piao and some provincial secretaries, were mainly bureaucrats at the Center concerned exclusively with party functions, such as organization, propaganda, and the party equivalent of secret police work.

The nature of the coalitions brings up what has been perhaps the most decisive contradiction in the history of the People's Republic, that between party and leader. A bureaucracy perhaps requires leadership, but as Han Fei teaches, this inevitably will cause stress. Bureaucracies function through routine, and "power to innovate is reserved for superior figures with prestige."[201] Objective considerations aside, it is probably often in the superior figure's interests to innovate, lest he become superfluous. But innovation—change—disrupts things for the bureaucrat, not only when the change is at his expense. Bureaucrats may come to resent the intrusion of leadership into their routines, especially when they think they have the situation well in hand. The Cultural Revolution brought to light some mildly amusing instances of bureaucratic antipathy to charismatic leadership: A reporter had captioned a photograph of 1954, "The glorious creator of New China, the most beloved and respected leader of the Chinese people, Comrade Mao Tse-tung, casts his ballot, acting as a model in the exercise of his great civil rights." A Propaganda Department functionary changed this to: "Comrade Mao Tse-tung casts his ballot."[202]

The conflict between dynamic leadership and stodgy bureaucracy is probably general, but in China it was especially acute between Mao and the top leaders of the *party* bureaucracy, again because they represented alternative foci of legitimacy, occupying, as it were, the same ecological niche. The conflict could be covered over if Mao were willing—or could be made—to remain in the background or, as in 1958, if Mao and the party were in ideological agreement. After 1958, however, the party became increasingly given to the moderate tendency, while Mao, perhaps by conviction but also by circumstance, was more or less stuck with his radicalism.

Liu Shao-ch'i fell victim to the cult of Mao, but in the 1940s he had done perhaps more than anyone else to create it. Even then, however, Liu made it clear that Mao was glorious mainly because he led such a glorious party and was fully devoted to its interests and obedient to its discipline. The party constitution in 1945 took the "Thought of Mao Tse-tung" as the party's "guiding thought." This phrase was eliminated from the 1956 constitution, Teng Hsiao-p'ing explaining, in general terms, that changed conditions require a changed guide.[203] The constitution also made a provision for an honorary chairman of the party, a position for which there could have been only one candidate. It would seem that by 1956 the party bureaucrats were in the process of easing Mao out. Subsequent constitutions have restored the Thought to its old position and say nothing of honorary chairmen.

The general identification of the radical tendency with Mao is, within limits, valid. But while Mao's heart may have been on the left, he did not always behave in a radical fashion. Prior to attaining power in the party in 1935 Mao was mainly identified with the party's right wing,[204] and events of the 1970s would seem to show that Mao was still capable of temporizing. In the second chapter of this study the radical tendency was identified as a *quasi*-fascist political style, and some sort of *Führerprinzip* may be required for an effective voluntarist radical movement. From Mao's point of view, radicalism at one time served his concrete political interests against the party machine. In becoming closely identified with the radical tendency, however, Mao violated the Legalist maxim that the ruler should not reveal his biases. If a leader identifies himself with a partisan position his fate becomes to a certain extent tied to the fate of that position, and he may earn the enmity of those damaged by that position. He also makes himself vulnerable to those who cater to his desires (e.g., Lin Piao). As it happened, Mao's violation of Legalist prudence did not lead to his overthrow; but it did disrupt the Chinese political process, and it did not lead unequivocally to the victory of any Maoist goal other than the preservation of his position.

Probably in reaction to the growing strength of the party bureaucracy, in 1957 Mao supported the liberal phase of the Hundred Flowers movement, soliciting opinions from the educated public in order to rectify the party. This did not work out too well. In 1958 he turned to radicalism; as Mao's secretary, Ch'en Po-ta, verbosely elaborated, the Leap was carried out "under the banner of Comrade Mao Tse-tung." After 1956 Mao had become identified with at least two major movements, both of which were seriously flawed. Max Weber reminds us that the charismatic leader must be successful: "If his leadership fails to benefit his followers, it is likely that his charismatic authority will disappear.'' In December 1958 it was announced that Mao would resign as chairman of the People's Republic.[205] He was replaced in April 1959 by Liu Shao-ch'i. The position of state chairman is an honorific one, and it is likely the resignation had symbolic significance. It was probably one of those elegant compromises for which Chinese are supposed to be famous. Mao's resignation as party chairman, it was probably felt, would be too drastic a step; but his resignation as state chairman could be taken as a signal that he had become in effect honorary chairman of the party, with Liu doing the real work.

Mao made a comeback in 1959. That year the grosser excesses of the Leap were being gradually corrected, although in no systematic fashion. In late summer, however, P'eng Te-huai, the minister of defense, did attempt a systematic critique of the Leap in a manner more drastic than the party was then willing to accept. Mao took the lead in the defense of the Leap and the counter-attack on P'eng. As a result Mao resumed active leadership and the cult of Mao returned in 1960 to its 1958 level.[206] The cult died down in 1961 and 1962, but the embers were kept alive by Lin Piao, who had replaced P'eng as head of the army; it burst into flame again in 1963, blazing with ever-increasing intensity until 1970 or 1971 when (to finish with this metaphor) it burned itself out. The short-term consequence of the Lushan meeting, at which P'eng Te-huai was purged, was that China retained unworkable policies for another year, to be followed by two additional years of near-famine. The longer-term consequence was that Mao, in retaining his leading position, had nailed himself to the radical tendency. As long as the party bureaucracy retained any potency, he could not afford to abandon radicalism—to admit he had been wrong. As the party became increasingly moderate, the collision course was set.

The party machine as a whole was swallowed up in the Cultural Revolution. As of early 1976 it is difficult to get reliable information on its central organization. The party provincial committees were reconstituted in 1970 and 1971, most of them at that time being organized around the provincial military commands. Still, around 1970, things began to return to normal, with signs of renewed consideration for bureaucratic interests. At the second plenum of the Ninth Central Committee, held in the early fall of 1970, Mao's secretary, Ch'en Po-ta, the ranking (if not most influential) member of the radical Central Cultural Revolution Group, was purged. Ch'en, along with Lin Piao, had been an apostle of radical Maoism. The public report of the plenum said nothing of Ch'en (this is not unusual) but did say: ''The whole party must earnestly study Chairman Mao's philosophical works, promote dialectical materialism and historical materialism, oppose idealism and metaphysics.''[207] It soon became clear that Mao's philosophy and dialectical and historical materialism were code words for classical, nonvoluntarist Marxism. Idealism and metaphysics (or, sometimes, idealistic apriorism), a philosophy favored by ''phony Marxist political swindlers of the

Liu Shao-ch'i–Wang Ming type [i.e., Ch'en Po-ta—probably the radicals generally] who do no investigation, do no research, pour out rivers of words, create rumors to deceive the people, bind the state and paralyze the people,''[208] was the code for radical Maoism. Moderation and bureaucratic rationality had temporarily gained the upper hand.

Lin Piao, like Ch'en Po-ta, had built his later career on Maoism. When Lin was killed he too was translated into a ''phony Marxist political swindler of the Liu Shao-ch'i type.'' Lin's death was followed by an attack, indirect but unmistakable, on the cult of Mao itself. It was said that Lin (the ''political swindlers'') thought geniuses had something to do with history—typical idealist nonsense.[209] In the fall of 1971 there was a campaign to study the ''Internationale,'' a song showing that history is created by the masses. The lines (translating from the Chinese) ''There has never been any savior of the world, nor do we depend on gods or emperors'' were stressed. An exegesis pointed out, however, that the masses need help in creating history, a vanguard, ''the leadership of a Marxist-Leninist political party.''[210] The ideological position of the party was being restored and that of the leader downgraded. ''Superficially [the swindlers] wanted to establish the absolute authority of Chairman Mao, but actually they were trying to establish their own absolute authority.''[211]

Some apparently objected to this de-Maoification. Despite what the ''Internationale'' might say, grade school children in Kwangtung in 1972 were being taught: ''Chairman Mao is heroic and great; he is our great savior.''[212] Mao, however, was probably not among the objectors and apparently helped initiate this rejection of the cult. After the defeat of the old party bureaucracy he would no longer be under the same necessity to adhere to the radical tendency or to encourage his own glorification. He no longer had to be the stuffed idol that was the creature of Lin Piao. During the Cultural Revolution Lin's stooges would tell how Lin had creatively applied Mao's Thought to the concrete conditions.[213] But the Thought itself had originally been the creative application to concrete conditions of the universal truths of two dead men, Marx and Lenin. About a year before Lin was killed Mao told his apologist Edgar Snow (in Snow's paraphrase) that there had been a ''need for a personality cult'' to ''stimulate the masses to dismantle the old anti-Mao party bureaucracy.'' Anyway, Khrushchev had no personality cult, and look at what happened to him. But ''of course the personality cult had been overdone.''[214] In 1972 the party circulated within itself what was said to be a letter from Mao to his wife, written in July 1966. The text, published by the Nationalists, is certainly authentic, although we are not compelled to accept the date of composition. The purpose of the letter is to show that Mao had seen through his best pupil and closest comrade in arms from the very beginning. The Chairman is never fooled. Of his apotheosis at Lin's hands Mao says, ''I have never believed these few little books of mine could have that much magic power. . . . But they are forcing me up Liang Mountain [the bandit hideout in *Water margin*]; it seems it is no good disagreeing with them." "This is the first time in my life I have falsely pretended to agree with anyone," Mao is made piously to add. "Always when there is no tiger on the mountain the monkey becomes the great king. That is the kind of great king I have become." Still, Mao says, his tiger nature (*ch'i*) is stronger than his monkey nature.[215]

Radicalism at the level accepted within the regime will probably tend to become increasingly bureaucratized, if general order is maintained. The old Cultural Revolution radicals now have comfortable bureaucratic posts of their own. The campaign to study Marxist theory and philosophy itself would tend to work in favor of bureaucratic interests: it encourages orthodoxy. In 1971 and 1972 the campaign was directed against voluntarist radicalism, but as good dialecticians the radicals can turn the slogans around, using them to criticize a moderate sin, empiricism (an answer to those who "do investigations" and the like).[216]

At a lower level, there is the interest of bureaucrats to escape from control, of, as the Legalists point out, using bureaucratic position to obtain personal status, power, or pleasure: bureaucrats attempt to acquire special privilege. The current Chinese bureaucracy is perhaps as honest (in a bourgeois sense) as any in the world, but this is not a very exalted standard; the evidence would indicate that at times Chinese bureaucrats yield to temptation when they have reason to believe they can get away with doing so. The Lien-chiang documents contain complaints of peculation and minor grafting among basic-level rural cadres.[217] On a more serious level, we have already observed the debauching of schoolgirls by cadres in Ch'engtu. Corruption and moral turpitude aside, special privilege can come to be taken for granted as part of the holding of official power. One of the main targets of the Hundred Flowers dissidents was the special privileges of party members. The rightist Lo Lung-chi said: "A small number of professors have complained about the unfairness of adopting the grading system to improve the treatment of higher-level intellectuals on the grounds that more weight has been attached to political standing than academic attainment and that Party and Youth League members have been graded higher than non-Party personnel." A professor in Shanghai complained, "The Party members, due to their occupying positions of leadership and being favorably situated, seem to enjoy in all respects special privileges." A journalist who had been a party member since 1944 is alleged to have said: "The old ruling class has been overthrown but a new ruling class has arisen. The evolution of this will lead to an amalgamation with Taiwan."[218]

The special privileges of bureaucrats are not only galling to the general population but also indicate inefficiencies in political control—the ability of the bureaucrat to make his position serve his private ends regardless of the will of his master. The 1957 critics were called rightists, but their themes were taken up by radicals during the Cultural Revolution. As the furor died down, however, there appeared neither a new heaven nor a new earth, and the evils of bureaucratism reemerged, if they had ever in fact been subdued. In 1974 there was a campaign against cadres, particularly soldiers, who were able to gain university admission for their children through the back door, by political influence: "I am a soldier study-personnel who entered the university 'through the back door.' Last year, when the school requested applications, at my repeated requests Papa telephoned the cadre department of the military region and mentioned my name, getting me admitted to the university." In 1975 the radicals complained that the bureaucrats were engulfed in a bourgeois life-style, with the prevalence of material incentives leading to corruption.[219]

One of the radical means for controlling bureaucracy and limiting special privileges—a means advocated by the 1957 rightists as well—has been mass supervision. Here the old radical dilemma with the mass line comes up again: the cadres should be close to the masses, but not *too* close. In good dialectical fashion they should avoid both commandism and tailism: they should do things just right. Close relations with the masses, gaining support from below, is in fact one technique for avoiding too close supervision from above.

> Last year's [1968] Lunar New Year came at the high tide of the Cultural Revolution. Thus, the Maoists [*Mao-kung*] directed that the people of the whole country must "smash the old and establish the new" and did not permit a vacation at the Lunar New Year. This met opposition not only from the broad masses, but the basic-level Communist cadres were also equally dissatisfied. They did not, however, dare disobey the order from the upper level. Thus, a brigade secretary called a mass meeting and said to the commune members present, "Do you want a vacation or not?" The commune members answered with one voice, "We do." Some even put up both hands. The secretary said: "If you want a vacation, we will take three days off. When the upper level sends inspectors to determine who is responsible, you must admit it was your own demand. When they ask me, I shall say I was practicing the living study–living use of the Thought of Mao Tse-tung, according to Chairman Mao's teaching, 'Discuss things with the masses,' and walking the mass line." As a result, that brigade really took three days' vacation.[220]

This story comes from an exile source vehemently hostile to the regime, but the behavior described is probably common enough.

This example is relatively innocuous. In some places, however, basic-level cadres seem to have been able to establish themselves within the local social nexus in such a way as to become the functional equivalents of the traditional elites. Wang Jen-chung, then first secretary of Hupei, reported at the beginning of the *su-fan* campaign that "landlords and rich peasants" regularly "cause their old ladies [*lao-p'o*—their wives] or daughters to have sexual intercourse with or marry cadres. They invite them as guests and send money to buy off and corrupt the cadres."[221] This, we take it, is not what the regime means by "intimate relations with the masses." In 1961 and 1962 the cadres in Lien-chiang would "take advantage of house-raisings, marriages, and births to hold large-scale parties, invite guests, eat and drink heartily, and engage in waste and extravagance."[222] This was objectionable in part because the feasts were occasions for the soliciting of bribes (guests would bring presents of money) but was also held to be objectionable in its own right. This behavior is interesting sociologically. The small-time gentry used to finance the celebrations of the various yearly and special festivals in their neighborhoods, and these celebrations provided some of the few touches of gaiety in the arduous lives of Chinese peasants. When the landlords and rich peasants were expropriated, the celebrations ceased.[223] Aside from the element of extortion (which, however, may have been pretty much taken for granted and not really perceived as such) many peasants may have been pleased to see the new class assuming some of the more benign functions of the old.

This brings up a final bureaucratic interest, one that might be called the interest in normal life. Part of the radical critique of bureaucracy is that it encourages the bureaucrat to see his job as just that, a job. The bureaucrat becomes content to do his work sufficiently well to satisfy his superiors and to extract whatever gain he can from his position. He opposes anything that might make his job more difficult, makes compromises with those he has to administer, and lets alone those aspects of life he cannot conveniently control. Caught up in his daily work and his personal concerns, he loses sight of the broader goals of the revolution. For revolutionary ferment he would substitute strict rules and leave the rest alone. As Michels might say, his own social revolution has been effected.

We have already seen Wang Jen-chung, the boss of Hupei, in a vulgar mood. Wang was one of an interesting group of cadres from the South-Central Region allied with that region's overlord, T'ao Chu. The group as a whole was a curious combination of crude peasant toughness and urbane sensitivity. In 1966 T'ao Chu and his friends seemed to be on the way to replacing Liu Shao-ch'i, Teng Hsiao-p'ing, and P'eng Chen as heads of the central party bureaucracy. The forces against the consolidation of the party were then too strong, however, and by January 1967 T'ao and his faction were swept away. After his fall, Red Guards rifled Wang Jen-chung's papers and printed excerpts from his diary. From these we learn that Wang, a "gangster, bad stick, and counterrevolutionary," was himself not averse to a pretty face. He liked to philosophize about love, his comments ranging from the touching to the sappy. At one point he revels in his own nobility of soul: he will not appropriate or possess (*chan-yu*) a certain girl but will help her find her ideal lover who will make her happy. This is very fine, but it is also a reminder that the main thing preventing him from appropriating the girl—or anything else he wants from anyone weaker than he—

is whatever nobility he might have. Elsewhere Wang jots down his thoughts on public policy:

> What is socialism? It is no man oppressing another, no man exploiting another, no poverty, no unemployment. Everyone lives a happy and prosperous life. Isn't this sort of life good? Some people think poverty and hardship are good, that good clothes should not be worn. . . . This is not right. If we live in order to undergo hardship, why make revolution?[224]

This is perhaps a typical bureaucratic reaction to the Great Leap mentality; and to the radicals, a sell-out of revolution, goulash communism. The radical may accept revolution as an end in itself, but not all would find this a very rational end; or the radical may believe that the good life will be attained through continuous upheaval and ferment. The bureaucrat, who must administer radical programs, comes to see little evidence that this is true. If hardship is the aim of life, there is sufficient hardship without revolution. Perhaps there comes a time when the revolution should be consolidated.[225]

Bureaucracy is probably as unpopular as it is prevalent, and not only among radicals. In a liberal or traditional state the growth of bureaucracy means the diminution of freedom. When we approach bureaucracies, public or private, it is usually to complain, to petition, or to answer for alleged wrongdoing—all situations of little dignity. We are sometimes greeted by arrogance, but perhaps more often by indifference from persons who seem to care little for their work and not at all for us (being what we are, it is this that we remember, rather than those functionaries who are kind and helpful). We rabble are easily roused by any demagogue able to conjure up the image of the bureaucrat, briefcase in hand, his fat behind tapering to his pointy head. One of the finest scholarly studies of bureaucracy of the past generation conceives of itself as an examination of the "maladaptations, the inadequacies, or . . . the 'dysfunctions' " of bureaucracy.[226]

The contradiction found by the radicals between politics and bureaucracy is a real one. Politics normally implies choice, freedom: we choose these policies over those; we will be ruled by this man rather than that. In ideal form bureaucracy excludes choice: the choices have already been made, and things are done predictably by rule and routine. The full bureaucratic ideal—administration without politics—is probably never attained, and a society in which it came close to being attained would probably be intolerable, at least until we became conditioned to it. But life in the absence of predictable regulation would also be intolerable: nasty, brutish, short. The bureaucratic prison excludes as well as entraps and keeps certain elements of life beyond arbitrary—political—choice. Bureaucracy, particularly in societies that are not free, may now serve to limit the scope of political power in the way that custom, convention, and consensus—

the Confucian *li*—did in older societies. It may be a poor substitute but, within reason, may be better than nothing. From another point of view, while politics involves choice, those who win a political battle—who have their own way—would like to see something like their choice enforced routinely as policy. Totalitarian politics may be the combination of what is worst in both spheres: politics without freedom and bureaucracy without predictability. Many Chinese would probably like to see the evolution of a more liberal system, but perhaps the best they can expect in the short run will be a more routinized, rational, bureaucratic one.

The Army

The CPC recruited and developed its own army during the two decades prior to Liberation and thus did not have the same problems as did the Bolsheviks when the former czarist officers supposedly had to be flanked by two of Trotsky's commissars with drawn pistols. KMT units were incorporated into the PLA during the civil war, but there was already a well-established military framework. The interrelationship of the party and army has meant, however, that military interests are strongly represented within the hierarchy of the party, and the interests of the military and civilian members are not always alike.

In China as in other countries, there is the problem of political control of the army, of insuring that the "party commands the gun," not "the gun the party." The Chinese, like the Americans, tend toward the exercise of what Samuel Huntington calls subjective civilian control. Rather than encouraging apolitical professionalism, the two regimes try to exert direct political intervention in military affairs and attempt to see that military leaders share the ideological and policy preferences of the rulers. The Chinese carry out subjective control more thoroughly than do the Americans, and the PLA could hardly be expected to become a completely professional force in the Western sense, with the mission to kill whomever the current rulers wish killed: as far as the regime is concerned, there will never be any political authority other than the party. In Huntington's analysis, however, subjective control may be deficient as a means of control: by blurring the distinction between political and military, not only is politics brought into the army but the army is also brought into politics.[227]

In China, resistance to the prevalent type of control has come from two directions. Some soldiers have felt that their work is of a specialized, technical nature and have wished to limit political intervention in military affairs. Other soldiers seem to have felt that as high-ranking Communists they are in at least as good a position as any civilian apparatchik or bureaucrat to perceive the laws governing the development of things, and they have worked to make the army the dominant force in society. The first minister of defense, P'eng Te-huai, seems to have desired the PLA to become more professional; his successor, Lin Piao, rather more successfully took the second route. The moderate tendency is perhaps inclined to support a greater degree of military professionalism. The radicals did support Lin Piao's near-total politicization of the army but were never completely reconciled to his attempted militarization of society. As a consequence of Lin's activities, the Chinese in recent years have been concerned with the growth of the power of local military commanders, apparently fearing they might not always be responsive to orders from the Center.

The first overt manifestation of civilian-military tension after Liberation came with the purge of Kao Kang, who had occupied the top state, party, and military positions in Manchuria. In the denunciation of Kao and his partner in crime, Jao Shu-shih, in 1955, they are depicted as unprincipled ambitionists:

> The special characteristic of . . . Kao Kang and Jao Shu-shih . . . is that they never brought up in any party organization or meeting or publicly in any way any program opposing the party Center. Their only program was to seize supreme power in the party and state by means of a plot.

But while Kao may have lacked a program, he at least thought he had a constituency:

> Kao Kang's antiparty sect violated the party Center's policies in its work in the Northeast [Manchuria]. With all its might it downgraded the function of the party and sabotaged party solidarity and unity, turning the Northeast into Kao Kang's personal independent kingdom. . . . He even tried to instigate party members working in the army to support his plot against the party Center. To this end he developed an extremely absurd "theory," saying our party has two parts. One is the so-called base areas and military party, the other the white areas party. He said the party was created by the army, and he considered himself the representative of the so-called base areas and military party. Thus, the party and government should be reorganized according to his plan, with himself as general secretary of the party Center and vice-chairman and also premier of the State Council.[228]

Kao's theory does not seem to have been all that absurd and points to a divergence between the party soldiers and the former underground ("white areas") workers, protégés of Liu Shao-ch'i, who until 1966 controlled the central civilian apparatus. The talk of Kao's clique as antiparty and of his downgrading the function of the party does not mean he wished to do without the party, but, rather, that he wanted to limit the role of the central apparatus. The talk of his independent kingdom conjures up the specter of regional militarism—warlordism. It was left for Lin Piao to carry out Kao's program almost to the letter. Were it not for differences of interest within the army itself, China might today be under military rule—perhaps geographically incohesive military rule—with the party as an appendage of the army.

Lin did not get a chance to pursue his ambition until 1959. From 1954 until the fall of 1959 the minister of defense was the veteran Communist warrior, P'eng Te-huai. P'eng had commanded the Chinese army in Korea during the latter part of that conflict (Lin had been in command during the more pleasurable first part) and came to be impressed by, and appalled at the consequences of, American firepower. During his tenure as defense minister he attempted to modernize and regularize the PLA. A conventional (European) system of military ranks was introduced, along with fancy uniforms patterned after the "proletarian Graustark" style of the Soviet army (Lin Piao abolished both of these practices in 1965). Conscription was introduced. P'eng attempted to limit the role of the military commissars and the amount of time spent on political indoctrination. He apparently opposed the split with the Soviet Union, since that country was then the only source of hardware.

It is possible, of course, that some of P'eng's alleged devotion to professionalism was retroactive calumny by Lin Piao; at any rate, P'eng was not very successful in limiting the politicization of the army. The antirightist campaign of 1957 saw the intensification of party activity in the army as well as in other sectors of Chinese society. P'eng's 1959 purge had nothing directly to do with his military line but was a consequence of his opposition to the communes—behavior that may speak well of his courage and humanity, but not for his military professionalism.

In any case, shortly after his purge, P'eng was accused of professionalism:

> From the time it was created our army has destroyed, under the leadership of the party and Chairman Mao, the oppressive system of the armies of the exploiting class. . . . However, during the period when Comrades X X-x [P'eng Te-huai] and X X-x [Huang K'o-ch'eng, P'eng's chief of staff] were in charge of the work of the Military Affairs Commission they violated Chairman Mao's military building principles, promoted dogmatism with all their might, and followed the bourgeois military road of unadulterated military outlook and warlordism.

Lin Piao was not about to make the same mistake. "Since Chief Lin took charge of the work of the Military Affairs Commission, he has instituted a systematic management according to the military thought of Chairman Mao."[229]

Rhetorically, at least, this meant that Lin's military doctrine stressed radical voluntarism. This is summed up in his once-famous "four firsts": man is more important than weapons; political work is more important than other work; thought (*ssu-hsiang*—ideological) work is more important than other political work; and *living* thought work is more important than *book* thought work.[230]

While it may be somewhat artificial so to view it (Lin could probably not have thought things out so well in advance), Lin's politicization of the army can be seen as the first part of a subtle and complex plan for his own advancement. First of all, this politicization was a stick with which to beat those soldiers loyal to P'eng Te-huai, thus eliminating his rivals in the army.[231] Second, Lin's stress on politics would, paradoxically, limit the role of Liu Shao-ch'i's apparatus in a way that P'eng's professional passivity could not. The post-1958 expansion of the scope of the party actually weakened the party's organizational cohesion outside the army. Within the army the role of politics was similarly increased, but the politicization was carried out entirely by party organizations already within the army, particularly by the army's General Political Department, staffed by career PLA men and headed by Lin's then right-hand man, Hsiao Hua. Lin was thus able to run the army autonomously from the civilian party machine and, in fact, along fairly conventional military lines. In spite of all Lin's talk of the precedence of politics over other work, apparently soldiers who required military training (pilots, soldiers stationed in shore defense installations) spent 60 to 80 percent of their time in military training.[232]

Lin also took advantage of the dual focus of legitimacy in pre-1966 China, stressing Mao much more than the party in his political indoctrination.

> Comrade Mao Tse-tung is a great Marxist-Leninist of the present age. . . . Therefore, raise to the heights the red flag of the Thought of Mao Tse-tung; go a step further in using the weapon of the Thought of Mao Tse-tung as the guide of the brains of all our fighting personnel; firmly let the Thought of Mao Tse-tung take command of all our work—this is the most basic duty of political work in our army.[233]

Lin's support of Mao in 1961 and 1962 was timely, since at that time the civilian party was fed up with radicalism and increasingly fed up with the Chairman. It was probably Lin's support that gave Mao the clout necessary for rallying all those opposed to Liu's apparatus. At the same time Mao provided protection for Lin from the civilian party and also gave Lin the opportunity to expand the influence of the army and himself at the expense of the party. In 1964 the whole country was told to "learn from the PLA."[234] The army was also told to "learn humbly from the locality," that is, from the local party branches. This part of the slogan was revived at the time of Lin's death, but originally it implied a broadening of military involvement in the national economy, as the following tortured passage indicates:

> Especially in the past few years the whole army has firmly responded to the summons of the Military Affairs Commission and Marshal Lin Piao and has actively and enthusiastically thrown itself into the state's construction of socialism and the revolution of the popular masses. It has provided powerful help and has absorbed nourishment from joining [socialist construction and mass revolution], riding the "east wind," raising the thought of the troops and tempering the style of the troops, propelling forth the bright function of the work of the troops. There is a

> popular saying among the broad masses of soldiers: Communes and factories are the best classrooms, the local cadres and the popular masses the best teachers, the production struggle and class struggle the best teaching materials. This is exactly so.[235]

In 1961 Lin Piao had said: "Historically, our army has been the school of our party cadres. . . . In fact, our army is able to train cadres for the localities. . . . Our party has grown out of the barrel of the gun."[236] As Kao Kang had put it, the party was created by the army.

There is a further wrinkle in Lin's plan. Through his stress on Mao, Lin gained autonomy from the party apparatus; but Lin's "fourth first," his stress on living thought—what he liked to call living study–living use (*huo-hsueh huo-yung*) of Mao's Thought—gave him a certain autonomy from Mao as well. As we have seen, the Chairman was later made to claim that he did not fully approve of Lin's apotheosis of him—and he had reason to dislike it. For Lin, it was not sufficient that the good pupil of Mao simply read the works of the master: he must be able correctly to apply them in a living way. The arbiter of correct application was, of course, Chief Lin.

Lin raised the position of the army as a whole within Chinese society. Within the army, however, there were interests other than Lin's, and this disunity in the military seems to have been the condition for Lin's ultimate failure. Lin had tried to purge the army of professionalism, but professionalism was not limited to supporters of P'eng Te-huai and as a style of thought probably develops spontaneously among soldiers. Many soldiers may have objected to Lin's injection of the army into politics and into the running of the economy, seeing this as a dissipation of military strength (and many of these were perhaps just as glad when a more conventional role for the military was reemphasized in the early 1970s). Lin's spiritualism did not really entail a neglect of all "concrete" factors: under Lin Piao, China continued to enjoy a fine infantry and developed as good a nuclear weapons program as could have been expected. Lin's line did involve, however, a relative neglect of the intermediate range of modern conventional weapons—artillery, tanks, airplanes, trucks, and the like. It is probably not coincidental that his line was pushed most strongly after the break with the Soviet Union, China's supplier of modern weapons. Both Korea and Tibet had shown Chinese soldiers the utility of modern conventional weapons, and many soldiers may have felt that Lin's line was threatening national security. Under Lin's system, China's ability to fight beyond its borders was limited, and pessimistic soldiers could imagine circumstances when it might have been imperative to do so—should the Americans invade North Vietnam, for example. The Chinese arsenal was sufficient against Tibetans, but not against Americans. If China itself were invaded, particularly before the development of a reliable nuclear weapons delivery system, the Lin program seemed to call for protracted "people's war," a strategic retreat in the face of invaders who would be swallowed up just as the Japanese had been.[237] To many Chinese soldiers this must have seemed the height of imbecility. Despite Mao and his paper tigers, most Chinese soldiers probably realize that Japan was not defeated by China but by the United States, in the air and on the Pacific islands, not on the China mainland (although the need to occupy large areas of China certainly served to tie down Japanese troops). The potential new invaders, the Americans or the Russians, would not need to occupy much Chinese territory; it would be sufficient to cripple China, to render it harmless. People's war would mean great hardship for the Chinese people without much prospect for gain. It could also be politically costly to the regime, since if the invaders and their collaborators behaved with a modicum of decency in the areas they did occupy, the position of the Communists might come to resemble that of Chungking more than that of Yenan. It is likely that Mao and Lin did not really think of people's war as a serious *military* strategy. Rather, its espousal was a rational political act based on the calculation that there would be no major war. To prepare to fight the United States or the USSR would entail coming to terms with the power not to be fought. Since (that was another age) the United States then appeared to be the more dangerous power (it had fought in Korea and was fighting in Vietnam; it was allied with Taiwan; in Cuba the United States had humiliated the Russians), to choose a more conventional military strategy would mean coming to terms with the Russians, something Mao was not then prepared to do. The Chinese had apparently reached a tacit agreement with the United States on the limits of the war in Vietnam. The Mao-Lin strategy was to do nothing really to provoke the United States, while exhorting the Vietnamese to fight a protracted war. The Americans would be harmlessly bogged down in that way and unable to bring to fruition the détente with the Russians. As a kind of side-benefit, the Vietnamese would be too busy to get ideas about their own sphere in Southeast Asia. If, by chance, the Americans should win—that is, the Saigon regime should survive—China would not have lost anything. If this was the plan in Peking, in retrospect it seems a good one; the American defeat was perhaps more decisive than the Chinese would have liked, but one can rarely have everything. Certain Chinese soldiers, however, might have seen the strategy as carrying great risks.

The professional soldiers found their spokesman in 1965 in Lo Jui-ch'ing, Lin's chief of staff. This in itself is a bit of a surprise. In this and the previous chapter we have had occasion to use Lo as a guide in his capacity as head of public security. Lo became chief of staff when Lin became defense minister, and as Lo was skilled at purging and liquidating, one of his missions was certainly to purge the army of professionalism. As with P'eng Te-huai, the extent of Lo's commitment to professionalism may have been exaggerated later. To the extent that it was not, it is testimony to the potency of bureaucratic roles in the Chinese army, which some would stress over factional relationships.[238] During the early

1960s Lo seems to have been happy enough to voice publicly the Lin Piao line; he endorsed, for example, the concept of the Thought of Mao as a "spiritual atomic bomb."[239] As chief of staff, however, he would have a bureaucratic interest in China's acquisition of a modern army, and given Lin's preemption of the opposite position, a political interest in this as well. In the summer of 1965, in opposition to Lin's people's-war line, Lo indirectly urged that China acquire the military means to fight the United States in Vietnam, at the same time urging a relaxation of tension with Russia.[240]

Lo was dismissed from his post in November 1966. After that, the story goes, he and his sympathizers in the army, mostly former subordinates of the legendary bandit-turned-party-soldier Ho Lung, got together with P'eng Chen, the boss of Peking, who was himself beginning to come under attack from Lin and Lin's radical civilian allies. Lin says P'eng and Lo plotted a coup to remove him,[241] although this was never formally alleged and the Chinese media have expressed doubts about the truth of this since Lin's death. In any case, Lin struck first, and P'eng Chen fell in May 1966. Lin's military opposition had been crushed, and later the Red Guards crushed what remained of the party machine. The army was required to fill the vacuum. It might have seemed that Lin's work was complete.

Lin, however, ran up against another contradiction within the army, that between the central headquarters and the regional and provincial commands. William Whitson has identified the old Communist field armies as a natural basis for factionalism within the PLA, and in the 1960s this factionalism also had an institutional basis in that most of the military regions contained heavy concentrations of officers from the field army that had conquered that part of China.[242] This perhaps provides a potential for renewed regional militarism, as the chaos of the Cultural Revolution led to a concentration of power in the hands of the local soldiers. Unlike in warlord days, however, the local soldiers, except in isolated instances, did not fight each other; rather, they formed a common front against the Center.[243] The local soldiers were responsible for bringing order out of Red Guard chaos; they were not always inclined to treat the Red Guards gently and in any case were often provoked. Lin Piao, cramped by his alliance with the Cultural Revolution Group radicals, was forced to limit the degree to which the local soldiers could suppress the Red Guards. The *Liberation Army Daily* told the soldiers "sternly to guard against bad men using the tools of dictatorship to suppress the revolutionary masses and revolutionary cadres." The little red generals "from beginning to end embody the great direction of the revolution."[244] Unless the little red generals were tamed, however, order could not be restored. The turning point came with the Wuhan "mutiny" in July, in which the regional commander allowed conservative Red Guard organizations to crush the leftists. The radicals in Peking were already disenchanted with the local soldiers, and while they and Lin were allies and devoted to the same ideological line, this does not mean the radicals were delighted with the prospect of Lin's rule. The

Wuhan mutiny became the occasion for a radical attack on the army generally, and probably on Lin in particular. Radicals in Peking denounced a "handful of bad men in the army" who had caused the Wuhan problem, warning the handful that they, together with their "strong backstage supporter," would be "ground to despicable piles of dog shit by the wheels of history."[245] Others in Peking had come to believe, however, that the support of the military was more important than the support of the Red Guards, and this attack on the army was turned against the radicals. Most of the Cultural Revolution Group—the "May 16 Corps"—were purged. This purge did not leave Lin unscathed, however. Hsiao Hua, Lin's top aide and the prime spokesman for Lin's radicalism, fell along with the radicals, perhaps as punishment for not having supported the local soldiers against the Cultural Revolution Group and the Red Guards.

Hsiao's role as Lin's military spokesman was taken over by the acting chief of staff, Yang Ch'eng-wu. Yang worked to restore both discipline in the army and society and the power of the Center, calling in November 1967 for obedience to the absolute authority of the "great generalissimo" (*t'ung-shuai*) Mao Tse-tung and the absolute authority of Mao's thought—the absolute authority being, it was understood, what "Vice-Chairman Lin" says it is.[246] Yang's turn came in the spring of 1968. He was accused of ambition—he did not like being *acting* chief of staff. He was also accused of collaboration with the May 16 Corps, something outside observers have found hard to credit. The most genuine charge is probably that Yang wished to remove the more important regional commanders: Hsu Shih-yu (Nanking); Han Hsien-ch'u (Foochow); Huang Yung-sheng (Canton); Ch'en Hsi-lien (Shenyang); and Yang Te-chih (Chinan). Yang Ch'eng-wu may have been objectively concerned with the growth of local military power, and the local soldiers resentful of Yang's attempts to restore authority. If his affiliation with the May 16 Corps is a fabrication, it was probably introduced to symbolize the victorious local commanders' rejection of radicalism. One local soldier, Huang Hung-sheng, replaced Yang—as real, not acting, chief of staff. The surviving Peking radicals also attacked Yang, one of them, Chiang Ch'ing, calling also for the purge of his "backstage boss"—again, almost certainly Lin Piao.[247]

Lin's position was institutionalized in a curious way in the party constitution adopted in April 1969: he was named sole vice-chairman of the Central Committee and explicitly designated Mao's successor. Less than two and a half years later he was dead and disgraced. It is unlikely that justice will ever be done to him. Former Red Guards who have left the mainland report being extremely unimpressed by Lin Piao.[248] Since late 1973, when Lin came to be denounced by name instead of code, a common cliché has been that he was a warlord who "never read books, never read newspapers, was utterly unlearned." On the whole Lin probably did his country more harm than good, and his demise was greeted with general relief. Still, he had been an excellent, perhaps even a brilliant, soldier, despite efforts to denigrate his abilities; and he had been popular with troops under his command. His unimpressive appearance in his last years was a consequence of ill-health, which may have had its roots in war wounds. Disregarding considerations of the common good and his shameless toadying to Mao, there was a certain elegance in his attempt to climb the greasy pole. Lin failed because he could not gain full control of the circumstances, and in strengthening himself in some places he weakened himself elsewhere. In the end, Lin had achieved the *ming*, name, largely at the expense of the *shih*, reality. His alliance with the radicals alienated him from the local soldiers, and then the radicals turned against him. In 1970 his main support, Mao Tse-tung, turned against him as well.

Lin's last program does not particularly stress military interests and is best discussed in the next chapter. What is known of the story of his plot, however, is relevant to an analysis of the general political position of the army. Lack of support among the major regional commanders seems to have sealed Lin's doom. The role of Huang Yung-sheng in Lin's last crisis may be another illustration of the importance of bureaucratic roles. When Huang became chief of staff it was apparently with the intention that he represent the local soldiers at headquarters, but Huang seems to have spent much of 1971 attempting to win the local soldiers to Lin's side.

The official public account of Lin's purge is rather sketchy.[249] At the second plenum of the Ninth Central Committee, held in August 1970 (at Lushan, where P'eng Te-huai had been purged—although the location was not given at the time the plenum was announced) Lin and his followers attempted a coup (*cheng-pien*). The radical line was then under attack, and it is possible that Lin (with Chou En-lai?) was able to force the purge of the highest-ranking radical, Ch'en Po-ta. Mao broke with Lin at this meeting.

> After the plot was smashed, [Lin's gang] drew up the "571 Engineering" Outline, a plan for a counterrevolutionary armed coup. They attempted a counterrevolutionary armed coup on September 8, 1971, expecting to kill the great leader Chairman Mao and establish a separate Center. When this failed, they fled to the wilderness, defecting to the Soviet revisionists, betraying the party and state and seeking their own destruction.[250]

The official story hardly clarifies things. The famous plane crash in Mongolia (the "wilderness") took place on the night of September 12/13, four days after the "armed coup." What was happening in the meantime? Some rumors of Russian reports say that none of the bodies at the crash site fit Lin's description. There is much that is fishy in the story and in the plane crash itself.

At the time of the alleged coup there was either general ignorance of what was going on or confusion as to whether Lin had succeeded or not. On September 12 the *People's Daily* carried a story about a book of photographs of Politburo members.

> Several of these pictures show Chairman Mao together with his closest comrade in arms, Vice-Chairman Lin Piao. This makes people feel very deeply the degree to which Comrade Lin Piao always raises high the red flag of the Thought of Mao Tse-tung and firmly carries out and protects Chairman Mao's proletarian revolutionary line. He is a glorious model from whom the whole party, the whole army, and the people of the whole country should learn.[251]

As late as October 15 Lin's favorite phrase, the "living study–living use" of Mao's Thought, continued to be used.[252]

A more detailed account of what might have happened can be derived from intraparty documents, particularly a series of speeches delivered (it is said) by Mao to military men in various regions prior to Lin's alleged attempt. From the context one gathers Mao was countering Huang Yung-sheng's attempts to gain support in the regions: "I don't believe that you, Huang Yung-sheng, will be able to order the Liberation Army to rebel." (According to another document, Lin himself had made an inspection of the military regions earlier, in late July.)[253] Mao mentions his falling out with Lin at Lushan: "And now there is another Lushan conference in 1970. At the 1970 Lushan conference they went in for a sudden attack and underground activities. Why didn't they dare attack openly? Obviously they had the devil in their hearts." The "sudden attack" was conducted by what Mao calls the five big generals, the active-headquarters soldiers who were also on the Politburo: Huang Yung-sheng, Wu Fa-hsien, Li Tso-p'eng, Ch'iu Hui-tso, and Yeh Ch'ün. (Yeh Ch'ün was not really a big general. She was director of the Work Office of the Military Affairs Commission; more importantly, she was Lin Piao's wife.) The occasion for the argument was whether the new constitution should provide for a state chairman. "Someone was in a hurry to become state chairman; he wanted to split the party; he was in a hurry to seize power."[254] "He" is Lin Piao; but it is not obvious what the real issue is. Clearly Mao would have been named chairman, not Lin Piao.[255] While Mao might have had personal reasons to dislike the idea of that post, it is not explained what there was to get so excited about. Mao's objection was probably to private consultations among the five big generals (the sudden attack). The draft constitution adopted by the meeting makes no provision for a state chairman but names Mao head of state and Lin as his successor. The 1975 constitution follows the draft, omitting, of course, the business about Lin Piao.

At the same meeting Mao says he circulated a little essay showing that the masses, not geniuses, are the creators of history. Here Mao is turning against his own cult, undermining the position of Lin Piao, which depended upon that cult.

Mao then says he returned to Peking and spoke individually with Lin's followers, but with no results. He then chose "three types of method": "throwing stones" (adding remarks critical of Lin Piao to documents used in the criticism of Ch'en Po-ta); "mixing in sand" (adding new members to the staff of the Military Affairs Commission, diluting Lin's control of that organization); and "digging in the corner of the wall" (an allusion to the purge in late 1970 of the commander of the Peking Military Region). By late spring, Mao says, he was able to make the five big generals conduct self-examinations, albeit insincere ones.[256]

At this time Lin began his last plot, which despite the sanctimonious horror shown at Lin's devious ways after he had failed, was clearly a defensive reaction to the intrigue undertaken against him:

> During the collection of reports in the Criticism of Ch'en Rectification, Huang, Wu, Ch'iu, Li, and Yeh had all made self-examinations. Moreover, the Chairman had sanctioned their being made to conduct self-examinations. The director [Yeh Ch'ün] was extremely tense, and at that time decided to do the "571." She also discussed this with Huang Yung-sheng.[257]

Lin's son, Li-kuo, an air force officer, went to seek support in the Nanking Military Region (probably in Shanghai and Hangchow). Lin Li-kuo drew up the actual program, a plan to arrest (or kill?) Mao and other top leaders, after which Li-kuo felt the conspirators would be able to dictate their own terms.[258] (The 571—the title of the program—is a pun in Chinese: *wu-ch'i-i,* using different characters with different tones, means "armed righteous rebellion.") There is much less information on what happened after that. On September 12, according to one version, there was to be an attempt to blow up a train Mao was riding on, but the assassin lost his nerve at the last minute (but then, what happened on September 8?). Lin panicked and attempted to flee but was betrayed by his daughter to Chou En-lai.[259] This last, if true, is as fitting as it is melancholy. The whole affair may help explain the Chinese inability to comprehend why Americans got so wrought up over Watergate, why an American ruler so useful to them should be deposed over such a trivial incident.

So much for Lin Piao. There are, however, a couple of footnotes. Lin was vilified on a daily basis in the press during the years following his death, but there also seem to have been a few covert defenses, if not of Lin personally, then of what different writers took him to stand for. (If these are defenses, however, they imply very different interpretations not only of what Lin stood for—which can be explained by the ambiguity of his position—but also of the facts of the case.) The first appeared in July 1972 as the brief period of moderate dominance was coming to an end, in an expanded English version of an article that had appeared earlier in Chinese. The English version discusses Robespierre, a man who did some fine things, all in all, but who, "after all, . . . was a bourgeois revolutionary." He began to ignore the masses, and so "he himself was finally sent to the guillotine by the reactionary forces."[260] For *Robespierre* we should probably read *Lin*. The implication is, no doubt, that Lin deserved what he got, but his bungling resulted in the rule of reaction in China. This would be a defense of Lin's Cultural Revolution radicalism and an attack on Chou En-lai. During the campaign to criticize Lin Piao and Confucius there seem to be certain defenses of Lin from the opposite, moderate point of view. One perhaps questionable instance is a discussion of the Sung statesman Wang An-shih. Wang was a great man who carried out Legalist policies. Unfortunately, his opponents won the support of the empress (and the inner court generally) and had Wang dismissed. They wanted to kill Wang. The references to the empress and the like are (probably) slaps at Chiang Ch'ing. The essay adds that Wang's enemies accused him of "ten big crimes,"[261] as, apparently, did Lin's enemies in the months following his death.[262] Other essays in the campaign explain that the collapse of the Ch'in dynasty did not come because that dynasty was so tyrannical, but because, after the death of the First Emperor, the eunuch Chao Kao usurped power and the otherwise able prime minister, Li Ssu, lacked the backbone to stand up to Chao. The idea, one gathers, is that Chou En-lai is being criticized for temporizing with the radicals. One of Chao Kao's crimes, however, was to cause the death of the legitimate heir apparent (a good military man) and the execution of all the able generals of Ch'in.[263] This is all rather slight, and perhaps not too much should be made of the defenses. Their purpose would be less to rehabilitate Lin than to belabor current enemies.

At the time of the purge of Lin, the local soldiers as a group seemed stronger than ever. Lin's alleged attempt followed the completion of the rebuilding of the provincial party committees, and the great majority of those committees were then headed either by the provincial commander or by the commander of the military region that included the province. There were some provincial purges following Lin's death, but the soldiers removed were in general replaced by other soldiers. Some of the local commanders had been in the same position since the mid-1950s, and the addition of the top party posts to the military commands seemed to institutionalize military control at the local level. It is small wonder that outside observers should be impressed with the entrenched nature of local military leadership[264] and speculate on the possibility of the revival of some sort of warlordism.

The devolution of power to the regions clearly worried some in Peking as well. The commanders had behaved in a conservative fashion during the Cultural Revolution and were probably generally disliked by the radicals. Moderates such as Chou En-lai also seem to have been concerned with the possibility of disunity, say in some future succession crisis. A confession by one of the more insignificant of Lin Piao's fellow plotters looks like an attempt to get Hsu Shih-yu, perhaps the most impressive of the regional commanders, then commander of

Nanking. According to the confession, Lin Li-kuo planned to use shock-troops to occupy Shanghai and arrest the radical leadership there. Once that was done, it is implied, Hsu Shih-yu could probably be persuaded to join in peace talks.[265] Li-kuo was not certain about this; still, Hsu could hardly relish having it broadcast among the comrades that he is the sort of man with whom traitors think they can do business.

The complex campaign to criticize Lin Piao and Confucius was at least in part directed against regional militarism.[266] This is seen particularly in essays praising a T'ang dynasty scholar, Liu Tsung-yuan, who, in opposition to the more generally orthodox Confucian view, praised the Ch'in empire for its abolition of decentralized feudalism and the establishment of a strong centralized state. One essay on Liu goes so far as to put national unity on at least a par with continued revolution and even has kind words for the Ch'ing dynasty: had the Ch'ing been unable to maintain centralized rule, the imperialists would have dismembered China. The author of this essay implies that he is worried about military decentralization in China today—this will allow the Soviets effectively to intervene in Chinese politics. Hitting at the radicals as well as the soldiers, he also mentions Liu's dislike of eunuchs' having military or political power.[267]

These attacks on regional militarism came at a time when, superficially at least, the Center was finally able to do something about it. At the end of 1973 there was a massive reshuffling of the regional military commands,[268] the results of which are most easily presented in tabular form.

Commander	*From*	*To*
Ch'en Hsi-lien	Shenyang	Peking
Tseng Ssu-yü	Wuhan	Chinan
Yang Te-chih	Chinan	Wuhan
Hsu Shih-yu	Nanking	Canton
Ting Sheng	Canton	Nanking
P'i Ting-chün	Lanchow	Foochow
Han Hsien-ch'u	Foochow	Lanchow
Li Te-sheng	Anhwei (Military District)	Shenyang

(Unaffected regions: Ch'eng-tu, Kunming, Sinkiang)

It is not clear what should be made of the even swap, even trade pattern that holds except for the case of Peking, which previously had been without a regional commander. The apparent ease of the shuffle should perhaps refute any hypothesis predicting loss of control by the Center, although we do not know how easy the shuffle really was. We do not know what negotiations, if any, went on beforehand. The transfers affected only the commanders; their subordinates (cliques?) remain in place, and we do not know who is on the telephone to whom. None of the transfers was a purge; one, that of Li Te-sheng, was actually a promotion, from a provincial to a regional command. (Li, one of the few local commanders who seems to have been close to the radicals in the Cultural Revolution, was then also head of the PLA's General Political Department; in the spring of 1974, right after his promotion, he apparently came under a cloud, although he remained at least a nominal member of the Politburo into 1975; he was replaced as head of the General Political Department by Chang Ch'un-ch'iao.) The commanders did, however, give up their positions as provincial first secretaries, redressing, at least on paper, the civil-military balance.

For a final note on regional militarism we may refer again to the criticism of Confucius, this time for what might be construed as a defense of some local military autonomy. This is an essay by someone calling himself Shih Hsueh-chi'ing, "History Studies Ch'ing" (Chiang Ch'ing?). It is an apology for Sun Ch'üan, who ruled the state of Wu during the Three Kingdoms period, a time of disunity following the collapse of the Han dynasty. Shih says that Confucian historians have considered Sun an utter incompetent and a paranoid murderer to boot, but this is not entirely fair. Sun did oppose the unification of China and in this was very reactionary. But in ruling Wu he used Legalist methods and was very progressive. He "consolidated and developed East Wu. His overall activities, from the main standpoint, were in support of unity." At least, because of his strong rule, there was no disunity in Wu.[269] Shih does not elaborate this curious argument; it seems he could as well argue that Chiang Kai-shek, by strengthening and developing Taiwan, contributed to the unity of China. Shih's would appear, however, to be an esoteric argument to the effect that some measure of regional autonomy, under military control, will somehow be good for the country and not inhibit overall unity. Most of the army is probably just as glad to have its political functions decreased. Some of the regional commanders—those with ambitions for more political power—may not be; and some regional commanders, given the nature of Chinese politics over the past decade, may feel they need to acquire political power just for self-defense. The Shih article may be an expression of this interest, although even this does not give a principled defense of it.

This section has concentrated upon the military elite, upon high politics, albeit sometimes the low side of high politics. There are little data on the feelings and opinions of the ordinary soldier. The army is technically recruited through conscription, although there seems to be no shortage of volunteers. The manpower pool, naturally, is several orders larger than what the army can take in, and this means that the army gets, from the military point of view, the cream of Chinese youth. The soldiers are mostly of peasant background, and, especially since the PLA is a rather pampered sector of Chinese society, life in the army is in many ways better than life at home.

The peasant background of the soldiers means, however, that hardship in the villages will influence morale in the army. Most of the 1961 issues of an intra-army publication, *Work Bulletin,* have become available outside China, and these testify to widespread discontent among soldiers in that very bad year.

> The present condition of political thought among the vast majority of personnel in stricken areas or whose homes are in stricken areas is basically positive and solid. . . . However, among some comrades there still exists a situation of insufficient faith and hidden anxieties. A minority of people have doubts about the three red flags and are wavering; still others openly attack the party. Aside from this, there are certain units where reactionary bulletins are written, reactionary cliques are organized, and other counterrevolutionary activities occur.[270]

Lo Jui-ch'ing reported that in a "certain division" the "thought condition of the troops is basically good," although not as good as before the food ran out. Now, "26.6 per cent" of the soldiers still have had bad thoughts. Most of it is "related to the condition of the warriors' families."[271]

The *Work Bulletins* also contain some horror stories of the mistreatment of men by officers. In one company

> last year [1960] eleven soldiers committed suicide. Two of these had political problems and feared punishment; nine others had committed petty theft and killed themselves because the cadres mishandled their cases. One leading personnel, in order to interrogate a soldier who had stolen another's [character unclear], mobilized the higher cadres of the whole company and, using the method of cart-wheel war [unceasing interrogation in relays], "chatted" with him for twenty-eight consecutive hours. This soldier was forced to kill himself.[272]

The year 1961, however, was a year of general social demoralization, and it would not be fair to take the situation described in the available *Work Bulletins* as typical.

Lin Piao's solution to the morale problem was political indoctrination, and this included the urging of decent treatment by officers of those they commanded. Lin's program, combined with a return to relative prosperity, no doubt did much to appease discontent among the rank and file. We may wonder, however, whether the troops were entirely pleased by everything in Lin's program, particularly by his ever-growing collection of dead heroes. Any comment here must be speculative, not to say moralistic. Still . . . One hero, Chin Hsun-hua, was canonized for his death in attempting to save some equuipment that was being washed away in a flood. A philosophically minded Western historian observes:

> It is difficult for outsiders to take such accounts seriously. No one would scoff if Chin had lost his life trying to save another's, but could so mundane, so pointless an act be truly heroic? Two attributes of the deed may relieve it of absurdity: its

> relevance to everyday (and therefore petty) life, and its expression of total commitment to Mao's thought.[273]

Maybe. But if Chinese today are not completely different from outsiders or from Chinese in the past—and I think the evidence of this chapter shows they are not—the celebration of such a deed might also tend to render the whole enterprise absurd. An act of courage, of course, remains an act of courage regardless of its end; and few will scoff at the death of any man, although some may scoff at the use others make of that death. The problem is the scale of values that promotes Chin's act as an example for emulation. The production of dead heroes seems to have come to an end with Lin Piao. Chinese soldiers may be just as happy no longer to be explicitly told that their lives are of less value than a telephone pole.

6

Opposition Movements

The fact needs to be stressed that once it is the State which is carrying out the revolution and those who are opposed to the State are the ones who are called "counterrevolutionaries," it becomes very easy to understand that the ordinary person is confused and does not quite know where he is.[1]

—JACQUES ELLUL

The previous chapter discusses some specific manifestations of opposition but focuses upon an attempt to discover possible lasting sources of opposition, areas in which the regime and some of the persons it rules might have different opinions or interests. This chapter treats actual opposition movements, concentrating upon persons or groups that have criticized the regime in a relatively programmatic way. The previous chapter concentrates upon interests; the present, upon ideology or, more simply, ideas.

The discussion follows a rough chronological order. The first major opposition movement, the Hundred Flowers campaign, was largely liberal in orientation; its most prominent spokesmen were the liberal democratic personages who had allied themselves with the Communists against the KMT and had come to object to the regime roughly for the same reasons they had objected to the KMT. The crushing of this movement meant the end of effective opposition by the upper social strata outside the party. The other opposition movements are related to the two tendencies within the party, although the radical opposition has also spilled out into nonparty society. The Marxian Confucian opposition of the capitalist road period involved a classical Marxist critique of Great Leap Forward radicalism combined with a reassertion of traditional Chinese and universal human values. Radical opposition came to the fore in the Cultural Revolution (although there was precedent for it in 1957), beginning as a criticism of the Marxian Confucian critique of radicalism. What is here called establishment radicalism (the radicalism of Mao's inner court and perhaps of Mao himself) may be pseudo-opposition (or largely factional opposition), but the ideas of the establishment radicals were picked up by others and developed into a true oppositional stance. The final movement considered, the rational modernist critique of establishment radicalism, is in effect a more hard-line version of the Marxian

Confucian critique, expressing similar policy preferences but (overtly) without the humanism of the former movement.

While liberalism has been eliminated as a distinct ideology on mainland China, there seems to be a convergence of all these movements toward liberal demands. This is perhaps not surprising: the oppositionists want toleration at least for themselves. The world views of these dissidents differ greatly, but in many concrete points their criticisms are similar; while people may differ in their interpretation of their discomfort, the agreement on what constitutes discomfort is perhaps more widely shared.

LIBERAL OPPOSITION: THE HUNDRED FLOWERS

The decision to allow a hundred flowers to bloom, a hundred schools to contend, was almost certainly Mao's own, as part of a plan to undercut the growing strength of an increasingly bureaucratized party machine.[2] The year 1955, with its *su-fan* and the purge of Hu Feng, was not a happy time for Chinese intellectuals. The first hints of a more relaxed policy come in a speech by Chou En-lai in January 1956. In this speech Chou hints that greater liberty for intellectuals will contribute to the weakening of dogmatic conservatism among the comrades: "The party has decided to make opposition to rightist conservative thought the central question of the Eighth Party Congress and demands that the whole party in all offices take up this struggle." A few months later Lu Ting-i introduced the actual slogan about the flowers and the schools, attributing the slogan and the policy to Mao.[3] In 1956 Mao was being frozen out by the party machine, then apparently dominated by Liu Shao-ch'i and Teng Hsiao-p'ing. Mao's plan, apparently, was to widen the scope of debate, forcing the party to reform itself in response to criticisms from educated nonparty public opinion. Mao was going over the heads of the party bosses to the people—a policy he followed with greater success in the Cultural Revolution, when he chose his people with more care and made sure of the support of the army. Mao may also have figured that this soliciting of outside opinion would be fairly safe, the intellectuals having been remolded by thought reform and cowed by the 1955 campaigns. Chou En-lai estimated that only 10 percent of the intellectuals were counterrevolutionary; 40 percent were firm supporters of the regime, while the rest were "basic supporters" but lacked "sufficient political awareness."[4]

There was little immediate response to these promises of liberalization. The intellectuals were understandably wary, and the party machine was probably actively hostile. While 1956 was not a particularly radical year, neither was it a year of great free debate. Despite what Chou (and Mao) might have liked, the Eighth Party Congress marks, if anything, the triumph of rightist conservative thought within the party. Mao's main allies in his plan to rectify the party by means of the intellectuals included Chou En-lai and probably P'eng Chen, at least after some dickering. Chou, as head of the state bureaucracy, would have a natural interest in causing trouble for the apparatus, and he also had practical and probably personal reasons for disliking the stultifying intellectual atmosphere of People's China. The assignment of P'eng Chen as a supporter of Mao is more problematic and controversial.[5] P'eng did, however, publicly support party rectification, albeit belatedly and with reservations.[6] Lu Ting-i, Mao's spokesman on the Hundred Flowers policy, had become, at least by the late 1950s, a factional ally of P'eng's. P'eng ranked second to Teng Hsiao-p'ing on the party Secretariat, and Teng showed no enthusiasm whatsoever for either liberalization or rectification. Should P'eng support rectification and should rectification come, it could only help him at Teng's expense. Less crassly, P'eng's support for liberalization in 1957 is consistent with the later, relatively liberal, attitude attributed to him during the Cultural Revolution. P'eng Chen was a thug, but thugs do not have their own party line.

The real blooming and contending began gradually in the spring of 1957, reaching a climax in the month of May. On June 8 the party struck back, claiming for itself, as well, the right to contend.

> We must accept correct criticisms, rectify our mistakes, and reform our work. Sometimes this kind of criticism is not totally correct but must be strictly distinguished from rightist opposition to our social and political system and opposition to the leadership of the Communist Party. Do you want socialism? Do you want people's democratic dictatorship? Do you want leadership by the Communist Party? These are the most basic questions of right and wrong in the life of our state.[7]

The more vocal critics were labeled rightists thirsting for a "Hungarian incident."[8] The campaign to rectify the party became in effect a campaign by the party to rectify the people.[9] "The Communist Party's rectification movement is also a struggle against bourgeois thought. Bureaucratism, sectarianism, and subjectivism [the original targets of the rectification campaign] are all bourgeois things."[10] The campaign within the party continued as well but came to concentrate upon those members who had shown sympathy with the views of the rightists outside the party. As one comment had it, "The spring of 1957 was an unusual time for our country's political and intellectual circles."[11]

We have already referred in various places to many of the specific criticisms of the regime made during this period. The major ones have been translated and compiled by Roderick MacFarquhar.[12] As a guide to what the regime apparently considered the most telling criticism, it is useful to rely on the regime's most detailed point-by-point refutation, a speech by Chou En-lai delivered in June 1957. It will be noted, however, that Chou ignores some of the harsher criticisms, responding mainly to those published openly by the rightists prior to

June 8. These tend to be milder than later allegations of what the rightists said. The distinction is indicated below by a rather clumsy syntactical device. For what had been published openly, the rightist "said." For allegations, the rightist is "said to have said" (or words to that effect). There is no reason to think that the post–June 8 quotations from rightists are inaccurate, although many may be out of context. It should also be noted that Chou's speech is a criticism of bourgeois rightism from a party moderate point of view.

Chou begins with praise for the purge campaigns of the early 1950s. On June 5 a rightist had said:

> Since 1952 campaign has succeeded campaign, each one leaving behind a great wall in its wake, a wall which estranges one man from another. In such circumstances no one dares to let off steam even privately, let alone speak his mind in public. Everyone has now learned the technique of doubletalk; what one says is one thing, what one thinks is another.[13]

Chou, however, thinks the campaigns are fine things. "It is obvious and easy to see that without the victories in these movements we should not have attained the victory of socialism in such a short time after the establishment of New China." There may have been some mistakes, but the rightists exaggerate them.[14]

Chou then turns to the economy. Some say the five-year plan is "all screwed up" (*kao huai-le*). They are wrong. "Some people think that unified purchase and sale [forced levies of grain and other crops] is too crude. This is a direct attack on the socialist system." Those who object "are either covetous for free enjoyment by a minority, or are dazzled by free competition, or have the aim of making a personal fortune."[15] Actually, opposition to the grain levies would be an *indirect* attack on socialism, if it is an attack on socialism at all (rather than just specific opposition to a concrete policy). I have seen no direct, public attacks on socialism itself among the criticisms published before June 8. Later, however, such attacks were "uncovered." A member of the Communist Youth League was said to have said: "Bureaucratism is a product of socialism. Capitalism is highly efficient, and doesn't produce bureaucratism. One must get down to the 'system' itself."[16]

Chou then defends the party's policies on education and science. There will be, he says, no more monopoly of the school by bourgeois intellectuals. The rightists say our science is now more backward than in the days of the KMT, that the people we train are less qualified than those trained prior to Liberation. "This is simply a denial of the excellence of the socialist system. Some people think that the CPC and the People's Government cannot lead scientific work, that 'amateurs' cannot lead 'professionals.' Some even think the existence of the State Council Science Planning Commission is an expression of distrust toward

Chinese scientists.'' How malicious can some people get? Party leadership is required in thought (i.e., ideology), policy, direction, and planning. Chou concedes, however, that scholarly questions cannot be resolved by administrative fiat.[17]

Despite what some people say, the standard of living of ''most'' workers and peasants has risen. Consumption has increased an average of four Chinese dollars a year, but there is a limit to how fast it can be increased. The living standard of some ''high-level intellectuals'' has fallen, but ''this is entirely proper.'' ''Some people say the living standards of workers and peasants are too unequal.'' But it is cheaper to live in the countryside, and anyway, workers are more productive. The rightists exaggerate the pay differentials between those of high and low rank. ''In a socialist system the state must still make a differentiation in compensation between complex and simple work, between brain work and physical work.'' To call this exploitation, as the rightists do, is ''extremely ignorant, infantile talk and not in good faith.''[18] Perhaps wisely, Chou refrains from quoting Mencius: ''Those who labor with their hands feed those who labor with their minds; those who labor with their minds rule those who labor with their hands.''

In his discussion of the economy Chou attempts to answer those critical of China's reliance on the ''Soviet experience.'' Some ''even think the mistakes and defects of our socialist construction are a consequence of learning from the Soviets. This is an extremely harmful viewpoint.'' We cannot take over the Soviet experience uncritically, but would the rightists have us learn from the United States?[19] Chou does not mention the harsher anti-Russian attitudes. Lung Yun, the former warlord of Yunnan province, was said to have voiced the following opinions: the Russians did not give sufficient aid during the Korean war; the interest on Russian loans is too high; the Russians plundered Manchuria in 1945; China spends too much on foreign aid.[20] These ''absurd views,'' and the rightists' views of the Russians generally, were to become the commonplaces of a few years later.

After his discussion of economics Chou turns to the question of political and civil liberties, the heart of the liberal critique. The rightists had complained about the lack of a rule of law. Actually, Chou says, China has lots of laws: the family-reform law, the land-reform law, and the like. A criminal code has been drafted, and a civil code and a code on public security are being drafted. But, Chou says, we still need dictatorship to deal with counterrevolutionaries, thieves, swindlers, murderers, arsonists, and gangsters[21] (persons, is one to gather, who cannot be properly punished by law?). The regime in fact lost interest in law codification in 1957, and nearly twenty years later all the proposed codes Chou mentions had yet to be promulgated.

Chou is most upset by the criticisms of one-party rule, just as the fact of one-party rule had been upsetting to the democratic personages who technically formed a part of the people's democratic dictatorship. Chu An-p'ing, the editor of the *Kuang-ming Daily,* had said: "I think a party leading a nation is not the same thing as a party owning a nation; the public supports the Party, but members of the public have not forgotten they are the masters of the nation."[22] Some professors in Shenyang were reported to have said that a

> system of general election campaigns should be put into effect alongside the abolition of the absolute leadership of the Party. The people should be allowed freely to organize new political parties and social bodies, and to put out publications so as to open the channels of public opinion, supervise the government, combat cheap phrases, and encourage them to oppose an undesirable status quo, even if this means opposition to the Communist Party, providing they do not stand against the people and socialism.[23]

Chou tears into this sort of thing. The rightists do not think they have enough freedom. "It seems you have freedom only if the state protects all opposition to the basic state system stipulated in the constitution and allows all speech and action opposed to socialism." They say, "Only elections like those in capitalist countries are most free." Here we do not want democracy for the sake of democracy, but only "in order to unite all forces in the joint construction of socialism and the development of the social productive forces." No anarchist or petty bourgeois absolute democracy for us, thanks. "Could it be that aside from the Communist Party there are other parties that can lead the Chinese people to the realization of this great ideal?" What an absurd idea. The rightists complain of *tang t'ien-hsia,* the "party world." It is, in fact, the *t'ien-hsia* of the workers and the people. The rightists treat the party "as if it were a sect divorced from the masses." Why, everyone knows the party opposes sectarianism: that is what the rectification was all about. The rightist clamor for a two- or multi-party system is simply a ruse to swindle the people. The party will retain its branches in state offices and schools; it will continue to organize among intellectuals (i.e., to pressure intellectuals to adhere to the regime's discipline in their work); it will continue to operate beyond the sphere of government; and it will not step down.[24]

The "unusual spring" was unprecedented among Communist regimes (Hungary aside—but that was a rebellion) and is perhaps matched only by the "Prague spring." The criticisms published prior to June 8 tend, however, to be rather mild, in absolute if not relative terms. Later the rightists were alleged to have said some very rough things: "Our Party's massacre of intellectuals and the mass burying alive of the literati by Ch'in Shih-huang will go down in China's history as two ineradicable stigmas."[25] The criticisms published directly in the press, however, are never integral and rarely fundamental. (This campaign may show, however, that it is arbitrary to try to assign degrees of intensity to opposition. The regime could apparently construe a demand for free competition among parties not opposed to socialism as opposition to socialism. Given that the critics, both as Chinese and as subjects of this kind of regime, were familiar enough with the uses of Aesopean language, it is hard to say that the regime was wrong. Its members were better placed than any outsider to interpret the critics correctly, although they also had an incentive to lie.) Perhaps the most ferocious directly published criticism is that by K'o P'ei-chi, an economics teacher.

> I believe that the relations between the party and the masses are 18,000 miles further apart than before Liberation. . . . Unified purchase and sale has screwed things up, so there is a shortage of supply. The "*su-fan*" movement screwed things up; the party made mistakes. . . . There is a shortage of pork. The common people [*lao-pai-hsing*] never eat any. Some people call this an improved standard of living. Whose standard of living has improved? . . . That of the party members and cadres. Speaking honestly, the shortage of supply is a result of mistakes by those carrying out party policy. For example, where has all the pork gone? The common people don't eat it up. It is that because of unified purchase and sale, the common people are not willing to raise pigs.
>
> [The CPC was welcomed in 1949]. Today the common people avoid them as if they were ghosts or devils. This has happened before. There are many examples in Chinese history. . . . For example, after the victory in the War of Resistance in 1945, the common people who had suffered eight years of Japanese oppression welcomed the KMT. . . . The situation now is not the same. The common people have mixed opinions about the Communists. If the Communists are not aware of this, it will be very dangerous.
>
> Formerly in underground work in the schools there was progress through unity, taking the middle position. Now party members take the lead. The success of a party member depends upon how many reports he turns in. . . . In supervising the masses the party members have taken on the functions of the police. The party members cannot be blamed for this, since the party organization orders them to collect intelligence; it is the responsibility of the party organization.
>
> China is the China of 600 million people, including counterrevolutionaries. It is not the China of the Communist Party. It is fine if the Communists take the attitude of lords and masters [*chu-jen-weng*], but it is not permitted for you to say, "We [*chen*—the 'royal' we] are the state." . . . If you do well, fine. If not, the masses may [*k'o-i*—"are permitted to"] overthrow you, kill the Communists, push you down. If the Communist Party is destroyed, China is not destroyed. Just because people do not want communist leadership does not mean they are traitors.[26]

This is extremely harsh, but the harshness is more in the tone than in the content. Whatever his real feelings may have been, K'o says the economic troubles are a result of mistakes made by those carrying out policy, for example, not the result of party policy itself. A not unsympathetic critic characterized much of K'o's speech as "loyal words that grate upon the ears."[27]

The most visible criticism of the Hundred Flowers period came from the bourgeois intellectuals and democratic personages. There was also criticism from party members, particularly younger ones and localists, and also from students. The students were perhaps the most outspoken; they would even express disgust with the timidity of the older critics. The regime gathered the most vitriolic student criticism into a booklet intended for internal circulation as a "negative example"; this has been translated into English by Dennis Doolin.[28] The ideas of the most articulate of the student critics, Miss Lin Hsi-ling, are discussed below, under radical opposition. Most of the student critics, however, apparently thought of themselves as liberals.

At its mildest, the student criticism matches that of K'o P'ei-chi:

> The Party takes everything into its own hands and decides everything; the Party is the whole people; the Party is the state; the Party is the law. So-called "democracy" has, in fact, been replaced by Party rule. . . .
>
> The Party can only strive to win the masses of people to accept its leadership; it cannot demand they must necessarily obey its leadership.

Often it is harsher:

> They are a group of fascists who use foul means, twist the truth, band together in evil ventures, and ignore the people's wish for peace both at home and abroad.

The students also criticized personally high-ranking leaders, including Mao, something the more mature critics either chose or dared not to do:

> What do they mean when they speak of suffering now in order to have a happy life later? These are lies. We ask: Is Chairman Mao, who always enjoys the best things of life . . . having a hard time? . . . Everyone was told that [Chairman Mao] was leading a hard and simple life. That real son of a bitch! [*T'a ma-te*] . . . When he wants to kill you, he doesn't have to do it himself. He can mobilize your wife and children to denounce you and then kill you with their own hands! Is this a rational society? . . . Dictator, you've turned into a brute.

The students were also in some cases willing to translate their opposition into action. There were student riots in several cities, and a riot lasting several days at the First Wuhan Middle School resulted in the only announced executions coming from the movement.[29] Some of the older rightists apparently also tried to organize their opposition. The colorful ex-warlord, politician, and

Buddhist layman Ch'en Ming-shu allegedly tried to reorganize his old Social Democratic Party, presenting a "10,000-word manifesto," "attacking Chairman Mao," and organizing branches of his party in Shanghai, Shantung, and Wuhan. The attacks on Ch'en speak of his setting fires, but this turns out to be metaphorical; his opposition does not seem to have gone beyond consultation with his friends and the expression of opinion.[30]

MacFarquhar believes the Hundred Flowers experience shows that the "idea that free discussion can take place in a totalitarian society is . . . metaphysical."[31] Perhaps a better word is *contradictory,* since part of the meaning of "totalitarian society" would be a society in which free discussion cannot take place. The real problem is whether a totalitarian society can become non-totalitarian, and the Hundred Flowers may show some obstacles to this. On the other hand, it may not be a completely ideal test of the possibilities of evolution. The bulk of the criticism came from a fairly narrow elite. The student leader, Lin Hsi-ling, said: "The present 'blooming and contending' is confined to the upper strata only. This won't do. I think the top layer is made up of old men who are not bold enough, who are too experienced in life and dare not speak up."[32] In many cases this elite tended to concentrate upon its own problems and concerns (one critic said K'o P'ei-chi was in a snit because the government was no longer providing servants for professors;[33] this, however, is probably largely slander). There was no direct criticism from the lower strata, from, say, peasants—according to the students, not because the peasants were so happy, but rather because intellectuals did not deign to speak for them: "There has not been a single mention made in the press about the peasants in the fish-and-rice producing areas who contracted dropsy from eating pumpkins or those who starved to death because they had nothing to eat but grass roots."[34]

The students themselves were also an elite, and one relatively cut off from the rest of society. The bourgeois intellectuals were even more cut off—a social elite which the regime had once been able to use, but which had been reduced to utter political impotence. The critics lacked a social base, and, given the structure of the regime, had no opportunity to acquire one. It is easy to believe that the regime was originally as scared of their criticism as it claimed to be, but it is also easy to believe later analyses that imply the original fright was unwarranted: the attacks came largely from the "warlords, politicians, gangsters, and celebrities of yesteryear"[35]—from what Lenin sometimes liked to call the "useful idiots."

This, of course, says nothing about the soundness or justice of the criticisms, nor would this particular critique apply to the student or party dissidents. It is also possible to take a more charitable view of the bourgeois intellectuals. Chinese liberalism in this century has often been a shallow thing. The liberalism of many of the warlords was simply a consequence of their having been excluded from power by Chiang Kai-shek. More serious liberals have tended to be nationalists as well and may have had mixed feelings when they saw nationalist goals being achieved by antiliberal means. Joseph Levenson notes, after a discussion of the degrading self-examinations conducted by the rightists throughout the summer of 1957:

> There was not just the pressure of outside force against liberal sentiments, but a genuine questioning of liberal sentiments. A nagging doubt might intrude: were these sentiments hollow, while the material achievement was ''real''? This was the inner schism that seemed to corroborate the communist charge of ''*bourgeois* egoism''—the schism expressed in feeling that what might be good for China was hell to me.[36]

This should not be taken too far, of course, Levenson, in common with many American academics, perhaps underestimates the efficacy of the pressure of outside force. Also, his contention might not be very pertinent to much of the criticism set out in this section. K'o P'ei-chi, for example, had no trouble distinguishing between the party and the country and also questioned the reality of the material achievement. Levenson's analysis does show, however, one of the reasons for the weakness of Chinese liberalism.

The Hundred Flowers campaign perhaps marks the end on the China mainland of liberalism as a distinct school of thought, aside from sporadic manifestations (and, as analyzed below, some of the other critiques of the regime tend to converge upon a kind of liberalism).[37] It may be fitting to conclude this section with one of the sporadic manifestations, an example of moral courage. Ma Yin-ch'u, an economist and former president of Peking University (China's outstanding institute of higher education before its debasement in the Cultural Revolution), had managed to avoid trouble during the unusual spring. He had said he did not really mind having the actual running of the university done by the Communist vice-president, since this gave him more time for research and mountain climbing.[38] In 1958 he was attacked for two of the fruits of his research, a study of the Chinese economy and a study of population policy. He held firm, and in late 1959, amidst another antirightist campaign, published a reply. He concludes:

> Last year more than two hundred critics attacked me . . . but their criticisms did not hit the mark. In the heat of the debate, some friends strongly urged me to admit a mistake; otherwise it would inevitably influence my political standing. . . . But I would not do it. I do not think this is a political question, but a purely scholarly one. . . . One must know the difficulties and go forward and never bow the head because of difficulties. . . . I do not ordinarily teach and am not in direct contact with students, but I want to educate students by my behavior. I always hope that the 10,400 students at Peking University will know the difficulties and go forward in their pursuit of learning and in their work.

> Lastly, I want to express thanks to another friend and also apologize to him. When I met difficulties at Chungking University he helped me in a thousand ways with a hundred tricks. When I came north from Hong Kong in 1949 to join the government, it was in response to his invitation. For this I am grateful without end; I still keep this in my heart. I have not accepted his sincere advice. I am unhappy because I have a fairly firm grip on my theory and cannot let go. Reverence for scholarship must be maintained; I must refuse to make a self-examination. I hope my friend will continue to be understanding and not take my refusal to make a self-examination as audacious defiance.[39]

His friend, without doubt, is Chou En-lai. Ma may display bourgeois egoism, even arrogance—the egoism and arrogance of one who places limits on the extent to which he will play the whore. While Ma talks of scholarly questions, he surely knew that a political question is anything the regime chooses to regard as one. The preservation of his own integrity—and the encouragement of integrity in others—is a political act, the only political act remaining for the bougeois intellectuals and one that most chose, or were forced, not to do. Ma was dismissed as president of Peking University in 1960 but continued to hold an honorific position as delegate to the National People's Congress until he was swallowed up by the Cultural Revolution.

The bourgeois intellectuals were suppressed, but many of the issues they raised were real ones and later came to be taken up by certain Communists themselves. There may be something in the structure of the regime that encourages the expression of such ideas and their subsequent suppression. In 1976 some party members were attacked for a slogan to the effect that universities should be led by "amateurs ardent for science." This sophistry, it was explained, is exactly equivalent to the 1957 rightist demand that amateurs should not lead professionals, since it implies there are party members not ardent for science.[40] These later critics of the prevailing ethos are probably less handicapped by any inner schism than were the bourgeois intellectuals, although this does not mean they will be any more effective.

MARXIAN CONFUCIAN OPPOSITION: THE CAPITALIST ROAD

As noted many times, the tendencies discussed in this study are not necessarily the same as factions. Several factions have adhered to the radical tendency, and the Lin Piao case shows that a faction can switch tendencies. There have also been divisions among the moderates, both in factions and in ideas. The moderate opposition movement of the early 1970s, under the perhaps half-reluctant leadership of Chou En-lai and Teng Hsiao-p'ing, took as its ideology what I call rational modernism. The movement of the early 1960s criticized the radical tendency from the point of view of what might be called Marxian Confucianism, although the term should not be taken in too strict or technical a sense. The main spokesmen for this movement were the party intellectuals, Teng T'o and Wu Han, under the patronage of P'eng Chen, who, in turn under Liu Shao-ch'i, apparently dominated the central party apparatus at that time. We have already met Wu Han, a democratic personage who had cooperated with the Communists prior to Liberation. He had come to hold the honorific position of vice-mayor of Peking (the mayor was P'eng Chen) and at some point must have joined the party, since the first attacks on him in 1965 call him comrade. Teng T'o's party credentials are much older. In the 1930s he had been a member of the famous underground Northern Bureau (headed by Liu Shao-ch'i and P'eng Chen). From 1955 to 1959 he had been chief editor of the *People's Daily,* the party's central newspaper. He then became a secretary of the Peking Party Committee (first secretary, P'eng Chen). The philosophical position developed by Teng and Wu, it must be noted, was not necessarily shared by Liu and P'eng. Liu, like Teng Hsiao-p'ing, seems to have favored, as far as we can tell, a rather hard-line, authoritarian "rational modernism," a position some people seem to identify (incorrectly) with Stalinism. P'eng Chen's position is perhaps even harder to reconstruct. We can probably say that, as long as he was on his way up, he had an objective interest in the Marxian Confucian position; he might have found it less palatable had he come to power. (We will never know, of course, whether Teng and Wu would have been willing to turn against a victorious P'eng Chen faction the kind of criticism they directed at Mao and the radicals.)

The position developed by Teng and Wu must be understood in the context of both the political and intellectual situation in the late 1950s and early 1960s. Politically, their critique of radicalism might be considered a tale of two P'engs—of P'eng Chen, but also of P'eng Te-huai. The 1957 campaign against rightism set the stage for 1958's Great Leap Forward. At the end of 1958 Mao was forced into semiretirement, and during the first part of 1959 many in the party began cautiously to express second thoughts about the blind enthusiasm of the previous year. In June, Wu Han, under the pen name of Liu Mien-chih, published a vernacular translation and commentary on Hai Jui's diatribe against the emperor.[41] There are indications that P'eng Te-huai had been dissatisfied with party policies for some time, but (apparently) the example of Hai Jui inspired him to show courage and make his dissatisfaction known.[42] At the Lushan plenum in July he addressed a letter of opinion to Mao, criticizing the party's petty bourgeois fanaticism. "In the view of some comrades, putting politics in command could be a substitute for everything."[43] Mao took the offensive against P'eng, and after a slanging match lasting several weeks P'eng was removed as minister of defense.

After the Lushan plenum, elements of the P'eng Chen faction made contact with Wu Han, expressing further interest in Hai Jui:

> As soon as the Lushan meeting was over, Hu Ch'iao-mu [a Propaganda Department functionary], a right opportunist element who had escaped the net, sought out Wu Han and said, "Some people brought up Hai Jui at the Lushan meeting, but lots of people don't know who Hai Jui is. You do [*kao*] Ming history. Write an essay on Hai Jui, and add some discussion." Wu Han's spirits jumped, and he wholeheartedly agreed. A few days later, the big poisonous weed, "On Hai Jui," was written and sent to Hu Ch'iao-mu for approval. Hu Ch'iao-mu busily revised it, making many changes. . . .[44]

"On Hai Jui" was published in September, and it tells how Hai Jui was a brave man who opposed those who oppressed the people. The conclusion of the essay may come from the politic hand of Hu Ch'iao-mu (or maybe from Wu Han, who was only a partial Hai Jui himself):

> Some people [i.e., P'eng Te-huai] proclaim themselves Hai Juis, calling themselves oppositionists. But they are the opposite from Hai Jui. They do not stand on the side of the people, do not stand with the enterprise of today's people: the socialist enterprise. They do not oppose bad men and bad deeds, but only good men and good deeds. They say this is "too soon," "too fast," "all screwed up," "extreme," "too rigid"; that is "biased"; this "has defects," that has "flaws," the sun has black spots; among ten fingers they find the one with a flaw . . . pouring cold water on the heads of the masses, dousing the spirit of the popular masses.[45]

Hai Jui's courage perhaps rubbed off on Wu Han as well. In 1960 Wu began work on a Peking opera, *Hai Jui is dismissed from office*.[46] The September 1959 essay explicitly dissociates itself from P'eng Te-huai, but the opera was later held to be a plea for the rehabilitation of P'eng. Criticism of this opera was the occasion for the initiation of the Cultural Revolution.

At the end of 1960 the regime admitted the extent of the country's economic collapse (problems with the weather, it was explained), and many reforms were introduced: greater use of material incentives, less collectivization on the communes, and a more liberal policy on culture. P'eng Chen apparently wished (along with many others) for the liberalization to go further. With the approval, it is said, of Liu Shao-ch'i, in November 1961 P'eng Chen directed Teng T'o to undertake a general review of all party policies since 1958. Teng produced a report highly critical of the Great Leap Forward, moving P'eng Chen to predict the collapse of the communes and urge that peasants be allowed to farm their own land.[47] During 1961 and 1962 Teng also published in the *Peking Daily* (the organ of the Peking Party Committee and the local paper for Peking city, not to be confused with the *People's Daily*—which, of course, is also published in Peking) a series of urbane and witty essays, mostly on traditional culture, "Evening talks on Swallow Mountain" (*Yen-shan*—an old name for Peking). Together with Wu Han and the journalist Liao Mo-sha, he also published a series with a bit more bite, "Random notes from a three-family village," in *Front Line,* the Peking Party Committee's theoretical journal. *Three-family village,* a term taken from a poem by Su Tung-po, of the Sung dynasty, is a rather more literary equivalent of the American one-horse town, and this was later said to be a reference to P'eng Te-huai's exile to his native Hunan countryside. In these essays Teng, in an elegant, extremely indirect manner, voiced his criticism of the policies of the previous few years. At one point he neatly combined an explanation of his method with an illustration of it. He was discussing caricatures of ghosts in old paintings:

> [We] know that [some painters'] satires of ghosts were in fact satires of people. But in the society of that time, if painters had used caricature directly to satirize living men, they would have gotten into trouble. If they only satirized some dead ghosts there would be no danger.[48]

As Teng would soon find out, times had changed.

Meanwhile, P'eng Te-huai, with the support now, it is said, of Liu Shao-ch'i as well as P'eng Chen, continued to adhere to his old views—which had in fact been tacitly adopted by the party. Other considerations aside, the central apparatchiks would have a motive in supporting P'eng simply as a check to the growing ambitions of his successor, Lin Piao. Te-huai drew up an "80,000-word essay" reiterating and developing his Lushan criticisms, and the submission of this essay was apparently the occasion for the calling of the tenth plenum of the Eighth Central Committee in September 1962.[49] The plenum left the concrete economic policies of the capitalist-road period untouched; but politically it was a victory for the Mao-Lin line, and the cultural atmosphere began once again to turn cold. The "Three-family village" series continued to run into 1964, but the later essays are apparently relatively innocuous. Teng's last chat on Swallow Mountain was published in September 1962, a meditation on the famous "thirty-six tricks," a set of strategems dating from the Warring States period. Teng concludes that all the thirty-six tricks are summed up in the last one: *tsou wei shang,* "the best is to run away."[50]

The criticism of Wu Han began in November 1965 and led to the criticism of Teng T'o and thence to P'eng Chen, the real target. Given the general Western impression of the Cultural Revolution as a radical assault on bureaucracy, it is tempting to view Teng and Wu as apologists for some bureaucratic "new class." This, however, would mean ignoring much of what they actually said. Given their affiliation with P'eng Chen, Teng and Wu may in fact have served the interests of the party bureaucracy; their vision of the good society was probably one in which there is more routinized order than most sincere radicals would like. But neither Teng nor Wu was an uncritical exponent of bureaucratic arbitrariness that disregards the ideas and aspirations of ordinary people. In 1957 Wu Han's only contribution to the blooming and contending had been an attack on the "rightist" head of the Democratic League, Chang Po-chün.[51] Teng T'o, however, quoting a T'ang saying, "When there is basically no problem under heaven, the valet will still fuss about it," wrote an essay on "valet politics." Too many comrades busy themselves doing needless work, running around after subordinates, holding endless meetings, issuing thoughtless orders. In one county the bureaucrats ordered that all cotton be picked in one day, even the cotton that was not ready for harvesting (i.e., the bureaucrats are arbitrary and stupid, not just busy—an example of Teng T'o's indirectness). This is bureaucratism, not politics (i.e., leadership). "I thought, if all that is considered politics, then it is 'valet politics.' " The real valets are those who are afraid of the masses. "Our popular masses have received years of revolutionary education; we can trust them not to fail here."[52]

It is even possible that the relatively liberal outlook of Teng and Wu was shared by P'eng Chen—although P'eng was not very squeamish about his choice of allies, for example, Lo Jui-ch'ing. P'eng, it will be recalled, took a liberal line in 1957 as well as 1961. His, no doubt, was the policy of the capitalist road, but even here his spokesmen do not show themselves blind to the more idealistic aspects of the communist enterprise. Thus, in 1962 one of P'eng's economists, Lo Keng-mo, discussed the principle of "distribution according to labor," recognizing this as a "basic principle of the socialist stage." The alternative is "poverty communism." "The material wealth produced by production will for a long time be insufficient to satisfy the demands of consumption; it can only satisfy the people's demands to a degree." Therefore, we can have no communist distribution system yet. There are, however, many dangers in the practice of this necessary policy—the same dangers the radicals find. Pay differentials and the like can become a form of "bourgeois right." Inequality resulting from differences of ability can become too broad. A new "high-salaried class" may develop. We have no choice in the policy but must guard against its abuse.[53] This, perhaps, is a defense against accusations—to be made explicit years later—that P'eng and his friends were selling out communism. The radicals, however, tacitly admit the validity of the argument given, and their differences with the P'eng Chen line on this point would seem to be mainly rhetorical.

The chief difference between Teng and Wu and the radicals would be the humanism implied by the Confucian part of *Marxian Confucianism*. This term (which is, of course, mine, not that of those to whom I attribute the position) should perhaps not be taken too seriously, although it does refer to much more than Teng's and Wu's easy familiarity with the classical tradition. Teng and Wu were not the only ones discussing traditional philosophy in 1961 and 1962. The papers carried almost daily articles on ancient thinkers, discussing them from the Marxist point of view, of course, but also (unlike in the 1970s) in a fairly detached and scholarly manner. Joseph Levenson, in his brilliant *Confucian China and Its Modern Fate,* argues that this revival does not mean the resurgence of any eternal China triumphant over communism. Rather, it signifies that Confucianism had become harmless. For the progressives of the early part of this century Confucius was still a living enemy, the representative of all that was dark, weak, and reactionary in China. Ku Chieh-kang, one of the first historians to apply Western critical methods to the classics, took the conventional historicist view of systems of thought as reflections of changing social conditions. His Hegelianism, however, had its limits: Ku "would not deem Confucianism historically appropriate under any conditions."[54] The use of Confucian forms by the KMT and the Japanese further discredited that philosophy in the eyes of progressives. By 1961, however, Levenson argues, the Communists could afford to take a more lenient view: the battle had been won, and now there were others to fight. "Any contemporary assault against Confucius, while still a sort of ritual exercise for some writers in Communist China, was ideologically superfluous." Though "early Christians might break the images of pagan gods, centuries later the Vatican Museum would shelter its Apollos."[55]

Levenson's argument is persuasive, but in gross terms it must be partly false. The Cultural Revolution and later the "campaign to criticize Lin Piao and Confucius" would indicate that in some sense the Sage is not quite the mummy he seemed. To take a dialectical view, it is perhaps precisely because Confucianism seemed so innocuous in 1961 that it could be used as a vehicle for political criticism. To praise, say, parliamentary democracy might have seemed to be toadying to U.S. imperialism, but the sages and emperors are safely dead; it is better to caricature—or idealize—a ghost. Confucianism could serve as political criticism, however, only because it has a certain content. *Confucianism* is one word, but its denotations are many. It may refer to the ideology of the traditional Chinese state; that state is gone, and Confucianism as a state ideology is equally gone. Confucianism also refers to a philosophical mode or tradition containing within itself many different schools of thought. This was once a living tradition but probably is no longer. There are relatively few, for example, other than specialists, who get too excited over the philosophical issues dividing the schools of Chu Hsi and Wang Yang-ming. This is surely for social and historical reasons, not because the philosophical issues are trivial.

Confucianism may also mean a description of the moral attitudes traditionally accepted by the Chinese people. It also refers to a system of thought that seems to underlie all the different strains of what has been, historically, considered Confucianism. Subtending from these varieties, Confucianism would include such propositions as: there is an objective moral order autonomous from expediency or social conditions generally; human society ought to, but does not always, embody this moral order; human beings have the capacity to know this moral order, at least in part; and (in the orthodox line) human beings have a natural inclination to the objective good. Whether anyone believes this sort of thing is perhaps a function of social conditions, but the truth of these propositions does not depend upon social conditions. These are all metaphysical propositions and thus not subject to empirical demonstration—but if the propositions are in fact true, this truth will certainly have empirical consequences.

Disregarding the problem of the metaphysical validity of such propositions, it seems that they do contain at least some psychological or pragmatic truth. These propositions, it might be noted, are hardly confined to Confucianism, and if they are in fact true it should be expected that they would crop up in varying historical or social circumstances. Modern Western philosophy—since Descartes, and perhaps since Occham—has tended to undermine these platitudes, but we often act as if they were valid. I think that one who holds a relativistic or emotive theory of ethics will feel, at least when off-duty, that the values of, say, a sadist are somehow perverse, quite apart from the consequences of the sadist's indulging his values—even when the sadist finds a congenial masochist. Strict Marxists are also relativists: "The only applicable norm of what is right and just is the one inherent in the existing economic system." Capitalism is just on its own terms.[56] This does not, however, prevent Marxists from denouncing capitalism as unjust, and their purpose is not merely to bamboozle the unsophisticated. Marxism as a science negates all ethics in the Confucian (or any other traditional) sense, reducing morals to utility and rendering morality a redundant concept; yet, "contrary to the myth inspired by Marx and Engels themselves . . . both men came to communism out of ethical conviction, not scientific discovery."[57] Chinese communists bring up their own relativism either explicitly to answer critics who attempt to justify themselves by appeal to universal moral norms or to justify their own deviations from universal norms but they seem to act in their daily lives as if they were subject to universal norms. During the Cultural Revolution, Red Guards were apparently much more indignant at the moral failings of the revisionists than at their political shortcomings (although normal human salaciousness might help explain this).[58] After Lin Piao's death his enemies revived a fine piece of traditional invective (usually used of places, not groups): *Nan tao nü ch'ang*—the men are thieves and the women whores—a criticism that would seem, somehow, to transcend class.[59]

Communist regimes are based upon a denial of a Confucian kind of morality, as are, perhaps, modern or modernizing regimes generally: in the democratic West we have at least the technical separation of law from morality. But communists are as responsive (or as unresponsive) to the moral demands postulated in Confucianism as is anyone else. Modern regimes subvert traditional morality, but an assertion of the ethical impulse Confucianism holds to be natural and universal in man is subversive to a modern regime. In Wu Han and Teng T'o, I think, there is an attempt to fuse a kind of watered-down Confucianism, very broadly construed as an assertion of ethical absolutes in a Chinese idiom, with Marxism, construed as a humanistic system.

As noted above, the writings of Teng T'o and Wu Han form only a part of the revived interst in Confucianism in the early 1960s. Their version of the current meaning of Confucianism seems close to, and probably derives from, that of Feng Yu-lan, long-time professor of philosophy at Peking University. Feng's own philosophical system—developed in the days when Chinese were allowed to develop their own systems—consists of an analysis by Western philosophical methods of Sung and Ming neo-Confucianism, arriving at neo-Confucian conclusions.[60] After Liberation, Feng made the necessary adaptations in his point of view but kept up a constant guerrilla war to defend, on one level, philosophy as a discipline autonomous from day-to-day politics and, more timidly and at a deeper level, to defend what he thought valid in traditional Chinese philosophy. We have already met Professor Feng—on his hands and knees, banging his head against the floor. This was a familiar posture for him. In 1958 he said he had made 135 self-examinations since 1949, none of them satisfactory.[61] Many more were to follow.

In the early blooming and contending period, Feng had argued for a more positive approach to Confucianism, distinguishing abstract and concrete meanings of the words of Confucius. Confucius urges us to study; concretely he means study the *Book of Songs* and the like, but in the abstract this is good advice anyway. When Confucians talk of the equality and goodness of man, concretely they are saying that feudal ethics are natural to man. But these same concepts can be used to criticize feudal ethics.[62] In effect, Confucius is making what purport to be valid general statements about human beings, which may be true or false. It seems that if abstraction is taken too far Confucianism would become vacuous, but Feng is arguing that it be treated as a philosophy, not simply, as in the Ku Chieh-kang and party tradition, as an ethnography. Three years later Feng attempted again to defend the philosophical respectability of Confucianism, this time in a more satirical manner. The essay begins, "Chairman Mao teaches us. . . ," and continues in the same vein throughout. Marxism holds that all philosophy is either idealistic or materialistic. Materialism is true philosophy; and dialectical materialism, true materialism. Since we already have Marxism, why study the history of philosophy, a history of error? The reason is that New China developed out of the old. But because China had no true capitalist stage, it turns out that the Marxist categories are not relevant to the study of Chinese philosophy (Feng does not convincingly explain why not—perhaps deliberately). We must avoid a "mistaken tendency to modernize ancient philosophy, to explain ancient philosophy as if it were the same as modern philosophy," although we may, if we wish, criticize ancient philosophy from a Marxist point of view. As a parting shot, Feng reminds us it is only "slaves of imperialism" like Hu Shih who deny all merit to traditional Chinese philosophy.[63]

Other attitudes toward Confucius were expressed in the 1961–62 period. Yang Jung-kuo, a kind of vulgarizer of the Ku Chieh-kang school and the guiding light of the 1973 attacks on Confucius, probably represents the rational modernist strain. In 1962, unlike before and after, Yang allowed that while such Confucian concepts as *jen* (benevolence, love, goodness) have a class nature and served the ruling class, there is in them some potential for progress. Similarly, while Mencius was a reactionary, he had a "certain positive influence and a certain positive influence on posterity." On the radical side, Kuan Feng and Lin Yü-shih (purged in 1967 as members of the "ultra-'left' May 16 Corps") published a rather good Marxist critique of Confucius. They conclude that politically Confucius was a reactionary, despite some positive aspects—after all, he was out of sympathy with the political developments of his time. He did make a positive contribution in the transmission of earlier culture. On the whole, Confucius did not really have a philosophical system; he was "eclectic." These, perhaps, are examples of Levenson's "museumification" of the once-influential sage. Feng Yu-lan took Confucius more seriously. Against Kuan and Lin he argued that Confucius was not a reactionary, but a conservative reformer (and thus that, in the abstract, his political views have some limited merit); that he believed in human equality; and that his philosophy was not an eclectic (*tsa-par*—an untranslatable term referring to the mixed warlord armies of the earlier part of the twentieth century), but a coherent system—a mistaken system, no doubt, but coherent nonetheless. His *jen* may have had a class character, but he thought of it, not as the ideology of a class, but as part of a universally valid moral system.[64]

There were, in fact, limits on how seriously Confucius and what he stood for could be taken. In 1961 Feng wrote a rather impertinent essay on ethics, defined as the problem of "what is good," giving an exposition of Marxist ethics in an unusually vulgar fashion. There are two approaches to ethics: one stresses intention and what is right (Confucius); the other stresses consequences and utility (Mo-tzu, the utilitarians). Chairman Mao is credited with the discovery that a satisfactory ethical system must take both views into account. Feng also discovers a passage from Mao asserting that all ethics are utilitarian. The English utilitarians, of course, denied that each class has its own notion of utility; they are swindlers. But the utility of the proletariat is the same as that of "more than 90 percent of humanity." (Feng elsewhere says that all ruling classes identify their own good with that of humanity.) "Proletarian ethics," however, boils down to the proposition that "what is currently expedient is the standard of good and evil," although proletarians are hardly the only ones who believe this. Now this, in fact, is what the comrades think (officially), but they do not always like it so plainly expressed. Feng's critics were upset by the analogy between communist ethics and bourgeois utilitarianism, but they were most upset by his seemingly innocuous definition of ethics as the "problem of what is good."

This, apparently, raises the question that there may be such a problem. Ethics is simply the historical study of the "laws of development of communist ethics" and also the study of methods for overcoming old ethical systems.[65] There is no ethical problem. The hostility to any absolute, universal ethical norms comes out strongly in the condemnation of Liu Chieh, a philosopher apparently less crafty (and less well connected) than Feng Yu-lan. Liu argued that *jen* has no class character in itself—it transcends any concrete context. It is an "abstract ethical term," the "summary of all concrete human social phenomena from ancient times to the present." This, of course, goes against the "iron historical fact" that there never has been any universal love.[66] Confucius will not be completely tamed until people are unable to conceive of transcendent norms.

Teng T'o and Wu Han, like Feng Yu-lan and Liu Chieh, took their Confucianism seriously, not as a museum piece. Their Confucianism is more outspoken than Feng's, partly, perhaps, because of their lower degree of technical philosophical sophistication but probably also because, being closer to the centers of power, they could get away with more. Teng and Wu did not make a systematic attempt to develop a Confucianism that would fit the modern context but confined themselves only to hints in this direction. They attempt to retain the Marxist historicist approach to morality while at the same time introducing universal moral principles. Their philosophy is more eclectic than that of Kuan and Lin's Confucius and is probably contradictory.

Wu Han says of Hai Jui:

> Naturally, simply to be familiar with our dead classics, to talk of antiquity, and to follow the former kings could not solve the problem. To ask that the officials not plunder the area, not do bad things, not be corrupt, not ask for bribes . . . could not succeed unless based on a program for basic social change. Similarly, without a change in the relations of production, simply to ask that the big landlords return to the peasants the few fields they had usurped, that they exploit a little less, that they relieve the peasants' hardship somewhat . . . would still leave the exploitative relationship of peasants and landlords, and the problem was not and could not be solved.[67]

Hai Jui was limited by his times and his class and could not envision the necessary basic social change—and probably would have opposed it had he been able to envision it. Nevertheless, Hai Jui's character has value transcending time and class, and his courage and concern for the people are worthy of emulation.

In *Hai Jui is dismissed from office* the implicit assumption is not only that Hai Jui is admirable as a person but also that the moral system to which he adheres is admirable. The theme of the work is the violation of accepted norms by those in power. The development of this theme seems to embody a kind of Empsonian ambiguity. On the one side is the assumption that the violated moral system is a valid one; on the other side, given the status of the play as political satire directed toward current problems, is the implication that the Commuist officials today violate the ideals they profess. This ambiguity can perhaps be reconciled: in their different ways and on an abstract level, both traditional and communist society should embody the same moral norms. As the play begins, some local gentry unlawfully seize the land of peasants and kidnap a peasant's daughter. The peasants protest this violation of human and natural law: "Where is the law of the king? Where are the principles of heaven?" They seek redress from the local magistrate, but this worthy, in the fashion of the Peking opera, describes his own character with a little song: "What are documents to an official? When I see money, my heart begins to itch; if you have no money, there is nothing to discuss." The magistrate is bribed by the gentry and the case dismissed. The peasants hear that "Blue-sky Hai" is making an inspection of the area, and they take their problem to him. It turns out, however, that the father of one of the evil gentry is Hsu Chieh, Hai Jui's old benefactor: years before, when Hai Jui had scolded the emperor, Hsu had defended Hai. Hsu does not approve of his son's doings but, for family reasons, feels he must stand by him. As Hsu expresses it in song: "Family affairs are more important to me than affairs of state; I must reconcile myself to being an ox or horse for my children. . . ." Torn between his duty to the state and his duty to his benefactor, Hai Jui consults his mother, who sings to him: "Read the books of the sages and worthies, do as the sages and worthies do; the law of the country must be observed, the distress of the people redressed." Hai Jui then condemns Hsu Chieh's son to death. Hsu Chieh and the other gentry begin to plot against Hai Jui. They decide it would be imprudent to murder him, since Hai Jui "has in the past held military power"—a hint, perhaps, that Hai Jui really is P'eng Te-huai.[68] Instead, Hsu uses his influence at court to have Hai dismissed. Hearing of this, Hai executes Hsu's son before the order dismissing him arrives. (This last part is historically inaccurate, but Wu Han feels it is artistically necessary. In real life, Hsu's son was exiled to the border regions. I think the play's ending is not that great, artistically.)

The play, then, contains at least an implicit defense of an eternal moral order. In their 1961–62 essays Teng and Wu elaborate on the problem of the role of feudal morality. In 1961 Teng discussed the Confucian concept of *li*—ritual, propriety. "Confucius said many things we basically cannot agree with, but his explanation of 'overcome the self and restore ritual' [*k'o chi fu li;* this has been the standard interpretation of the phrase since Sung times, and the interpretation the communists follow, although it is probably not what Confucius meant] . . . has some good sense if you give it a correct explanation." *Ritual* means rules, limits, laws; it is close to the homophonic word *li,* meaning reason or principle.

> No matter what you are doing, there must be certain rules. Probably no one will argue with this. In this sense we also have our ritual. It is absolutely not only the ancients who understood ritual. Our ritual is the sum of moral standards, the rules of life everyone observes.[69]

Teng reduces this to a standard communist morality (the subordination of individual interests to those of the collective) and even to banality (do not talk about state secrets). His critics found less banal implications—that there are, in fact, moral standards that everyone observes, regardless of class. The "Three-family village" wrestled with this humanistic approach throughout 1962. "Ordinarily the moral theories of the ruling class become the moral theories of the ruled class, thus consolidating the rule of the ruling class." In China, Confucian theories "became the standard of right and wrong." But even the ruled shared these values, and they are worth preserving, at least in altered form. Thus, we still need loyalty—now to the country, not to the emperor. There is also obvious good in filial piety: "Could it be children should not take care of their parents?" "The proletariat can absorb certain parts of feudal morality and bourgeois morality, cause its nature to change, and allow it to serve proletarian politics and production."[70]

> If the proletariat is not good at absorbing certain excellent things of the former ruling classes . . . it seems it can only take over [the morality] of the ancient proletariat or depend upon itself and create out of nothing. The problem is, in ancient times there was no proletariat, and to create out of nothing is impossible. . . . If we cannot regard the words and deeds of those feudal times as standards of proletarian morality, we can at least critically succeed to them.[71]

Marxian Confucianism, in sum, would appear to be the Chinese version of the humanistic strain in Marxism, of "communism with a human face."

All of this is what Feng Yu-lan would call abstract. Teng and Wu were condemned not only for their critique of radical relativism; they were also accused of attacking concrete party policy. Yao Wen-yuan, who began the Cultural Revolution with his attack on Wu Han, finds the theme of Wu's play to be the return of the land. Should the people's communes 'return the land'?" To whom? The landlords? Wu Han clearly wants to dismantle the commune system.[72] If Wu Han did in fact advocate returning the land, the circumstances suggest he meant it should be returned to those who had owned it prior to collectivization, not to the landlords; and it seems likely that the faction Wu was affiliated with wished for even more decollectivization than had become party policy. In the preface to *Hai Jui is dismissed from office,* however, Wu is rather coy about the problem of returning land:

> The first four drafts stressed the theme of Hai Jui's order forcing the local elite [*hsiang-kuan*] to return the land they had stolen from the common people. This aroused the common opposition of the local elite, and he was dismissed from office and returned home. The extirpation of tyrants [*ch'u-pa*] was only part of the story, secondary to the return of the land. But many friends pointed out that while Hai Jui's order to return the land is a historical fact, under the conditions of the

> times this could not and did not solve the peasants' problem. In the balance of history, this policy is definitely reformist. What is the point today of writing plays making propaganda for historical reformers? After much discussion, finally the extirpation of tyrants was made the main theme, with the return of the land put in the secondary position. This was a very big change.[73]

Reading between the lines, one gathers Wu did not think much of the regime's agricultural policies but was persuaded by his "many friends" that it would be impolitic to say this too openly. Instead, he concentrates upon the more general issue, tyranny. If peasants may not have their own land, at least their rulers might treat them decently. Overinterpretation is the vice of the Kremlinological method, but one can find further meanings between the lines: Wu may also be suggesting that peasants' problems even now will not be solved by reformist policies such as ending collectivization, unless there is an extirpation of tyranny as well.

Yao, of course, is not happy with Wu Han's "extirpation of tyrants" either. Wu Han calls Hai Jui a virtuous official (*ch'ing kuan*). But in reality, Yao explains, virtuous officials were even worse than corrupt ones, as they disguised the nature of the feudal rule over the peasants. Wu Han claims to be criticizing *hsiang-yuan,* hypocrites, particularly hypocritical upholders of conventional morality. But, Yao reminds us, the rightists of 1957 used the term *hsiang-yuan* to describe "proletarian revolutionary cadres and left-wing democratic personages."[74] If the shoe fits . . .

The writings of Teng T'o and the "Three-family village" concentrate upon the Leap. Sometimes the criticisms are fairly specific (remembering always, of course, the indirect nature of the whole critique). This, for example, is clearly a reference to the "voluntary" labor drafts of 1958–60:

> As early as the Spring and Fall many of the ancient great statesmen knew the important significance of cherishing labor power. Naturally the people of that time, especially ordinary feudal rulers, did not really cherish labor power; but they had to act as if they did in order to obtain and maintain their feudal ruling position. However, from their own experience they discovered the "limits" on the "use of the people's labor"—in fact, they discovered the objective laws of the strengthening and weakening of labor power.

In effect, even if the radicals care nothing about the people, it is in their own interests that they not make the people work too hard. Teng quotes from the *Book of Ritual* to the effect that people should not be made to spend more than three days on public works, and to drive his point home Teng renders "public works" into contemporary jargon as "basic construction."[75]

More commonly, instead of satirizing policies directly, Teng and Wu make fun of the attitudes that underlie them, perhaps, as their enemies say, attempting to create counterrevolutionary public opinion that would eventually permit a formal repudiation of the policies. Teng T'o tells a version of the fable of counting chickens before they are hatched. A poor farmer comes home with an egg and tells his wife he is going to become rich by raising chickens. In ten years' time he will be wealthy; they will have many fine things; he will take a concubine . . . Hearing this, his wife "flared in anger and smashed the egg with her hand."

> That dreamer of wealth knew it takes a long time to accumulate a family fortune. Thus, he planned with his wife to take ten years to get it. This seems reasonable enough. However, his plans simply had no reliable basis, but were founded completely on supposition. . . . Thinking of things ten years hence he completely substituted empty thought for facts. . . . He aroused his wife's anger, and with a blow of her hand she smashed the fortune.[76]

This, we are later told by Teng's critics, is a parable of the Great Leap, with its grandiose, empty plans and its alienation of the peasantry.

Big words are among the most constant targets of these essays.

> [Some people] talk for half a day and you don't know what they are saying. The more they explain the more confused things become, until it is equivalent to no explanation at all. This is the characteristic of big empty words.
>
> A child of our neighbor wrote a poem:
>
> *Old heaven is our father;*
> *Great earth is our mother.*
> *The sun is our nurse.*
> *The east wind is our benefactor,*
> *The west wind our enemy.*
>
> [These are fine-sounding words—but are also overused, empty clichés.] We urge our friends who enjoy great empty talk to read more, think more, speak less. When it is time for you to speak, go rest. Don't waste your own time and the time of others.[77]

The reference to the winds, of course, implies that the Chairman is the big empty talker. Elsewhere Teng suggests that all traditional stories about braggarts be gathered into an anthology and "in that way further arouse attention and raise awareness; this will have an educational significance."[78] This was written in June 1961, but there may be a reference to the work Teng was to undertake for P'eng Chen that fall.

Some of the Teng-Wu critique refers to policies and attitudes that go beyond the Leap. The "Three-family village" discusses a recently published book, *Stories about not being afraid of ghosts*. This is a pretty good book, they say; the only problem is that in all the stories the ghosts people are not afraid of are presented as real. Perhaps there might be a further collection, "stories about people who brag about not being afraid of ghosts but are really scared to death of them." This is probably a reference to the party's talk of how much it trusts the masses, while at the same time it maintains tight control over the population. Teng T'o discusses the traditional concepts, the king's way and the tyrant's way (*wang-tao, pa-tao*). Traditionally, Teng says, the king's way has meant the "combination of a regard for human feelings and the morality of the law." The tyrant's way is rule by violence. Today, "the so-called king's way can be explained as an utterly honest mass-line thought style that proceeds from reality. The so-called tyrant's way can be explained as a raucous, monomaniacal, isolated thought style that depends upon subjective arbitrariness." The critics claim, of course, that Teng was calling People's China a tyranny. He certainly must have considered the radical trend tyrannical. During this period another writer published in the *Kuang-ming Daily* an essay on the Legalist philosopher Han Fei, one of the heroes of the 1973–75 campaign against Confucius. Han Fei was a materialist—if only a "vulgar materialist"—and thus progressive. He opposed the aristocracy. But unlike Confucius, Han Fei was not democratic: he opposed the people as well. He was an advocate of totalitarian rule (*chi-ch'üan t'ung-chih*). His "untrusting psychology and oppressive methods" may have been helpful in consolidating Ch'in, but they also led to the fall of Ch'in.[79]

On the positive side, and most broadly, Teng and Wu strongly defend the notion that there are values in other things than work and politics, asserting, we might say, the interests of normal life:

> What are interests [*hsing-ch'ü*]? . . . They are what the individual enjoys doing. . . . Some like to paint, some like to sing, some like physical exercise, some like to dance, some like to fish, some like to play bridge, and so forth. Doesn't the practice of these secondary interests help cultivate interest in work? Moreover, these secondary interests do not hinder the first interest. . . . You can retain your enjoyment of literature, and your spare time becomes your first interest's broad and lively world of freedom.[80]

Another example comes from Yao Wen-yuan, at his offensively prudish best:

> [Teng T'o] received a letter from a student at the Peking Broadcasting Academy. This "schoolmate" had been undermined by bourgeois thought. His whole brain was full of low tastes; he could only pay attention to the length of the hair of a certain girl on the bus. He wanted Teng T'o to "explain why this kind of long hair has such an effect on me." Teng T'o immediately wrote a typical putrid hoodlum [*Ah Fei*] essay not only supporting that "schoolmate" but also writing an advertisement for the "long hair" of the palace "beauties" of the most lascivious emperors in history.[81]

Most despotisms, perhaps, would like their subjects to be politically apathetic, to find their amusement in things other than politics—in the long hair of girls, for instance—provided restraint is present as well. China, however, is not a simple autocracy, but a totalitarian system in which anything is potentially political. Teng's assertion of value outside politics becomes as much a political act as Ma Yin-ch'u's defense of his scholarly integrity against the claims of politics. Despite his advocacy of depoliticization, Teng himself covertly admits his political aims, praising the Tung Lin scholars of the Ming dynasty for their combination of learning and political activity and their courage in standing up to "reactionary and corrupt power."[82]

During the Cultural Revolution Teng and Wu were accused of wishing to maintain good relations with the Soviet Union, and Merle Goldman, an astute student of contemporary Chinese culture, agrees with this accusation. If true, this would not necessarily mean, as the critics claim, that the two men were traitors. P'eng Chen, supposedly their backstage boss, was in public perhaps the leader most hostile to the Russians in the 1960s; but P'eng may have been dissimulating, and in any case there is nothing to indicate that P'eng and Teng agreed on all things. Teng T'o does seem to have taken exception to the manner of the split with the Soviets. He urges that foreign guests be treated courteously (as they were by the ancients) and that we learn humbly from them. "We must respect the function of the teacher." To show how pro-Soviet Teng was, his enemies quote one example that would seem, however, to have the opposite import. In 1962 he wrote a poem including these lines: "The freezing season brought by the north wind has ended; instead there is the warm east wind. The great earth will quickly thaw." Look, says Yao Wen-yuan: Teng T'o wants a thaw; he is just like Khrushchev.[83] The north wind in Peking blows in from Siberia; the east wind symbolizes China. Teng would seem to be expressing the hope that now that China has broken the Stalinist yoke of dependence upon the Russians, a more human and Chinese kind of communism might begin to flower.

Given Mao's commitment to radicalism at that time, it was perhaps inevitable that Teng and Wu would come into conflict with him. There seems to be a gradual evolution in their attitude toward Mao. In "Hai Jui scolds the emperor" Wu Han follows closely the original text from the *Ming History* (discussed above in chapter 3). This text, it will be recalled, is critical of the emperor but not hostile to him; and the portrait of the emperor is not unsympathetic ("This fellow is worse than Pi Kan, but I am not King Chou [who had Pi Kan dissected to test the theory that the heart of an upright man has seven orifices].") The old text is remarkably appropriate to conditions in the summer of 1959, particularly Hai Jui's strictures against the waste of labor in public works—in basic construction, as Teng T'o would put it. Mao had retired at the end of 1958, and part of the pretext for this was that it would give him more time to study Marxist-Leninist theory, for what Hai Jui calls "cultivating the Way." This essay would be an appeal to Mao as the leader of the party or nation, not of a faction or tendency, to return to court, to reassert his leadership and correct a bad situation.

The emperor does not figure at all in *Hai Jui is dismissed from office,* except as a remote force. The gentry leader Hsu Chieh, however, may symbolize Mao. There are certain parallels: Hsu had formerly supported Hai Jui and had overthrown and replaced the notoriously wicked prime minister Yen Sung (Chiang Kai-shek?); Hsu Chieh, like Mao, is living in retirement (the contemporary time of the play would be 1959) but still takes an active interest in things and has great influence. The picture of Mao, if Hsu Chieh is Mao, is not entirely unfavorable: Hsu's concern for his family is in itself good. It seems Mao is here being criticized for allowing personal considerations and considerations for his "family" (the party) to stand in the way of what he knows is good for the nation.

Hsu Chieh is a good man gone bad. By 1961 the picture of Mao has become more unambiguously hostile. Teng T'o, in an essay, "Study more, criticize less," talks about Wang An-shih, a Sung dynasty statesman who has usually received a good press in People's China. Wang is probably Teng's stand-in for Mao. Wang talked a lot about water conservation (*ta chiang shui-li*). He had many big plans but did not always think things through. Once he proposed draining a lake. Fine, someone said; we'll just dig another hole the same size beside it to hold the water. In the story, Wang had the grace to laugh; his contemporary analogue may have been less amused. Wang was a great man, but he was "very unhumble; we can say this was his big defect [*ta mao-ping*]."[84] Perhaps the "Three-family Village" series' most notorious essay is "Curing amnesia," published in July 1962, as the Maoist counterattack on the capitalist road was coming to a head. "There are many sick people in the world." Those with amnesia are unreliable. People think they are crazy. Amnesia can, in fact, degenerate into idiocy. A Ming dynasty work recommends bathing the patient in a tub of dog's blood (the critics pedantically point out that the work in question is a political satire, not a medical book). Western doctors simply bash the patient over the head with a club. In any case, the patient "needs complete rest: he must say nothing, do nothing. If he is forced to speak or to work, the result will be great chaos."[85] The implication is that Mao has forgotten what happened the last time he had his way, and now it is really time for him to step down.

By 1965 Wu Han seems to have become completely disillusioned, perhaps pushing from fundamental to integral opposition. Wu's major scholarly work, first published in 1944, had been a biography of Chu Yuan-chang, the founder of the Ming dynasty. In 1965 Wu prepared a new edition of this work. There are many similarities between that peasant emperor and Mao—particularly the natures of their last years, although Wu could not have known this in 1965. His last edition, of course, has never been published and probably never will be. It allegedly contains the following passages (culled from criticisms of Wu Han):

> The generals of the red army from a peasant background, after taking power, became a new landlord class. . . . Chu Yuan-chang changed from a leader of a peasant rebellion to a representative of the political interests of the landlord class. . . . [He] was a bureaucrat in the feudal system. . . . His thought changed daily. . . . Finally, he betrayed the peasant revolution, usurping the benefits of the victory of the peasant revolution. He changed from an opponent of the landlord ruling class to its boss . . . and in turn suppressed the peasant revolution. No matter what, this serious crime cannot be lifted from him.[86]

Wu's and Teng's opposition is part of the moderate tendency, in that their policy preferences seem to coincide with those of the rest of that tendency. The rest of that tendency, however, does not necessarily match their more humanistic views. Wu and Teng share with the radicals a *quasi*-libertarian trust in the masses. It is impossible to say what would have happened had their elite sponsors triumphed. Perhaps they would have been less liberal in victory than they were in opposition. This Marxian Confucian movement combines the general tolerance for depoliticization—and hence the potential for evolution away from totalitarianism—of the moderate tendency with the courage to oppose the tide of the radicals. This style of thinking was the first target of the Cultural Revolution. Its political base within the party has been destroyed, and there have been no new manifestations of it. If the ideas of the two men have merit, the ideas may emerge again, although in the near future any proponents of this style of thought are likely to lack the breadth of culture of Teng T'o and Wu Han.

RADICAL OPPOSITION

The radical opposition movements discussed here are a rather miscellaneous assortment. The problem in this section is not merely that at least one such movement (the "May 16 Corps") may never really have existed as such. The major problem is attempting to define just what constitutes radical opposition to a radical regime. If we take the term literally—opposition that goes to the root—we might consider that traditional critics (those, say, who would bring back the Ch'ing dynasty—emperors, examinations, concubines, opium, bound feet, and all) are the real radicals. More moderately, we might proclaim Chiang Kai-shek the foremost Chinese radical of the third quarter of the twentieth century. This, clearly, would be more than a little eccentric.

Most commonly, *radicalism* these days seems to be a term associated mainly with the left (although in some contexts we still hear of the radical right—one common point being, perhaps, the imputation of fantaticism and rejection of the status quo). Radical opposition, then, might be considered opposition from a Marxist standpoint. This, however, would make Teng T'o a radical (as, in some senses of the term, he was, but not in a sense useful here). Also, one group discussed later in this section, the Voice of China, explicitly rejects Marxism. Are they, then, properly radical? If not, how *Marxist* are the groups and movements that are usually considered radical in the world today? Gregor, it will be recalled, pronounces contemporary radicalism to be more nearly fascist than Marxist. One study of the Red Guard movement finds that the radical groups tended to define *class* politically, not economically[87]—and this, if it is Marxist, is a sloppy Marxism. Ritualistic incantation of Marxist terms would not seem to be a sufficient or necessary condition for radicalism.

The easiest course is probably to use *radical* as a term of convenience, as we have heretofore been doing, and then describe the groups and ideas so classified. Still, if movements or groups are called by the same name, it is more elegant if they are found to have at least something in common. We can perhaps give a semioperational definition of radical opposition. Radicalism implies a rejection of much of the status quo and perhaps even an element of fanaticism and monomania; therefore, radical opposition is fundamental or integral. Radical opposition is also nontraditional. While radicals may well share certain values and policy preferences with traditionalists, they will view these in a different way. Radicals are either hostile or indifferent to tradition as such. Radical opposition should also perhaps be seen as directed against established institutions.[88] The Teng-Wu critique constituted strong opposition to certain policies and attitudes, but not (aside, perhaps, from very ambiguous hints by Wu Han) to the system itself; a radical critique would be much more systematic. While radical opposition cannot be identified with Marxism, general radicalism does share certain concepts and attitudes with Marxism. Although it is probably no favor to Marx to harp too much on Marxist ideals, what are commonly taken as Marxian values are certainly generally radical as well: an end to class rule (eventually, and however defined), to material human misery (and hence all human misery), to inequality. Like Marxism, radicalism is generally historicist: our values are reflections of our material conditions, and history moves through stages. Radicals generally hold also that what corrupts a man comes from outside him. Radicals also seem to believe it is possible to build a new heaven and a new earth: radical opposition, then, tends to be voluntarist.

More generally the radical mind is said to be characterized by an "uncompromising denial and rejection of existing reality."[89] This turn of mind is not new (Taoism; in a way, Christianity), although the notion that through politics all things can be made new is probably fairly recent. Perhaps the key word in radicalism is *liberation,* a freeing from external restraint (or internal restraint coming from an external source), even from necessity. Teng T'o could speak of freedom, the ability and opportunity to do as one pleases; but he also liked the *li*—manners, rules, restraints. Radicalism stresses the freeing of the human person from all restraint and all alienation. This vision is no doubt impossible, and attempts to realize it have had more than their share of viciousness; but for all that, it is still noble.

In the Chinese context the obvious target of radicalism is bureaucracy, since it is the bureaucracy that imposes restraints and stands in the way of the realization of the vision. Radicalism is nourished in China because the official ideology is in part hostile to bureaucracy, while at the same time the regime requires bureaucracy: it is both criticized and omnipresent. Ralf Dahrendorf argues that the experience of Communist countries decisively refutes any assertion that private property is a necessary condition for human bondage; any working society is a society with inequalities of power: "The origin of inequality is thus to be found in the existence of all human societies of norms of behavior to which sanctions are attached. . . . There is inequality because there is law; if there is law, there must be inequality among men."[90] In China, bureaucratic routines are at least a partial substitute for law. The establishment radicals (those who compose the radical tendency) seem to be the most consistent radicals in their opposition to law. We have discussed the 1975 radical attack on *fa-ch'üan,* legal rights. The term and the criticism of it go back to 1958, to Chang Ch'un-ch'iao, then an obscure propagandist in Shanghai. Chang reflects on the tradition of the soldiers of the Red Army, who cared for neither comfort nor promotion:

> After liberation of the whole country this "common supply system" characteristic of military communism still had a very sweet savor. . . . Some revolutionary youths immediately joined the revolution and also hoped for a "common supply system," wishing to be like the old comrades. . . . Originally the comrades under the common supply system did not covet any salary system but enjoyed it as an expression of a life-system of equal relations. However, not long after, this life-system was attacked by bourgeois legal-rights thought. . . . The nucleus of bourgeois legal-rights thought is a system of unequal distinctions. . . .

People have begun to call the good old ways a rural or guerrilla style. They say it "does not give incentives for production activism," that people need material incentives. These people sound just like Chiang Kai-shek and the rightists. They are no doubt corrupt. The Red Army did not need material incentives; neither did the Paris Commune; neither do the workers of Shanghai.[91]

The workers of Shanghai may in fact not be that uniformly enthusiastic. Since what is "commonly supplied" turns out to be rather little, some may see the system as exploitation. Chang here falls into what might be called the Jesuit fallacy—the assumption that a life-style that may suit some, say, a volunteer army, suits everyone else just as well. More seriously, Chang ignores (but hardly forgets) that inequality of power is necessary to maintain economic equality, just as it would be required to maintain any other distribution of income. The establishment radicals are concerned with enforcing their will and do not falsify Dahrendorf's generalization about law. The liberation of the establishment radicals comes at the expense of that of others, and to that extent their radicalism is limited, a pseudoradicalism—although some of the time they have been in opposition, and some of their ideas have influenced other radicals, even inside China. Other radicals discussed in this section have attempted to meet the problem Dahrendorf poses in another way—in effect, in Dahrendorf's own way. They recognize the need for law but argue it should be both regularized and flexible, able to permit and regulate spontaneous competition within society. Cynics may say these radicals (Lin Hsi-ling, Li I-che) feel the way they do because they are in no position to impose their own wills. Whatever their motives, in their radicalism we see a dialectical convergence of radicalism with liberalism or with some of the positions of the Marxian Confucians, a Chestertonian revolt into sanity.

There was no discussion of radical interests in the last chapter, since radicalism can be a response to the failure to satisfy many particular interests. To a certain extent, however, radical interests can be seen as the converse of bureaucratic interests. Opportunism, of course, may lead some, such as, perhaps, the provincial party secretaries in 1958, to espouse radicalism (although this was hardly radical *opposition*). Taking opportunism more broadly, radical movements may be a way out for the dispossessed. The Cultural Revolution, for example, provided an opportunity for redress by cadres who considered themselves unjustly treated by their superiors.[92] In a study of radical Red Guards in Kwangtung, it is hypothesized that the radicals were children from bourgeois families, who are targets of discrimination by the regime.[93] Youth in general, particularly educated youth, are also a source of radicalism, for reasons discussed in the last chapter. The structure of party rule itself may work to make radicalism all the more appealing to young people. In 1961 it was reported that 80 percent of the party had joined since 1949, 70 percent since 1953, and 40 percent since 1956.[94] The bulk of the party, then, was extremely young, but positions of influence were held by the old 20 percent. Since the Cultural Revolution all party committees are supposed to include the old, middle-aged, and young, but it is likely that in general promotion remains slow. The young both within and without the party may feel they have an interest in shaking things up.

A further condition making for radicalism is that young persons most temperamentally inclined to radicalism are often those who have been extended the dirty end of the stick. In 1957 *China Youth* published a bitterly outspoken letter from a disappointed young man. "In 1950, when Kwangtung was liberated, I was in my first year at the university. Because I wished to make revolution, I responded to the summons of the organization, left school, and joined work." He participated in land reform and spent three years in the army, fighting in Korea. Now he is stuck with low pay as a low-level cadre. "I am not even a section head." "I have seen my schoolmates over the years. At school they were not as successful as I, and their thought awareness, of course, is much inferior to mine; but since they did not break off their studies" they all have interesting and important work and "have a broad future." Even his little brother gets to go study in the Soviet Union (this seems especially galling). His friends live in luxury, while "I have given my spring-green youth to the revolution." People tell him all the old platitudes: "reward according to contribution," he is unqualified, etc., and accuse him of individualism. But precisely by joining the revolution he showed he did not care about selfish interests. "I think that in the past I was a perfect melon-head [*sha-kua*] and they were the intelligent ones."[95] We might dismiss this as a spectacle of selfless dedication finally shuffling up to the back door, holding out its hand for a tip; but we can also, I think, appreciate the boy's sense of the injustice of things. He and those like him could no doubt be easily persuaded to join a movement denouncing the new class of educated (sneer) "experts." He could possibly even bring himself to rail against material incentives.

There was a similar letter in 1973—following the trend of the times, less interesting and probably less honest. This was from a boy, sent back to his home on a commune in Liaoning, who found himself unable to pass a college entrance exam, as he had been out of school three years. While he had been serving the people, the brats back in the cities had been going to school, and they were allowed to test directly into the universities—and both tests and direct entrance into college had supposedly been abolished by the Cultural Revolution.[96] This young man, Chang T'ieh-sheng, happened to write at an opportune moment and now has himself comfortably established as a house radical. He is studying to become a veterinarian, although he seems to spend as much time censoring the morals of his schoolmates and teachers as he does learning how to help sick animals.

The analysis so far is, in good social-science fashion, a diagnosis of Chinese radicalism. It concentrates upon who the radicals are and what their motives might be, not upon what they say. This is also the approach the regime itself takes toward radical opposition: it can hardly admit the validity of radical criticisms of the system, so the fault must be in the radicals themselves. The establishment radicals are willing to criticize the system to some degree, but what if someone is more radical than they? The moderate tendency can find good Marxist categories to turn against the radicals: infantile leftists, petty bourgeois anarchists, reactionaries, and the like. This reaction is more difficult for the establishment radicals, since criticisms of this nature reflect upon them as well. Given the usual predominance of radical ideology, Chinese radicals who run afoul of those in power come to be denounced in rather classless personal terms. The propagandist Jack Chen (who seems to be a rather bourgeois type) was treated roughly by the leftists in the Cultural Revolution, and he unburdens himself about those leftists who failed to stay on top:

> They were sociopaths. Aberrants in the new society. They were deficient in conscience and morality. They lacked the feeling of sympathy, of suffering sympathetic pain or anguish. They lacked sympathetic imagination. Their arrogance and self-confidence, their over-weening belief in their own probity, their personal ambition founded on self-righteousness, their self-love and blind self-admiration left them insensitive to the feelings of others. Their ruthlessness was seen by themselves as determination; their egoistic drive as vitality; their amorality as realism.[97]

They must have been formed evil in their mothers' wombs.

This kind of criticism, of course, serves many functions, including that of showing that Mao, Uncle Chou, and the rest had nothing to do with the atrocities of the Cultural Revolution: could they help it if there happened to be monsters loose in the land? The explanation is not completely satisfactory, however, even to a non-Marxist. These people may be aberrants of the new society, but they are also *products* of the new society (which explicitly taught them, by the way, that one is to feel no sympathetic pain or anguish for those belonging to the wrong class). Oppositional attitudes can spring from personal discontent or from moral deformity, but they usually have some objective basis as well.

A Prelude: Lin Hsi-ling

The mainstream of the Hundred Flowers dissent—that by professors and assorted celebrities of yesteryear—was liberal. Some of the criticism by the young, however, was of a radical nature, directed against the party's bureaucratism, one of the official targets of the campaign. Many of the younger generation perceived the party as having lost its élan and, after consolidating its rule, having settled down to become the new ruling class.[98] The youths felt the party remote from them; to use a term fashionable in the West, but not in China, they felt alienated. A college student wrote to Tung Pi-wu, one of the party's grand old men, that "our leaders do not pay sufficient attention to our spiritual lives." "I hope that our leaders, Chairman Mao, Premier Chou, Comrade Liu Shao-ch'i, and others, will from time to time give speeches to us university students."[99] Tung's reply is less than helpful: the leaders give lots of speeches; anyway, if you want to know what they think, all you have to do is read the editorials in the newspapers. They are too busy to give speeches to students. The student seems to feel that editorials are not enough: "I think our leaders and chiefs are very mysterious." No one knows what they are doing; even county-level cadres work in secret. In a pattern fairly common in Chinese dissident writings, the author of the letter makes the loudest complaints about something relatively trivial and then mentions the real horrors in passing. Thus, students are not alone in being neglected by the regime. He cites a published story of a worker who was forced to commit suicide by some cadres. In his own village a whole family fell sick, no one was able to work, and "no one came to see them." They apparently starved. "I think that 90 percent of the workers and peasants are too hard-pressed. . . . Everyone knows that our laboring people have an outstanding tradition of being able to bear hardship, of frugality. But because of this we cannot take lightly the lives of the worker-peasant masses."[100]

In late April 1957, as the flowers were coming into bloom, Chou En-lai took a stroll through Hangchow with Klimenti Voroshilov and some other Russians. "The walls of Peking are high," Chou says. "They easily create a division between the leaders and the masses." Voroshilov says walls at least keep bureaucratism from spreading outside. They are also a temporary defense against the masses, Chou says, "but walls can be breached." He point to two children: "If our bureaucratism is not reformed, someday they will smash our walls." He then addresses the children: "After ten years, if there is still bureaucratism in the leadership, you must rebel."[101] Some children, in fact, did rebel ten years later; in 1976 they rebelled again. Some also rebelled in May 1957.

The most notorious student rebel of that time was Lin Hsi-ling (per pen name; her real name was Ch'eng Hai-kuo). Miss Lin had joined the PLA at the age of fifteen and was discharged in 1953—perhaps against her will, since she complains the PLA no longer takes women comrades.[102] In 1957 she was a fourth-year law student at China People's College, a party school founded in 1950; she was thus the equivalent of what would now be called a worker-peasant-soldier study personnel, not the sort of person the regime would expect trouble from. She had published her maiden essay in 1955, when she was about nineteen, a piece of standard Marxist scholasticism discussing Balzac, Tolstoy, and the "counterrevolutionary Hu Feng." Hu Feng says a realist style has nothing to do with a writer's worldview. He is wrong: realism is always progressive. "Some comrades" hold there is a contradiction, however, between the [advanced] style and [reactionary] world views of the "critical realists," people like Balzac and Tolstoy. Actually, their style does reflect their world views: it is simply that their world views are contradictory. Balzac knew all about exploitation, but he was a royalist. Tolstoy knew the Russian people defeated Napoleon, but he believed in God. The contradictions of their thought reflect the contradictions in their societies, and we must evaluate them from the point of view of the proletariat.[103] One would like to find in this a covert defense of Hu Feng, of realism, and of writing that can transcend the officially set mold; if a defense is there, it is mighty covert. No one in 1955 denied literary merit to authors who were not orthodox Marxists, but similarly in 1955 no one in mainland China had the excuse of Balzac or Tolstoy of living in a backward society. Miss Lin should probably be taken at her word: "In the past I too wrote articles criticizing Hu Feng. Now I believe this was very childish and shameful on my part."[104]

Miss Lin began to bloom only when the schools began to contend. In May she delivered a series of public addresses at Peking University (in those days a more serious institution than China People's College), developing a Marxist-like critique of a Marxist society. The Stalinist tyranny, she argued, cannot be explained by Stalin's personality; it is a distortion of socialism in a backward country, and China has the same problem.

> Marxism tells us that all social phenomena have their social and historical origins. The problem of Stalin is not the problem of Stalin the individual; the problem of Stalin could only arise in a country like the Soviet Union, because in the past it had been a feudal, imperialist nation. China is the same, for there has been no tradition of bourgeois democracy. This could not have happened in France. I believe that public ownership is better than private ownership, but I hold that the socialism we have now is not genuine socialism; or that if it is our socialism is not typical. Genuine socialism should be democratic, but ours is undemocratic. I venture to say our society is a socialist one created on a feudal foundation; it is not typical socialism, and we must struggle for genuine socialism!
>
> . . . After some study, I have come to believe that all ruling classes in history have one thing in common: their democracy is limited. The democracy of the Communist Party has limits too. During the tempest of the revolution party members stayed together with the people, but after the victory of the revolution they climbed up to the ruling position and ideological limits were imposed. They want to suppress the people; they adopt policies aimed at deceiving the people.

"A real solution to problems depends," not upon any self-rectification by the party, but "on the actions of the masses of the people, the creators of history."[105]

Like the Maoists of the Cultural Revolution, Miss Lin finds no problem with the economic relations; the trouble is the superstructure. For Miss Lin this means, in particular, the "contradiction between the rulers and the ruled":

> All ruling classes have common limitations; this is an objective law. I have studied this for a long time but didn't dare discuss it before. . . .
>
> In the present socialist society, the interests of the working class coincide with those of the people. But there are still contradictions among the people that are expressed in relations between the ruler and the ruled. . . . The ruler and the ruled are in different positions; they look at problems from different angles, and their interests are not the same. . . . This is a nonantagonistic contradiction. But when it develops, from a quantitative change to a qualitative change, it will erupt as an antagonistic one.

Miss Lin expresses in literal terms the radical rejection of existing reality:

> To feel dissatisfied with reality, I believe, is a good thing. People should be encouraged to feel this way. The philosophical foundation of being contented with reality is the soul of Hegel coming back to life. Hegel had absolute ideas. Now some of the leaders have also become Hegels.
>
> Socialism is the best, highest, and most beautiful form of society. The word "most" is metaphysical. In the future there will be a better form of society. If I were to live in "X" society five hundred years from now, I would be dissatisfied, for society is progressive. . . . Had the apes been content with reality we would not be men today. . . . But now some gentlemen chant cheap anthems, continually making comparisons with the Kuomintang and capitalism, always looking back rather than ahead.[106]

Most of Miss Lin's specific criticisms come from the left, and many were revived (without attribution) by the Red Gaurds of the 1960s. Interest paid to expropriated capitalists should be abolished; party members should not enjoy special privileges; "the ranking system has permeated every aspect of life"; the Soviet style adopted by the army "makes for bad relations between the officers and the soldiers"; the party is penetrated by feudal, fascist, even slave ideology. Some of her complaints, however, might be considered rightist. Thus, she objects to party control of literature. Hu Feng was correct; he has been vindicated by the Hundred Flowers policy. He should never have been jailed; his case should never have been for the courts and the police. The problem is, the case "concerns the Chairman."[107] There is no rule of law in China. We have killed 770,000 people—720,000 of them on the basis of false charges.

> The problem is that the Party has taken the place of the government. The Communist Party is the party in power. . . . The law is only a matter of formality. The Soviet constitution is even more specious [than ours]. . . . We have no judicial system; the judge's verdict is final. . . .
>
> When you disagree with the leadership you are opposed to the leadership; to be opposed to the leadership is to be opposed to the organization; to be opposed to the organization is to be antiparty; to be antiparty is to be opposed to the people; to be opposed to the people is counterrevolutionary. Applying this formula in rendering a verdict is nothing but the method of Stalin.[108]

Here we see a convergence between radicalism and liberalism; we shall see it again.

Lin Hsi-ling graciously allowed that the contradiction between her and her rulers was nonantagonistic. Her rulers disagreed. She disappeared after the crackdown on the bourgeois rightists.

Establishment Radicalism

Those who are called here the establishment radicals have often spoken of rebellion, but it is not clear to what extent they should be considered opposition, that is, taken at their word. On the other hand, someone once suggested to me that Chairman Mao was China's most outstanding oppositionist, and if we refrain from sentimentalizing him, there may be a sense in which this is not entirely fatuous. While the radical tendency has usually dominated ideology, it has rarely dominated concrete policy; and attempts by radicals to have their way in actual practice constitute opposition of a sort. Also, particularly in the early days of the Cultural Revolution, the behavior of Mao and his radical supporters was in gross violation of the norms of a Leninist party. From the point of view of their victim, Liu Shao-ch'i, this seemed a species of counterrevolution. Liu Shao-ch'i had, he says, taken over the direction of the Cultural Revolution in May 1966. Rather than allow the mass movement among students to go its own way (remembering 1957), he sent party work teams into the schools. The work teams were far from gentle in their methods (Liu must not be sentimentalized either). Teachers and some students were humiliated; some were killed. The teachers were bourgeois intellectuals, the sort of people who would sympathize with what P'eng Chen had seemed to stand for, and thus could be anyone's goat. The students were treated roughly because they resisted outside direction by the regular work teams (some students were probably already in contact with anti-Liu segments of the party). To Liu, the disciplined Leninist, opposition to the work teams meant opposition to the party and (to complete Lin Hsi-ling's sorites) to the people and to the revolution:

> I did not understand that the Great Proletarian Cultural Revolution was a deeper and broader new stage in our country's socialist revolution. In order to implement the Great Proletarian Cultural Revolution . . . it is necessary truly to walk the mass line, to go deeply and broadly into the masses, promote the proletarian rebellious spirit of the masses. My method at that time was not to trust the masses, not to rely on the masses, not to dare to unleash the masses that they might achieve their own liberation. I believed in the function of work teams, sending in work teams as a substitute for mass revolution. I was afraid of chaos, afraid of big democracy, afraid that the masses would rebel against us, afraid that counterrevolutionary elements would mount the stage.[109]

Liu, a good comrade bound by norms that his enemies scorned, confessed and banged his head. Some of his fears have not been realized: big democracy, for example, did not last all that long. Still, he may have continued to think that the triumph of his enemies was in fact the triumph of counterrevolution; the Cultural Revolution did bring a qualitative change to the regime.

There have been many studies of the origins and development of the Cultural Revolution, although it would be silly to pretend we understand everything about it.[110] The fights that culminated in the Cultural Revolution date, according to official interpretations, into the 1930s and even 1920s; more concretely, they date from the 1959 Lushan plenum or the Eighth Party Congress of 1956. The Cultural Revolution began as a reaction to the Marxian Confucian opposition of 1961–62. This opposition to opposition can be construed as valid opposition, at least initially, since the radicals were attempting to overthrow the leadership of the Propaganda Department that had tolerated the earlier opposition to radicalism, and their ultimate goal was the overthrow of the party establishment generally. In the area of concrete policy, the party establishment had the situation fairly well in hand throughout the early 1960s. The rural socialist education movement initiated by Mao in late 1962 soon came under the control of Liu Shao-ch'i, who pursued a policy " 'left' in form, right in substance,"[111] which probably means Liu's policies could not be faulted ideologically, but the wrong people were being purged. The ideological line became harshly leftist, but the capitalist-road policies remained generally unchanged.

The struggle in the field of culture, where the Marxian Confucian dissidents had carried out their attacks, was perhaps more principled, and here the radicals had more success. The cultural revolution narrowly construed took its inspiration from the most colorful of the establishment radicals, the Chairman's wife, Chiang Ch'ing. In 1966 Miss Chiang said she had been ill some years earlier (1961 or 1962?)—trouble with what she calls the "functions of my organs of hearing and sight." Her doctor told her she ought to "spend more time in cultural pursuits." The culture of the time was not the sort of thing to bring peace to her soul, however: the stage was full of plays about ghosts, emperors, princesses, and Hai Jui getting dismissed from office. "I began to feel that if our literature and art did not correspond to the social-economic base, they would inevitably wreck it."[112]

Chiang Ch'ing encouraged the writing of modern, revolutionary Peking operas focusing on contemporary events and expressing a socialist world view. The monsters in the Propaganda Department put up resistance, but she won the support of K'o Ch'ing-shih, the boss of Shanghai.[113] K'o died in 1965, and Shanghai passed into more conservative hands; but Miss Chiang continued to enjoy the services of two of the younger Shanghai apparatchiks, Chang Ch'un-ch'iao and Yao Wen-yuan. Miss Chiang also won the support of Ch'en Po-ta, editor of *Red Flag* and the Chairman's long-time spokesman and personal secretary, and of K'ang Sheng, a native of Shantung like herself, perhaps her original sponsor in the party, and reputedly head of the secret police and espionage system. She also had the support of Lin Piao's army.

In addition to promoting new plays, Chiang Ch'ing's group conducted a kind of guerrilla warfare against the Liu Shao-ch'i–P'eng Chen establishment. In

1963 Ch'i Pen-yü, an underling of Ch'en Po-ta's, attacked one of the leaders of the Taiping rebellion who had signed a confession when captured by the imperial forces. The accepted party interpretation of this had been that the confession was a means of buying time for the rebels. Not so, Ch'i said; the man was a traitor.[114] This, it later transpired, was an attack upon persons (including P'eng Chen) who had entered the party under the sponsorship of Liu Shao-ch'i and who, captured while undertaking messy and dangerous "white areas" work, had written anti-communist confessions to secure their own release.

The open attack on the establishment began in November 1965 with Yao Wen-yuan's criticism of Wu Han. The case, for some reason, was turned over to P'eng Chen, who then headed the first Cultural Revolution Group. It is impossible to say whether this shows P'eng's influence or the organizational strength of the established party machine, or whether it was simply a matter of giving P'eng enough rope. The radicals were represented on P'eng's group by K'ang Sheng. In February 1966 P'eng Chen submitted a Report Outline on the case. What Wu Han did is inexcusable. He misinterprets history. But this is an academic question, and a hundred flowers should bloom. Problems such as this should not be resolved by fiat from the school lords (*hsueh-fa*). "Everyone is equal before the truth."[115] After a further series of intrigues—perhaps by P'eng Chen, certainly by his enemies—P'eng was purged in May.

Then Liu Shao-ch'i, of all people, took direct charge of the Cultural Revolution, purging the supporters of his fallen disciple from the schools and from party organizations. The Chiang-Ch'en-K'ang cabal gained partial control of the Cultural Revolution Group but had to share this control with T'ao Chu, the former boss of the South-Central Region and now the new Propaganda boss. By one of the ironies of the times—ironies so numerous as to become tedious—T'ao's ideological and policy preferences seem to have been identical with those of P'eng Chen, although T'ao was probably a political ally of Lin Piao's.[116] In July Mao, who had been away (probably sick), returned to Peking after his fantastic swim in the Yangtze and ordered the work teams withdrawn.[117] Liu Shao-ch'i was demoted in August and purged, along with Teng Hsiao-p'ing, in October. Liu's name began appearing on wall posters in December, and the following spring he was attacked in the public press,[118] although until 1968 he was not publicly called by name but by code words ("The greatest person in power within the party walking the capitalist road" [Teng Hsiao-p'ing was "another person in power . . ."]; "China's Khrushchev").

By December 1966, Red Guards, no doubt inspired by Chiang Ch'ing, had begun to criticize T'ao Chu, and T'ao was overthrown within the month. This gave the Chiang-Ch'en-K'ang clique full control of the Cultural Revolution Group (aside from a shifting and not very effective series of military representatives) and also prevented the rapid reconsolidation of civilian party control. The Cultural Revolution Group acted as a kind of general headquarters for the radical

Red Guard groups, and the actions of the radicals brought the group into conflict with the military. By early fall 1967, a consensus had apparently been reached among Mao, Lin, and Chou that the Red Guard anarchy had lasted long enough; over the following months all of the lower-ranking members of the Cultural Revolution Group beneath the big three, with the exceptions of Chang Ch'un-ch'iao and Yao Wen-yuan, were purged as part of the "ultra-'left' May 16 Corps." In early fall 1968, the surviving radicals abandoned the Red Guards to their fate.

The radicalism of the establishment radicals is found in its most pristine form prior to the sell-out of 1967: the purge of the May 16 Corps is a symbol of the rejection of radicalism by the evolving power constellation in China and of the at least opportunist compliance in this by the establishment radicals. In chapter 3 we examined the radical critique of party discipline and democratic centralism. In their rejection of the institutionalized authority of the party, although not perhaps in their submission to the person of Mao, the establishment radicals seem truly radical. The departure from Leninist norms was justified in the same terms as those used by other disgruntled leftists from Robert Michels through Leon Trotsky to Milovan Djilas or Lin Hsi-ling: the party had become a new ruling class; the institution had become an end in itself and had betrayed the ends it was originally intended to serve. Ch'i Pen-yü said:

> The navigation by these people is no good. They spend the whole day thinking how to coexist peacefully with the Soviet revisionists. They don't want tension. They say: you are causing tension; you are ruining relations with Soviet revisionism; you are isolated; the imperialists oppose you; many countries oppose you; we'll never get into the U.N. They are scared to death. They want to surrender to the enemy. They say the villages are not doing well: we need to set quotas at the household! Divide the land up among the peasants! Let Wu Han . . . prepare public opinion for a capitalist restoration. If these people take the helm of our country they will become a new nobility. Some of you Communists can turn your backs on your class and become a new nobility. There are only a few, but the broad masses of the workers and peasants are still treated as horses and cattle. Our state can become a revisionist state, compromise with imperialism, not help Vietnam, compromise with Soviet revisionism. Isn't this the restoration of capitalism? Our broad laboring people will once again become horses and cattle.[119]

This statement is eloquent in a way, but it also shows some of the limitations of establishment radicalism. Instead of a rejection of existing reality there is in part a stubborn defense of existing reality, such as collectivized agriculture—a policy which, it can be plausibly argued, encourages the treatment of peasants like horses and cattle. The appeal of establishment radicalism seems to have been limited among the broad laboring people, although the tendency found favor among students.

To overthrow the new class and prevent its reemergence, the radicals originally urged direct mass action and participatory democracy along the lines of the Paris Commune as interpreted by Karl Marx. "The masses must liberate themselves." In February 1967 the Shanghai Commune was formed, and there were also moves by some to set up a Peking People's Commune.[120] In common with the radical Red Guards, the establishment radicals tended to define class in political terms and to focus upon the mechanics of seizing power: "Chairman Mao has taught us again and again that the question of revolution is the question of political power. The purpose of every revolutionary struggle in the world is to seize and consolidate political power."[121]

This outspoken, almost libertarian, radicalism did not survive the clamping down on the Red Guard movement. Since then, establishment radicalism has become more tame—not to say conservative. After the Cultural Revolution the establishment radicals tended to concentrate upon rather defensive defenses of specifics, particularly of "revolutionary new-born things" (*ko-ming hsin-sheng shih-wu*). The list of these varies but usually includes Chiang Ch'ing's model operas, the educational revolution, the rural health-care movement, the May 7 Cadre Schools, and the sending of educated youth "up to the mountain, down to the farm." Sometimes even the people's commune is considered a new-born thing. These programs, in themselves, would not all seem to be meaningfully radical, but they are the programs with which the radical tendency has associated itself. The phrase *new-born things* is meant to imply that they are not perfect; as Marx says, "All developing things are imperfect."[122] This stress on imperfection is less an incentive to improve the new-born things, however, than an excuse to attack those who criticize them: since it is impossible for a new-born thing not to have defects, anyone who finds fault with it must be acting in bad faith.

Certain ideological lines seem to have been associated with the establishment radicals since the Cultural Revolution, although it is difficult to be too certain of this. A cornerstone of the radical position has perhaps been the concept of "continuing revolution under the dictatorship of the proletariat," a phrase introduced by Lin Piao. The idea of continuing revolution (*chi-hsu ko-ming*— or, more rarely, uninterrupted revolution, *pu-tuan ko-ming*) goes back to the Great Leap; the term is said not to be the same as Trotsky's similar-sounding one, although the distinction is not clearly explained. Lin Piao called the combination of continuing (or continuous) revolution with proletarian dictatorship one of Mao's "great theories," although the phrase is not in quotes, nor is it ever put in heavy type, as all the Chairman's pronouncements have been since the Cultural Revolution.[123] Mao apparently never used the words. It is tempting to say this theory is Lin Piao's own, although Lin's son denounced it and it has continued in use since Lin's death, if less frequently than before.

The purge of Ch'en Po-ta in 1970 seemed to signal a general crackdown on the left. But while the year preceding Lin's death is a low-mark in the fortunes of the Chinese radicals, even then they do not seem to have been silenced completely. Most of the criticisms of Ch'en interpreted his idealism as a refusal to face facts, as a contention that revolutionary spirit could overcome all things. But one strain criticized Ch'en for his "humanism," for his belief that human nature transcends class.[124] Applied to Ch'en this sounds like a joke, since his public position had been just the opposite.[125] This may have been a way of criticizing Ch'en's enemies under the pretext of criticizing Ch'en.

Chiang Ch'ing was inactive prior to Lin's death and quite active afterward. Lin's failure may have been her salvation. Radicalism continued to have a bad press, however, for another year. In the summer of 1972 the radicals had apparently developed their new soteriology, explaining their past misfortunes (and unhappy alliances) and promising new glory. The new line, which would seem to tie in with continuing revolution, is expressed in Mao's purported 1966 letter to Chiang Ch'ing. Mao says he cannot voice his doubts about Lin Piao, since this will only encourage the rightists. The struggle will not be completely victorious; there will be others.

> Great chaos under heaven leads to great order under heaven. After seven or eight years it will come again. The cow-devils and snake-spirits will jump up by themselves. This is a function of their class nature; they cannot help but jump up. . . . Our current task is to beat down the rightists in the whole party and all parts of the country (naturally we cannot get them all). After seven or eight years there will be another movement to sweep away cow-devils and snake-spirits. We must do this many times.[126]

The leftists will have hard times, but their own times will come again. In the fashion of the older Chinese dialectic, order breeds chaos, chaos order. The fight goes on forever. This involves at least a partial retreat from radical voluntarism: the cow-devils and snake-spirits, at least, are puppets of their class nature. An exegesist notes that Mao treated Lin with benevolence and righteousness (*jen-i*), but Lin just couldn't help himself; "he didn't reform a bit."[127]

By early 1973 there was a major change in the evaluation of Lin Piao. After his death Lin had been condemned mainly as a leftist. In 1972 the radical preoccupation with the seizure of power had been condemned as "empty-headed politics."[128] In the context, this was an attack on radical voluntarism generally. A year later, however, it was explained that the comrades who developed this critique are "muddled." Lin's politics were not at all "empty-headed" but were "concrete landlord-bourgeois reactionary politics." Some say Lin was an "extreme 'leftist,' " or "first 'left,' later right." Those who say this are stupid.

Lin may have pretended to be a leftist, but he was "right in his bones." He was "an unadulterated big rightist."[129] All of this, of course, tells more about the evolving balance of forces than about Lin Piao. From this point the establishment radicals seemed to have returned to their accustomed position, dominating (although not completely) ideology, but not policy. After this it is probably no longer meaningful to consider them as opposition. In August the radicals began to speak of opposing the tide; but by that time they themselves were once again a strong tide.

The May 16 Corps

In September 1967, Yao Wen-yuan wrote an essay on his former ally, T'ao Chu, a very wicked man. In 1955 T'ao showed sympathy for counterrevolutionaries. In 1957 he said, "The function of dictatorship should be weakened." In 1959 he said, "even the sun has blackspots," an obvious slap at Chairman Mao, the most red, red sun in our hearts. T'ao thought communism means "good food, good clothes, good housing"—a "hedonist" philosophy, and a "philosophy of the lowest traitors." He loved capitalism and hated socialism. In passing, Yao entertains us again with his thoughts on sex:

> Didn't T'ao Chu once archly and frivolously say to some young people, "There are men in the world, and women, so there is love." Huh? This immediately makes people think of China's Khrushchev's asinine saying, "If you put a cow with a cow it is still a cow . . . but if you put a bull with a cow you get a new relationship, the relationship of men and women together as husbands and wives. All things are necessarily a contradictory unity." As these scoundrels see it, relations between humans are the same as those between bulls and cows. In a class society people divide and unite along class lines. Sexual relations are no exception.

T'ao also thought writers should have creative freedom. He is a "Khrushchev-like ambitionist." Yao concludes, however, with a surprise: in 1966 T'ao appeared in the guise of an "ultra-'left' anarchist." He said: "Anyone can be opposed"; "Doubt everything." He was just like the members of the "May 16 Corps."[130]

As far as I know, this is the only mention in the national media of the mysterious May 16 Corps, although much has been said unofficially. Yao's depiction of T'ao Chu as an anarchist seems tacked on—it was probably added just prior to publication—and involves a distortion of what T'ao actually did say.[131] The main purpose of the ending of Yao's essay is not so much to attack T'ao as to signal a turn against the left, the ultra-"left" being depicted as a giant subversive conspiracy. Yao does not tell us who the May 16 Corps actually are, but other sources reveal they are Yao's friends: Wang Li, Ch'i Pen-yü, Kuan Feng, Chao I-yu, Lin Chieh, and Mu Hsin—the entire leadership of the Central

Cultural Revolution Group except for Yao, Chang Ch'un-ch'iao, and the big three.[132] The May 16 Corps was a "secret counterrevolutionary organization." It "directed the spearhead of struggle" against Chou En-lai, "not as an individual," but as part of an attempt to overthrow the government. It opposed the PLA, advocating the "dragging out of a handful in the army." It won a following among students: "Young students, being inexperienced, are prone to being taken in."[133] Its members had a "wolfish ambition to usurp the Party." They advocated "doubt all, oppose all," just like T'ao Chu, although, being scoundrels and opportunists, when T'ao fell they were the first to attack him. They burned the British embassy.[134] They opposed Lin Piao. They "collected black materials" on Chiang Ch'ing.[135] They colluded with Hsiao Hua and (later) Yang Ch'eng-wu in the army—Hsiao and Yang, in fact, were the men behind the group.[136]

This, at any rate, is the legend, the approved telling of the story. The purge of the May 16 Corps was obviously a triumph for Chou En-lai and the regional soldiers. The purge seems to have grown out of the Wuhan incident. In the summer of 1967 Ch'en Tsai-tao, the commander of Wuhan, had supported the Million Heroes, a conservative Red Guard faction, against their radical opponents. On July 14 Hsieh Fu-chih, the minister of public security, flew to Wuhan together with Wang Li. Wang Li behaved in an arrogant and obnoxious fashion, attacking Ch'en Tsai-tao. On July 20 some of the Million Heroes killed Wang's bodyguard and abducted him, while Hsieh was placed under house arrest. Lin Piao may have then sent in troops under direct central command, while Chou En-lai flew to Wuhan to negotiate. On July 22 Wang was released.[137] Returning to Peking, Wang, together with Kuan Feng, collaborated with Lin Chieh to write the July 31 article attacking the handful in the army.[138] The month of August was marked by violence in many parts of China, with fighting among Red Guards, between army units and Red Guards, and among army units. The British embassy in Peking was attacked. At this point Mao, Lin, and Chou seem to have agreed that things had gone far enough.

Barry Burton, an American student of the May 16 Corps, finds much of its story to be contrived. The purged were "scapegoats for party policies that misfired"; what had begun as a "clear case of removing six leading party intellectuals who had led the ideological attacks against the party revisionists" became an allegation of a "conspiracy that extended to the highest levels of the PLA as well as the party."[139] As Burton notes, the conspiracy was open ended: there was always room for finding new, higher back-stage bosses. In 1967 the boss of the May 16 Corps was said to be Hsiao Hua; the following year it became Yang Ch'eng-wu; by 1971 it was Ch'en Po-ta[140] (and here, finally, we are probably close to the truth); later, we are unofficially told that Lin Piao, in addition to Ch'en, was the real boss of the conspiracy.[141] This openness serves a definite political function. Given the situation, radical ideology was difficult to attack head-on. The postulation of the May 16 Corps allows persons whose ideas may not be openly attacked to be implicated in a treasonous conspiracy, and this, in turn, may provide leverage for attacks on their ideas.

While the conspiracy may be contrived, this need not mean that all statements about the May 16 Corps lack objective basis. What is contrived, for example, is probably not the idea of the existence of a radical organization: it is likely that the Cultural Revolution Group had an extensive and complex organizational network among Red Guards all over China. What *is* probably contrived is the idea that those named as members of the May 16 Corps were organizationally or ideologically distinct from the Cultural Revolution Group as a whole. In their attacks upon Chou En-lai and upon the regional soldiers they were no doubt acting for the Cultural Revolution Group's leadership. The summary of the ideas of the May 16 Corps as "doubt all, oppose all" is a not very distorted caricature of the position of the establishment radicals prior to the purge of the May 16 Corps. The association of the corps with Hsiao Hua makes some sense, as Hsiao was Lin's liaison with the establishment radicals. Burton finds the association of the corps with Yang Ch'eng-wu to be the "most fabricated aspect of the whole conspiracy," and he speculates that the association made was a function of the common hostility of the regional soldiers to both Yang and the radicals.[142] This is plausible. But the commissar of the air force, Yü Li-chin, who was purged with Yang Ch'eng-wu, had accompanied Wang Li and Hsieh Fu-chih to Wuhan,[143] and the possibility of unprincipled political combinations should not be excluded.

Also, while it seems likely that there never was a distinct political organization called the May 16 Corps, we should not exclude the possibility of objective factional or personal differences between the radicals who fell and the radicals who survived. The May 16 people may not have wished to remain stooges all their lives. Wang Li, in particular, seems to have been nourishing a little cult of himself. Here is a description of him at Wuhan:

> Firmly holding the booklet *Quotations from Chairman Mao Tse-tung* close to his breast, Comrade Wang Li stood erect as a sturdy pine, raising his head. His figure loomed large in the breaking dawn. . . .
>
> Comrade Wang Li remained firm and calm, his composure reflecting his contempt for the rough treatment accorded him. Raising his head, he stood on the terrace erect, his silver-gray hair gleaming in the rising sun. . . .[144]

It is surprising to see this little mediocrity described in such allusively redolent symbols as pine trees and rising suns. In those days, glorification of persons, aside from Mao, was limited to Lin Piao and Chiang Ch'ing. Even Wang's friends may have felt he was getting too big for his breeches.

Chang Ch'un-ch'iao and Yao Wen-yuan had managed to secure for themselves a power base as rulers of Shanghai, where they ruthlessly suppressed leftists who violated public order, and this may be sufficient to account for their survival. Among the May 16 Corps, however, Wang Li, Ch'i Pen-yü, and Lin Chieh were employed by *Red Flag,* working for Ch'en Po-ta, while Chang and Yao were close to Chiang Ch'ing. The May 16 Corps collected "black materials" on Chiang Ch'ing. Miss Chiang and Ch'en were, in their different ways, close to the Chairman, and there may have been jealousy between them—jealousy the Chairman might not have wanted much to discourage. The suppression of the May 16 Corps could have been in part a consequence of this possible rivalry.

The May 16 Corps may have been largely a fake. Its suppression, however, shows the limitations on radical opposition. The establishment radicals accommodated themselves to the suppression of ideological radicalism; but the establishment radicals remained active, and if the ideology of the May 16 Corps is in fact identical with theirs, the ideas may reemerge—and in fact they do reemerge from time to time, as we shall see. The corps was also said to have had a following among students. In the May 16 Corps, then, we may see the link between establishment radicalism and the less-adulterated radicalism of some of the Red Guard groups.

Radical Red Guards

In October 1967 the Hunan media thundered against an "extreme 'left' thought tide," a "reactionary thought tide." The "class enemy" in Hunan swindles the people, fishing in muddy waters (a saying that carries about the same meaning in Chinese as in English, as it happens), inciting the masses. He "creates rumors" about the PLA, slanders members of the preparatory committee for the Hunan Revolutionary Committee as "neutralists" and "speculators," incites armed struggles. He says: "There must be civil war"; "Civil war is the decisive strategic battle for our country's Great Proletarian Cultural Revolution." He says, "The revolutionary great alliance means the restoration of capitalism."[145]

This diatribe does not give specific details, but its subject is the Provincial Proletarian Alliance (*Sheng Wu Lien*), an abbreviation for the Hunan Province Proletarian Revolutionary Great Alliance, a coalition of radical middle-school Red Guard groups. This alliance came under full attack from the Center in January 1968. In early Red Guard writings there is an overplus of radical attitudes but little real political thought, much less political philosophy. As the establishment radicals came to terms with the realities and radicalism was abandoned, many Red Guards felt betrayed and, as it were, struck out on their own. The ideology they developed does not much transcend that of early establishment radicalism; and, for opportunist reasons if no other, they usually claimed to be carrying out the correct line of Mao, Lin Piao, and the Cultural

Revolution Group. Still, they do represent a true oppositionist tide. The Provincial Proletarian Alliance is the most prominent of these groups.

K'ang Sheng names as the leaders of the alliance two middle-school students, Yang Hsi-kuang and Chou Kuo-hui. K'ang believes, however, that the program of the alliance is too sophisticated to come from students: "I have the feeling that the arguments set forth could not have been written by middle-school or even university students. Behind them were counterrevolutionary black hands." The black hands include those of the Liu-Teng clique, of course, but also the followers of P'eng Te-huai and Ho Lung and the KMT. K'ang finds the ideas of the alliance similar to those of the May 16 Corps, but he does not say there is an organizational connection.[146] It is possible that P'eng Te-huai's people did have something to do with the alliance: Chou Hsiao-chou, until 1959 the first secretary of Hunan, had been one of the main elements of P'eng's clique, and Yang Hsi-kuang's father had worked for Chou Hsiao-chou. There is also a chance that KMT agents were involved in the alliance.[147] What causes K'ang to wonder is a citation of Lenin by the alliance: "Our state organs . . . are to a very large extent remains of old organs which have rarely been seriously reformed." What student would know about this quotation? K'ang wonders. The alliance distorts Lenin's words, using them to oppose proletarian dictatorship.[148] The quotation proves nothing about whether the students had outside help. It requires no great erudition to flip through Lenin and find a quotation appropriate to your circumstances. Yet the use of this quotation is interesting and may show some relationship between the alliance and the establishment radicals—K'ang Sheng and his friends. In 1975 the regime trotted out the very same quotation, this time embellished by Mao, who is made to say that what Lenin said of the Soviet state is true of China today as well—exactly what the alliance had said.[149] It is unlikely that in 1975 the establishment radicals were picking up from the alliance. More probably, the program of the alliance represents some kind of trial balloon launched before the big sell-out of September 1967, what the establishment radicals had planned to be the next phase of their own attack; the alliance would then be continuing a theme planned by the establishment radicals but abandoned by them before it had been made public. Chiang Ch'ing's remarks at the purge of the alliance are interesting: "I propose that ordinary hoodwinked masses must be distinguished from the few bad elements or behind-the-scenes teachers and bosses of that organization. . . . But not all the leaders are bad elements."[150] Miss Chiang tended to behave with more honor toward her tools than did the other establishment radicals. Like Lewis Carroll's walrus, she at least had the grace to cry.

As usual, the attempt to define concrete political groupings leads to ambiguities. In the alliance's two major documents—a program and a manifesto ("Whither China")—we have at least their concrete ideas (if words may be used this way): a reaction against the reimposition of discipline. The alliance's program begins with a standard denunciation of Soviet revisionism and praise for Mao, the "greatest Marxist-Leninist of the present age." "In the 16 years after the founding of the state, the majority of cadres have embarked on or passed through the capitalist road." The quote from Lenin follows, but the program adds that the army at least is "basically in the hands of the proletariat." A "privileged stratum" has emerged. The Cultural Revolution has concentrated too much on the dismissal of officials belonging to this stratum, while the problem is the system itself:

> The seizure of power was regarded as dismissal of individuals from their offices and not as the overthrowing of the privileged stratum and the smashing of the old state machinery. Moreover, the proletarian revolutionaries were childish. As a result, the seizure of power was only a superficial reform.

The revolutionary committees are "only a reprint of the old political power." But the revolution goes on:

> Through the practice of revolution, the broad revolutionary masses have learned the . . . Thought of Mao Tse-tung and will eventually unmask the distortion of the Thought of Mao Tse-tung by the bourgeois privileged stratum for maintaining its rule and fooling the masses, shake off the trammels of the habitual forces, and carry the revolution through to the end.[151]

The alliance also put out a manifesto, "Whither China," which is even more outspoken than the program, as well as more problematic (see note 147). "Contemporary China is the focus of world contradictions and the center of the storm of world revolution." Mao wants all China to become a great people's commune, a "new society" in which "intellectual youths" can achieve "liberation"—revealing (as if anyone could doubt it) at least the putative source of these ideas. Particularly hard on intellectual youths is the "revisionist movement on going to hilly or rural areas." Like the program, the manifesto speaks of a new class; unlike the program, it names names: Chou En-lai is the "general representative of China's Red capitalist class."[152] The manifesto is also more directly hostile to the army than is the program. The program says the army is "basically in the hands of the proletariat," which, of course, could be regime jargon for "not much in the hands of the proletariat" (cf.: a "basically good harvest"). The manifesto, however, says outright that the army has changed since Liberation. "The January storm has not touched in anything the vital problem of all revolutions—the problem of the army." Chairman Mao's call for the army to support the left was really part of an ingenious plan to radicalize the army. "It is education for the armed forces and cultural revolution for the army, rather than support for the left." The Great Leader miscalculated, however, and now the army is taking over. The revolutionary committees "inevitably . . . will be the form of political power to be usurped by the bourgeoisie, at which the army and the bureaucrats are to play a leading role.''[153]

The manifesto rehearses the great events of 1967. The January storm—the Red Guard seizures of power—was wonderful, but then came the bureaucratic reaction, the February Adverse Current led by Chou En-lai. Things picked up later in the spring, however, reaching a climax in August, a glorious month with lots of killing and stealing of weapons from soldiers. ''The creative spirit and revolutionary fervor displayed by the people in August was very moving.'' In September, reaction set in again. The reactionaries had become more clever. ''One after another, Red capitalists . . .—bloodthirsty vampires who used to ride on the backs of the people—suddenly displayed 'fervor' for the slaves' revolutionary struggle.'' Mao himself came to terms with reaction: ''The Chairman went so far as to say that Ch'en [Tsai-tao] studied very well and could come back to work.'' Like the Chairman, the left must also adapt to the circumstances and accept for the time being the new structure of power; to do otherwise is left infantilism. But this acceptance is only temporary: ''In the not too distant future the revolutionary people will surely smash to pieces with their own iron hands the new-born red political power which they have secured with their own blood and lives.''[154]

The manifesto warns against ''left infantilism'' several times, but both the program and the manifesto reek with just this quality. While not denying the puerility (and even nastiness) of the Provincial Revolutionary Alliance and its rather one-sided concern with the problems of intellectual youths (a not always very sympathetic category), we might remember that these youths were oppressed in a way their contemporaries in other parts of the world who made similar noises were not. Also the ideas of the alliance show, inadvertently, some limitations on the degree to which human liberation can be achieved by movements such as the Cultural Revolution, even assuming this is the goal of those who instigate such movements. When the rebels have overthrown the old classes they will strive to consolidate their newly won power with as much jealousy as any decaying reactionary force.

The alliance was the most famous of the dissident Red Guards, but it was not the only such group. After the leaders of the radical Flag Faction in Canton decided to join the revolutionary committee, some of their followers broke away, forming what was called the August 5 Thought Tide, accusing the bosses of the Flag Faction of ''reformism.'' The Tide was accused, in turn, of being the ''Provincial Proletarian Alliance of Canton,'' although there seems to have been no organizational connection.[155] In Shanghai the Eastern Consultative Committee (*Tung Hsieh Hui*) is described as a radical organization of those who had been targets of radical attacks, apparently bourgeois intellectuals. The attack on them quotes from the program of the alliance, with the implication that the two groups are alike. The committee said: ''Break the shackles of proletarian dictatorship. . . . No matter what class, where there is oppression there will be revolution.'' Chekiang also had radicals who said the revolutionary committee in that province was a form of ''peaceful transition,'' reformist and regressive. They wanted to smash the old state institutions. The method for doing this was perhaps more truly radical, in the circumstances, than anything thought up by the alliance: ''No rebels, no conservatives, no capitalist roaders; . . . they want elections by the whole people''[156]

The Voice of China

The Provincial Proletarian Alliance shows great unhappiness with the system, but in some ways its criticism is as conservative as it is radical. It argues in the idiom of the regime, and the argument is structured as an outgrowth of ideas that at least one segment of the regime had once officially professed. Outright rejection of the regime as a whole would probably have been too imprudent even for the most infantile leftist. Not only would this have resulted in immediate suppression; the vulnerability of such behavior to suppression would have denied it any audience. This is not so much because such radical opposition would lack popular appeal; even if it did have appeal, there are few who would voice their approval, simply because, given the outrageousness of the ideas, no one could reasonably expect them to have any effect. Even when all can see the emperor is naked, if everyone else behaves as if he were clothed, one is more inclined to doubt one's eyes than to doubt what seems to be the general consensus. In the story, the child's cry causes everyone else to give voice to the obvious. In real life the comrades hustle the child off for reeducation, to teach him to see clothing dialectically. Still, it is only a step from the position of the alliance to an outright rejection of the regime—and within China itself, part of this step seems to have been taken by the Eastern Consultative Committee and the Chekiang children. For an extended example of what form this outright rejection might take, however, we examine a group of exiles in Hong Kong.

The material for this section comes from the *Voice of China* (*Chung-hua Hu-sheng*), a magazine that published five issues from January 1969 to May 1971 (in preparing this study I have had access to only the first, third, and fifth issues; I saw all the issues some years ago). The magazine's format is like that of *Red Flag,* and so is its tone. In the European and mainland manner, the writing runs from left to right across the page, not in the traditional manner, in columns from up to down and right to left. Regular rather than simplified characters are used, perhaps in part because cheap Hong Kong printing shops do not have the proper fonts. Since the Cultural Revolution, each issue of *Red Flag* carries on its first few pages some quotations from Mao in large type. The *Voice of China* has a similar section, ''Our Beliefs.'' Some of these beliefs include:

> China is a large agricultural country. To change the poor face of China, it is necessary fully to develop the strength of the peasants, with the peasants as the masters to cause China rapidly to move toward industrialization.
>
> Among the current contradictions inside China, the most intense and complex, the most sharp contradiction is that between the peasants and the Maoist privileged class. When the peasants of the south, north, west, and east of China suddenly arise, the Maoist privileged class will collapse. [January 15, 1969]
>
> If we do not meet the test of the age, the age will weed us out. If we do not create history, history will abandon us. [December 20, 1969]
>
> . . . China will certainly take the great way to freedom, equality, democracy, and science. [May 15, 1971][157]

The editors say that their average age is twenty-five and that they all left the mainland between 1965 and 1968. They claim to come from all different kinds of background, but judging from the contents of the journal they seem to be disproportionately of "black element" heritage. Their goals are to give a true account of what they have seen, to reflect the complaints of those still inside, and to think about the future of China. They claim to receive no money from "any party or group."[158] They are, in fact, very defensive about allegations of outside support; they do not want to be seen as a front for some other group. They say they pay for the publication of the journal out of their own pockets. They complain: Some say, since the magazine looks like *Red Flag,* we must be part of the Liu Shao-ch'i clique. In fact, we reject all communism, whether Mao's, Liu's, or Trotsky's. Others say we must be affiliated with the United States or the "John King Fairbank clique" (a Taiwan code phrase for the CIA or the U.S. government generally). Others think we are propagandists for the KMT. All this is false. On the other hand, the *Voice* considers the United States a friend and does not oppose the "Republic of China," which is the "only legal government of China" and the "anticommunist center of Asia."[159] Over its life-span the journal seems to have moved ever closer to the Taiwan position. The first issue talks of Peking. By the fifth, this has become Peiping.[160] There is no evidence, however, that the group was simply a loudspeaker for Taiwan, and the fact that the journal folded after five issues is perhaps evidence that if it was receiving outside help it was not receiving much.

Despite its rejection of Marx and all his works, the *Voice* is still very much under his influence or, rather, that of his disciples. It analyzes the problems of China in terms of class, defined, as with the radicals inside China, in political terms. In fact, for the *Voice* it makes sense to describe the Chinese class structure in political terms only, since the economic privileges of the ruling class derive from its political power. The ruling class is the leading cadres, .01 percent of the population. Another 2 percent are the ordinary cadres, the *nu-ts'ai,* house slaves, as it were, or drivers. The rest of the population is the "enslaved class."[161] "Proletarian dictatorship" is the false ideology whereby the ruling class justifies its power and privilege:

> In capitalist society the laboring people are exploited in all kinds of ways by the capitalists. . . . Marx characterized them as "proletariat" [*wu-ch'an-chieh-chi:* "no property class"], and this was apt and reasonable. But after they are emancipated and become the masters and rule the whole country, the wealth of the whole country is under their control. How, then, can they still be called "no property"? But a look at the facts shows that the "emancipated" worker and peasant masses under the Maoist regime are still model proletarians, even poorer than before "emancipation." We might ask, Where does the wealth they produce go? Is it exploited by the capitalists? No, the capitalists have been beaten down. Is it plundered by the imperialists? No, even less so. The imperialists have long since been driven out. Well, then, where does the wealth produced by the people go? If it goes to the state or the collective, then according to the theory of "proletarian dictatorship" the proletariat controls the wealth of the entire people. They no longer have "no property." How, then, can they still be called the "no property class"? Thus, we say proletarian dictatorship is nothing but a misleading swindle. The dictatorship in China today is not by the proletariat but by a small privileged class headed by Mao Tse-tung. . . .[162]

Mao, Chou En-lai, and the rest are in fact "petty bourgeois intellectuals." The role of Mao's "old lady," a woman of "neither virtue nor ability," helps give the regime a "feudal" tone. The workers have traded "weak and corrupt" capitalists for "blood-thirsty new capitalists." But where there is exploitation there must be class struggle. "The Maoist society, naturally, is no exception."[163]

The ideology of the *Voice* is a kind of naïve populism; their concern for the peasants is a refreshing change from the typical Chinese intellectuals' preoccupation with themselves. The peasants are those who suffer the gravest exploitation, and they are also the foundation of the state:

> In an agricultural society the peasants are the main force. The production of other sectors is built upon the base of the peasantry. Following the needs of the peasants they gradually develop into classes apart from agricultural production. We may say that the forerunners of Chinese workers, merchants, intellectuals, and other classes were all peasants.[164]

Their plans for the reform of Chinese agriculture are somewhat vague. The communes are simple slavery, but it is impossible to return to the system that held prior to Liberation, and to attempt it would be unjust. Private ownership of land leaves the peasant vulnerable to natural disasters and leads to inequality. The *Voice* finds much merit in a program by Tseng Hsi-sheng, once first secretary of Anhwei, who overcame famine in his province by instituting a "responsibility field [*tse-jen t'ien*] system." Under this system, quotas are apparently set at the level of the household, not a larger unit. The household does not technically own the land it farms but is responsible for producing a certain quota and is allowed to retain for itself any surplus. This gives the peasants an incentive to produce. Under the current system, the *Voice* reports, the peasants say: *Kan-pu-kan, san-liang-pan*—work or not, three and a half ounces. In any case, the peasants should manage their own affairs. As the peasants become richer a market will be created for manufactured goods (currently the Maoists export all manufactured goods to Hong Kong, the *Voice* says). The country will thus industrialize naturally.[165]

The *Voice* contends there is no hope for an amelioration of the regime. It will not reform itself; the masses must overthrow it. It is critical of what it calls the new left, not hippies or the SLA, but the erstwhile "third force," particularly old anti-KMT liberals who now live in exile. These people see the common failings of capitalism and socialism but think Mao offers the best hope for China. They are impressed by the recent (1971) moderation of Maoist policies, but they are misinformed about the real level of material well-being in China. Also, "Historical experience tells us, to walk the reformist road always fails," a lesson the children of the *Voice* learned at the Chairman's knee.[166]

In worldly terms the *Voice* itself is insignificant, perhaps even more insignificant than the general run of exile political groupings. It is doubtful these boys will ever rule China. The ideas they express are not profound, and the journal rarely transcends the vitriolic cries of hate that disfigure so much Chinese political discourse in this century. It is plausible to argue, however, that the *Voice* does express ideas that other youths inside China would express had they opportunity to do so. The ideology of the *Voice* is an extrapolation of many themes of the radical tendency, particularly when these themes are taken up by persons who are really oppressed. The *Voice* does not seem to object to a great deal of the regime's concrete economic program; rather, they object to what they take to be the harshness, inhumanity, and cruelty of the regime and argue that these features are built into its structure. It seems probable that in the early 1970s the alienated sent-down youth in China were more given to apolitical melancholy than to blood-boiling radicalism.[167] But should the opportunity for genuine political action arise, there may be many who would come over to the attitude represented by the *Voice of China*.

Socialist Democracy and the Rule of Law

Another tactic taken by dissident Chinese youth may be represented by a wall poster published under the name of Li I-che, entitled "On socialist democracy and the rule of law." The poster was put up in its final form, after three revisions, on Peking Road in Canton in November 1974. The first draft had been completed and apparently circulated in September 1973, right after the Party Congress. Li I-che is a pseudonym for a group of young persons, the main leader apparently being one Li Cheng-t'ien, aged about thirty years, orginally from Wuhan and formerly a student at the Canton Fine Arts Academy. Taiwan military intelligence, which has reproduced a copy of the text,[168] speculates that at the time the poster was written Li Cheng-t'ien was some kind of party functionary. The poster is extremely long: it took up yards and yards of wall. Crowds of people are reported to have read it intently, in silence. While Li I-che is a group, for convenience in exposition I shall speak of "him" (although in summarizing certain passages I shall follow the style of the poster and say "we") and treat *Li I-che* as if this were the proper name of a person.

Some may consider it arbitrary—or downright wrong—to treat the Li I-che poster as an instance of radical opposition. At least ostensibly, Li I-che is a reformist (as the *Voice of China* or the Provincial Proletarian Alliance would say), "working within the system," hoping for change from what pass for the established institutions, particularly the National People's Congress. His main targets are the establishment radicals, and he seems to approve of the concrete policies of the moderate tendency and even some of its personnel (in particular, Teng Hsiao-p'ing).[169] Affiliation with a particular faction, however, should not be a measure of radicalism, nor should there be any reason in principle why the radical tendency cannot be subjected to a radical critique.

Li I-che uses many of the terms of the establishment radicals, as well as their mode of analysis and certain of their assumptions—for example, that Lin Piao was an "extreme rightist" (although Li equivocates on this). To a certain extent this may be "waving the red flag to oppose the red flag," another of the many manifestations in China of "persecution and the art of writing."[170] But to go too far in failing to take Li I-che at his word may mean to allow the rulers to set themselves up as the standard of radicalism, and this seems somehow perverse. Li I-che also notes that his criticis contend his position is the same as that of the 1957 rightists. There is a difference, however: "The revolutionary rebels and popular masses" have been using the same slogans as the old rightists since 1966, but their meaning is not the same. Times have changed. The Hungarians used democratic slogans in 1956, and "we" thought it proper for the Soviets to suppress them; but when the Russians did the same to Czechoslovakia in 1968, the "Chinese people" protested.

> In 1957 the rightists used democratic slogans to oppose the leadership of the Communist Party and the socialist road. But since 1966 the popular masses have used democratic slogans to oppose the bourgeois reactionary line of the capitalist roaders in the party, particularly the extreme "left" in form but extreme right in fact feudal social fascist line promoted by Lin Piao. Their purpose

> was to consolidate proletarian dictatorship. This reasoning should not be too hard to understand.[171]

The reasoning is perhaps not very persuasive, either, and it is hard to know how serious Li I-che is; but the relativism may be radical enough. In 1957, we might remember, there was a coincidence of interests between liberals and some radicals.

Li I-che also claims a genetic connection with Red Guard radicalism: "The many movements since 1968 have all been intended to beat down the persons who rose in rebellion since 1966; they simply had to beat them down to the eighteenth level of hell."[172] Li I-che's is a moderate radicalism, however. With him we seem to be back to Lin Hsi-ling and the convergence of radicalism and liberalism. Li I-che may represent Red Guard radicalism come of age.

The poster is in two main parts: the poster proper, written in 1973; and an introduction, longer than the poster proper and answering criticisms of it, written in 1974. The last section of the poster proper, "Our hopes for the fourth national people's congress," was rewritten in 1974. In summarizing the poster we use the following order: the poster proper, minus the last section; the introduction; then the rewritten last section of the poster proper.

Li opens with "New problems of the socialist revolution." The new threat to the revolution does not come from landlords or compradors, but from within the party—just as in the Soviet Union the capitalist restoration was not brought about by the Whites. Liu Shao-ch'i and "especially Lin Piao" did not try to set up an "ordinary bourgeois dictatorship," but a "fascist dictatorship of a feudal nature." Chairman Mao has warned of this since the early 1960s, but it took the experience of Lin Piao's line to show the Chinese people what the Chairman really meant. The fight against Liu Shao-ch'i tempered the people, developed their "revolutionary democratic spirit of liberating themselves." The people enjoyed (Li I-che says) free speech, free press, free assembly, free association, and free *ch'uan-lien*—freedom to travel around and make linkages with other groups; this last "has not been put into the [draft] constitution." But the people did not hold firmly to their democratic rights, and in 1968, when the Red Guards were suppressed, "social fascism" emerged (this term is sometimes used in China to characterize the Soviet dictatorship). Also the old constitution is defunct and a new one has not been promulgated; this means there is "no law and no heaven" (*wu-fa wu-t'ien*—is the quote from *Hai Jui is dismissed from office* deliberate?). That the Lin Piao system (*t'i-hsi*) came to be "worshipped" as the "orthodox Thought of Mao Tse-tung" was an "unavoidable historical mistake of the Chinese people in the Great Proletarian Cultural Revolution." This mistake allowed Lin to subvert "great democracy" and reimpose a "feudal 'order.' "[173]

Lin Piao's program constitutes a definite, interrelated system of idealism in philosophy, genius in history, suppression in politics, common property (*kung-ch'an*—pronounced similarly to, but written differently from, the word for *communism*) in economics, chauvinism in foreign affairs. Mao's letter to Chiang Ch'ing shows the Chairman knew all about this, but he could do nothing. The systematic nature of Lin's program means that the fuss about Lin cannot be regarded as "nothing but a power struggle at the Center." The struggle concerns the people's welfare, and the people will now protect their welfare. "The struggle at the Center is nothing other than the centralized expression of the struggle in society."[174]

The fourth section of the program proper, "The situation since the criticism of Lin," throws an interesting light on the 1973–74 criticism of Confucius. The earlier criticisms were directed against Confucius's concept of government by ritual, *li-chih,* which meant government by the arbitrary will of the ruler—that is, the sort of thing Lin Piao approved of. Lin Piao's fall, however, did not wipe out his system, and the criticism of Confucius has been distorted into praise for the book-burning, scholar-killing First Ch'in Emperor. Those who praise this emperor might remember that the people overthrew his dynasty. Currently the policies of Ch'in are being followed, while the popular masses are accused of wanting a restoration. This is a flagrant distortion of the facts. "The main current danger in the criticism of Lin is the mistaken tide of protecting the Lin Piao system under the banner of 'opposing a restoration of the old.' "[175]

This last sentence is important. The establishment radicals could agree with much of what Li I-che has said about the systematic and reactionary nature of Lin Piao's program and about its social base within the party. Here, however, Li I-che begins to argue that it is in fact the radicals, not the moderates who currently embody the Lin Piao system, that the radical opposition to restoration is a cover for a desire to restore the Lin Piao system. In the fifth section, "Talking about opposing the tide," Li criticizes the establishment radicals directly. The radicals hold up the student Chang T'ieh-sheng as a model in opposing the tide. "As a result, (1) he has not been jailed; (2) he has not been beheaded; (3) it seems he hasn't divorced his old lady." But those who have opposed the Lin Piao system have, in fact, been jailed and killed. "The popular masses are not Ah Tou," the stupid son of Liu Pei, ruler of Shu in the Three Kingdoms period. "They demand democracy; they demand socialist legality; they demand the protection of the revolutionary rights and personal rights of the popular masses." The standard for determining who are the true revolutionaries is who protects the interests of the people, and the people themselves should decide who best protects them. China now has at best "factional democracy," the tide and the antitide factions opposing each other, each wishing to eliminate the other. This squeezes out "class democracy" (i.e., real democracy—elections and that sort of thing) and lays the foundation for social fascism. "Comrade Wang Hung-wen" makes much of the "five no-fears." In fact, "since ancient times China has always had persons willing to speak out without fear of execution.'' But who has the opportunity to speak out today? Lu Hsun lived under the warlords and the KMT, but he was still able to publish his writings. Even when they were suppressed in China he could get friends to publish them in Japan. ''Today, where can the 'five-no-fear' people publish their writings?'' ''Has the Cultural Revolution died?''[176]

In the lengthy introduction, Li I-che notes that this poster has aroused great fear, and responds to those who say he is developing his own system. Maybe so, although his system contains nothing outside the sphere of Marxism. This is a Marxist weapon to oppose the Lin Piao system. But over the past year (1973–74) the Lin Piao system has grown even stronger. People now are scared ''first of all, because we discuss this topic at all.'' But so many socialist countries have undergone capitalist restoration, and new bourgeois elements are emerging in China. (The establishment radicals, of course, agree with this; but Li I-che includes the establishment radicals among the new bourgeois elements.) The new bourgeoisie in China is collecting ''special privileges'' and has even become able to extend its special privileges to family and friends. Officials have ceased to be public servants but have become the ''masters of the people.'' The emergence of new bougeois elements is ''inevitable,'' and the people need law and democratic rights in order to oppose this. Currently, the rights of the people are suppressed. ''Western news agencies'' talk of ''Chinese-style wall posters'' in Ethiopia; ''but 'Chinese-style wall posters' in China have met disaster.''[177]

People are scared because we say the Lin Piao system was established during the Cultural Revolution. By this we mean primarily ''(empty-headed) politics to the fore.'' Lin's use of the Thought of Mao had a ''religious color and atmosphere.'' The ''common-property wind'' damaged the interests of the peasants. Class struggle became ''formalistic''—but Li I-che really means ''bloody'': ''In Kwangtung province alone close to 40,000 revolutionary cadres and masses were killed, while more than a million were jailed, put under supervision, or struggled.'' Those who firmly opposed the Lin Piao system were slandered as active counterrevolutionaries, members of ''May 16.'' ''The production of the Lin Piao system is a consequence of the historical conditions of Chinese society.'' We have dictatorial habits left over from feudal times, and these infest even the brains of party members. We give weight to ''genius.'' Lin Piao implemented his ''government by ritual,'' recapitulating the experience of Yuan Shih-k'ai and the warlords.[178]

People are afraid because we criticize the slogan, ''Oppose restoration,'' ''Oppose the countertide.'' But those who use these slogans wish to restore the discredited system of 1969. ''They are perfectly nostalgic for the climax of the Lin Piao system, the 'glorious days'—days when tens of thousands of heads rolled on the ground.'' They criticize the ''reversal of verdicts''—well, shouldn't the tens of thousands of unjust verdicts be reversed? They hold up as glorious examples people like Chang T'ieh-sheng, an exemplar of "empty-headed politics," and also "Huang Shuai" (Li I-che's quotes), a horrible little girl who terrorizes her teachers.[179]

People are afraid because we are less than enthusiastic about the First Ch'in Emperor. Of course, the Legalists performed a "great historical function" in ending slavery and in uniting China. But the slave owners destroyed primitive communism and the European bougeoisie destroyed feudalism—they also were revolutionary, but we do not go into rhapsodies about them. There must be "severe limits to our affirmation of Ch'in, and beyond these limits we must undertake merciless criticism." Also, in 1965 Wu Han's Hai Jui was criticized: we thought it was ridiculous to hold that Hai Jui "loved and protected the people."

> But now people are saying, "The Legalists loved and protected the people." Isn't this a countertide that should scare people to death? Hai Jui, without a doubt, was a Legalist; moreover, historically he was a Legalist from a poverty-stricken national minority. Now some people are compiling great lists of those whose policy took root, from the First Ch'in Emperor to Sun Yat-sen. Why, then, must Hai Jui be regarded with such hatred and contempt? . . . Recently, he has been attacked in the papers again. This shows clearly that there are still those who curse the Legalists. Why, then, can't the First Ch'in Emperor be cursed?

The praise for Legalism is patently hypocritical anyway, since those who engage in it may want harsh dictatorship, but they do not want a rule of law. The campaign should be "linked to the many years of no law and no heaven of Lin Piao."[180] (The quote from Wu Han, then, is deliberate.)

The final section of the poster contains Li I-che's suggestions to the National People's Congress. His first demand is for a rule of law, not a rule of ritual; the law must protect the revolutionary people, who have been oppressed since 1968. We need to overcome our feudal heritage and our tradition of blind obedience. There is a need to "limit special privilege." The main danger is that the radicals' "new-born things" will become "the sacred ground of special privilege." We must "guarantee the people's right to manage the state and society." "Power is what corrupts people most," and to prevent corruption we need mass supervision of cadres. We must "consolidate proletarian dictatorship over the reactionaries." At present there is no proletarian dictatorship, only a developing fascist dictatorship in the hands of reactionaries who slaughter, torture, and unjustly imprison. "Policy must take root." Over the past few years policy has changed "from morning to evening." People are confused. Policy must "become embodied in the form of law." There must be "distribution according to labor." The reasonable economic interests of the people are neglected, while among officials there is an "inflation of special privilege."

> The workers have not received wage increases for many years and have even lost the reasonable bonuses that used to come with their wages. The peasant masses eat a rewardless "loyal" grain . . . and in the midst of movements to "cut off the tail of private ownership" have suffered even greater losses. This is the danger carried by Lin Piao's extreme "left" line [then in some ways, Lin's system is *left* after all], which is increasingly becoming ever more manifest.

In the Cultural Revolution we opposed high wages and bonuses, "but should we deny absolutely the function of bonuses?"

> Didn't the 1954 constitution stipulate democratic rights for the people? Hasn't Chairman Mao said many times, "Without broad people's democracy, proletarian dictatorship cannot be consolidated?" However, on the one hand there still remain the antidemocratic forces represented by the Lin Piao gang's suppression of the people. On the other hand the popular masses have made too little use of their democratic rights. (This is a consequence of the depth of China's feudal tradition, and also the low level of our country's production and of the people's culture; thus, we are relatively lacking in democratic spirit.) For many years, Chairman Mao has had the goal of "creating a lively and active political situation." This goal is far from being reached. . . . A mass movement thoroughly to smash the Lin Piao system must develop very soon. [The people] must once again restore and develop the spirit of the first Great Proletarian Cultural Revolution.[181]

Feng Yu-lan once said that Confucianism is a tool of the rulers but can also be turned against the rulers. Li I-che and other dissidents demonstrate that the same is true of radicalism. In the end, the Li I-che critique amounts to the recognition of the banal but important truth that power tends to corrupt—a truth rarely palatable to those with power. Since power corrupts, it must be restrained by institutions: law and democracy. Chinese radicalism has come a full circle: Li I-che converges with Lin Hsi-ling, and both converge with liberalism.

In 1974 there was a spate of officially approved wall posters in Peking and other cities, mostly attacking petty corruption. The Canton officials apparently did not know what the appropriate response to Li I-che was, and they referred the case to the Center. (The local people, after all, would not want to persecute a new Chang T'ieh-sheng.) The Center delivered its opinion in another wall poster, signed "Hsuan Chi-wen" ("Propaganda Collection of Documents").

> This reactionary wall poster wears the garb of "criticizing Lin" but undertakes instead a systematic and extremely malicious attack on the Great Leader Chairman Mao, the party Center, the socialist system and proletarian dictatorship, the Great Proletarian Cultural Revolution, and the movement to criticize Lin Piao and Confucius. With all its might it drums up bourgeois democracy, freedom, and the rule

> of law, in the vain hope of gathering together all the cow-devils and snake-spirits, inciting the masses, and instigating a "Hungarian incident" in China. . . .[182]

Li Cheng-t'ien himself was arrested, of course.

It is, as usual, impossible to know how widespread are ideas like Li I-che's. If these ideas are at all representative of the opinions of the younger and educated proportion of the population (and party) we may be seeing an ongoing realignment of the tendencies, with an increasing isolation of the establishment radicals. The ideas of Li I-che perhaps give some insight into the psychology behind the 1976 Ch'ing Ming riots.

RATIONAL MODERNIST OPPOSITION

The final set of opposition movements discussed here might be called rational modernist opposition. This, perhaps, is the mainstream of the moderate tendency. Although in China rational modernism manifests itself within a Marxist framework, its spirit is close to that of the technocratic elites of richer countries. The rational modernist strain lacks the overt moral focus of the Marxian Confucian strain of the moderate tendency, as well as the stress on spontaneity and activism that is somewhat present even in establishment radicalism. These deficiencies may inhibit its attaining any lasting legitimacy, although in the short run many may prefer it to be the status quo. This strain stresses, against Maoist voluntarism, a strong appreciation for the limits of the possible. It is more willing than at least establishment radicalism to tolerate a certain amount of diversity in society and to make concessions to existing interests, at least as long as these concessions do not endanger general political control. The tendency stresses "expertise" over "redness," or rather, takes a broad view of what is red. It is perhaps elitist, although not necessarily in a pernicious sense: as Lin Hsi-ling once said, "The masses don't necessarily want [intellectuals] to come to work; they want them to run things as they should be run."[183] The motto of the rational modernist strain may be that of the Legalists: *Kuo-ch'iang min-fu,* a strong state and wealthy people. In personal terms this tendency is perhaps represented by Liu Shao-ch'i after around 1959 and by Chou En-lai almost always (except when tactical opportunism led Chou away from it). Liu, more than Chou, however, seems to have combined his views on China's destiny with a strong, deeply felt sense of the historical mission of the Leninist party. Some, particularly Western radicals, seem to identify this tendency with Stalinism, focusing on its stress on bureaucracy, material incentives, expertise, and the like. This, however, would seem inaccurate. The Chinese tendency lacks Stalin's gratuitous bloodlust (and surely this, not bureaucracy, is the distinctive feature of Stalinism); also, Stalin's despotism was built upon the perpetual insecurity of every human being he ruled. The Chinese tendency has more respect for routine and order. It is post-Stalinist, Brezhnevist, or, in Chinese parlance, revisionist.

"If [Maoism] has not led to anything resembling a Marxist dictatorship of the proletariat . . . it has at least prevented a dictatorship of bureaucrats, as many foreign observers would seem to like to have it."[184] There is some point to this: the establishments of this earth may have a fellow-feeling at least as profound as that among proletarians. The early foreign comments on the madness of the Cultural Revolution expressed horror at what they took to be an atavistic return to the Yenan spirit, at the upsetting of established social order, at the probable retardation of China's modernization, that is, technological embourgeoisement. There seemed to be little concern that the upheaval was at least in part a reflection and consequence of an unjust system nor much concern that the movement was directed against an incipient humanizing, liberalizing trend potentially as hostile to rational modernism as was radicalism, a trend that might have eliminated dictatorship altogether. The triumph of the rational modernist trend would probably mean, in the short run at least, the consolidation of the dictatorship of bureaucrats.

The February Adverse Current

Since the elimination of Liu Shao-ch'i, rational modernist opposition has revolved largely around Chou En-lai and the "old cadres"—mainly high-ranking state bureaucrats—who took their cue from him. Around the middle of 1975 leadership of this tendency was taken over by Teng Hsiao-p'ing, Liu's onetime alleged henchman ("the other person in power within the Party walking the capitalist road"), who was rehabilitated in 1973 by Chou. Teng, less secure than Chou, was more aggressive and less subtle. Since the Tsun-i Conference in 1936 Chou's political strategy had been to put himself in alliance with the Chairman—and, after Mao had become radical, to try to pick up the pieces afterward. Chou apparently never aspired to do anything but whisper in the prince's ear and thus was never (after 1935) a political threat to Mao. Chou's intelligence, tact, guile, and (despite his opportunism) dedication to the good of China made him a useful man to have around. In the Cultural Revolution Chou found himself allied with persons whose policies he could hardly approve of and who soon came to find him a cramp on their style.

Chou, as premier, was responsible for maintaining social order and the smooth flow of goods and services. The initial target of the Cultural Revolution radicals had been the party machine, not the state bureaucracy. As the chaos spread, however, the radical push began to encroach upon the area of Chou's interests. Chou himself liked to get along by going along, but his subordinates lacked his patience, particularly after the "January storm."

In February 1967, part of Chou's following met together and denounced the radical faction, particularly Chang Ch'un-ch'iao, Chiang Ch'ing, and K'ang Sheng. This "adverse current" included the great names of party history: Chu Te, Ch'en Yun, Ch'en I, Li Hsien-nien, Teng Tzu-hui, Yeh Chien-ying, Hsu Hsiang-ch'ien, Nieh Jung-chen, and T'an Chen-lin. These old men were bitter not only at the way they themselves were being treated but also, perhaps sharing some of Liu Shao-ch'i's view of unrestrained mass movements, at seeing their life's work destroyed. The apparent ringleader, T'an Chen-lin, said, "I should not have lived 65 years, should not have joined the Party, should not have followed Chairman Mao in making revolution for 40 years."[185]

Mao himself apparently had no desire to purge these people; he expressed dismay at their attitude while, in Bismarckian style, bringing moral pressure to bear upon them:

> "Whoever opposes the Central Cultural Revolution Group, we shall oppose him. You may call Wang Ming and Chiang Kai-shek back, and I and Comrade Lin Piao, together with Yeh Ch'ün, will go to the south. Comrade Chiang Ch'ing shall be left with you, as will the comrades of the Central Cultural Revolution Group. You may behead Comrade Chiang Ch'ing and banish Comrade K'ang Sheng. All this you may do." Chairman Mao felt truly sad when he said this.[186]

Chou scolded his followers while also sympathizing with them, trying to smooth things over. The incident, however, was made to order for Chou's enemies and put Chou on the defensive. In the months that followed, Red Guard groups attacked "T'an Chen-lin," T'an being a transparent symbol for Chou.[187] These attacks more or less came to an end with the purge of the May 16 Corps, which, of course, was blamed for the attacks. There is no reason to think that the attitude of the corps toward Chou was much different from that of the radicals who survived, and there are fairly clear indications that hostility continued between Chou and the radicals until his death. By September 1967, however, Chou had made friends with the regional soldiers, and his political position became more secure. In 1969 all participants in the adverse current, with the exception of T'an Chen-lin (who was rehabilitated later) were reelected to the Central Committee, although some were dropped from the Politburo. China began to move fitfully—until late 1972—toward rational modernism.

The 571 Engineers

The program identified with Lin Piao fits within this emerging trend. It is a rational modernist denunciation of Maoism, the last thing that would have been expected to come from Lin Piao. We have already discussed the mechanics of the plot; here we shall consider the program that was circulated within the party as a negative example, said to have come from Lin's son.

The program says the situation has become tense since the second plenum (when Mao and Lin quarreled), that "dissatisfaction is increasing daily," and that the "ruling clique is incompetent and corrupt." "A political crisis is brewing. . . . China is in the process of undergoing a coup by peaceful evolution. . . . If we cannot use 'Project 571' to block this peaceful evolution, one morning they will attain their ends, and who knows how many heads will roll?" Such a coup is necessary. Mao—"B-52"—"is weakening; he cannot wait several years to arrange what will follow him. In his heart he is uneasy about us." We must act now. The "pen-barrel" (i.e., not "gun-barrel") Trotskyites—the radicals; Yao Wen-yuan and the like—are taking over. Their theory of continuing revolution is pure Trotskyism. They are social fascists.[188]

The authors of the program try to explain why Lin, after toadying to Mao for so long, should now betray him. The answer is: times have changed.

> We do not, of course, deny his historical function in uniting China. It is just because of this that in the history of the revolution we have given him his proper position and support. But now he has squandered the trust and position given him by the Chinese people and has become historically retrogressive. He has, in fact, become the First Ch'in Emperor of the present age.
>
> Because of our responsibility to the Chinese people and to Chinese history, our patience has limits.
>
> He is not a true Marxist-Leninist, but a follower of the Way of Confucius and Mencius, one who, borrowing a Marxist-Leninist hide, carries out the laws of the First Ch'in Emperor. He is the greatest feudal tyrant in Chinese history. . . .
>
> Those he entices today with honeyed words tomorrow are led to the execution ground, victims of trumped-up charges. Today you are the guest of honor, tomorrow a criminal at the foot of the throne.
>
> What political force can work with him from beginning to end? His few intimate comrades in arms and trustworthy aides have been sent to prison. He even drove his own son insane.
>
> He is a paranoid, a sadist. . . . Others are blamed for all the bad things he does. . . . In the past there has been propaganda for B-52. Some of this was historical necessity; some of it was required for unifying the whole people, uniting the great whole, or to resist foreign enemies. Some of it was a result of his fascist pressure; some of it was from lack of understanding of his inner feelings.[189]

The criticism of Mao may or may not be entirely just, but it should at least caution us against being too impressed by statements about how respected and beloved he was. (Lin Li-kuo also says, however: "The superstition of the masses concerning the person of B-52 is very deep.")[190] The references to the various ancients were to become very significant later on.

The program identifies what its authors take to be various sources of discontent in China. "A small handful of *hsiu-ts'ai*"—examination passers; not very intelligent intellectuals—"have established hegemony. Their heads are swollen; their estimation of themselves is too high." The Center is rife with intrigue; the military and high-raking cadres are unhappy. "The peasants lack food and clothing." "The sending of young intellectuals up to the mountain and down to the farm has become a type of labor reform." The Red Guards were first used and then suppressed, made into scapegoats. The May 7 Cadre Schools are a type of unemployment. "The wages of workers (especially young workers) are frozen; this is a type of exploitation."[191]

We must, therefore, use the following slogans: "Down with B-52, the First Ch'in Emperor of the present age." Overthrow his feudal dynasty that masquerades as socialism and establish true socialism. Unite with all true Marxist-Leninist parties; adhere to peaceful coexistence abroad and protect the safety of foreign diplomats. Rely on the Soviet nuclear umbrella.

> Substitute a "rich people and a strong state" for a "rich state and poor people." Let the people live in peace and be happy in their work, with good clothing and sufficient food, that politically and economically they attain true liberation. Use Marxism-Leninism as our guiding ideology, establish true socialism instead of B-52's social feudalism.

Preserve public order and protect state property. *Ch'uan-lien* is forbidden. Those who have been unjustly harmed by B-52 must "all be given political liberation. Comrades who have praised B-52 must be analyzed in terms of historical materialism."[192]

This text, published by Taiwan, is certainly genuine, that is, it did circulate after Lin's death within the party with the blessing of the party center; but it might not be authentic—that is, it might not come from Lin's circle. The text, of course, purports to be the work, not of Lin Piao, but of his son, Li-kuo, an air force officer; and the ideas expressed may be representative of those held by cadres in the modern sector of the military and perhaps by middle-level cadres in the modern sector generally. It is interesting that the concrete policies in the program, except for the part about the Soviet nuclear umbrella—improved relations with foreign countries, rehabilitation of cadres, a better standard of living for the people—seem to describe the program that was actually being implemented by Chou En-lai during the year following Lin's death. It is possible the program was cooked up by radicals to discredit Chou's program. Alternatively, the program could be a forgery by Chou En-lai, in which he puts into the mouths of traitors some hard truths that could not be otherwise expressed. No doubt even more Byzantine complexities suggest themselves. The personal animus against Mao and the Shanghai radicals may be evidence of the program's authenticity, although not decisive evidence. In any case the document is, in form, a concise oppositional statement (with the policy arguments embedded in much puerile talk of poison and secret weapons and the like; this aspect of the program is a sideshow and has not been discussed here). Whether the program is a forgery or not, there is no reason to doubt that the discontents it identifies are real ones, and it remains a valuable view of Chinese politics different from that given in the open media.

The Criticism of Confucius

The revival of the criticism of Confucius in the 1970s is one of the more puzzling aspects of contemporary Chinese politics. Implicitly from the beginning and explicitly since February 1974, the campaign linked criticism of Confucius with criticism of Lin Piao, with the implication that Lin was a Confucian—which is only a little less than ludicrous. Like many of his generation and status, however, Lin had a feel for the old tradition and at least a vestigial admiration for it and to a certain extent continued to define his world according to it (just as another old-fashioned gentleman, Mao Tse-tung, continued to define high politics in terms of the traditional alternation of *chih* and *luan,* order and chaos.)

Lin's active Confucianism is dated from October 1969, when he allegedly circulated among his clique a scroll, ''In the anxieties of ten thousand things, this alone is worthwhile: overcome the self and restore ritual'' (*yu-yu wan shih, wei tz'u wei ta: k'o chi fu li*).[193] The circulation of this excellent piece of pious wisdom may have been a move in a political game or the occasion for a new political game, since the following month a pamphlet was compiled, *Collection of statements praising Confucius and advocating the restoration of the old by reactionary and landlord-bourgeois scholars since the May Fourth period.* The pamphlet was not published until 1973, however, and then in supplemented form. The supplement includes sayings by imperialist and revisionist scholars and attracted attention in the West for this rather graceless description of Owen Lattimore: ''A U.S. reactionary scholar, international spy, former advisor to the Chiang Kai-shek government.'' In addition to the foreigners, the supplemented version must have contained the reflections of at least two additional Chinese scholars, Ch'en Po-ta and Lin Piao. The biographical information on Ch'en shows how seriously that on Lattimore should be taken: ''A KMT anticommunist element, Trotskyite, renegade, agent, revisionist.'' The pamphlet lists only two quotations from Lin Piao (''A bourgeois ambitionist, plotter, counterrevolutionary two-faced element, he never read books, never read newspapers, knew nothing of Marxism-Leninism and less of ancient China. . . .''), both taken from his ''anticommunist diary.'' In 1969 Lin wrote that Confucianism was a type of historical materialism; and in 1964 he wrote, ''I often ponder that I must behave toward people in the manner of Master Chu [Chu Hsi].''[194] This does not make Lin a very impressive Confucian. At the time the pamphlet was released, however, it had not yet been discovered that Lin's love for Confucius was his most conspicuous quality.

As we have seen, in 1971 Lin Li-kuo (allegedly) accused Mao of Confucianism, as well as Legalism. Mao "carries out the Way of Confucius and Mencius" (*hsing K'ung-Meng chih tao*), the very phrase that was to be used again and again of Li-kuo's dad. By this Li-kuo meant simply that Mao was a feudal tyrant, just like the First Ch'in Emperor, who was not, however, a Confucian. In September 1971, about two weeks after Lin's death, there appeared an attack on Confucius's concept of *jen* and its use by "political swindlers of the Liu Shao-ch'i type." These "fake Marxists" talk of love, but there is no love that transcends class. Lu Hsun showed how all the old Confucian talk of *jen* was nothing but cannibalism.[195] This comes too early to be directed against Lin Piao. The political swindler must be Ch'en Po-ta, who was then being represented as a sentimental humanist. This, then, is perhaps an arcane attack on the radical tendency.

In July 1972 Kuo Mo-jo published an article rehearsing his old thesis that the transition from the Spring and Fall to the Warring States (around 500 B.C.) marks the change from slave to feudal society. Kuo's real purpose is apparently to answer the Lin contention that Mao is just like the First Ch'in Emperor. On the one hand, the First Ch'in Emperor was not all that bad. His triumph marks the triumph of feudalism, which is better than slavery. He was a progressive man. On the other hand, in those days the people "did not become the true masters. One system of exploitation was replaced by another system of exploitation."[196] Since the people are now the true masters, there is no point to a comparison of People's China and the Ch'in dynasty.

In December 1972 a relatively obscure scholar, Yang Jung-kuo, published a long essay setting forth what were to be the main themes of the coming campaign. Confucius was a representative of the decaying slave-owning class. Mencius was no better. The Legalists were progressive; Ch'in was very progressive. The subject was dropped for many months, until just before the party congress, when Yang published two more essays.[197] After this, the flood gradually began. In February 1974 the movement acquired an official title, the "criticism of Lin Piao and Confucius," and was said to be under the "personal instigation and leadership of Chairman Mao,"[198] although Mao was never quoted directly on the campaign. In the manner of all such campaigns, this one became increasingly boring and more or less petered out around the time of the National People's Congress in January 1975. It was revived about a year later as a minor part of the struggle against "unrepentant capitalist roaders," Teng Hsiao-p'ing.

The most common interpretation of the campaign has been that it was an attack by the radicals on the moderates, particularly on Chou En-lai. This is certainly a reasonable interpretation. After all, Confucius was a moderate gentleman with a liking for order and restraint; he believed in the golden mean; and so forth. It is possible, however, to construe at least part of the campaign in just the opposite sense—as an attack on radical Maoism from a rational modernist position.[199] In this interpretation Maoism is seen to be related to Confucianism in much the same way as non-Marxist rational modernists seem to hold that communism is related to religion: these are irrational, superstitious, authoritarian systems that get in the way of making money. Legalism, which is in fact an ultramodern system of thought even in its original form, is seen as a doctrine that can help achieve social order and material prosperity. I shall argue that in its origins the campaign against Confucius was a rational modernist attack on radicalism, although it soon became complex and confused, and shall concentrate upon an explication of what I take to be the rational modernist themes in the campaign.

That one can plausibly interpret certain parts of the campaign in a moderate sense is, of course, no evidence that such an interpretation is valid. Most of the evidence that can be adduced is indirect and negative. The little positive evidence comes from unofficial or semiofficial sources. Thus, Lin Li-kuo accused Mao of Confucianism, identifying this Confucianism with social feudalism and social fascism. Just as in 1972 the moderates seemed to be implementing Li-kuo's program, so, possibly, in the campaign they were developing this particular theme of his. Li I-che also, it will be remembered, uses the same concepts (taken, no doubt, from Lin Li-kuo), identifying the first part of the campaign against Confucius as an attack on the radicals, on "government by ritual." According to Li I-che (who may know: Yang Jung-kuo teaches at Chung-shan University in Canton), Yang "and his helpers" had been placed in the "cow brigade" by Lin Piao during the Cultural Revolution. It was then that Yang began his study of the evils of rule by ritual. "This white-haired dignified old professor is a true rebel." But the campaign has been distorted, no longer criticizing rule by ritual but instead praising the tyranny of Ch'in.[200]

Yang was not the only white-haired old professor involved in the campaign. We recall that Feng Yu-lan and Fei Hsiao-t'ung were trotted out to say their piece. In a campaign run by radicals, these are usually the sort of people who disappear or come under attack. The campaign also referred favorably to themes and historical personages attacked during the Cultural Revolution. Thus, both Liu Tsung-yuan of the T'ang dynasty and Li Chih of the Ming dynasty were held, in the 1970s, to be true Legalist heroes; in 1967 they were "feudal mummies."[201] One of the marks of Li Chih's rebellion against conventional morality was said to be his compiling of an edition of *Water margin*. This shows he "reflected the demands and aspirations of the lower-class masses and newly rising urban class."[202] The 1975 attack on *Water margin,* however, was certainly from the left and held that novel to be thoroughly reactionary, an apology for the betrayal of revolution.[203] For what it is worth, while the campaign against Confucius never quoted Mao directly on itself, the campaign against *Water margin* issued straight from the Master's mouth.

Throughout most of 1974 Chou En-lai was the only high-ranking leader publicly to mention the campaign (he was later joined by Teng Hsiao-p'ing). At the People's Congress Chou said: "Our *primary task* is to broaden, deepen, and persevere in the movement to criticize Lin Piao and Confucius."[204] In his speech at that congress Chang Ch'un-ch'iao virtually ignored the campaign. While it was going on there were other campaigns of obvious radical inspiration—against bad plays, "untitled music," and the like—as if the radicals were trying to change the subject. In the criticism of Antonioni—surely a radical ploy—we read, "When he says stuff like the Chinese people 'think of the past' [*hsiang-nien kuo-ch' ü*], this is even more insulting. Who 'thinks about the past'? . . ."[205] Well, look at just about any issue of any Chinese newspaper of the time . . .

The language and themes of part of the campaign also have moderate implications. The slogan "Oppose the tide" had radical connotations when it was introduced. The campaign against Confucius began at about the same time, but article after article tells how Confucius "stubbornly opposed the tide of history." In 1972 Lin Piao as well was said to have opposed the tide of history—and in those days Lin was an "extreme 'leftist.' " Perhaps the "tide" and the "tide of history" are not the same thing, but the contrast in themes is intriguing. The condemnation of Confucius for opposing the tide would seem to be a criticism of radical voluntarism from the perspective of a more classical Marxist historicism. Also, Confucianism was identified as a species of a priori idealism, from the fall of 1970 a code word for radicalism (the radicals call the moderates "empiricists"). As a kind of final note, it is interesting that, following the adoption of the constitution in 1975—itself something of a Legalist measure—after more than a year of praise for Legalism, there should be a leftist attack on *fa-ch'üan,* legal rights.

The interpretation of the campaign as a moderate, rational modernist one must be modified, of course. First, however, it may be appropriate to speculate on the source of the campaign. As noted above, Chou En-lai was one of the few leaders publicly to mention the campaign. There are indications, however, that much of the pressure may have come from persons lower than Chou—say, middle-ranking cadres in the modern sector—who were using Chou much as a symbol of what they desired, not entirely to Chou's pleasure. One of the most famous essays of the campaign was first published in November 1973 and then reprinted in English in the spring of 1974, when Chou began to receive visitors "in hospital." The essay discusses, among other themes, a Ch'in politician, Fan Sui, the prime minister. Fan Sui was a good Legalist and a clever diplomat. His foreign policy was to "ally with the far to attack the near."

> However, although Fan Sui was the prime minister, he was in fact sitting on a volcano that could erupt at any moment. In Ch'in at that time the influence of the old nobility was still relatively great. In this background of class struggle Fan Sui also wavered, and in 256 B.C. he "requested to give up the prime minister's seal on account of illness."[206]

We now know, of course, that Chou's illness was no pretext. But this essay virtually digs its elbow into our ribs. It would seem to be a criticism of Chou for equivocating, for refusing to take a strong stand against the radicals. Of course, it was partly by refusing to take strong stands that Chou was able to die full of honors and of days.

This obviously is not to say there was no radical input into the criticism of Confucius. The campaign was revived in early 1976, when the leftists seemed in clear control of the media.[207] Some radical themes had been a part of the campaign nearly from the beginning, and I think that with the beginning of the campaign under the title of "criticism of Lin Piao and Confucius" in February 1974 the radicals had succeeded in co-opting the campaign (although it did retain some moderate themes even after this—this campaign, more than most, was a common carrier). The editorial announcing the criticism of Lin Piao and Confucius uses that part of the campaign with the clearest reference to Chou En-lai, criticizing one of Confucius's heroes, Chou Wen Wang, the "Civilian King of Chou."[208] This certainly turns our minds to another highly placed civilian by that name. The editorial says the relations between Wen Wang and his successor, Wu Wang, the Military King, were just the same as those between Lin Piao and his son. Wu Wang, however, may well be a symbol for Chou's intended successor, Teng Hsiao-p'ing. Teng had been a civilian since 1949, but in January 1975 he became chief of staff of the PLA. He may have been performing that function a year earlier (one assumes someone must have been). A hypothesis might be that by attaching the criticism of Confucius to the ongoing campaign against Lin, the radicals were able to deflect the attack from themselves.[209]

This is not the place for a complete redaction analysis of the campaign. Still, there are important differences in the radical and the moderate treatment of the subject. The radicals, I think, tend to concentrate on the political and personal vileness of Lin Piao, while the moderates are given to pedantic and tendentious distortions of ancient history. In a closed speech in January 1974, Wang Hung-wen praised a *People's Daily* article attacking Lin Piao's alleged attachment to the golden mean and the "rites of Chou," but then he adds: "Some refuse to undertake the criticism of Lin Piao and Confucius. Most recently we solved the problems of twelve factories in Szechwan. What were the problems? *They had not implemented the criticism of Lin deeply enough. That was the crux.*" A radio broadcast from Honan in April 1974 also purports to talk about the criticism of Lin Piao and Confucius, but on Confucius restricts itself to the comment that he was an "extremely rotten [*tsau-te-hen*] theoretician." The bulk of the broadcast is a diatribe against Lin's suppression of the "rebels."[210]

There is another major difference of usage between the radicals and the moderates, and this difference leads into an exposition of some of the rational modernist themes. Both the radicals and the moderates focus upon Lin's use of Confucius's saying, "Overcome the self and restore ritual." The two sides, however, mean different things by *li,* ritual. The radicals (like Teng T'o in 1962) use *li* in its traditional sense, as natural law, as it were—objectively valid social norms (which both radicals and rational modernists hold do not exist), reflections in human behavior of the Way of Heaven. For the radicals, to advocate restoring *li* means to wish to restrict dictatorship (dictatorship being, for the radicals, a Good Thing). Such advocacy is an "evil attack on revolutionary violence," a plot to restore capitalism.[211] But as Li I-che points out, for the moderates (or at least Yang Jung-kuo), *li* means the arbitrary class code of the slave owners, their demand for "blind obedience by slaves."[212] For Yang, in effect, *li* means dictatorship and is a Bad Thing. As an alternative to *li* he upholds the Legalist *fa:* objective, codified, positive law. In 1976 the moderates were accused of wishing to broaden *fa-ch'üan,* legal rights, the radicals identifying *fa-ch'üan* with *li.*[213] In sum, the radicals see *li* as a restraint on dictatorship and would substitute for it dictatorship; the moderates identify *li* with dictatorship—lawlessness—and would substitute for it a rule of law.

Another moderate theme would seem to be the criticism of crude class dictatorship in education, something we now know with a fair degree of certainty the moderates were opposed to. One essay shows that while Confucius pretended to teach anyone, regardless of class, he really tended to take as pupils only scions of the slave-owning aristocracy, and to these he charged tuition. What a hypocrite![214] If someone accuses another of being a hypocrite, he usually means to affirm what the person pretends to be but to criticize the person. If someone claims to be a murderer, a drunkard, a wife-beater, and a pederast, but it turns out he is none of these things, it is only as a joke that we would call him a hypocrite. The implication of this essay, then, is that equal opportunity to education regardless of class is something to be desired, but the radicals wish to bias the educational system in favor of the proletariat, the new aristocracy. The radicals are just like Confucius.

The radicals fear *li* will get in the way of "revolutionary violence." The moderates—or rather, Li I-che, whose position here seems to coincide with that of the moderates—identify *li* with violence. The campaign against Confucius did, of course, exalt the violence of Ch'in. But also Confucius, of all people, is accused of maintaining his *li* by violence. Many tears are shed over Confucius's fabled execution of Shao-cheng Mao, promoted for the purposes of the campaign to a Legalist statesman who "proposed reform; this suited the development of history at that time and the wishes of the popular masses.'' Confucius prated about *jen,* but when the chips were down, look at what a bloodthirsty scoundrel he was.[215] Here again is the argument from hypocrisy.

Another line of argument focuses upon the excellence of the Legalists—their rule of law, also their policy of employing government functionaries on the basis of ability. Yang Jung-kuo writes:

> This is to say, no matter how mean and despised the enslaved persons might be, whether they work in agriculture in the mountain, forests, or swamps; whether they have been locked in jail; whether they have been cooks or herdsmen; or whether they have been doing other kinds of work: if only they have ability they must be liberated and promoted to engage in [political] work.[216]

The list of the conditions and occupations of the ''enslaved persons'' is a paraphrase from Han Fei but also seems to show how the cadres purged in the Cultural Revolution had been passing the time. The passage is a clear reference to the ''liberation'' of these same cadres, the later ''unrepentant capitalist roaders.''

Lin Li-kuo revived the old Legalist slogan, a ''strong state and a rich people.'' As far as I have seen, this slogan was not used in the campaign against Confucius—it was probably too tainted by its association with the Lins and had in fact come under explicit criticism prior to the onset of the campaign.[217] The Legalist policy summed up in the phrase, however, was praised. Yang Jung-kuo informs us that under slavery land was organized according to the well-field (*ching-t'ien*) system, which traditionally was held to imply communal ownership under an overlord who received a ninth of the product. Yang, however, takes this to mean some kind of plantation economy. The Legalists advocated breaking up the well fields and turning the land over to private ownership by landlords: a very progressive policy. Ch'in did this, and so ''Ch'in was able to develop its agriculture.''[218] What is appropriate to the development of feudalism, of course, need not be appropriate to the development of socialism, and one would have thought that by now the question of whether land should be collectively owned would not even come up any more in China. Still, this does cause us to wonder. An article in January 1975 argued that the emperors Ching and Wen of the Han dynasty seemed Confucian but were really Legalists. One mark of their Legalism was their use of rewards to encourage agricultural production.[219] In its moderate aspect the campaign seems to argue at most for some decollectivization and at least for material incentives to peasants to stimulate production.

The attitudes seemingly implied by this part of the campaign are hardly radical. They also have, on their face, little of the moral conservatism found in, say, Teng T'o; in fact, they explicitly repudiate moral considerations. They are ''modern,'' much in the sense in which that term is used by the ideologues of modernization in the West. Their program seems to be Orwell's utopia of fat little men—which, in the context, should perhaps not be sneered at: fat little men are as entitled to happiness as anyone else, and for the others, this program may carry more promise than available alternatives. The support for this program probably comes from middle- and lower-level cadres in the modern sector. That such attitudes are voiced at all is evidence that they are widely shared; that they are expressed in the manner they are is evidence that those who hold them were hardly in a position to dominate China. Should this rational modernist trend triumph, it would probably entail a more rationally bureaucratized system in China. There would be more stress on material incentives and less on what foreign observers are pleased to call equality. Education would become elitist: academic competence (along with basic political reliability) would become again the criterion for admission to schools. Policy changes would become less erratic and the ordinary man better able to predict what his rulers demand of him. In agriculture there might be limited decollectivization or, in the absence of structural changes in agriculture, at least no further collectivization. Chinese would become more free to follow their personal interests. If a rule of law were really adopted, the system would cease to be totalitarian (or revolutionary), but this does not mean it would become liberal. As Judith Shklar notes of the Western variety of legalism, "Legalism, as an ideology, is capable of being combined with the politics of repression, although not in its extreme form."[220]

It may be unfair and shortsighted, however, to view these attitudes as nothing but an amoral utilitarian modernism. While they do not tend toward a liberal system, they do support what in the context can only be considered liberalization. Once liberalization acquires a political and social base—that is, generates vested interests—it can also acquire its own momentum. Also, the rational modernists, like other dissidents, face limitations on what it is possible to say. Yang Jung-Kuo's own past is suggestive. A generation ago his hero was no hard-nosed Legalist, but Mo-tzu, a utilitarian theist who preached universal love. He, not Confucius, was the representative of the forces of progress and the champion of human well-being. Unlike Confucius, he believed in a "total love without regard to class distinctions."[221] It is often noted, however, that in practice Confucian and Mohist ethics amount to much the same thing.[222] By the 1970s the Chairman had revealed that there is no such thing as universal love—and Mo-tzu's ideas would have been even more obnoxious than those of Confucius. One wonders, however, since Yang's attacks on Confucius in 1973 are the same as in 1950, whether his position might not be an implicit and cryptic advocacy of some kind of "Mohist" humanistic utilitarianism.

The praise for the tyranny of Ch'in, of course, does little to strengthen this speculation. In fact, the praise for Ch'in might lead us to question the sincerity of the commitment to the rule of law. The First Ch'in Emperor, we are told again and again, was simply too child-foolish for this world. He did not suppress his enemies with enough ferocity. Actually, however, the position on Ch'in is complicated. The radicals praise the Legalists for their power politics, not their rule of law, and for them Ch'in presents no special problem. The progressive nature of Ch'in had its limits, of course. But the burning of books and burying of scholars was necessary for the consolidation of Ch'in's rule; too bad there was not more burning and burying.[223] The moderates also take this line, but for them the affirmation of Ch'in seems in part satirical (after all, fulsome praise for the sagacity of an emperor whose dynasty collapsed after fifteen years must be at least implicitly satirical) and also historicist. Ch'in's harsh tyranny was necessary, but it did not last. While it was probably dangerous to attack Ch'in's tyranny head-on, at least one article attacks the tyranny of Sui, another harsh, short-lived dynasty that united China after a long period of chaos and that has often been coupled with Ch'in. The ruling clique of Sui was "corrupt." To satisfy its voracious appetite, it "seized the land of the peasants." "Half the population died of exhaustion" from work on public projects. It was overthrown by a peasant insurrection that "swept away the obstacles to the economic prosperity of the T'ang."[224] One of the last major articles of the campaign informs us that Ch'in did not collapse because of Legalism, but as a consequence of the machinations of the eunuch Chao Kao (references to eunuchs in the current context carry connotations of radicalism). These precipitated a peasant rebellion, and the rebellion eliminated the vestiges of slavery, something the "landlord class" (the First Ch'in Emperor) "could not and did not do." It was through rebellion that feudalism became consolidated (although the peasants did not come to rule the state). The Han, which succeeded Ch'in (and is associated with internal peace, external strength, economic prosperity, cultural flowering, and mild government) was really a Legalist, not a Confucian, dynasty.[225] All this should probably be construed to mean: perhaps the tyranny of the past few decades has been necessary to destroy the old social order—although those in power now seem to embody what was worst in that order; but if the system does not change, the people will rebel; just as the fall of Ch'in did not mean the end of feudalism, so the fall of the current system will not mean the end of socialism.

The most extended discussion of Ch'in in this vein was perhaps most safely left to a thinker more than a millenium dead. In 1974 the regime reprinted in the original and in a vernacular translation Liu Tsung-yuan's brilliant essay, "On feudalism."

> All within the four seas were brought under control. It was as if all could be held and manipulated with one hand. Ch'in was correct in doing this. But after a few years there was great destruction under heaven. The reason for this was that 10,000 persons were put into forced labor, the punishments were severe to the point of cruelty, and financial reserves had become exhausted. Men were sent to the borders, carrying rakes and hoes on their shoulders. At Huan-shui they gathered and with a great yell became a mob. At that time there were

> rebels, but no rebellious officials. . . . The cause of failure, then, was in the complaints of the people. . . .
>
> The changes in the system made by Ch'in resulted in the common good. The motive was one man's will for personal power, a desire to centralize power and have everyone submit to him. But in this he acted in the interests of all under heaven. . . . The failure was in the policies, not the system. So much for Ch'in.[226]

The Denouement

There are hints in the campaign against Confucius of pressure from below on the high-ranking moderates. By the mid-1970s there also seem to have been similar pressures on the establishment radicals. This does not in itself imply that the political process was becoming more open (only that there may be a foundation for an opening) but does imply that the leaders had to look after their clientele—a result of the general factionalization dating from the Cultual Revolution. Not all young Chinese radicals have gone the way of Li I-che. Many no doubt hope to make their fortunes (their contribution to the building of the new society) through the system, through the triumph of their own tendency. And many of these seem to find, as others have before them, that those who most scrupulously meet the demands of the system are not always those who reap its rewards. During the 1970s decisions were supposed to be made by the triple unity of old, middle-aged, and young cadres at all levels. But in many cases it turned out that the young cadres, particularly those recruited by the radicals, were shunted aside as incompetent and ignorant, with the really important work being done, perhaps, by "unrepentant capitalist roaders," persons the youngsters had helped purge some years earlier.[227] The resulting frustration is perhaps reflected in a 1974 broadcast from Honan: Lin Piao "mercilessly attacked" revolutionary cadres and masses, calling them counterrevolutionaries. What Lin didn't realize is that "communists are rebels." "The Communist Party must rebel against the old world, against the bourgeoisie and all exploiting classes, against revisionism." "The Cultural Revolution caused chaos everywhere," the Lin gang says. "It is better to have peace." But chaos leads to order. "The malicious attacks on the Cultural Revolution by the class enemy are a function of their class nature." They, at least, can't help themselves. But even within our own ranks there are some who are not pleased with the Cultural Revolution and the new-born things, but "trail along behind the butt of the class enemy."[228] It is as if the Provincial Proletarian Alliance had been rehabilitated and moved north a few hundred miles. The power struggle between radicals and moderates at the Center was certainly continuing, but the establishment radicals do not seem to have shared their underlings' eagerness for rebellion (the Gate of Heavenly Peace Incident—see below—perhaps shows why). Both the radicals and their opponents seemed agreed in a desire to maintain social discipline, to carry out their intrigues and await the old man's death in relative peace and quiet. The establishment radicals, again, had their own positions of power and prestige; should disorder come, they could not be sure they themselves would not be its victims.

The regime held its Fourth National People's Congress in January 1975, after many delays (the Congress seems to have been originally scheduled to have been held before October 1, 1973). Mao did not attend the gathering but while it was in session had his photograph taken with Franz-Josef Strauss, indicating it was not poor health that was keeping him away. At the congress Chou En-lai stressed mainly economic questions, the "four modernizations" of agriculture, industry, defense, and science and technology.[229] The congress also adopted a new state constitution.

A few days after the congress closed, the national press began to publicize the theme of proletarian dictatorship, complete with new quotes from Mao, one agreeing with the Provincial Proletarian Alliance's interpretation of Lenin, although the children were given no credit.[230] The stress on the need to suppress the "spontaneous capitalist inclinations" of the "petty bourgeoisie" (the peasants) was a clear attack on some provisions of the new constitution. A couple of weeks later Yao Wen-yuan published a major article attacking bourgeois legal rights. These legal rights help support the "social base of the Lin Piao anti-party clique." Here Yao is correcting the older moderate interpretation of the Lin Piao incident. In 1972 Lin was held to have been a leftist adventurist who, lacking a social base, had to resort to plots and tricks. In speaking of Lin's social base and saying that the conditions for it remained, Yao was laying the ground for more purges. But Yao wanted a quiet purge, with no fuss: in addition to struggle there must be peace and unity, *an-ting t'uan-chieh*.[231]

The peace and unity slogan was made to order for the moderates. In his article, published a month after Yao's, Chang Ch'un-ch'iao does not mention peace and unity.[232] The dialectical nature of the radical theme also helped the moderates. The radicals admitted that legal rights could not be abolished outright; rather, when possible they must be limited, and in no case must they be expanded. But, then, efforts to limit legal rights could plausibly be interpreted as attempts inappropriately to abolish them.

By summer (July, August, September) the moderates had gone on the offensive, now under the leadership of Teng Hsiao-p'ing. They had a "theory, a program, an organization."[233] Teng seems to have drawn up a document, "General program for the work of the whole party and whole country," which set out what he took to be the tasks of the party "for the next twenty-five years." Teng, it is said, had sworn upon his rehabilitation never to seek revenge, and he paid lip-service to this: "Those problems of the Cultual Revolution must be forgotten. We must simply not think of them, nor must we bring them up. My memory is no good; I have forgotten them." But if the criticism of his program does not overly misrepresent it, the radicals could not take much consolation in Teng's loss of memory. Teng's program would seem to echo Li I-che's, but without the democracy. Thus, Teng's program is full of "criticize Lin" and "oppose the 'left' "; it complains of the harm done to "experienced cadres." "Oppose anti-Marxist class enemies," those who have "inherited the suit of Lin Piao." "Recover leadership power."[234] The heart of Teng's program was a slogan, "The three directives as the guide," these directives being the study of Marxist theory, peace and unity, and the development of the national economy.[235] Teng said the directives "are mutually related. They cannot be divided." Mao, on the other hand, said, "Peace and unity does not mean no class struggle. Class struggle is the guide rope [of a net], everything else is the eyes." During the same period Teng allegedly gave his opinion of Chiang Ch'ing's model plays: they are "a flower blooming alone"; they "hinder the development of literature"; "no tickets are sold"; they are "extreme 'left' "; "life is not all class struggle." Teng also delivered other witticisms calculated to drive the radicals up the wall: "If people say you are attempting a restoration, that means you are doing a good job."[236]

Some have wondered why Teng, so close to succession to the premiership, should apparently gratuitously injure his chances, say, by insulting the Chairman's wife.[237] One of Teng's more appealing qualities, however, has always been a kind of blunt, scrappy courage. Also, his actions appear quite rational. We might assume he began his offensive at the time of Chou En-lai's incapacitating illness. Despite the impression of the U.S. State Department, Teng's position was intrinsically weak. He had been purged and degraded; he was the coleader of the "Liu-Teng line." As perhaps the prime critic of the cult of the individual in the 1950s, he seems to have been disliked by the Chairman. His return from disgrace in 1973 would cause resentment by the radicals and possibly jealousy among those who shared Teng's policy preferences but who had not themselves been purged. Decisive action was required if Teng were to build any kind of base that could support him after Chou was gone. His attempt, of course, failed: he was purged before Chou En-lai's ashes had cooled.

The program attributed to Teng fits the man (except, perhaps, for an uncharacteristic concern over the quality of literature by this not very reflective person). He had been a hard-line party disciplinarian but was apparently willing to be pragmatic on economic questions (his famous white cat and black cat—who cares, as long as he catches mice).

Teng's offensive seems to have been initially successful. In October, Honan, which a year and half earlier had praised rebellion, took a different tone, broadcasting a direct attack on the radical slogan "Oppose the tide":

> Whoever . . . intentionally treats revolutionary discipline as the restoration of revisionism, treats his sabotage of revolutionary discipline as "opposing the

> tide'' or something like that stands on the side of the bourgeoisie and opposes the Party and proletarian dictatorship.[238]

In the fall of 1975 the regime held a great Tachai Conference to plan the future of China's agricultural development. This seems to have been Teng's show, although the high-ranking radicals attended the meetings. Both Teng and Chiang Ch'ing made speeches, although these were not published. The main published speech was by Hua Kuo-feng (a luckier man than Teng) and presumably represents the general consensus. Hua sets forth the basic tasks: develop Tachai-style farming, with the county party committee as the leadership nucleus; struggle against capitalist tendencies, suppress the class enemy, and expand collective agriculture; encourage cadre labor; mechanize agriculture; and encourage handicraft industry.[239] This program seems largely moderate, rational modernist. There is little stress on the mass line: agriculture is to be reformed from above, by the county. The general emphasis is on increasing yield. There may be some concessions to the radicals, such as the encouragement of cadre labor. The goal of expanding collective agriculture may also be such a concession. The moderate voice in the anti-Confucius campaign, we have argued, was against further collectivization, and those who wrote these articles were probably political allies of Teng's. But Teng (white cat, black cat) may well have had no objection to collectivization—may in fact have preferred it as leading to easier social control—if structural changes such as mechanization of agriculture would remove the obstacles collectivization places in the way of increased yield.

A counterattack on the consolidation of the moderate position also began in the early fall, apparently under the direct inspiration of Mao Tse-tung. The first sign was an attack by Mao on *Water margin,* a work the world had heretofore been given to understand was one of the Chairman's favorite books. It is a tale of Robin Hood–like bandits in the Sung dynasty. According to Mao, however, their leader, Sung Chiang, is a ''surrenderist'': he made peace with the court and accepted an amnesty to fight other bandits—although in the end he was betrayed and killed. *Water margin* ''opposes corrupt officials, but not the emperor'' (which may be said of many contemporary dissidents as well). Sung Chiang is a ''landlord element'' who sneaked into the revolutionary ranks in order to betray the cause. The story is a ''negative example,'' teaching us not to surrender.[240] Some of the resulting discussion of the novel is decidedly strange. One of the traditional versions of the work omits the part about the amnesty; Sung Chiang and his friends are simply captured and executed. This, it turns out, was done ''so the people would not clearly perceive Sung Chiang's surrenderist line.''[241] In 1976 it became clear that Sung Chiang was a figure for Teng Hsiao-p'ing,[242] although if one looks at a picture of Teng (short, squat, grinning; Peter Lorre with a crew-cut) the analogy is not very compelling. Sometimes Sung Chiang may also have been a figure for Chou En-lai, and it is also possible that some of the talk of surrenderism was Mao's criticism of the establishment radicals for temporizing with the likes of Teng.[243]

In December the radical offensive became more open, with students from Peking and Tsinghua universities criticizing "strange talk and bizarre theories." This was a reference not to the campaign against *Water margin,* but to moderate criticisms of the "educational revolution."[244] On January 1 Mao published two poems he had written in 1965. The poems are classical in form, but perhaps of less than classical refinement.

> *Didn't you see that in the fall of the year before last*
> *The three families made a treaty.*
> *There's stuff to eat—*
> *Some stir-fried potatoes,*
> *Throw in a little beef . . .*
> *Stop this farting:*
> *Just look at the turmoil of heaven and earth.*[245]

This, of course, is an attack on the moderate program as "goulash communism."

When Chou En-lai died in January the radical counteroffensive was well under way. Chou's death removed what was probably the main obstacle to Teng's purge but did not really result in a qualitative change in the nature of the growing campaign against him. Hua Kuo-feng became premier instead of Teng; the speculation in the West was that Hua was a compromise choice (the radicals would have preferred Chang Ch'un-ch'iao). After Teng had definitely fallen, the press continued to say, "Cure the illness, save the man," but it seems unlikely there was any real desire to save Teng: this had already been tried. Instead, the phrase was an inducement for those who might be inclined to defend Teng to desert him before it was too late. The campaign increasingly began to refer to the glorious tradition of the Red Guards, but the references were in part insincere: this campaign was to be an orderly one; there must be no *ch'uan-lien,* no wandering about causing trouble.[246]

Trouble did, of course, come. The Ch'ing Ming ("bright and clear") festival falls two months after the lunar new year, about the time the Chinese spring really begins to warm up. The festival was described in the Western press as a "feast of the dead," but the reality is gayer than this implies. Ch'ing Ming is the time for the sweeping of family graves and has something of a picnic atmosphere to it. Wreaths had been placed at the monument to Chou En-lai on Ch'ing Ming, and these were removed over the weekend. On April 5 "a small handful of class enemies" (100,000 persons, according to the regime, but most were said to be curiosity-seekers) gathered in front of the Gate of Heavenly Peace in Peking to protest. According to the regime, the crowd, mostly students, like the Chairman, took to poetry:

> . . . China now is no longer the China of the past. Also, the people are not utter dolts. The feudal society of the First Ch'in Emperor is gone and will not come back. We believe in Marxism-Leninism. Those *hsiu-ts'ai* who have castrated Marxism-Leninism can go see the devil! What we demand is true Marxism-Leninism. For the sake of true Marxism-Leninism we do not fear getting our heads smashed and our blood spilled. We offer it as wine in a sacrifice to the day of the four modernizations.

As the regime points out with horror, they sound just like Lin Li-kuo[247]—or, we might add, Li I-che. During the demonstrations there was some violence. Some cars were burned and some near-by buildings damaged. "Worker-peasant-soldier study personnel" from Tsinghua and urban militia-men were badly beaten up (I have heard speculation that the regime students were sent in in order to provoke violence). Following the riots in Peking, disturbances were also reported in Nanking, Canton, Taiyuan, Shanghai, and Chengchow.[248]

Teng, of course, was blamed for the riots (he is said to have fancied himself another Imre Nagy), although it is unlikely that he had anything directly to do with them—if nothing else, he would have had little opportunity to engage in many plots. The demonstration would seem to have been spontaneous. This is not unprecedented—only the summer before there had been turmoil in Hangchow. Even before the riots there were hints of popular restiveness, of hostility to the establishment radicals. Travelers say that in Canton Chiang Ch'ing had been attacked in wall posters for an interview she had given to the American writer Roxane Witke, in which Miss Chiang apparently claimed to have been the power behind the Chairman's throne, a claim that would not ring well on any Chinese ears. Chiang Ch'ing should step down along with Teng Hsiao-p'ing, the posters said.[249]

The Ch'ing Ming riots may never rival the May 4, 1919, riots in historical importance. "China now is no longer the China of the past," and the 1976 riots were suppressed much more easily. The short-term consequence of the riots seems to have been the very temporary strengthening of the establishment radicals—the *hsiu-ts'ai* against whom they were directed—and the very temporary rallying together of the ruling elite of both tendencies, as during the 1957 antirightist campaign. The riots may, however, be symptomatic of broader trends. They probably do not show real popular enthusiasm for the person of Teng Hsiao-p'ing (although in 1975, it is said, some were proclaiming Teng as a savior of the "type of Hai Ch'ing-t'ien"—Sky-blue Sea, Hai Jui),[250] or even, really, for Chou En-lai, although Chou was certainly genuinely popular. They do indicate a weariness with the radical line and an increasing isolation of the establishment radicals. The moderate line is seen as preferable, although the preference is possibly a very relative one. It is perhaps appropriate to apply to these riots (and to the other instances of opposition described in this study) the conclusions of Eugene Genovese on slave rebellions in North America:

> The significance of slave revolts in the United States lies neither in their frequency nor in their extent, but in their very existence as the ultimate manifestation of class war under the most unfavorable conditions. . . . The panic of slaveholders at the slightest hint of slave insurrection revealed what lay beneath their endless self-congratulations over the supposed docility, contentment, and loyalty of their slaves.[251]

I am not sure whether this reasoning—Genovese's or any *mutatis mutandis* application of it to China—is sound, but it is plausible.

This section is the denouement. The Ch'ing Ming riots are a good place to end the study. This last section traces a defeat—perhaps the last one*—of the old moderate tendency. "China now is no longer the China of the past," and the Chinese people, whether as a consequence of indoctrination in the virtues of rebellion or as a manifestation of the traditional eventual wearing out of patience with misgovernment, seem less docile than they have been, and the radical victory may be hollow. This section, and this study as a whole, may be merely an introduction to a period in which opposition and dissent in China become more overt and obvious. The regime may either liberalize or repress, but the Chinese people have stood up.

*October 1976: one way or another.

7

Conclusions

i own and own it with
a sigh
my point of view
is somewhat wried
i am a pessimistic
guy
i see things from the
under side

—archy the cockroach
in "ballade of the under side"
DON MARQUIS

One who adopts the point of view of a cockroach is not apt to see things in their most becoming aspect. This study of Chinese politics from the under side reveals only a part of the Chinese reality. Much of ordinary life must surely go on without too much reference to politics, and many Chinese must surely be completely dedicated to the regime and its works, whatever the regime may do.

The approach taken here does, I think, provide insights into Chinese politics that might be missing in other approaches, such as studies of elites or of bureaucratic decision making. It might also help to correct some of the more romantic interpretations of Chinese society popular in the West during the early 1970s. It shows interpretations of Chinese politics alternative to those approved by the regime, but by those subject to the regime. From a narrow point of view the interpretation, say, of Chang T'ieh-sheng by Li I-che perhaps tells us little we would not guess anyway; but it is nice to have internal confirmation for this guess. The interpretations of Chinese politics by dissidents within China are not necessarily valid, of course—in some ways they may be inevitably warped—but it contributes to our understanding even to be aware that such interpretations exist. We are certainly not compelled to assent to the dissident attitudes. If a man complains about his society, the fault may well be in himself (although I think the dissident attitudes discussed here do have some objective basis). We may, at the extreme, regard the Chinese dissidents as sociopaths, men unfit to live in the society fit for men to live in. It is a rather universal principle, however, that government exists for the sake of the governed, and in Chinese dissident attitudes we learn what some Chinese think of their government. The dissidents are no doubt flawed in their persons and in their ideas, but many of them have also shown great moral courage. This in itself is probably worth commemorating, especially since it may be some time before their countrymen will be able to indulge in such commemoration. In the fashion of the traditional novelist, we might reiterate by listing some of the more outstanding dissidents: Hu Feng, Kung P'in-mei, Lin Hsi-ling, K'o P'ei-chi, Ma Chen-wu, Pen-huan, P'eng Te-huai, Teng T'o, Wu Han, Li Cheng-t'ien—heroes under heaven.

This study is intended as a critique of totalitarianism. Since a totalitarian regime is one that does not consider itself subject to any standards external to itself, this study does not constitute any transsubjective rational criticism a totalitarian would accept. It does show empirically, however, that unhappiness remains and that people remain capable of forming visions of the good life that do not accord with the regime's.

This study shows most clearly, perhaps, the limitations of opposition. The physical limitations are plain enough. There would also seem to be intellectual limitations. Most of the dissent discussed here has been in the idiom of the regime. There has perhaps been a secular trend away from overtly integral opposition. In 1957 the rightists could still demand a multi-party system; by the 1970s Li I-che speaks only of a vague democracy. Li I-che and the 1976 Peking rioters present their demands as true socialism, something their rulers presumably want as well. Human imagination is limited enough in any case, and most rebels probably tacitly affirm as much of the status quo as they reject. The Communists, for example, argued that they better embodied Chinese nationalism and were better able to modernize China—that they could accomplish the goals of the KMT better than the KMT. Much of the new left ideology in the United States seems to be eighth-grade civics taken seriously, filtered through an existentialist gauze. Huey Long used to urge that when fascism comes to the United States, it will be as one hundred percent Americanism. In China, indoctrination and the sheer lack of opportunity to develop a really radical stance exaggerate this propensity. Solzhenitsyn could not have developed his radical criticism of the Stalinist society in Stalin's day, and in fact his integral opposition seems to have developed only after the experience of many years of a relatively mild regime. Existence may not *determine* consciousness, but we must not underestimate the force of circumstances on the human mind.

This study also shows the ability of political power to eliminate certain interests it perceives to be antagonistic to itself. The Chinese regime would appear to have thoroughly crushed organized religion, for example, as any kind of oppositional interest (without, perhaps, destroying the sentiments served by organized religion). But while the regime can do very well without any organized religion, it does require certain other potentially dissident interests, such as agriculture. As the country modernizes, more interests will be generated. In the absence of utter economic stagnation, for example, it seems that at a minimum the set of attitudes identified as rational modernism will grow stronger.

Here, perhaps, we see the limits of the force of circumstances and of totalitarianism: despite all, opposition persists. Chalmers Johnson says of prewar Japan that "a political order that proclaims discussion to be useless is one that invites treason, or, conversely, one that makes the concept of treason unintelligible."[1] This is probably true only of a modernized and politicized order, but China is politicized and increasingly modernized. Discussion is not really permitted—even the most innocuous specific opposition may suddenly be denounced as hostility to socialism. This probably tends to increase the intensity of opposition, and in fact, while opposition may have become in some ways less integral, it also seems to have become more intense. This trend may continue. Much of the regime's earlier appeal had been its ability to restore and maintain civil peace, but after two decades the regime itself encouraged disorder: it deliberately denied protection to some of its subjects. This sets a precedent. Also, the population of China is very young. When on the defensive the regime urges its subjects to "remember the bitter, think of the sweet." The bitter increasingly numerous Chinese remember is the Great Leap Forward, the "temporary economic difficulties," and the Cultural Revolution. The regime may not much longer be able to impress people with tales of the wretchedness of former alternatives to itself.

We should be wary of overestimating the limits of totalitarianism, however. While opposition does persist in a totalitarian regime, it is likely that a *revolutionary* totalitarian regime requires opposition—it needs enemies to suppress, the suppression of enemies keeping alive its dynamism. Historically, new campaigns have generally begun with the digging out of the class enemy. In China, I argue below, were enemies suddenly to disappear, the regime would have a hard time justifying dictatorship. The point may be, however, that the opposition required by the regime also, as an unintended consequence, keeps alive alternatives to the regime.

The opposition movements discussed in this study seem to converge toward liberalism. All of the major opposition movements have been liberalizing in tendency. Rational modernism, the most narrow of these, makes no provision for liberty but does promise order, regularity, some personal privacy, perhaps, and a higher level of material well-being. Marxian Confucianism may not have any institutional democratic implications; it does emphasize some cultural spontaneity and nonpolitical freedom and would have political programs limited by the felt needs of the population. In radical opposition there is an argument, of varying degrees of vagueness, for political democracy. Some may find this convergence toward liberalism surprising. There is no real liberal tradition in China, and liberalism in China has been weak. Explicit liberalism was wiped out on the Chinese mainland in the 1950s. From a more abstract and general point of view, liberalism seems a discredited ideology if there ever was one. It is a product of modernization and also, it seems, a way station, a rest stop on the way to totalitarianism. Liberalism serves to undermine all authoritative—and hence moral—systems but does not itself seem able to substitute anything of general appeal. In the absence of strong liberal institutions liberalism decays, and it seems to decay only more slowly where there are democratic institutions. In Europe it appears to be an honorable but ineffective sect. In the United States the right wing of liberalism (conservatism) seems often to amount in practice to an apology for corporate greed (no longer even human greed). Mainstream liberalism seems to lack any confidence in the principles it professes[2] and to underpin a system increasingly without either order or liberty[3]—although (the totalitarian implication) we may be fairly confident that order will be restored (order is of lower value than liberty, but in its absence it is in fact more desired; and liberty over any long term requires order—but not vice versa—although there is always tension between the two). In China, liberalism would seem regressive.

We might return to basics, however, and see liberalism as an appeal against arbitrary and unreasonable power. As the Chairman teaches us, "Where there is oppression, there must be resistance." The cynic would add: Where the oppressed have no real chance of becoming oppressors themselves, they will demand toleration.

This study does not yield any direct predictions about future developments in China. There is little reason to think any opposition position will ever become the dominant one, and less reason to think it will be unchanged in its triumph. The analysis of the political dynamics used in this study is predicated on the presence of Mao in the system, which is no longer the case. Anyway, the empirical rule of thumb in predicting is that no prediction ever works out.

Still, the temptation remains, and we may at least engage in general speculation, confined to the possible consequences of principled opposition without worrying about the whole range of alternative futures. The most obvious question is whether opposition will lead to rebellion—whether, as some seemed to hint in the campaign against Confucius, the present order will be violently overthrown and a new, milder order established, one which will retain what is good in the present dynasty. The easy answer is that numerous rebellions have in fact taken place—most recently, as of this writing, in April 1976. There is no reason to expect a successful rebellion. In this century it seems that strong regimes are overthrown only as a consequence of foreign war. War can hardly be excluded, but neither can it be predicted—and even less could it be welcomed. Peking is not Saigon, and in the absence of general chaos it would seem impossible for potential rebels to organize on any large scale. They would have few prospects for foreign support. Taipei or Moscow might be willing to help out, but neither of these regimes is well situated to provide large-scale support for subversion in the interior of China. The consequences of rebellion could well be worse than the evils causing it. As usual, it would be the innocent (including the soldiers on the various sides) who would suffer most. Large-scale rebellion might lead to warlordism, as it usually has in the past, or to foreign intervention. The evil consequences of rebellion, of course, say nothing about whether it will happen. The probable consequences of the battle of Verdun could have been easily foreseen, and no one desired those consequences; yet that battle was fought. Finally, there is no guarantee that rebels tough enough to overthrow the present order would be any gentler with the people than are the current rulers, but there is precedent in Chinese history for mild rule following harsh.

More prosaically, we might consider the possible consequences of the triumph of one of the two major tendencies. It is hard to know what the triumph of radicalism would mean. Given that tendency's hostility to vested interests, as a ruling ideology it would seem to be inherently unstable. The triumph of the radical tendency would probably be the triumph of radicals, not radicalism; there are already clear signs that the establishment radicals have their own comfortable vested interests; and the most radical among them could probably survive only by alliances with persons or groups, less radical by temperament than they, in the army or the police. Should the radicals become completely deradicalized, the triumph of the tendency would be its extinction. It is likely, however, that the radicals will retain some of their old ideology, particularly the stress on class struggle. It is also unlikely that the radicals will wish to deprive themselves of the sources of wealth and power and will therefore continue the modernization of China. This will provide the social base for new bourgeois elements and thus targets for the struggle the radicals require. Radical rule may become increasingly terroristic, and, when terror fails, the system may yield to disorder. Some such cycle could, in the abstract, go on forever, but one intuitively feels that radical rule will be transitional to something else.

The triumph of the moderate tendency—which in the short run would be rational modernism, not that tendency's Marxian Confucian strain—would probably be welcomed at first by the general population, even by those persons outside the ruling circles who are radical by temperament or conviction. This would probably mean the rule of a bureaucratic, Brezhnevite state that would grant limited autonomy to various social groupings and would aim at a higher material standard of living than has been normal since 1949. It is likely, however, that limited grants of autonomy will generate demands for more, and the rulers will probably be willing neither to yield to such demands nor to eliminate the conditions that give rise to them. Over the long run the moderate regime is likely to have serious problems of legitimacy. Once it finishes congratulating itself on having overcome the "petty-bourgeois, phony Marxist, idealist, feudal-fascist adventurers" (or whatever it chooses to call the radicals), or once the people become tired of hearing about this, the moderate regime would seem to lack any real moral content. The state will no doubt be strong enough to handle the inevitable carping of intellectuals and might have little to worry about as long as good times last. But it is inevitable that trouble come. The moderates will probably down-play the idea of struggle, perhaps turning to some Khrushchevian notion of the state of all the people. The problem here (as the Russian rulers have discovered, and probably would have discovered even without the shrill help of the Chinese) is that in Marxist terms, if there is a state of all the people there is no longer any excuse for dictatorship. But it is unlikely the moderates will be willing to grant democracy. The consequence will be a more or less repressive, probably capricious, regime, one which may last for a long, long time, but not to anyone's great enthusiasm.

There is another general possibility, one that might be called the Machiavellian solution. The hypothesis is that neither tendency will be able to defeat the other, although the struggle between them will continue. Each unable to eliminate the other, and each unwilling for the other to eliminate it, the tendencies may learn to tolerate each other. In pursuit of tactical advantage they might be willing to broaden the scope of political struggle, bringing in more people; their common interest in maintaining a chance at power will lead them to preserve public order (lest, at the extreme, the people throw them both out). This may lead to an evolution, in Li I-che's terms, away from factional democracy to class democracy. The clash between the forces of, say, order and equality will insure that each part is kept in consideration, while the clash itself will generate liberty. The struggle will provide an incentive for those engaged in it to develop institutions (laws) to regularize and contain the conflict, to assure the participants that their tactical defeats need not be strategic personal disasters. It is idle to speculate on what form such institutions might take—whether there would be a multi-party system, for example. There would be, in any case, an evolution away from totalitarianism, with the realization that in politics one can attain only a relative good.

This last prediction is probably fantasy. There is no doubt much merit in the Chinese radicals' warnings against reformism. The two tendencies have been coexisting for twenty years or so, and there does not seem to be any evolution toward democracy yet. Still, there is perhaps a base from which this condition could develop. In the mid-1970s the establishment radicals seemed isolated and the moderates increasingly able to appeal to mass discontent. Any coalition that overthrows the establishment radicals is likely to contain discordant interests—those, say, of bureaucrats and of educated youth. The common participation in victory may give each element of the coalition sufficient power to prevent its immediate defeat by an ally.

Those who have sponsored this study wish it to have policy implications. It has no direct ones, and this is probably just as well. There may be some innocuous indirect implications, however. For one thing, it might be good for foreign governments sometimes to ignore the instinctive fellow-feeling of establishments. One has in mind here the anile dithering of the *New York Times* over the possibility of disorder resulting from the Ch'ing Ming riots. The simple point is that not all order is just (or an unjust order is no true order). Disorder may be a symptom of injustice (which is not to impute justice to those who directly instigate disorder), and it may be inexpedient as well as immoral to invest too much worry over someone else's inability to maintain an unjust order. This certainly does not mean foreign governments should support Chinese dissidents in any material way. The behavior of the Peking rioters indicates some dissidents themselves would not welcome such meddling.

Another indirect policy implication concerns the Chinese "great experiment," the sad utopia. Those who admire the Chinese experiment by and large do not yet want to incorporate it directly into their own societies. But, then, what were abominations to our fathers are commonplaces to us, and God knows what we are preparing for our children. The Chinese system has a special appeal to those who combine concern about the inequitable distribution of resources with worry about the limits to growth, the possibility that unrestrained material advance is bringing catastrophe to the planet.[4] In China, some see a solution: collectivism, restricted consumption, equality, "poverty communism." Life is not very comfortable, but (allegedly) "no one is starving" (at any rate, starving people are not on visitors' agendas). There may not be much freedom, but who cares about that? China, in this incarnation, has all the advantages of a well-run jail.

The first comment here is that, despite what we hear, it is not because of totalitarianism that China is not like India. Despite missionary propaganda, China has rarely been the land of the starving masses. People certainly starved in China—just as people starved in preindustrial Europe—but for long periods China apparently enjoyed a standard of living higher than most preindustrial countries, including those of Europe. This century's misery has been a consequence of war and the absence of strong government, but not a consequence of the absence of totalitarianism. Since Liberation, material misery has resulted precisely from the imposition of totalitarian policies, as in the 1959–62 period. When the regime worries about its belly, it liberalizes. That the nation of the most skilled farmers in the world should ration its staple foods (and even import some of them) is a comment on the welfare inefficiencies of totalitarianism. It is unlikely, of course, that China will ever attain the material standard of living that prevails in the United States—just as it is likely that Americans must somehow learn to abate their standard of living. But objectively there seems to be no reason Chinese could not be both more comfortable and more free than they now are.

The advocates of the limits of growth who admire the Chinese system hardly share the same vision as the Chinese rulers, of course. We hear of "Chinese," but these often seem like the irritating "Chinese" or "Persians" or "Iroquois" who people the literature of the European Enlightenment, whose function is to point out the irrationalities of their creators' home societies. The current "Chinese" seem less witty than their ancestors—as do their creators, who sometimes tend to approach the philosophy of Chairman Mao with a pretentious air that would seem affected if directed toward that of Immanuel Kant—but the world changes. The real Chinese rulers are rather fundamentalist Marxists and consider the foundations of "ecologism"—limitations of resources, entropy, that sort of thing—to be the products of the fetid wet dreams of a dying bourgeoisie. The Chinese have, however, developed the social techniques for attaining what some concerned with the limits of growth would consider a viable society. The solution may not be a good one, but it may be all that human imagination can devise. This study might lead to a rethinking of the facts behind some of the modish evaluations of the Chinese experiment; at least it can show some of the costs of the experiment and demonstrate that in some respects programs we may take to avert catastrophe may lead to no more human happiness than the catastrophe itself.[5] The viable society will not be a happy one nor, in the short run, a stable one. People will continue to hope for something better. My own personal feeling is that China will show, in the not too long run, that such hopes are not vain.

prince ere you pull a bluff
and lie
Before you fake and play the snide
consider whether archy s nigh
i see things from
the under side

—archy the cockroach
"ballade of the under side"
DON MARQUIS

Appendix

Notes on Opposition on Taiwan

The government in Taipei claims Taiwan is an integral part of China, and the government in Peking agrees. As this is a study of opposition in contemporary China, it is proper to include something on Taiwan. This can only be "notes," however. Despite its greater accessibility, Taiwan has been studied much less systematically than the mainland. In some ways the politics of Taiwan are as obscure as those of the mainland, and on Taiwan we do not even have the advantage of a near-monolithic party line from which we can derive clues about what is going on. The ability of Chinese scholars on Taiwan to conduct objective political studies is still somewhat limited by the nature of the regime, and American scholars have too often regarded Taiwan as a poor substitute for the "real China,"[1] as a kind of cultural zoo.

Foreigners are less than impressed by the claims of the government of the Republic of China to be a bastion of liberty and democracy in Asia. An introductory text on Chinese government informs us: the KMT regime is "at least as oppressive and insensitive to the civil rights and liberty of its citizens as its mainland neighbor."[2] *At least*. It is hard to know how to respond to this sort of thing. If someone, staring directly at an object you perceive as white, pronounces it black, the difference would seem to be one of perception and interpretation of the facts, not one that can be settled simply by reference to the facts. In 1975 Freedom House agreed with the textbook evaluation, classifying Taiwan as "unfree," putting it in the same category as the mainland. Taiwan publicists find this disturbing. One article explains that in the West freedom has acquired a new meaning, implying that the opposition should be more powerful than the government, that people can openly support enemy countries, that those who are opposed to the existing system should enjoy license—the writer, in fact, sounds rather like Chou En-lai in 1957 (or like Aleksandr Solzhenitsyn). The article quotes a professor of government at Taiwan National University who says that "half-free" would be a better designation for Taiwan than "unfree." "In some respects civil rights in the U.S. are not as well developed as in China [i.e., Taiwan]," the professor says; for example, women's rights. An "American merchant'' says, ''At least I can walk the streets at midnight without fear of being assaulted,'' and this is freedom of a sort. At first the merchant thought this was because Taiwan was such a police state, but later he changed his mind.[3] All this is less than convincing, in that the examples of freedom given do not distinguish Taiwan from the mainland. Mainland women are also ''liberated,'' and the streets of mainland cities are also safe at night—and not just because the mainland is a police state.

Rodomontade aside, any classification system that does not distinguish between Taiwan and the mainland is not a very subtle one. The KMT makes no attempt to control every aspect of its subjects' lives. The inhabitants of Taiwan enjoy a wide range of nonpolitical liberties. While Taiwan is a one-party (or ''hegemonic party'') state, the KMT is not ''monolithic,'' and there is perhaps almost as wide a range of disagreement within the party as there is in the society at large. Taiwan is relatively open to the outside and enjoys a fair, if limited, amount of cultural freedom. Students from Taiwan coming to the United States will peruse the *People's Daily* in college libraries for a time, partly out of curiosity, partly because, since the anticommunist propaganda at home is so vehement, they feel that the Communists must have something to offer. After a while, however, even many radical students abandon the *People's Daily* but continue to read the official KMT organ, the *Central Daily News*: the latter is, in fact, a much more interesting paper, and this probably says something about the quality of life under the two regimes. There is much less political freedom than other kinds of freedom on Taiwan, but even political freedom is not totally absent. There are competitive elections (while the KMT is effectively the only party, independent candidates may run against it), and the votes are usually counted (although there are complaints of irregularities in all elections).

In 1975 the Taiwan regime did little to mollify its liberal critics, at the end of that year sentencing a dissident politician to life imprisonment and suppressing an opposition publication.[4] The suppression of the publication, *Taiwan Political Review,* shows the capricious nature of the repression on Taiwan. The journal was ordered to suspend publication for one year on the pretext that it had violated copyright laws—the regime likes a facade of legality; but the regime admitted that the suppression was political.[5] The journal's error, we are told, was to publish a letter from a Taiwanese scholar abroad. The scholar reports his conversation with two mainlanders he met. One was a musician who fled the mainland about seventeen years ago. The musician thinks totalitarianism was necessary for China in order to destroy two thousand years of feudalism and autocracy and establish a basis for freedom and equality (on the mainland he would perhaps be a rational modernist). Mao has swept away feudalism, but in the process he has destroyed creativity. Mao's culture is even worse than that of Confucius. The KMT, on the other hand, might be somewhat better but is afraid of democracy (this is typical—communist tyranny is given some excuse; that of the KMT, none). The musician refuses to go to Taiwan because the regime would simply use him for his propaganda value (alas, true enough). The second interlocutor grew up on Taiwan. When he came to the United States he was impressed by the mainland, now the world's third great power. His political thought is childish, the letter writer says: he thinks the mainland is a democracy. Taiwan, on the other hand, is a totalitarian system with economic inequality, poverty in the midst of plenty. The KMT represents minority privilege. Now comes the offending passage: "He believes that if the Taiwan people really want to be 'masters of their own house,' they have only two roads: The first is an armed rebellion by the Taiwan people to overthrow the KMT dictatorship; the second is for the Taiwan people to get united and struggle for an early peaceful reunification of the fatherland."[6]

These views can hardly be represented as those of the journal, and the writer of the letter also dissociates himself from them (but after studying Teng T'o, say, we perhaps cannot be too sure the censor did not know what he was doing). The letter as a whole, of course, does not correspond with the regime's public-relations image of itself. Still, the impression is that this specific political motive for the suppression is itself a pretext. The journal, which had been established only a few months earlier, was run by Taiwanese intellectuals with previous records of criticism of the regime. Its editor, a Taiwanese member of the Legislative Yuan, the national parliament, had been reelected a few days before the suppression on a platform calling for an end to martial law, an independent judiciary, freedom of the press, a multi-party system, and less spending on the army and more on welfare. Because of the touchy international situation, the editor, K'ang Ning-hsiang, said he was pulling his punches. It had been suggested that after the December 20 elections the regime would bring pressure on the magazine, "although K'ang himself thinks it would not be so stupid as to do such a thing."[7] Whom the gods would destroy . . . The suppression appears to have been an act of spite, one which, because the regime is structured as it is, it could get away with. Still, it does not indicate a total absence of political liberty. Thus, there was no thought of denying K'ang his seat in the legislature. Perhaps we may say that domestic opposition to the Taiwan regime is normally at least as outspoken as that on the mainland in May 1957.

An even more egregious case of repression is that of Po Yang (Kuo I-tung), a satirist jailed in 1968. This shows the regime at its worst (this is not to say the jailing of Po Yang is the worst thing the regime has ever done; rather, it is typical of the worst things it does). Po Yang was tried in secret on charges of being a communist agent. He had always publicly been an anticommunist liberal; this hardly precludes his being an agent, but, as his friends point out, the regime has not seen fit to publish any convincing evidence against him.[8] Po Yang came to grief by guilt through association with Popeye, the sailor man (see cartoons, pp. 248–50). Po Yang had been responsible for translating Popeye for a newspaper. His friends say the cartoons that brought him down have nothing to do with politics and profess to fail to understand how Po Yang could have let himself have anything to do with someone as vulgar as Popeye, anyway. As the cartoons stand they are a nice (but certainly unintended) comment on the situation on Taiwan. In his translation Po Yang made the comparison a bit more explicit. As he told the Garrison Command, "In order to relax and intensify the humor, as usual I did not make a completely literal translation, but did some revising and reorganizing."[9] It is hard to believe that Po Yang's mind was not in fact turning to Chiang the father and Chiang the son. Still, the satire is fairly good-natured, and it is equally hard to believe this is the sort of thing for which a person should go to jail. It is likely that Po Yang, with his liberalism, his hostility to the traditional culture (especially in its KMT version), and his attacks on official corruption, was regarded as a gadfly, and Popeye provided the occasion to swat him. To preserve the legalities—it is not against the law to translate cartoons—the charge of espionage was thrown in.

These are the dregs. Perhaps we should also examine, in general terms, the political atmosphere, the ambiance, of Taiwan and some specific opposition movements.

POPEYE By Bud Sagendorf

Po Yang's Translation:

①走吧，到咱們王國去.
②我想了一個國名。

③先掛起招牌來……
人間樂園，
歡喜王國，
妙呀！

1. LET'S GO TO OUR KINGDOM.
2. I'M THINKING OF A NAME FOR OUR STATE.
3. FIRST I'LL PUT UP THIS SIGN . . .
A PARADISE ON EARTH
A DELIGHTFUL KINGDOM.
HOW WONDERFUL!

10-7

①父王，我們住啥地方呀

別亂叫！

②啥都妥妥貼貼！

③瞧！

1. KING-FATHER, WHERE SHALL WE LIVE?

2. I'll PUT UP A PALACE.

3. THERE.

10-9

①好美的王國。

②我是國王，我是總統，我想是啥就是啥！

③我哩！

1. WHAT A BEAUTIFUL KINGDOM.

2. I AM THE KING; I AM THE PRESIDENT; WHAT I SAY GOES.

3. WHAT ABOUT ME?

10-10

①你算皇太子吧！

我要幹就幹總統

②你這小娃子

③口氣可不小。

1. YOU ARE THE CROWN-PRINCE.

I WANT TO BE PRESIDENT.

2. YOU LITTLE PUNK . . .

3. YOUR GALL IS NOT LITTLE.

10-11

①老頭，你要寫文章投稿呀！
我要寫一篇告全國同胞書。
②全國只有我們兩個人，你知道吧！
③但我還是要講演。

1. OLD FELLOW, WHAT ARE YOU WRITING?
   I AM WRITING AN ADDRESS TO ALL
   MY FELLOW COUNTRYMEN.
2. IN THE WHOLE COUNTRY THERE ARE ONLY THE TWO OF US.
3. I'M STILL GOING TO GIVE A SPEECH TO YOU.

10-12

①敝國乃民主國家，人人有選舉權！
人人！只兩個罷啦。
②等我想想……
③我要跟你競選！

1. THIS IS A DEMOCRATIC COUNTRY. EVERYONE MUST VOTE.
   EVERYONE! THERE ARE ONLY TWO OF US.
2. LET ME THINK . . .
3. I'LL RUN AGAINST YOU!

10-13

①等我先發表競選演，
好吧！
②全國同胞們……
開頭不錯。
③千萬不要投小娃的票。
這算幹啥！

1. LET ME WRITE MY DECLARATION OF CANDIDACY.
   OK.
2. FELLOW COUNTRYMEN . . .
   IT STARTS OUT ALL RIGHT.
3. YOU BETTER NOT VOTE FOR THE LITTLE PUNK.
   WHAT'S GOING ON?

THE AMBIANCE

The Taiwan regime calls itself the Republic of China, considering itself the same state that was formed after the collapse of the Ch'ing in 1911. The regime does not think that Taiwan *is* China; rather, Taiwan is a province of China and the government in Taipei is the legitimate government of all China. Unfortunately, the other Chinese provinces are under the temporary control of a rebel bandit gang. Actually, the KMT controls more than just Taiwan. The offshore islands of Chin-men (Quemoy) and Matsu are part of Fukien province, and one reason the KMT does not abandon them is that to do so would undermine the regime's claim to be more than just the government of Taiwan. The pretension to be the government of China is the means by which the regime justifies its rule of Taiwan, but it is also the source of many of its political problems.

There have been Chinese on Taiwan for more than a thousand years, although the major settlement did not begin until around the seventeenth century. The island for a time was an outpost for Ming loyalists (doubling as pirates) opposing the Ch'ing, but eventually the island was brought under central control. It was originally administered as part of Fukien province but became a province in its own right in 1885. Ten years later it was ceded to Japan and remained a Japanese colony until 1945. Taiwan was thus isolated from the more general Chinese turmoil that shaped the minds of those who now rule it. Misgovernment by the occupying mainland forces led to an uprising on February 28, 1947, which was brutally and treacherously suppressed. Soon after the uprising Chiang Kai-shek decided to make his last stand on Taiwan, and after rattling around various mainland cities the National Government finally settled in Taipei in December 1949. Accompanying the government came large numbers of soldiers and refugees. These and their families are the "mainlanders" and now constitute about 10 percent of the island's population.

On walls all over Taiwan, usually in faded paint, one sees the slogan, *Chien-she T'ai-wan, Kuang-fu Ta-lu*—"Develop Taiwan, gloriously recover the mainland." In spite of what most observers feel to be exorbitant spending on the military, the regime's main stress has been on the development of Taiwan into a model province, a preview of what all China will be once the bandits are pacified. Land on Taiwan was distributed very unevenly in 1945 (much more unevenly than was the norm on the mainland), and the government instituted a land-reform program based upon Sun Yat-sen's idea of "land to the tiller." This has virtually eliminated landlordism. The government purchased all land the owner did not himself farm, paying in slow-maturing bonds on government corporations, and resold the land to the tenants through long-term, low-interest loans. While Taiwan is not a welfare state—as on the mainland, families expect and are expected to look after their own—the island has well-developed educational, health, and social programs. The rise in the standard of living on the island—

which survived the world recession of the early 1970s[10]—is well known. It is less well appreciated that the spectacular growth has not led, as in Brazil and other countries, to increased inequality on the island.[11] Poverty still exists, of course, and perhaps the regime does not deserve all the credit for the progress. The Japanese did much to establish a base for the economic and social programs (and in fact the island was already one of the most modernized areas of China even before the Japanese took it), and until 1965 the regime received large amounts of developmental aid from the United States. Still, while hardly a government of the people, the regime has some claim (at least as much as the Communists) to be a government for the people.

Politically, the conditions are darker. Taiwan is in effect a one-party state. In addition to the KMT there are two tolerated minor parties, the Youth Party and the Social Democratic Party. These, however, are of no account; their position is rather like that of the democratic parties on the mainland: dwindling groups of old men. There are elections on Taiwan, however, and independent candidates may run against the KMT. The expenses of campaigning and the organizational advantages of the KMT as the single party perhaps account as much as its general popularity for the fact that the KMT usually wins.[12] Until 1971 the only elections were those at the local and provincial levels. The national Legislative Yuan remained the one elected in 1948, when Taiwanese did not vote. (It was inconvenient to hold new general elections all over China, it would be explained throughout the subsequent years.) In 1971 time had done its work on the old legislature, and the constitution was amended to allow supplementary elections in those parts of China under government control. Since then, Taiwanese have enjoyed at least minimal representation and have the opportunity to run for national office. Taiwanese have more representation in the government (including its appointive branches) than in the party, and while the various branches of the government are not just rubber stamps, the main locus of power is the party.

The political atmosphere is capriciously repressive. Periodicals are not usually subject to prior censorship but are subject to suppression for publishing objectionable material, and it takes a certain amount of courage to test the fluctuating limits of political tolerance. On the cultural level many post-1919 literary works are banned because of their leftist content; even nonpolitical works by leftist writers—or even by writers who simply chose to remain behind in 1949—are banned.[13] In general the heavy hand of oppression does not fall on ordinary people. Unlike the Communists, the KMT does not usually interfere with established life-styles.[14] Active dissent has been limited mainly to students and intellectuals,[15] although this does not mean that others, in the abstract, might not also desire some major changes.

Because of the national emergency, Taiwan is under martial law. Ordinary criminal cases are handled by the regular courts, but political offenses are turned over to the Taiwan Garrison Command (or, more ominously, to the Investigation

Bureau, which is reputedly nastier and more efficient than the relatively easy-going soldiers). At least in the 1960s and 1970s political cases have tended to be tried *in camera*, although the family of the accused may be permitted to attend. The charges against political offenders usually have to do with communism, although Taiwan independence activities, at least in the past, were probably of greater day-to-day concern to the regime. There are, naturally, allegations of the abuse of political prisoners, and given the way of the world some of these allegations must have foundation. The Taiwan independence advocate, P'eng Ming-min, reports being subjected to lengthy interrogation but not to physical brutality. The students arrested with him (persons of lesser status than he) were slapped during questioning but not tortured.[16] P'eng himself, perhaps because of American pressure, was soon released from prison on condition that he cease his political activities. He professed repentance—he wanted to "get out of prison by any means" and had decided that martyrdom would be "totally futile"[17]—but was not allowed to resume his teaching position at Taiwan University and was kept under loose supervision (house arrest). He fled the island during the 1970 lunar new year, eventually making his way to the United States. Dissidents less well known (particularly by Americans) than P'eng are probably treated more harshly. The regime, however, generally prefers to co-opt opposition rather than suppress it. Thus, P'eng was offered a position at the Institute of International Relations (Chiang Ching-kuo's "brain trust," he says), which he declined.[18]

The career of Kao Yü-shu (Henry Kao), another Taiwanese politician, may show more successful co-option, with give on both sides. Kao was elected mayor of Taipei in 1954 over KMT opposition. In 1957 he was defeated in what may have been a rigged election. Three years later he was involved in an attempt by Lei Chen and other mainlander intellectuals to organize a viable opposition party. After Lei was jailed on charges of communist sympathy, Kao publicly condemned "political influence" in the court system.[19] In 1964 Kao was again elected mayor of Taipei.[20] This time the regime attempted to solve the problem by finesse, making Taipei a special municipality (like Peking, Shanghai, and Tientsin on the mainland), administratively apart from Taiwan province. Thus, the mayor of Taipei, like the governor of Taiwan, is appointed directly by the president of the republic, nullifying Kao's popular appeal. But the first mayor appointed was the incumbent, Kao Yü-shu. In 1970 the machinery to have Kao impeached for corruption was set under way, but nothing came of this. In 1972 he was made minister of communications—kicked upstairs, perhaps, but he probably remains the most potent local leader on the island.

Unlike the Communists, the Taiwan regime is content with public silence and outward compliance, and it is probably easier to maintain a dissident stance on Taiwan. This does not, of course, detract from those who have maintained such a stance.

The gravest problem for the regime derives from its pretension to be the legitimate government of all China. Just as the CPC would find it hard to legitimize its dictatorship should it give up the notion of class struggle, so the KMT would find it difficult to legitimize its should it give up the goal of mainland recovery. But while the CPC members who stress class struggle seem to have few doubts about themselves or their righteousness, even the narrowest KMT man probably feels in his heart of hearts that reunification on anything like KMT terms is not too likely in his generation. This self-doubt makes the regime vulnerable and also inclined to act with a capricious viciousness against anyone who says out loud what everyone really thinks. The KMT position should not be dismissed simply as a cynical desire to hold onto small power after having lost the big, while pretending never to have lost the big. Many feel a sincere horror at what they perceive to be the disaster that has overcome their country; their inability to do anything about this only increases the frustration. Many combine homesickness with a passionate devotion to China. I was once a passive spectator at a conclave of American and Chinese pooh-bahs in Taipei. The Chinese, as is their wont, were trying to turn the meeting into a propaganda show; the Americans, who had naïvely fancied that the Chinese valued their opinions for their own sake (as if they had been scientists or economists), were rebelling against this. In the midst of this subdued, nerve-jangling tension, a friend said to me (in effect): "You think we are stupid. We know how we seem. What you don't understand is that we want to go home. We know we will probably never be able to go home, but we know for certain we never will unless we stay united. That is why we act the way we do: we want to go home." The regime likes to carve on mountainsides overlooking army camps: *Wu wang tsai Chü*—"Never forget we are in Chü," in exile. Alas, most of those the regime rules are natives of Chü; they are already home.

Mainlanders, as well as educated Taiwanese—there is not always that much to do—tend to assuage their homesickness in rather mindless, but harmless, hedonism. One-word summaries of situations are unfair, but if the atmosphere on Taiwan is to be summed up in one word, it would be *frivolity,* not *oppression.*

There is another important aspect to the ambiance of Taiwan. While Taiwan may be a province of China, for the past generation it has been the equivalent of an independent state, and, like many small states today, it has been a penetrated one. Franz Schurmann writes, "the real political history of Taiwan since 1949 would be virtually equivalent to a history of American covert war in Asia."[21] Well, maybe *virtually* . . . Schurmann is thinking about the petty harassment of the poor, defenseless mainland by Chiang Kai-shek and the CIA, but his insight is capable of refinement. The Nationalist Party is, as its name implies, nationalistic, and it was galling for it to have to be a client, to have to bow and scrape and pretend to believe what it did not. Much of the American connection has not contributed to national dignity (the pimp as the image of the Westernized Chinese). Many of the older—and even some of the younger—liberals view the

United States as the embodiment of all things bright and beautiful, and Taiwan became something of an anomaly, an American client-state in which the opposition is more pro-American than the regime. American influence no doubt contributed to the tempering of the regime's treatment of dissidents. In the days when there was a free world, Americans did not relish seeing their clients behave in a fashion indistinguishable from that of their enemies. While this no doubt contributed to liberty on the island, it also may have hindered natural political development. The liberals could behave like the small boy who thumbs his nose at the bully from behind his mother's skirts—he is safe now, but wait until he is caught alone. The unofficial KMT conviction is that at times the United States has actively worked to subvert the regime, although, in the nature of things, neither Taipei nor Washington would choose to supply evidence for this. The various American administrations have rarely been as fond of Chiang Kai-shek as they pretended to be, and as American spokesmen used to reiterate, the United States did not accept the joint CPC-KMT claim that Taiwan was part of China (the Americans are even vague on this in the Shanghai communiqué). Rather, the status of the island was "unsettled." This, of course, did not prevent the American recognition of the Taipei regime as the legal government of China.

THE TAIWAN INDEPENDENCE MOVEMENT

It is common to see the regime on Taiwan[22] as the domination of the mainlanders over the native Taiwanese, as a kind of colonial situation. A mainlander student once told me, "To the extent there is repression, it falls on everyone equally, not just on Taiwanese." This is probably true. While no reliable figures are available, I would guess that a disproportionate number of political prisoners on the island are mainlanders. Still, if the mainlanders see themselves as sojourners in Chü, they may be better able to tolerate the repression than are the natives.

There is at least a residue of bitterness left over from the postwar days. The Japanese had run the island smoothly and efficiently. The occupying Chinese, under Ch'en I (the Fukien warlord, not the Communist general and foreign minister) treated the island as enemy territory (much as the National Army treated Nanking and other areas of the mainland held by the Japanese). On February 28, 1947, there were riots against the occupying forces. Ch'en I, after negotiating with the rebels and promising them amnesty, proceeded to slaughter some 10,000 to 20,000 of them, mostly young and educated.[23] Ch'en I was executed a few years later—in a figurative sense his bloody head was displayed to the crowd—but more for attempting to sell Chekiang (which he ruled after Taiwan) to the Communists than for his behavior on Taiwan.

Taiwanese intellectuals complain of their exclusion from political influence. There are numerous Taiwanese employed by the government, and in increasingly high positions since 1972, when Chiang Ching-kuo, little Chiang, took effective control of the island. There are relatively few Taiwanese in the party or in the higher ranks of the army. Entry into the bureaucracy is by competitive examination, and the examinations seem to be conducted fairly. Within the bureaucracy, however, there are complaints of discrimination in promotion—the Taiwanese lack background—*pei-ching*—that is, connections.[24] Mainlanders will sometimes point out that in any particular office there will be employed more Taiwanese than natives of any other province, but this may not be very comforting to those not already convinced of the justice of the situation. One also hears that in 1945 there were no Taiwanese qualified for administrative or political positions, since the Japanese had permitted them to receive higher education only in medicine if they attended schools on the island. Many Taiwanese had received university educations in Japan, however, and in any case in 1945 the KMT had little reason to pride itself on its own administrative competence. The basic reason for the lack of Taiwanese representation is the regime's need to present itself as the government of China, something it could do even less convincingly were it dominated by natives of Taiwan province.

Some speak of Taiwanese (or, usually, Formosan) nationalism. It is difficult to say whether the distinction between Taiwanese and mainlanders is a national one. Aside from the 2 percent of the population of aboriginal descent, the Taiwanese are Chinese in language, heritage, and culture. They are Han, more Chinese than, say, Tibetans. The customs of Taiwan are different from those of other provinces but similar to those of Fukien, from whence most of the Taiwanese came. Even the Chinese Taiwanese are not a homogeneous category. Thus, 13 percent of the population of the island is Hakka, and the Hakka were traditionally subject to discrimination by the Fukienese majority.[25]

It is possible to argue, however, that the Taiwanese have developed into a separate nationality. A handwritten manuscript at the Hoover Institution, dated 1950, seems to be at least a proto-Taiwan nationalist argument. The Taiwanese are said to be pure Han—even the aborigines have assimilated—from all over China, not just Fukien. The wretched climate and the wars against the aborigines weeded out the weaklings, so that by a process of natural selection a new people emerged. Later, the Japanese slapped this new people into shape, endowing it with further excellent qualities, discipline and respect for law. In jail P'eng Ming-min met a prisoner who "had devised his own scheme for the romanization of the Formosan dialect . . . so that we could cut ourselves off from the traditional Chinese writing. His hatred for the Chiangs was extraordinary." This is probably exceptional. Sheldon Appleton conducted a survey of attitudes among high school students on Taiwan, attempting to discover differences between Taiwanese and mainlanders. While each group associates mainly with its own members, no significant attitudinal differences were discovered. "The people of Taiwan are essentially Chinese in their social and political outlooks as well as their ancestry."[26] The data may instead imply a new Taiwanese nationality has emerged among the young of both groups. Also, the circumstances did not permit Appleton to inquire into the area where the most serious differences are probably found, that of concrete political opinion. Most Taiwan independence advocates admit to being Han, and some take pride in this; they do not, on that account, consider themselves Chinese, that is, as properly subject to any Chinese state. All in all, however, it seems that the hostility between Taiwanese and mainlanders is a manifestation more of localism than of nationalism, although the localism is exacerbated by the special circumstances.

It is difficult to judge the potential support for the independence movement on the island (or for that matter, to tell what, in the abstract, "Taiwan independence" means: at a minimum, presumably, the end of the KMT dictatorship and the renunciation of reunification). Open discussion of independence on the island is strictly forbidden. An American advocate of Taiwan independence has discovered a way of sampling independence sentiment abroad: "Occasionally one could locate a useful contact by repeating anti-Nationalist slogans in Japanese while walking along city streets at night: 'Taiwan under the pigs is hell,' or 'Taiwan is a police state but Japan is a democracy.'"[27] This is no doubt a useful way to find the sort of people one wants to talk to and to establish rapport with them (provided one does not feel oneself degraded by referring to human beings as "pigs"), but may not be so clever a way to obtain a random sample. There is reason to think that the advocates of Taiwan independence, if not the concept itself, may have a limited appeal on the island. At least in some of its manifestations it seems an elitist movement. P'eng Ming-min says the purpose of the KMT land reform was to "weaken oppositional strength. Since the Ch'ing dynasty the leading personages at the local level in Taiwan have all come from the landlord class,"[28] as does he himself. The peasants may not be too eager to have their "natural rulers" take the reins again. At a guess, independence sentiment is stronger in the cities than in the countryside. There is also the rumor, assiduously promoted by the regime, that the independence movement is a front for American and Japanese interests. American support for the movement, from a cold if not particularly honorable point of view, would make sense, even (or especially) before the rapprochement with China, as an easy way out of an anomalous situation: presented with an independent state ten or twenty years ago, the Communists would have had to like it or lump it. American officials always deny any involvement with the movement, however, and there is no evidence either way.

The most noted advocate of Taiwan independence in recent years, P'eng Ming-min, has a very moderate program, appealing not so much to Taiwan nationalism as to general discontents on the island, including those of the military. He wants the idea of any return to the mainland to be abandoned; he wants free elections to be held, opposition parties to be permitted, and domestic espionage to be ended; and he wants freedom of communication. The state of Taiwan should strengthen its ties with the United States and serve as part of the free world. P'eng does not say how all these wonderful things are to come about but does say that sympathizers have penetrated all levels of the government.[29] The right wing of the KMT would agree with the last statement, one that might serve to temper some of P'eng's talk of the regime's tyranny.

Douglas Mendel says, "While I am positive that underground political organizations exist, I do not know of any which is large or effective."[30] For all practical purposes the independence movement is a movement of exiles. It takes a certain amount of vanity to believe oneself qualified to rule others, and when vain and articulate men are thrown together in a distant and uncaring land, there is little for them to do except argue with each other. The movement is highly factionalized. Its prospects in the mid-1970s are not encouraging. Any U.S. support for it presumably ended with the Shanghai communiqué. With the deteriorating international situation, some independence advocates may wish to come to terms with the KMT, feeling their fates are bound together. While the circumstances create pressure for this, however, some prefer to continue to worry more about the devil they know than the devil they don't know: once the Chiangs are taken care of there will be time enough to worry about the Communists.[31] The Communists themselves have given no direct encouragement to the movement (why should they?). In 1972 Chou En-lai told a group of students from Taiwan who had been studying in the United States that the Taiwanese should, of course, become the "masters of their own house," but this refers to the Taiwan proletariat. The Chiangs have decades of counterrevolutionary experience, and out of consideration for the Taiwan people the Chinese will not encourage direct resistance on the island (Chou says).[32] Some younger Taiwan independence advocates think Taiwan could exist as an autonomous part of the People's Republic, rather like Tibet. It is likely they are carried away by their hatred of the Chiangs.

Chiang Ching-kuo has made concessions to Taiwanese sentiment since 1972, and the death of his father in 1975 may have given the regime more flexibility. That year "rumor among the regime's ruling circles, though yet to be substantiated, has it that the possibility of declaring the ROC a new independent political entity has been considered in discussions at the highest level of the party."[33] This would be what is known as "Taiwan independence, Chiang-style." If this is combined with liberalization it might meet most of the concrete demands of the independence advocates but possibly would not satisfy the advocates themselves.

An American advocate of independence would like to see blood flow: "The real test of nationalism is a people's willingness to fight for it. . . . No genuine Formosan nationalism could hope to come to power under mere modifications of the status quo, which preserves mainlander political dominance."[34] A new order established by violence, even assuming this does not entail a general massacre of mainlanders, would have to maintain itself by violence, and there is no reason to think such a regime would be any less a police state than the present one. This, presumably, is not what most advocates of independence want. At its more moderate, the aims of the movement coincide generally with those of the liberal opposition at large.

LIBERAL OPPOSITION

We have discussed the appeal of the CPC to many Chinese liberals; other liberals, however, chose the KMT as the lesser of the two evils and followed that regime to Taiwan. As Hu Shih allegedly said, after he had been denounced by his son on the mainland, there may not be freedom of speech in Taiwan, but at least there is the freedom to remain silent. Unlike on the mainland, overt liberalism is still a force on Taiwan, although the liberals on that island have not had an easy time. The regime, of course, has attempted to cultivate a liberal image but has been harsh with liberals who have tried to do something about their ideas.[35]

By the end of the 1950s the liberal opposition, mainly mainlander intellectuals and Taiwanese politicians, was attempting to come out in the open and to institutionalize itself. The leader of this effort was Lei Chen, once a member of the KMT but expelled because of his thought problems. Lei edited a liberal journal, *Free China,* which had long condemned the use of threats against non-KMT oppositional candidates and police interference in elections. In 1956 the journal demanded that the regime "restore the method whereby all parties present candidates for election."[36] Abstract advocacy of a multi-party system was one thing; when Lei actually tried to do something about it, that was something else. In 1960 Lei and his friends began to organize a loyal opposition party, and at that point Lei was arrested and given ten years on what is almost certainly a trumped-up charge of communist activities. *Free China* was suppressed.[37]

For the first part of the decade of the 1960s the oppositional line was carried out mainly by *Wen Hsing* magazine. Whereas *Free China* had been primarily a political journal, *Wen Hsing* took a more general interest in cultural matters as well. In politics the *Wen Hsing* line was much the same as that of *Free China*, although *Wen Hsing* was perhaps livelier and more impudent (it published, for example, a piece by P'eng Ming-min on "pan-Africanism," which, we learn, was an esoteric argument for Taiwan independence).[38] The journal's crimes, however, appear to have been as much cultural as political. On the mainland, dissidents have appealed to the Chinese tradition for a critique of the pretensions of the regime. On Taiwan, however, the regime arrogates the Chinese tradition to itself, and the tradition thus becomes identified with repression and reaction.[39] Teng T'o would talk about the ancients in order to criticize current rulers; on Taiwan, criticism of the past also becomes a way of criticizing the present. As one traditionalist on Taiwan said of the liberals: "Their opposition to tradition is real, but what they call tradition does not necessarily mean Confucius, but in particular means President Chiang."[40] *Wen Hsing,* against the approved line, was militantly modernist and Western-oriented. Its custom was to feature on its front cover portraits of the cultural giants of the age, and these turned out to be almost uniformly Western (Brigitte Bardot, William O. Douglas, Helen Gurley Brown, but also, for a change of pace, Herbert Hoover) and sometimes sinister—for example, the insidious Dr. Fei Cheng-ch'ing (John King Fairbank), the Taiwan regime's equivalent to Fu Man Chu. The journal was accused by traditionalists of having attempted to corrupt Chinese society, advocating, for example, "glass-of-waterism"—according to KMT propaganda, the pattern of sexual relations prevailing in the old Communist liberated areas: when one is thirsty, one drinks.[41]

In 1961 Hu Shih resurrected in *Wen Hsing* one of his ancient themes: Western culture, with its scientific civilization, is the truly idealistic and spiritual culture; Chinese civilization is built upon degrading human-labor power and is really materialistic. China should advance toward science and technology and overcome all ways of thought that hinder this progress.[42] The subsequent controversy might have remained at the level of tendentious debate among old and young fogies had it not been for Li Ao, the (one-time) *enfant terrible* of the Taiwan liberal opposition. A native of Manchuria, Li Ao is a kind of cult hero among university students of Taiwan and embodies in his person, his behavior, his opinions, and even his literary style all that the traditionalists find obnoxious. Thus, Li Ao sometimes carries to an extreme a vice of young Taiwan intellectuals of putting in parentheses the English translations of the terms he uses, a habit that is sometimes useful in the case of neologisms but is more often unnecessary (particularly when, as is often the case, the translations are inaccurate or misprinted). Li Ao, one suspects, does this mainly as a parody and also because he likes to annoy the conservatives. Behind the odious public persona he affects is a keen and subtle mind; more than most young Chinese intellectuals he is able to keep himself in perspective. Li Ao jumped into the Westernization controversy behind Hu Shih, accusing the traditionalists of being just like the communists (a mode of disputation the traditionalists are fond of using). In the passage below the underlined words indicate those Li Ao has rendered in English.

> Those who embody the ancient culture are in several respects close to communist ways of thought: their *prejudgment* [prejudice; "bigotry," Gibbon would say], their appeals to authority, their dogmatism, their emotionalism, their *egocentric predicament* [!], their preference for the philosophical over the empirical base, their *pan-politicism,* their uniform and *dwarf* [dwarfish] thought, their love of discussing morality and orthodoxy, their liking for *historical prophecy,* their use of *value-tinged terms*: in these eleven ways their thought is basically no different from that of the communists.[43]

Along the way Li Ao has harsh words for various KMT intellectual moo-cows and also for some scholars who do not deserve this appellation, such as Ch'ien Mu. His opponents held that he was engaging in personal attacks and responded in kind. Li Ao, feeling that if his enemies wanted personal attacks he would be glad to oblige, published a long review of the involvement of one of his opponents, Hu Ch'iu-yuan, in the Fukien rebellion of 1933. This, Li Ao tells us, was a revolt against Chiang Kai-shek; the rebels were in collusion with the Communists and the Japanese. Now this rebel, Hu Ch'iu-yuan, his vile ambition thwarted, has changed from a traitor to a scholar, a historian, a political theorist, and poses as the champion of traditional culture.[44]

This sort of thing increased the bitterness of the controversy and led ultimately to the arrest of Li Ao and the suppression of *Wen Hsing* in 1965. Li was soon released but was forbidden to publish. He was rearrested in 1972, along with the students previously arrested with P'eng Ming-min, and reportedly sentenced to ten years in jail for smuggling a list of political prisoners out of Taiwan.[45]

At the time it seemed as if Chiang Ching-kuo were clearing up old business prior to a gradual liberalization of the regime. It is still difficult to know how correct this interpretation is, although Taiwan is one of the few Asian polities to have become more rather than less liberal during the 1970s. After the suppression of *Wen Hsing* it remained possible to criticize traditional culture and to defend liberal ideas—particularly in the abstract: the regime does this last itself. After the suppression of *Wen Hsing,* criticism of the regime was carried on by *Ta Hsueh* magazine, an organ mainly of young Taiwanese intellectuals. It courted suppression for several years and apparently ceased publication in 1972, although I do not know whether it was actually suppressed. The editorial board of *Taiwan Political Review,* suspended in 1975, included several who had written for *Ta Hsueh*.

Liberalism on Taiwan continues to exhibit the philosophical and political weaknesses typical of Chinese liberals of this century—weaknesses perhaps not shared by the "convergent" liberals on the mainland, who come to liberalism as a conclusion rather than begin from it as a premise. There is certainly much that is valid in the liberal critique of traditionalism, particularly the politicized traditionalism of the KMT. The use of machinery to replace arduous, unskilled human labor is no doubt a condition for some kind of human liberation, and not simply because a technological society will define itself in this way. While it is hard to say whether the liberal gods, science and democracy, contribute to human happiness, science at least allows more persons to survive and thus potentially to be happy. But the KMT does not really reject Hu Shih's science and technology. The traditionalists as well as the liberals wish to modernize but also wish the modernization to be controlled by certain human (and, alas, political) values, rather than treating human feelings as simply artifacts of the social conditions. It is not clear that this is possible, and it is even less clear that the Taiwan traditionalists are approaching the problem in the right way; but the liberals do not even seem to be aware that there is a problem.

There is, then a certain moral hollowness in the liberal position. In the early 1970s *Ta hsueh* ran a series, the "Reexamination of traditional dogmas." One such dogma is filial piety: Filial piety is fine in a traditional society—it accords with economic necessity. But in a modernizing society there develops a generation gap (rendered in English). In modern society it is proper that each member of the family develop his own individual potential. Too much of the family concept inhibits social consciousness. Old folks should certainly be cared for by the family and by society, but age should never confer authority.[46] Our values are reflections of external conditions over which we have no control; we float with the tide. Human sentiment is reduced to its economic function. The person becomes the individual, the creature of society. This seems to lead only to the abyss.

The older Chinese liberals idealized the United States, which is certainly the model modern country. As the communists point out, the United States is the closest mankind has reached to "goulash communism." In a way this liberal attitude is refreshing: there is much cant in anti-Americanism, whether by Americans themselves or by foreigners. But it is also difficult for an American to take too seriously, say, Hu Shih's contention that American civilization is so spiritual because it is so technological. On a more pragmatic level, liberal pro-Americanism may hinder liberal political effectiveness in Taiwan, not only with the regime but also with segments of the society unhappy with the regime.[47]

The Taiwan liberals feel cut off from Chinese culture—for Li Ao it is self-evidently inferior in every way to Western culture. This is a rejection of KMT obtuseness and sanctimony but also means the liberals are somewhat rootless, which, even if it is a cliché, remains a psychological handicap. Cut off from the general culture, the liberals also seem cut off from the people, from the demos they claim they would like to see rule: ordinary people may be generally "liberal" on economic matters (they like to see money flowing their way), but are often culturally conservative. Would a Taiwan peasant really care to entrust his fate to a young whippersnapper who sneers at filial piety? Democracy is a liberal catchword on Taiwan, but it is an abstract, idealized democracy. By democracy, Taiwan liberals often seem to mean mainly that they should have their own way. They are of the temperament of, say, Henry Adams or maybe Plato; but Plato and Adams knew from personal experience what democracy is.

That the liberals are cut off from the people is not simply a matter of temperament: the regime is not structured in a way to encourage oppositional agitation. Still, by temperament, the liberals are elitist:

> Certainly only the unbroken pursuit of progress will bring long-term stability; but in order to preserve unbroken progress, it seems there is no choice but unceasingly

> to allow knowledge to bloom [*k'ai-fang chih-shih*]. Knowledge is the greatest treasure-house of the modern state and is also the motive force for the state's preservation of unbroken progress.[48]

To *k'ai-fang chih-shih,* of course, means to *k'ai-fang* the *chih-shih-fen-tzu,* the intellectuals. Like some dissidents on the mainland, the Taiwan liberals complain that the autocratic tradition prevents the people as well as the government from "respecting freedom."[49] On Taiwan this can lead to a kind of patronizing contempt for ordinary people:

> The peasants' political awareness is relatively backward. They put their main efforts into stuffing their bellies and having babies. When they have leisure they enjoy singing and watching puppet shows. Their political demands are very basic. They only hope that persons they consider fair will work to their direct advantage: nothing but this.[50]

The writer is trying to be ironic, and, tone aside, the passage may be factually true. But the tone is insufferable. One gets the impression that for Taiwan liberals, democracy and civil liberty are considered a kind of special privilege for themselves, the intellectuals' equivalent of the oil-depletion allowance.

The liberal position cannot be identified solely with moral nihilism. For many there is a fierce, if somewhat empty, devotion to China. Po Yang told the Garrison Command:

> I ardently love my country. What man, after all, does not love his country? However, people vary in the ardor of their love. For example, all parents under heaven love their children, but with different degrees of ardor. Some parents love their children mildly, but my love for mine penetrates my bones and flesh. Their every breath makes my heart leap; my heart is full of the passion to sacrifice for my children. As for my love of my wife and friends, I only hope August Heaven will give me the opportunity to die one death with them. My love for my country shows me that the greater the love is, so also is the greater sorrow. Yet my ardor does not become insipid. This is a pathetic natural phenomenon whose reason I cannot find, but my love is sharp and my criticism thorough. I spontaneously hate all that hinders the progress of my country, and it is hateful to think that tomorrow it will not become strong. But the way to achieve a strong country is to begin at the root, meaning that everything must be modernized; and the standard of modernization is the U.S. Just as Confucius always brought up Yao and Shun, so do I bring up the U.S. The strength, liveliness, honesty and frankness of the national spirit of the American people, their willingness to admit mistakes, are all in the style of a great country and truly arouse respect. But I am only "pro-American," and only advocate we learn from them. I do not sell myself or despise myself. Even less do I toady to them. We have our own respect for our personal and national character. For example, I once advocated that in naming typhoons we

> should not just follow the Americans and call them "Pamela," but we could name them after Chinese women, such as Hsi-shih or Shao-chün. I am not stubborn about this, but there is a distinction.[51]

We might disregard the flippancy about the typhoons—this is rather on a par with Hu Shih's permission to the Chinese people to continue to use chopsticks. Also, we should not be too harsh on a statement by a man who has been taken away from his children, his wife, and his friends and is abused by the rulers of his country. Still, it is no favor to Po Yang to slight the shallowness of his position. He loves China and would therefore make it like the United States. Some of the younger generation of modernists find a more convincing model for a modern China closer to home, westward across the straits.

RADICAL OPPOSITION

Almost all those who came to Taiwan in the late 1940s came by choice. The anticommunism of the Taiwan liberals is as strong as, if different from, that of the regime itself. In recent years, however, many younger people on Taiwan, particularly mainlanders, have come to feel sympathy for Peking. This radical opposition to the regime, of course, can only be manifested abroad. Young mainlanders are not in a completely enviable position on Taiwan. They generally do not care for the idea of Taiwan independence (although many no doubt feel they could live with it).[52] They have absorbed the regime's indoctrination in Chinese nationalism, but some find the claims of Peking to be the government of China more credible than those of Taipei. They are subject to personal frustrations. Outside the bureaucracy it is they who lack *pei-ching* in Taiwan society. Young mainlanders sometimes complain that if Taiwanese are discriminated against in bureaucratic employment, mainlanders suffer in a similar way in private employment. College graduates who have not managed to escape to the United States may be un- or under-employed. Those who are interested in politics will "lack both the votes and the cash to launch a successful campaign at almost any level of election."[53] The regime, feeling that student opposition was largely responsible for its loss of the mainland, keeps students under rather ham-handed supervision. The most common attitude toward politics by college students and graduates is probably apathy.[54]

The flap over the Tiao-yü-t'ai islands (Senkaku, in Japanese) in 1971, however, provided an opportunity for student political action. The Tiao-yü-t'ai are a chain of rocks north of Taiwan, administered as part of the Taipei prefecture when Taiwan was a Japanese colony; the chain has also been a resting place for Taiwanese fishermen. When it came to be thought that the seabed around the islands might contain huge oil deposits, the local powers cast their greedy eyes upon them. Japanese and ROC gunboats would cruise around the chain putting up their own flags and tearing down the other's. Peking in effect supported Taipei: the Tiao-yü-t'ai is a part of Taiwan province, and Taiwan is a part of China. Because of its dependence upon Japan and the United States (which gratuitously supported Japan, claiming the chain was part of Okinawa), Taiwan, while not relinquishing its claim, did nothing to support it beyond issuing wordy protests and vague threats. This provided the students on the island an opportunity to criticize the government from a patriotic point of view for its weakness in defending the sacred territory of the fatherland. In the demonstrations at the various universities in 1971, other antigovernment themes could also be cautiously developed.

The criticisms were much stronger among students abroad, particularly in the United States. The KMT claims the Tiao movement in the United States became infiltrated by communist agents. In any case, many of the activists in the movement rapidly became openly pro-Communist, urging the immediate reunification of the country: "The unification movement had its source in the Tiao movement. It was a natural product of the perception of the KMT clique's inability to protect the rights of the inhabitants of Taiwan."[55] It is also probably relevant that the student generation of 1971 had grown up with no memories of the mainland. In addition, the changing U.S. policy at the time gave many reason to believe the KMT clique would not be around long in any case.

The above quote speaks of the rights of the inhabitants of Taiwan. The Communists themselves have kept aloof from the Taiwan independence movement, but the Taiwan radicals wish to form a united front (the Taiwan independence movement, however, did not get very excited about the Tiao-yü-t'ai). Thus, the radicals claim the Chiang clique is responsible for the misery of the Taiwanese and is also the biggest obstacle to the reunification of the country. All opposed to the Chiangs should unite.[56]

As noted earlier, *radical* is a loose concept. These youths are radical because they are pro-Peking. This kind of radicalism seems a natural enough development of a liberalism empty of all moral content except modernism and patriotism, particularly when the patriotism itself is empty. It is, of course, proper to feel some attachment to one's own country simply because it is one's own, but this student nationalism seems to lack any other content. China is not valued for anything it has been (a Taiwan cliché: Our greatness is in the future, not in the past) or held to represent anything transcending itself. If liberalism is an instrument of national greatness, why be liberal if greatness is obviously achieved without it? At the same time, however, the commitment to substantive radicalism, to socialism, may be equally empty: socialism too is a tool for making the country strong. "The success of the Chinese revolution has changed the world balance of power. It carries the hope and faith of the oppressed peoples of the whole world."[57] Socialism brings wealth and power. In their illiberal nationalism the Taiwan radicals may have more in common with the KMT clique than they would care to think.

THE CONSERVATIVES

Since this is a study of opposition, there is not much to say about the conservatives, or traditionalists. They have developed no oppositional stance, and their main efforts are devoted to accusing those who disagree with them of treason. But in their defense of traditional culture the conservatives may be more and more out of step with the developments of the times, with the increasingly technocratic direction of Taiwan society.[58] Taiwan may not be embracing Mr. Democracy, but it is good friends with Mr. Science.

The conservatives are capable of sophistication, but it becomes a rather melancholy sophistication. Hu Ch'iu-yuan, Li Ao's antagonist, once told some students there is really no conflict between Taiwanese and mainlanders. The conflict is generational. Taiwan independence would be a disaster:

> I say, everyone is Chinese. It is necessary to talk about political reform, but to talk of Taiwan independence is a joke. From the point of view of costs and benefits, the movement will result in nothing but great chaos on Taiwan. Those who reap the advantage will be Japanese ambitionists and ultimately the Chinese Communists. The U.S. won't be able to do a thing. China will belong to the youth of China. If we return to the mainland, Taiwan is yours and so is the mainland. If we can't return, no matter what, as you age, Taiwan is yours.[59]

The conservative position is a potentially oppositional one, particularly if it should win some following among the younger generation. This position has lacked, however, any kind of convincing principled defense. That a position is poorly defended, of course, does not mean it is worthless. The Taiwan liberal position does not lead directly to Maoism, as the conservatives contend, but in its slavish adherence to the spirit of the times it provides no principled defense against Maoism or worse. The Taiwan conservatives probably do not have the right answers, nor, probably, will they begin to develop any decent answers at all until they are pushed onto the defensive; but they ask the right questions.

Notes

1: CONFLICT AND OPPOSITION

1. For excellent treatments of the problem of opposition in its liberal context see Robert Dahl, ed., *Political Opposition in Western Democracies*.

2. Robert Dahl, ed., *Regimes and Oppositions*, p. 1. In this work I shall use the term *regime*, despite its pejorative connotations, to refer to the locus of political power in China. Alternatives such as *party, state,* or *government* are, in context, misleading or inappropriate (Leonard Schapiro, *Totalitarianism*, p. 71).

3. Carl J. Friedrich and Zbigniew Brzezinski, *Totalitarian Dictatorship and Autocracy*, p. 162.

4. The erstwhile liberal Indian political system encouraged "fragmented oppositions, which are often hard to distinguish from the coalitions in power" (Rajni Kothari, "India: Opposition in a Consensual Polity," in *Regimes and Oppositions*, ed. Dahl, p. 306). In the United States, given the separation of powers, the distinction between government and opposition is also sometimes vague.

5. Hans Buchheim, *Totalitarian Rule*, p. 41.

6. Frederick C. Barghoorn, "Soviet Political Doctrines and the Problem of Opposition," *Bucknell Review* 12, no. 2 (May 1964): 5.

7. Frederick C. Barghoorn, "Factional, Sectoral, and Subversive Opposition in Soviet Politics," in *Regimes and Oppositions*, ed. Dahl, p. 39. This should perhaps be expanded to include ideology as well as interests. Franz Schurmann, *The Logic of World Power*, p. 38, makes an interesting distinction between interest and ideological politics. For the sake of simplicity, however, it is probably sufficient in most cases to consider ideology as a special sort of interest.

8. H. Gordon Skilling, "Background to the Study of Opposition in Communist Eastern Europe," *Government and Opposition* 3, no. 2 (Spring 1968): 295–99.

9. This, it might be noted, is not an overly rigorous exclusion. Few politicians today ground their criticisms of those they wish to replace *simply* by reference to their own ambitions—although they may have plenty to say about the ambitions of their opponents.

A general note: the title of this work includes the words *opposition* and *dissent*, whereas above I have spoken only of opposition. To me opposition implies an active attempt to replace certain rulers, whereas dissent (which may, like opposition, be integral, specific, etc.—but possibly not factional?) would imply simply some sort of protest against persons or policies without any necessary desire to participate further in the political game. The use of both terms in the title is to imply that this study concerns itself with all forms of protest. Given the scope of the study and the crudeness of the data, however, it did not seem analytically interesting to make too fine a distinction between opposition and dissent, and the two terms function in this study as synonyms for each other, or as a reference to the two combined.

10. Ralf Dahrendorf, *Essays in the Theory of Sociology*, p. 126.

11. Ibid., p. 227.

12. See, particularly, Richard Solomon, *Mao's Revolution and the Chinese Political Culture*; also Lucian Pye, *The Spirit of Chinese Politics*.

13. Barrington Moore, Jr., *Social Origins of Dictatorship and Democracy,* p. 486.

14. Some even contend that the "value-free study of revolutions is a logical impossibility for those who live in the real world" (John Dunn, *Modern Revolutions,* p. 2). This is probably an exaggeration; a study of revolution that is truly value-free, however, would perhaps be trivial and uninteresting.

15. Cf. Bernard Crick, *The American Science of Politics.*

16. Hannah Arendt, *Between Past and Future,* p. 17. While Miss Arendt is speaking of the Western tradition, it is also basic to Confucianism, the mainstream of the Chinese tradition, that society—those in power—is subject to evaluation by criteria external to itself.

For an extreme, sometimes perverse, but still persuasive statement of our current condition with respect to politics see Jacques Ellul, *The Political Illusion.*

17. Niccolò Machiavelli, *The Prince and the Discourses,* pp. 119–20. See also Neal Wood, "The Value of Asocial Sociability: Contributions of Machiavelli, Sidney, and Montesquieu," in *Machiavelli and the Nature of Political Thought,* ed. Martin Fleisher, pp. 290–91.

18. Dahrendorf, *Theory of Sociology,* pp. 227, 255.

19. For a profound criticism of Machiavellianism see Leo Strauss, *Thoughts on Machiavelli*; for a different (and, I think, less profound) perspective see Christian Bay, "Politics and Pseudopolitics," *American Political Science Review* 59, no. 1 (March 1965): 39–51.

20. A relatively harmless example of this truism might be the "democratization" of Germany and Japan after the war. "We are simply asking for the same *kind* of acceptance of something else," resulting in a "democracy of allegiance, a system in which all share the same conviction" (Jacques Ellul, *Propaganda,* pp. 245, 248). See also Hans H. Baerwald, *The Purge of Japanese Leaders under the Occupation.* It may, of course, be wrongheaded to reduce the *content* of democratic and nondemocratic politics to insignificance.

21. Wang Che, "How Engels Criticized Duhring's Apriorism," *Peking Review,* March 10, 1972, pp. 5–9.

22. *Hung ch'i* [Red Flag] 1972, no. 8 (August 1), p. 9 (this publication is the organ of the CPC Central Committee and is hereafter cited as RF).

23. Barghoorn, "Soviet Political Doctrines," p. 3. This would seem a relatively recent development in the Soviet Union, however, as Stalin liked to believe that the struggle would intensify as the final victory of socialism drew nearer (Roy A. Medvedev, *Let History Judge,* p. 190).

24. *Chung-yang jih-pao,* August 10, 1972.

25. *Jen-min jih-pao* [People's Daily], May 6, 1971 (hereafter cited as PD).

26. James Chieh Hsiung, *Ideology and Practice,* p. 151.

27. B. F. Skinner, *Beyond Freedom and Dignity,* p. 3.

2: PICTURES OF CHINESE POLITICS

1. Cf. Jürgen Domes, "New Course in Chinese Domestic Politics," *Asian Survey* 13, no. 7 (July 1973): 633–46; and Harry S. Bradsher, "China," ibid., no. 11 (November 1973): 989–1009. Each of these excellent analyses was probably valid for the time at which it was written, yet their implications seem to contradict each other. This illustrates the speed with which apparent changes take place in China and the need for a theory—or at least an interpretation—that could encompass these changes. (The necessity for such a theory does not, of course, imply its possibility; our being hungry does not guarantee our being fed.)

2. On the need for such general pictures see T. H. Rigby, "Crypto-Politics," *Survey,* no. 50 (January 1964), p. 186.

3. On totalitarianism generally see Hannah Arendt, *The Origins of Totalitarianism*; Friedrich and Brzezinski, *Totalitarian Dictatorship and Autocracy*; Buchheim, *Totalitarian Rule*; Leonard

Schapiro, *Totalitarianism*; idem, "The Concept of Totalitarianism," *Survey*, no. 73, (Autumn 1969), pp. 93–113.

4. For criticisms of the concept see the excellent collection by Carl J. Friedrich, Michael Curtis, and Benjamin Barber, *Totalitarianism in Perspective*, Barber and Curtis attacking, Friedrich defending. Also see Robert Burrows, "Totalitarianism," *World Politics* 21, no. 2 (January 1969): 272–94; Rigby, "Crypto-Politics"; idem, "'Totalitarianism' and Change in Communist Systems," *Comparative Politics* 4, no. 3 (April 1972): 433–53.

5. Hans Rothfels, *The German Opposition to Hitler*. Hitler may, of course, have had Machiavellian motives in tolerating certain appearances of independence.

6. Burrows, "Totalitarianism," p. 280.

7. Quasi-totalitarian systems can of course be found in earlier compounds of theory and practice, such as Chinese Legalism and the Ch'in empire, and perhaps in Calvin's Geneva (Barrington Moore, Jr., *Political Power and Social Theory*, pp. 52, 59 ff.). (One recalls here how People's China touched James Reston's Presbyterian soul.) Totalitarianism is perhaps a subtheme of the gnostic strain Eric Voegelin finds running through Western philosophy (*The New Science of Politics*). In Chinese philosophy as well, there are certain possibly totalitarian themes, not only in Legalism but in some varieties of Taoism and the (usually subdued and unstressed) utopian strain in Confucianism. For an extended treatment of utopianism in China see Wolfgang Bauer, *China und die Hoffnung auf Glück*.

8. David Apter, *The Politics of Modernization*, pp. 43, 15.

9. Ibid., p. 10.

10. Ibid.

11. Ted Robert Gurr, *Why Men Rebel*, p. 179.

12. Schurmann, *Logic of World Power*, p. 564.

13. Frederick Wakeman, Jr., "The Use and Abuse of Ideology in the Study of Contemporary China," *China Quarterly*, no. 61 (March 1975), pp. 151, 152.

14. Skinner, *Beyond Freedom and Dignity*, p. 164.

15. Buchheim, *Totalitarian Rule*, p. 15. A rejoinder might be that the new man will be a better sort than those we have now, although the criteria for "better" would have to be arbitrary. Most totalitarians would probably deny we have a nature in Buchheim's sense. If one denies that we have a nature or that, if we do, it has normative implications, there may be no rational grounds for opposing totalitarianism, although the hedonistic grounds may remain.

16. An innocuous example is the indoctrination of school children against sexual stereotypes. Changes in textbooks are said to reflect the changing values of our society, but obviously they reflect only the values of some, who would like to see the values of everyone change. The goal means the elimination of some of the diversity that supposedly characterizes a liberal society and an abandonment of the liberal tenet that it is not the business of the state to set the values of the society.

17. William van Etten Casey, S.J., "Mao's China," *Holy Cross Quarterly* 7, nos. 1–4 (1975): 10.

18. For a fine study of the American tendency to see the Chinese in terms of rather shallowly held stereotypes see Harold R. Isaacs, *Scratches on Our Minds*. The specific material is dated but the analysis is not, and subsequent events fit the patterns defined.

19. Cf. Edward J. Woodhouse, "Revisioning the Future of the Third World," *World Politics* 25, no. 1 (October 1972): 1–33; Robert L. Heilbroner, *An Inquiry into the Human Prospect*.

20. Mark Selden, *The Yenan Way in Revolutionary China*, p. 274. See also Ipjong J. Kim, *The Politics of Chinese Communism*.

21. Selden, *Yenan Way*, pp. 74, 116, 130.

22. Kim, *Politics of Chinese Communism*, p. 20, with specific reference to the Kiangsi period.

23. Chalmers Johnson, "Chinese Communist Leadership and Mass Response: The Yenan Period and the Socialist Education Campaign," in *China in Crisis*, ed. Ping-ti Ho and Tang Tsou, 1: 397–437.

24. Cf. Michael Walzer's interesting argument in *The Revolution of the Saints* that the prototypical radical ideology is Puritanism: "the idea that specially designated and organized bands of men might play a creative part in the political world, destroying the established order and reconstructing society according to the Word of God or the plans of their fellows" (p. 1).

25. Donald Munro, "The Malleability of Man in Chinese Marxism," *China Quarterly,* no. 48 (October/December 1971), pp. 609–40.

26. Richard M. Pfeffer, "Serving the People and Continuing the Revolution," *China Quarterly,* no. 52 (October/December 1972), pp. 620, 626.

27. Ibid., pp. 627–28. Pfeffer's main argument is that there have evolved since the Cultural Revolution institutions which help insure that the elite remains responsive to the felt needs of the general population. This argument is discussed below in chap. 4.

28. Bay, "Politics and Pseudopolitics."

29. Pfeffer, "Serving the People," pp. 627–28 n. 18.

30. James Chieh Hsiung, "The Substitution of 'People' for 'Individual' in the Ethic of the Maoist Polity," in *The Logic of "Maoism,"* ed. Hsiung, pp. 191, 197, 202, 203.

31. Ibid., p. 208.

32. J. Tinbergen, *Economic Policy,* p. 33.

33. Hsiung, "Substitution of 'People' for 'Individual,'" p. 191, 208.

34. Anthony Downs, *An Economic Theory of Democracy,* pp. 177–82. Downs allows that a government might hit upon an optimal position through pure chance. This, of course, is true for the Maoist polity as well.

35. James S. Coleman, "Foundations for a Theory of Collective Decisions," *American Journal of Sociology* 71, no. 6 (May 1966): 615.

36. Hsiung, "Substitution of 'People' for 'Individual,'" p. 205.

37. For a sympathetic discussion of Legalism see Ch'en Ch'i-t'ien, *Chung-kuo fa-chia kai-lun.*

38. Coleman, "Theory of Collective Decisions," pp. 622, 623.

39. Hsiung, "Substitution of 'People' for 'Individual,'" p. 205. Selden and Pfeffer have not "eschewed" ethical questions but have, I think, failed to resolve them coherently.

40. A. James Gregor, *The Fascist Persuasion in Radical Politics,* p. 398. See also idem, *The Ideology of Fascism.*

41. The term is taken from Burrows, "Totalitarianism," p. 276.

42. Gregor, *Ideology of Fascism,* p. 345.

43. Gregor, *Fascist Persuasion,* pp. 136–40.

44. For that matter, there are strong similarities between the Maoist strain of Chinese communism and the fascist strain in the Kuomintang. Cf. Lloyd E. Eastman, "Fascism in Kuomintang China," *China Quarterly,* no. 49 (January/March 1972), pp. 1–31.

Scholars have long noted a disintegration (or creative development) of Marxism as an ideology as it moved eastward (Benjamin I. Schwartz, *Chinese Communism and the Rise of Mao*). The CPC, the purported vanguard of the proletariat, came to lose any organic connection with the proletariat, becoming instead a free-floating revolutionary group organizing a movement on peasant grievances. Richard Thornton, *The Comintern and the Chinese Communists, 1928–1931,* argues, however, that the Maoist policy was in fact that of the Comintern. At the same time, Korean communists, who had probably never heard of Mao (and if they had, would not have cared) were also pursuing what has come to be considered a Maoist policy toward the peasants (Robert Scalapino and Chong-sik Lee, *Communism in Korea,* 1: 106.) This would not refute Schwartz's contention about disintegration but might show that it has to do less with local adaptations than with some inherent logic of Leninism.

45. Gregor, *Fascist Persuasion,* p. 197.

46. Frederick Wakeman, Jr., *History and Will.*

47. Ibid.; Hsiung, *Ideology and Practice,* p. 197.

48. Li Ta-chao, one of the founders of the CPC who may have had much influence on the thinking of the young Mao, would speak of China as a proletarian nation (Maurice Meisner, "Li Ta-chao and the Intellectual Prerequisites for the Maoist Strategy of Revolution," in *Revolutionary Leaders of Modern China,* ed. Chün-tu Hsueh, p. 388). Mussolini, around the same time, was using the same term (Gregor, *Ideology of Fascism,* p. 151). The proletarian nation theme was revived, in a way, by Lin Piao, *Long Live the Victory of People's War.* The theme is implicit, perhaps, in the Chinese appeal to the Third World against the hegemons.

Chalmers Johnson, *Peasant Nationalism and Communist Power,* argues that peasant nationalism in the face of Japanese occupation and the flight of the original local elites provided the party the opportunity to extend its base among the peasants in the occupied zones of north China. Johnson, however, may underestimate the *economic* appeal to the peasants of the communists' program (Donald G. Gillin, "'Peasant Nationalism' in the History of Chinese Communism," *Journal of Asian Studies* 23 [1963–64]: 269–89; Selden, *Yenan Way,* p. 120).

49. Maurice Meisner, "Leninism and Maoism," *China Quarterly,* no. 45 (January/March 1971), p. 4 (with particular reference to the Narodniks). Despite his populism, Meisner believes Mao is still a good Marxist, since he seeks to change the world (rather than interpreting it?) (p. 36). Genghis Khan also changed the world.

50. Ibid., pp. 21–22, 29.

51. Ibid., p. 7; Tetsuya Kataoka, "Communist Power in a War of National Liberation," *World Politics* 24, no. 3 (April 1972): 410–27.

52. Gregor, *Fascist Persuasion,* p. 244. Cf. Meisner, "Leninism and Maoism," p. 24. The idea of the manufacture, as it were, of human beings is typically totalitarian.

53. Gregor, *Ideology of Fascism,* pp. 13, 380.

54. F. G. Bailey, *Strategems and Spoils.*

55. Richard Thornton, "The Structure of Communist Politics," *World Politics* 24, no. 4 (July 1972): 495–517.

56. The phrase was coined by Andrew J. Nathan, "A Factionalism Model for CCP Politics," *China Quarterly,* no. 53 (January/March 1973), pp. 34–66.

57. Michael Oksenberg, "Policy-Making under Mao Tse-tung, 1949–1968," *Comparative Politics* 3, no. 3 (April 1971): 323–60.

58. Robert C. Tucker, "The Dictator and Totalitarianism," *World Politics* 17, no. 4 (July 1965): 555–83; Schapiro, *Totalitarianism,* p. 70.

59. Nathan, "Factionalism Model," p. 54. Also on factional politics see William Whitson, "The Field Army in Chinese Communist Politics," *China Quarterly,* no. 37 (January/March 1969), pp. 1–30; Phillip Bridgham, "Factionalism in the Central Committee," in *Party Leadership and Revolutionary Power in China,* ed. John Wilson Lewis, pp. 203–33.

60. Nathan, "Factionalism Model," p. 55.

61. Ibid., pp. 50–51.

62. Tucker, "Dictator and Totalitarianism"; also idem, "Toward a Comparative Politics of Movement Regimes," *American Political Science Review* 55, no. 2 (June 1961): 281–89.

63. The following analysis is abstracted from an earlier attempt of mine to sort out the dynamics of Chinese politics: *The Politics of the Eighth Central Committee of the Communist Party of China, 1956–1966.* See also Joseph Nyomarkay, *Charisma and Factionalism in the Nazi Party;* Leonard Schapiro and John Wilson Lewis, "The Roles of the Monolithic Party under the Totalitarian Leader," in *Party Leadership,* ed. Lewis, pp. 114–45; and the already-cited articles by Tucker.

64. Cf. Maurice Duverger, *Les parties politiques*, p. 245. One hesitates to agree, however, that in politics there *must* always be only two tendencies.

65. Nathan, "Factionalism Model," p. 51.

66. Schurmann, *Logic of World Power,* p. 29.

67. Cf. Joseph Levenson, *Confucian China and Its Modern Fate*, vol. 2.

3: CHINESE ATTITUDES ON DISSENT AND OPPOSITION

1. Solomon, *Mao's Revolution*.

2. See, e.g., David S. Nivison, "Communist Ethics and the Chinese Tradition," *Journal of Asian Studies* 16 (1956–57): 51–74.

3. Karl A. Wittfogel, *Oriental Despotism*; this was also more or less the view of the late Etienne Balazs, *Chinese Civilization and Bureaucracy*.

4. This was not always true. See Luther Carrington Goodrich, *The Literary Inquisition of Ch'ien Lung*. This particular persecution, however, was unusual and not very long lasting. I don't think Goodrich shows the Ch'ien Lung emperor to be more intolerant than his contemporary European rulers.

5. Ping-ti Ho, *The Ladder of Success in Imperial China*.

6. For a recent treatment of this ancient theme see William Kornhauser, *The Politics of Mass Society*.

7. Hsu Cho-yun, *Ancient China in Transition*.

8. Rushton Couborn, *Feudalism and History*, p. 231. Cf. Noah Edward Fehl, *Rites and Propriety in Literature and Life*.

9. Donald Munro, *The Concept of Man in Early China*.

10. Karl A. Wittfogel, "Chinese Society," *Journal of Asian Studies* 16 (1956–57): 350.

11. *Analects* 13. 18; *The Analects of Confucius*, ed. and trans. by Arthur Waley, p. 176. The law codes of the Ch'ing dynasty made it a crime for a child to bring even a correct accusation against his parents, except in cases of treason (Derk Bodde and Clarence Morris, *Law in Imperial China*, pp. 40–41).

12. Eric Voegelin, *Order and History*, 1: 61.

13. *Mencius* 1. B. 28. Chou was the last king of the Shang dynasty, overthrown by the King of Chou (the two terms are written with different characters).

14. *Mencius* 5. A. 5.

15. Cf. John Plamenatz, *Man and Society*, 1: 155 ff.

16. *Mencius* 5. B. 9.

17. Thus, the Ch'ien Lung emperor placed on his index the works of Ming dynasty officials who later held office under his own ancestors, who had overthrown the Ming (Goodrich, *Literary Inquisition of Ch'ien Lung*, p. 49).

18. For the theme of Legalist opposition see the *Han Fei-tzu*, chaps. "Nan yen," "Shuo nan," "Ku fen."

19. See, e.g., James T. C. Liu, *Reform in Sung China*.

20. This cosmological theory was elaborated by the Han scholar Tung Chung-shu ([Feng Yu-lan], *Chung-kuo che-hsueh shih*, p. 524).

21. Levenson, *Confucian China*, 2: 65–67; Joseph Fletcher, "China and Central Asia, 1368–1884," in *The Chinese World Order*, ed. John King Fairbank, pp. 206–24.

22. S. N. Eisenstadt, *The Political Systems of Empires*, pp. 159, 172.

23. Levenson, *Confucian China*, 2: 63–67.

24. Jung-pang Lo, "Policy Formulation and Decision-Making on Issues Respecting Peace and War," in *Chinese Government in Ming Times*, ed. Charles O. Hucker, pp. 41–72.

25. John Meskill, "Academies and Politics in the Ming Dynasty," in *Chinese Government in Ming Times*, ed. Hucker, pp. 149–74; Charles O. Hucker, "The Tung-lin Movement of the Late Ming Period," in *Chinese Thought and Institutions*, ed. John King Fairbank, pp. 132–63.

26. Meskill, "Academies and Politics," p. 174.

27. For Hai Jui's memorial see *Ehr-shih-wu shih ching-hua*, 4: 211–13. For what is in effect a vernacular translation see Wu Han [Liu Mien-chih], "Hai Jui scolds the emperor," PD, June 16, 1959.

28. James P. Harrison, *The Communists and Chinese Peasant Rebellions*.

29. Thomas Taylor Meadows, *The Chinese and Their Rebellions*, p. 25.

30. Hsiao Kung-chuan, *Rural China*, p. 511; Ralph Thaxton, "Some Critical Comments on Peasant Revolts and Revolutionary Politics in China," *Journal of Asian Studies* (1973–74): 283.

31. This is more or less the overt point behind Mao's 1975 criticism of the traditional novel *Water margin* [*Shui-hu chuan*]. The robber heroes of the book "oppose corrupt officials, but not the emperor." Mao scolds the gang's leader, Sung Chiang, as if that legendary bandit chieftain were Brezhnev. (PD, September 4, 1975.) The idea is that the traditional writings favoring peasant rebellions cover up the revolutionary nature of the rebellions; but it is more plausible to hold that they were simply not revolutionary. Of China-watching interest, a few days earlier an article had been published that used exactly the same phrase but argued that on the whole the novel was a good one (Hsu Yun-hsi, "An Informal View of a little literary history," Hsueh-hsi yü p'i-p'an, 1975, no. 8 [August 18], p. 59). For an interesting Western study of the evolution of this novel see Richard Gregg Irwin, *The Evolution of a Chinese Novel*.

32. Vincent J. C. Shih, "Some Chinese Rebel Ideologies," *T'oung pao* 44 (1956): 225.

33. Jacques Ellul, *The Autopsy of Revolution*, pp. 8, 43–45, 86; cf. also Eric Hobsbawm, *Primitive Rebels*.

34. Ralph Thaxton, "Tenants in Revolution," *Modern China* 1, no. 3 (July 1975): 323–57; Jean Chesneaux, *Peasant Revolts in China, 1840–1949*; Hsiao, *Rural China*, p. 514. On the "reactionary" component of the French Revolution see Alfred Cobban, *The Social Interpretation of the French Revolution*, p. 157; although the specific case is usually considered a counterrevolution, the argument of Charles Tilly in *The Vendee* is also relevant here. Closer to China, the Vietcong was apparently most successful in gaining peasant support when it could appeal to traditional grievances (Robert L. Sansom, *The Economics of Insurgency in the Mekong Delta of Vietnam*).

35. Samuel P. Huntington and Clement H. Moore, eds., *Authoritarian Politics in Modern Society*.

36. Willmoore Kendall, "The 'Open Society' and Its Fallacies," *American Political Science Review* 54, no. 4 (December 1960): 972–79; Herbert Marcuse, Barrington Moore, and Robert Paul Wolff, *A Critique of Pure Tolerance*.

37. Yü-sheng Lin, "Radical Iconoclasm in the May Fourth Period and the Future of Chinese Liberalism," in *Reflections on the May Fourth Movement*, ed. Benjamin I. Schwartz, pp. 25, 55.

38. Benjamin I. Schwartz, *In Search of Wealth and Power*. Yen Fu may perhaps have been more sensitive to the implications of the ideas he was expounding than was his mentor, Herbert Spencer. Similar considerations also motivated the Japanese adoption of liberal institutions in the nineteenth century (Robert A. Scalapino, *Democracy and the Party Movement in Prewar Japan*, p. 89).

39. Wolfram Eberhard, *Conquerors and Rulers*, p. 13.

40. Bauer, *China und die Hoffnung auf Glück*, pp. 425–35.

41. Chang Hao, *Liang Ch'i-ch'ao and Intellectual Transition in China, 1890–1907*, p. 202.

42. Gregor, *Ideology of Fascism*, pp. 247, 256, 260.

43. Michael Gasster, *Chinese Intellectuals and the Revolution of 1911*, p. 237.

44. Donald Gillin, *Warlord*; Robert A. Kapp, *Szechwan and the Chinese Republic*. These two cases are, however, in their different ways atypical, in that they are extreme cases of a general tendency.

45. Tien Hung-mao, *Government and Politics in Kuomintang China, 1927–1937*.

46. Arif Dirlik, "The Ideological Foundations of the New Life Movement," *Journal of Asian Studies* 34 (1974–75): 945–80; Mary C. Wright, *The Last Stand of Chinese Conservatism*, pp. 306–7.

47. John Israel, *Student Nationalism in China, 1927–1937*.

48. Chow Tse-tsung, *The May Fourth Movement*; Yü-sheng Lin, "Radical Iconoclasm in the May Fourth Period."

49. For an excellent intellectual biography of Hu Shih see Jerome Grieder, *Hu Shih and the Chinese Renaissance*.

50. Crick, *American Science of Politics*, p. 129.

51. Theodore J. Lowi, *The End of Liberalism*; Garry Wills, *Nixon Agonistes*.

52. John Hunter Boyle, *China and Japan at War, 1937–1945*, pp. 167 ff.

53. Hu Shih, Mao Tzu-shui, and Li Chi, *Hu Shih yü chung-hsi wen-hua*.

54. V. I. Lenin, *What Is to Be Done?*

55. Leonard Schapiro, *The Origin of the Communist Autocracy*.

56. Liu Shao-ch'i, *Lun kung-ch'an-tang-yuan te hsiu-yang* [On the cultivation of a Communist Party member], pp. 1–6 (hereafter cited as *Cultivation*).

57. Ibid., pp. 34–35.

58. Ibid., pp. 57 ff.

59. Liu Shao-ch'i, "On intraparty struggle," *Chieh-fang jih-pao*, October 9, 1942.

60. Mao Tse-tung, *Kuan-yü cheng-ch'üeh ch'u-li jen-min nei-pu mao-tun te wen-t'i* [On the correct handling of contradictions among the people], pp. 9–10 (hereafter cited as *Correct Handling*).

61. Ibid., p. 2.

62. Ibid., pp. 26, 27, 28.

63. Liu Shao-ch'i, *Cultivation*, p. 21.

64. Mao, *Correct handling*, pp. 4, 5.

65. Ibid., p. 30.

66. Ibid., p. 3.

67. Ibid., p. 5.

68. *Jen-min shou-ts'e*, 1955, pp. 344–45.

69. Chou En-lai, "Report on the work of the government to the first session of the third national people's congress," PD, December 31, 1964.

70. Dennis J. Doolin, *Communist China*, p. 36. Cf. Wakeman, "Use and Abuse of Ideology." For a general statement of radical impatience with "reality" see Henry S. Kariel, *Open Systems*.

71. PD, November 14, 1954.

72. PD, July 31, 1958.

73. Schapiro, *Communist Autocracy*, p. 292.

74. Juan J. Linz, "From Falange to Movimiento-Organizacion: The Spanish Single-Party and the Franco Regime, 1936–1968," in *Authoritarian Politics*, ed. Huntington and Moore, p. 183.

75. Liu Shao-ch'i, *Cultivation*, pp. 12, 21, 29.

76. P'eng Chen, "Speech at the meeting of actors in the modern Peking opera," RF, 1964, no. 14 (July 31), p. 22.

77. *CCP Documents of the Great Proletarian Cultural Revolution, 1966–1967*, pp. 355–60.

78. *Ching-kang-shan*, no. 21 (March 22, 1967).

79. *Ping-t'uan chan-pao*, no. 11 (March 12, 1967).

80. Chung Hsuan-tso, "Lu Ting-i's counterrevolutionary mug revealed by the hawking of the *Story of Wei Cheng*," PD, November 9, 1967.

81. Chiang Ch'ing, "Speech," PD, December 4, 1966.

82. Lin Chieh, "Down with slavism, strictly observe proletarian revolutionary discipline," PD, June 16, 1967.

83. PD, January 22, 1967.

84. PD, September 14, 1967.

85. PD, January 8, 1968.

86. *Chieh-fang chün-pao*, January 27, 1968, in PD, January 28, 1968.

87. PD, April 27, 1968.

88. PD, August 5, 1968.

89. PD, June 9, 1969; An Hsueh-chiang, "Firmly support the principle of 'a cup of water filled to the brim,'" PD, June 23, 1969.

90. Yang P'u, "The spirit of opposing the tide," PD, August 16, 1973. This article, like most since the Cultural Revolution, is signed with a pseudonym; there is some gossip to the effect that Yang P'u is really Mao Tse-tung.

91. Chou En-lai, "Report to the Tenth National Congress of the Communist Party of China," PD, September 1, 1973.

92. Wang Hung-wen, "Report on the revision of the party constitution," PD, September 2, 1973.

93. See, e.g., Ch'i Wen-i, "A history of coups or a history of class struggle?" PD, September 19, 1972.

94. Ch'iu Chiang, "We must have the revolutionary spirit of daring to oppose the tide," PD, November 7, 1973.

95. Kuo Hui and Chang Pao-chiang, "Develop the revolutionary spirit of opposing the tide," PD, October 12, 1973. The phrase *thought tide* harkens back to the "reactionary thought tide" of the Cultural Revolution—i.e., to radicalism.

For what it is worth, the phrase *sui hsin so yü* is taken from the *Analects*. Confucius said, "When I was seventy I could follow my heart's desire without departing from what is right." I don't know whether the use of the phrase here has anything to do with the campaign against Confucius that was in progress then; in any case, it is a common enough cliché.

96. Chang Ch'un-ch'iao, "On full-scale dictatorship over the bourgeoisie," PD, April 1, 1975 (italics added).

97. Ch'ing Yen, "Go a step further in strengthening party unity," PD, August 8, 1975 (reprinted from RF, 1975, no. 8).

98. Chang Ch'un-ch'iao, "Full-scale dictatorship."

4: THE HANDLING OF OPPOSITION

1. Richard Solomon, *Mao's Revolution,* sometimes gives the impression that he thinks this desire for order is a peculiarly Chinese attitude. It would appear, however, to be universal—present in all cultures, if not in all persons. Thus, much of the early post-takeover appeal of the Nazis was not their ideology but their success in restoring peace and quiet to German society (Terrence Prittie, *Germans against Hitler,* p. 32).

2. Cf. Lucian Pye, "Mass Participation in Communist China: Its Limitations and the Continuity of Culture," in *China*, ed. John M. H. Lindbeck, pp. 16–17.

3. Li Yu-ning, *Wu Han chuan,* pp. 23–44.

4. Aryeh L. Unger, *The Totalitarian Party,* p. 82.

5. Daniel J. Boorstin, *The Image*.

6. Ellul, *Propaganda,* pp. 124–26, 138.

7. Unger, *Totalitarian Party,* p. 32.

8. The best study of thought reform remains Robert Jay Lifton's *Thought Reform and the Psychology of Totalism*. See also Mu Fu-sheng, *The Wilting of the Hundred Flowers*; Theodore H. E. Chen, *Thought Reform of the Chinese Intellectuals*.

The Chinese published numerous collections on thought reform in the early years of the regime. See, e.g., Ai Ssu-ch'i et al., *Lun ssu-hsiang kai-tsao wen-t'i* [On the problem of thought reform] (hereafter cited as *Thought reform*); and *Tsen-yang kai-tsao ssu-hsiang*.

9. For a critique of the small-group experiments from the point of view of democratic theory see Sidney Verba, *Small Groups and Political Behavior*, esp. p. 220.

10. Lifton, *Thought Reform,* p. 388.

11. Ai et al., *Thought reform,* p. 2–4, 8.

12. Alan P. K. Liu, *Communications and National Integration in Communist China.*

13. A. Doak Barnett, with a contribution by Ezra Vogel, *Cadres, Bureaucracy, and Political Power in Communist China,* pp. 146–47.

14. Martin King Whyte, *Small Groups and Political Rituals in China,* p. 10.

15. Richard W. Wilson, *Learning to Be Chinese,* p. 20.

16. Ezra Vogel, "From Friendship to Comradeship: The Change in Personal Relations in Communist China," *China Quarterly,* no. 21 (January/March 1965), pp. 46–60. Vogel notes, "As a moral ethic, comradeship is very similar to the moral ethic governing work relationships in the West," except that in China this is not balanced by a private "ethic" (p. 59).

17. Whyte, *Small Groups,* p. 56.

18. Ellul, *Propaganda,* p. 81.

19. Ezra Vogel, "Voluntarism and Social Control," in *Soviet and Chinese Communism,* ed. Donald W. Treadgold, pp. 168–84. The Nazis were also given to voluntary coercion or voluntary compulsion. (Hans Buchheim, "Authority and Freedom: The State and Man," in *Freedom and Authority in the West,* ed. George N. Schuster, p. 78; Unger, *Totalitarian Party,* p. 30.)

20. Ai et al., *Thought reform,* pp. 27–30.

21. Mu, *Hundred Flowers,* p. 221.

22. Martin King Whyte, "Corrective Labor Camps in China," *Asian Survey* 13, no. 3 (March 1973): 253–69.

23. Bao Ruo-wang [Jean Pasqualani] and Rudolf Chelminski, *Prisoner of Mao,* p. 188.

24. Ibid., p. 12. One problem with this source is that one is never sure, when opinions are expressed, that one is hearing Bao instead of Chelminski.

25. Ibid., p. 249.

26. Ibid., p. 133. In translations of regime Chinese into Peking English, *to struggle* has somehow become a transitive verb. When appropriate I shall probably follow this practice in my own translations or even in the general discussion; it is a solecism, but it captures the flavor of the original.

27. Cf. Whyte, *Small Groups,* p. 75.

28. Bao and Chelminski, *Prisoner of Mao,* pp. 155, 221.

29. Leon Festinger, *A Theory of Cognitive Dissonance.*

30. Whyte, *Small Groups.*

31. *Fei ming ti,* nos. 11–12 (May 20, 1967).

32. In early 1974 there was criticism of high officials, particularly military men, who would get their children admitted to the universities through the back door, i.e., by pulling strings (e.g., PD, January 25, 1974). The stress on soldiers probably simply indicates that the regime was then disciplining the military, not that soldiers are more corrupt than anyone else. Other examples of nepotism pass without comment. PD, December 26, 1973 (the Chairman's eightieth birthday, although this is not explicitly noted), carries a story about Mao's home county (without explicitly mentioning it is Mao's home county). There are a suspiciously high number of Maos among the leadership of that area. Chiang Ch'ing, while no doubt an intelligent and competent woman, clearly owed her high political position to her husband and to nothing else.

33. Huang Huo-ch'ing, "On the reform of capitalist industry and commerce and of the understanding of capitalists," PD, September 30, 1956; Chang Ch'un-ch'iao, "Full-scale dictatorship."

34. Central Issue (1972) No. 12, in *Chung-yang jih-pao,* August 10, 1972.

35. Richard Solomon, "One Party and 'One Hundred Schools,'" *Current Scene* 7, nos. 19–20 (October 1, 1969); Roderick MacFarquhar, *Origins of the Cultural Revolution,* vol. 1.

36. Whyte, "Corrective Labor Camps," p. 265.

37. Ranbir Vohra, *Lao She and the Chinese Revolution,* p. 165.

38. Gene Cooper, "An Interview with Chinese Anthropologists," *Current Anthropology* 14,

no. 4 (October 1973): 480. Cooper wisely sent Fei the text of his article before he published it. The last page is a letter by Fei that, I think, subtly takes issue with the more asinine conclusions Cooper draws from his interview.

Renunciations of previous work, by the way, need not always be taken too seriously. Kuo Mo-jo, much more of an opportunist than Fei Hsiao-t'ung, had renounced all his past works in time, at the outset of the Cultural Revolution. In 1972, however, he reminded his admirers that as long ago as 1950 he had solved a basic problem in Chinese historiography. He claims his solution was inspired by Mao, but the quote from Mao that he gives, if it does anything, contradicts his thesis. (Kuo Mo-jo, "The problem of periodization in ancient Chinese history," RF, 1972, no. 7 [July 1], pp. 56–62.)

39. Feng Yu-lan, "Speaking from the point of view of personal understanding on the relationship of the criticism of Lin and Confucius to the unity, education, and reform of intellectuals," *Kuang-ming jih-pao,* February 1, 1974.

40. Feng Yu-lan, "On the criticism of Confucius and on my self-criticism of my former ideology of revering Confucius," *Kuang-ming jih-pao,* December 3, 1973; also, idem, "Whether to restore the old or to oppose restoration of the old is a struggle between two lines," ibid., December 4, 1973.

41. Feng, "Speaking . . . of Lin and Confucius."

42. Chao Hao-sheng, "Three Chinese scholars talk about the criticism of Lin Piao and Confucius," *Ta kung pao* (Hong Kong), July 14–20, 1974; pt. 2, July 15; pt. 7, July 20.

43. Ibid., pt. 7, July 2; pt. 2, July 15.

44. Ibid., pt. 3, July 16.

45. A. R. Sanchez and S. L. Wong, "On 'An Interview with Chinese Anthropologists,'" *China Quarterly,* no. 60 (October/December 1974), p. 790.

46. Jan S. Prybyla, "Notes on Chinese Higher Education, 1975," *China Quarterly,* no. 62 (June 1975), p. 296.

47. James R. Townsend, *Political Participation in Communist China,* p. 3.

48. Giovanni Sartori, "Concept Misinformation in Comparative Politics," *American Political Science Review* 54, no. 4 (December 1970): 1050.

49. Mao Tse-tung, "Bombard the headquarters," PD, August 5, 1967 (written August 5, 1966).

50. *Hung-i chan-pao* [Red Arts War Report], no. 1 (February 15, 1967). Miss Chiang's speech was delivered November 18, 1966.

51. Stuart R. Schram, *The Political Thought of Mao Tse-tung,* pp. 250–59.

52. Mao Tse-tung, "Introducing a cooperative," RF, 1958, no. 1 (June 1), p. 3.

53. Li Fu-ch'un, "Continue to advance, holding high the red flag of the general line," PD, August 17, 1960.

54. Lu Li, "Leadership of agriculture must begin from reality," PD, November 12, 1960; Chang Te-sheng, "With agriculture as the basis, propel our national economic development," PD, December 12, 1960.

55. Wu Te, "We must resolutely and thoroughly carry out party policy," PD, December 22, 1960.

56. Yao Wen-yuan, "On the social base of the Lin Piao antiparty clique," PD, March 1, 1975.

57. PD, September 29, 1962.

58. PD, August 9, 1966.

59. *Hung ch'i* (Peking: Peking Red Flag Fighting Team of the Red Representative Assembly), no. 39 (May 21, 1967). (This publication is not to be confused with the theoretical journal of the Central Committee [cited as RF], which has the same title.)

60. Frederick C. Teiwes, "The Evolution of Leadership Purges in Communist China," *China Quarterly,* no. 41 (January/March 1970), p. 130.

61. *Wen hui pao,* February 5, 1967. For a description of the Cultural Revolution in Shanghai in its early period see Neal Hunter, *Shanghai Journal.*

62. PD, August 9, 1966.

63. For descriptions of the Red Guard movement by former participants see Gordon A. Bennett and Ronald N. Montaperto, *Red Guard*; Ken Ling, *The Revenge of Heaven*.

64. *Kuang-ming jih-pao,* January 14, 1967; PD, January 16, 1967.

65. PD, February 17, 1967; PD, March 10, 1967.

66. *Ching-kang-shan,* no. 11 (January 19, 1967). The business of "power, power, power" was later attributed to Lin Piao, and condemned (PD, March 9, 1972).

67. *T'i-yü chan-pao,* no. 6 (January 28, 1967).

68. *Fei ming ti,* nos. 11–12 (May 20, 1967).

69. For the story of the Wuhan mutiny and subsequent military takeovers see Chien Yu-shen, *China's Fading Revolution*.

70. Yao Wen-yuan, "The working class must take the lead in everything," PD, August 6, 1968.

71. PD, September 10, 1968.

72. Ibid.

73. PD, October 19, 1968.

74. Ibid.

75. PD, August 29, 1968.

76. PD, June 5, 1969.

77. For the text of this draft see *Chung-yang jih-pao,* November 5, 1970.

78. PD, January 20, 1975.

79. Pfeffer, "Serving the People," pp. 636–53.

80. Pfeffer admits this: "Nor . . . can it be shown that 'mass representatives' do in fact represent the masses." He adds an interesting note, however: "The exact same point can be made with regard to the representatives of the PLA." "Although it still remains to be shown what operational significance, if any, the alleged domination of China by the military has had, analysts continue to write about it as if it had some self-evident significance." (ibid., pp. 652–53 n. 74). The easy answer is that it makes sense to speak of the military as an interest group in a way that it does not make sense so to speak of the amorphous masses—although this is contention, not demonstration.

81. Michael P. Gehlen and Michael MacBride, "The Soviet Central Committee," *American Political Science Review* 62, no. 4 (December 1968): 1232–41; John A. Armstrong, *The European Administrative Elite,* p. 73.

82. Martin King Whyte, "Iron Law versus Mass Democracy: Weber, Michels, and the Maoist Vision," in *Logic of "Maoism,"* ed. Hsiung, p. 55.

The futility of predicting political behavior from class background is illustrated by the study of Robert C. North and Ithiel de Sola Pool, "Kuomintang and Chinese Communist Elites," in *World Revolutionary Elites,* ed. Harold D. Lasswell and Daniel Lerner, pp. 319–455. The class background of the two elites is virtually identical. For the classic statement of the lack of relevance of class background see Robert Michels, *Political Parties*.

83. "Emancipation of Philosophy," *Current Background,* no. 932 (May 21, 1971), pp. 45 ff. This is a translation of a series that appeared in PD, March 25–29, 1971.

84. Central Issue (1971) No. 82, in *Chung-kung yen-chiu,* no. 69 (September 1972), pp. 100–102.

85. The major articles are Yao, "Lin Paio antiparty clique"; Chang Ch'un-ch'iao, "Full-scale dictatorship."

86. C. S. Chen and Charles Price Ridley, *Rural People's Communes in Lien-chiang,* p. 18.

87. PD, August 17, 1975. This article takes a moderate line, however, warning against the "wind of communism."

88. PD, August 7, 1975.

89. Unger, *Totalitarian Party,* p. 263.

90. Solomon, *Mao's Revolution*.

91. Alexander Dallin and George Breslauer, *Political Terror in Communist Systems,* p. 1.

92. Peter S. H. Tang and Joan M. Maloney, *Communist China,* pp. 316–17; John Wang, *Land Reform in the People's Republic of China,* pp. 92–95.

93. Gerd Ruge, "An Interview with Chinese Legal Officials," *China Quarterly,* no. 61 (March 1975), p. 123.

94. Roderick MacFarquhar, *The Hundred Flowers Campaign and the Chinese Intellectuals,* p. 251.

95. See, e.g., Radio Shanghai, city service, reported by Foreign Broadcast Information Service (FBIS) *Daily Report*, January 25, 1968.

96. Doolin, *Communist China,* p. 37.

97. *Guinness Book of World Records,* ed. Norris and Ross MacWhister, p. 195.

98. Richard L. Walker, *The Human Cost of Communism in China,* p. 13.

99. Lo Jui-ch'ing, "The success of our country's struggle to purge counterrevolutionaries and the future tasks," *Hsueh-hsi,* 1958, no. 1 (January 3), pp. 2–4.

100. Walker, *Communism in China,* p. 14.

101. T'an I-wu, "The fanatical activities of counterrevolutionary elements in Hunan," PD, July 5, 1955.

102. On the Communist legal system see Jerome Alan Cohen, "The Criminal Process in China," in *Soviet and Chinese Communism,* ed. Treadgold, pp. 107–43; Leng Shao-chuan, *Justice in Communist China*. For traditional Chinese law see Bodde and Morris, *Law in Imperial China*.

103. PD, September 25, 1954.

104. Lo Jui-ch'ing, "Raise vigilance, oppose numbness," *Jen-min shou-ts'e,* 1956, pp. 351–53.

105. *Jen-min shou-ts'e,* 1958, p. 178.

106. Lo Jui-ch'ing, "Success of our country's struggle," p. 8.

107. Ruge, "Interview with Chinese Legal Officials," pp. 118–19, 121; Victor H. Li, "The Public Security Bureau and Political Legal Work in Hai Yang," in *The City in Communist China,* ed. John Wilson Lewis, p. 53.

108. Bao and Chelminski, *Prisoner of Mao,* p. 78.

109. Lo Jui-ch'ing, "Explanation of the draft statute on labor reform in the People's Republic of China," *Jen-min shou-ts'e,* 1955, p. 365; Bao and Chelminski, *Prisoner of Mao,* p. 266; Whyte, *Small Groups,* p. 204.

110. *Jen-min shou-ts'e,* 1958, p. 332.

111. Whyte, *Small Groups,* p. 203.

112. Bao and Chelminski, *Prisoner of Mao,* p. 108.

113. [Lin Li-kuo], " '571 engineering' outline," *Chung-kung yen-chiu,* no. 67 (July 1972), p. 100.

114. On the May 7 Cadre Schools see Pfeffer, "Serving the People," p. 647; Theodore Hsi-en Chen, *The Maoist Educational Revolution,* pp. 112 ff.

115. Bao and Chelminski, *Prisoner of Mao,* pp. 45, 177.

116. *Chung-hua hu-sheng,* no. 1 (January 15, 1969), pp. 21–23 (hereafter cited in English: *Voice of China*); Lo Jui-ch'ing, "Success of our country's struggle," p. 4; Chen and Ridley, *Rural People's Communes,* p. 167.

117. Kuo Chia-hsiung, "Accusation," *Ching-kang-shan,* no. 21 (March 22, 1967).

118. *Hung-i chan-pao* [Red Medicine War Report], no. 3 (April 12, 1967).

119. *Ch'üan wu ti* (Peking: Capital Medical Revolutionary Committee), no. 11 (June 6, 1967).

120. PD, December 24, 1970, reports T'an "unfortunately left this world," giving no cause of death. It is customary to give at least some cause, if only "sickness."

121. Chalmers Johnson, "Chinese Communist Leadership and Mass Response: The Yenan Period and the Socialist Education Campaign," in *China in Crisis,* ed. Ho and Tsou, p. 436.

122. Lo Jui-ch'ing, "Learn from Lei Feng," PD, March 5, 1963.

123. Tung Chi-ping and Humphrey Evans, *The Thought Revolution*, pp. 160, 162.

124. RF, 1972, no. 2 (February 1), pp. 5, 8.

125. Donald Klein and Lois B. Hager, "The Ninth Central Committee," *China Quarterly*, no. 45 (January/March 1971), pp. 37–56.

126. Jürgen Domes, "Intra-Party Conflict and the Development of Communist Rule in China" (Paper delivered at the Fourth Annual Sino-American Conference on Mainland China, Airlie House, Va., December 12–16, 1974), p. 13. Domes identifies K'ang Sheng (since deceased), Wang Hung-wen, Chi Teng-k'uei, and Wang Tung-hsing as the main representatives of the security system on the Politburo. Added to this, perhaps, should be Hua Kuo-feng (made minister of public security in January 1975, premier a year later, and Central Committee chairman in October 1976) and Wu Te.

127. PD, September 29, 1973; PD, September 13, 1973.

128. *China News Service*, no. 574 (July 9, 1975), p. 3. The militia was apparently unable to cope with the riots and strikes in Hangchow in July 1975, and in that city the army was called back in (*China News Analysis*, no. 1019 [November 7, 1975], p. 4).

5: OPPOSITIONAL INTERESTS

1. H. Gordon Skilling, "Groups in Soviet Politics: Some Hypotheses," in *Interest Groups in Soviet Politics*, ed. Skilling, p. 24.

2. Ibid., pp. 19–45; Rigby, "Crypto-Politics"; Francis C. Castles, "Interest Articulation," *Survey*, no. 73 (Autumn 1969), pp. 116–32; Michael Oksenberg, "Occupational Groups in Chinese Society and the Cultural Revolution," in *The Cultural Revolution*, ed. Alexander Eckstein, pp. 1–44.

3. David B. Truman, *The Governmental Process*, p. 34.

4. Conversely, certain seemingly actual interests may develop that would be beyond the imagination of most observers. Whoever would have conceived, except as a joke, the politicization of sex in the twentieth century?

5. The discussion below of opposition among the ruled concentrates upon the Han, omitting the complex problems of the national minorities, who have many grievances but who constitute only a small and somewhat isolated part of the population. An adequate discussion of their problems might require a book in itself.

6. [Chiang Jen-te], "A secret diary," PD, August 9, 1957.

7. Shen Hsin, "The struggle between the two lines in the process of consolidating the people's communes," *Cheng-chih hsueh-hsi*, 1958, no. 10 (October), p. 41.

8. Chen and Ridley, *Rural People's Communes*, p. 41.

9. *Voice of China*, no. 5 (May 15, 1971), p. 41.

10. "Emancipation of Philosophy," p. 15.

11. See, e.g., *I-chiu-ch'i-ssu-nien chung-kung nien-pao*, sect. 2, pp. 285 ff.

12. "Emancipation of Philosophy," pp. 15–16. Similar groups were said to have operated in Hunan in the early 1950s (T'an I-wu, "Counterrevolutionary elements in Hunan").

13. PD, November 26, 1973.

14. Yao, "Lin Paio antiparty clique."

15. Chen and Ridley, *Rural People's Communes*, p. 39. This kind of classification, of course, says nothing about current economic conditions. Most "poor" peasants are probably economically better off than most former landlords.

16. PD, October 14, 1975.

17. Fan Chung-liu, "What kind of parents should we be?" *Hsueh-hsi yü p'i-p'an,* 1975, no. 7 (July 18), p. 55.

18. C. K. Yang, *The Chinese Family in the Communist Revolution,* p. 109.

19. PD, May 16, 1956.

20. PD, December 19, 1958.

21. Teng Tzu-hui, "Do a good job in managing public mess halls; sincerely carry through the principle of voluntariness," *Chung-kuo ch'ing-nien,* 1959, no. 12 (June 1), pp. 5–6.

22. T'ang Sheng-p'ing, "Actively cultivate female party members and female cadres," PD, May 18, 1973.

23. William H. Parish, Jr., "Socialism and the Chinese Peasant Family," *Journal of Asian Studies* 34 (1974–75): 613–30. This study contradicts earlier expectations of a more radical and rapid change in attitudes (Yang, *Chinese Family,* p. 213).

24. PD, January 30, 1971; "Emancipation of Philosophy," pp. 22 ff.

25. Thomas P. Bernstein, "Problems of Village Leadership after Land Reform," *China Quarterly,* no. 36 (October/December 1968), pp. 1–22.

26. "Emancipation of Philosophy," p. 13.

27. Statement by P'eng's wife, in *The Case of Peng Teh-huai, 1959–1968,* p. 124.

28. Shigeru Ishikawa, "Changes in the Structure of Agricultural Production in Mainland China," in *Agrarian Policies in Communist and Non-Communist Countries,* ed. W. A. Douglas Jackson, p. 347. See also Dwight L. Perkins, *Agricultural Development in China, 1368–1968*; Mark Elvin, *The Pattern of the Chinese Past.* Land reform would probably not be in itself such a disruptive change, as land was constantly changing hands in traditional China.

29. Anthony M. Tang, "Input-Output Relations in the Agricultural Economy of Communist China, 1952–1965," in *Agrarian Policies,* ed. Douglas Jackson, p. 296.

30. *Ts'ai-mao hung-ch'i,* February 3, 1967, in *Survey of the China Mainland Press,* no. 3899 (March 15, 1967), pp. 4, 5.

31. *Yang-ch'eng wan-pao,* July 7, 1966, in *Survey of the China Mainland Press,* no. 3650 (August 1, 1966), p. 4. See also Richard L. Walker, ed., *Letters from the Communes,* for peasant hardship.

32. Chen and Ridley, *Rural People's Communes,* pp. 26–29.

33. *Voice of China,* no. 1 (January 15, 1969), p. 11.

34. Martin King Whyte, "The Tachai Brigade and Incentives for the Peasant," *Current Scene* 6, no. 16 (August 15, 1969), p. 6; Unger, *Totalitarian Party,* p. 216.

35. *Ta kung pao* (Tientsin), April 30, 1955.

36. T'an I-wu, "Counterrevolutionary elements in Hunan"; Wang Jen-chung, "Speech," PD, July 28, 1955.

37. *Voice of China,* no. 1 (January 15, 1969), p. 11.

38. Yang Ch'eng-wu, "Speech at the January 12 telephone conference," *Kung-tso t'ung-hsun,* 1961, no. 6 (January 26), p. 8 (hereafter cited in English: *Work Bulletin*).

39. *Work Bulletin,* 1961, no. 21 (May 26), p. 2.

40. T'an Fu-jen, "Speech at the Yunnan province agricultural work conference" (August 1967), *Chung-kung yen-chiu,* no. 46 (October 1970), p. 122.

41. *Chung-kung yen-chiu,* no. 43 (July 1970), p. 116.

42. PD, October 12, 1975. PD, October 16, 1975, reports that the following counties have already been mechanized: Shao-shan, Chingkangshan, Tsun-i, and Yenan—all Mao's old stomping grounds.

43. Paul F. Harper, "Trade Union Cultivation of Workers for Leadership," in *City in Communist China,* ed. Lewis, p. 152.

44. MacFarquhar, *Hundred Flowers Campaign,* pp. 150–51.

45. PD, January 17, 1956.

46. Wen Ch'ien, "That the rate of increase in wages should be lower than the rate of increase in productivity is an objective demand for the speeding up of the realization of national socialist industrialization," *Ta kung pao* (Tientsin), February 3, 1955.

47. *Chung-kung yen-chiu,* no. 17 (May 1968), p. 94.

48. Mitch Meisner, "The Shenyang Transformer Factory," *China Quarterly,* no. 52 (October/December 1972), pp. 732–33.

49. Lai Jo-yü, "Go a step further in directing the functions of trade unions in building socialism," PD, September 24, 1956.

50. *Kung-jen jih-pao* (Peking), May 8, 1957, quoted in *China News Analysis,* no. 183 (May 31, 1957), pp. 1–2.

51. Sun Sheng-fu, "Criticism of several poisonous weeds in the seventh issue of *Jen-min wen-hsueh,*" *Jen-min wen-hsueh,* 1957, no. 10 (October), p. 33.

52. Li Kuo-wen, "Reelection," *Jen-min wen-hsueh,* 1957, no. 7 (July), pp. 1, 3.

53. See, e.g., Wang Meng, "The young newcomer in the organization department," *Jen-min wen-hsueh,* 1956, no. 9 (September), pp. 29–43.

54. Li Kuo-wen, "Reelection," p. 3.

55. Ibid., p. 4. Such a wind blew in 1953. Li's treatment of economism allegedly shows that he opposes basic party policy (Sun Sheng-fu, "Criticism of several poisonous weeds," p. 33).

56. Li Kuo-wen, "Reelection," p. 4.

57. Yao, "Working class."

58. Mitch Meisner, "Shenyang Transformer Factory."

59. See PD, April 24, 1973. The story features the slogan, "To rebel against reactionaries is justified"—a conservative radical revision of the original, "To rebel is justified."

60. Mao, *Correct handling,* pp. 32–33; Wang Hung-wen, "Report to the central study group," *Chung-yang jih-pao,* December 5, 1974.

61. PD, October 31, 1974; *China News Analysis,* no. 981 (November 22, 1974).

62. *China News Analysis,* no. 981, p. 3.

63. Hsiao Hui, "Analysis of the current chaotic situation on the mainland," *Chung-kung yen-chiu,* no. 105 (September 1975), pp. 8–15; Wang Shuo-ch'i, "Social order on the mainland viewed from the case of the suppression of counterrevolutionary sabotage activities in Yunnan," ibid., no. 106 (October 1975), pp. 66–79.

64. PD, October 6, 1975.

65. Kan Wen, "Consolidate the great basic law of proletarian dictatorship," PD, January 24, 1975.

66. PD, March 11, 1975.

67. Eberhard, *Conquerors and Rulers,* pp. 100–101.

68. The regime seems to understand the relationship between weak family ties and delinquent behavior, although its solution (increased politicization of the family) does not seem very promising (see *Kuang-ming jih-pao,* December 5, 1972; Fan Chung-liu, "What kind of parents?").

69. PD, November 14, 1954; PD, November 10, 1954.

70. Stuart R. Schram, ed., *Chairman Mao Talks to the People,* pp. 204–5.

71. Theodore Hsi-en Chen, *Maoist Educational Revolution,* pp. 207 ff.

72. PD, December 4, 1975.

73. Yang Hsiu, "This is the kind of communist spirit we should cultivate," *Chung-kuo ch'ing-nien,* 1960, no. 5 (March 1), pp. 5–6.

74. Tung and Evans, *Thought Revolution,* pp. 82, 92, 97. Here the phrase is rendered "willing tools."

75. PD, October 14, 1975.

76. Chang Yao-liang and Sun Shih-k'ai, "Welcoming spring in the home of a nightsoil worker," PD, February 3, 1965.

77. Ch'un-mei, "Self-criticism," *Ta kung pao* (Peking), December 19, 1964.

78. Tung and Evans, *Thought Revolution,* p. 105.

79. Hu Yao-pang, "Struggle for the revolutionization of the youth of our country," PD, July 7, 1964.

80. Washington *Post,* February 14, 1965.

81. Ronald N. Montaperto, "From Revolutionary Successors to Revolutionaries: Chinese Students in the Early Stages of the Cultural Revolution," in *Elites in the People's Republic of China,* ed. Robert Scalapino, p. 603.

82. For a survey of some of the Red Guard organizations see Wang Hsueh-wen, *Chung-kung wen-hua ta ko-ming yü hung-wei-ping,* pp. 185–94. For factions in Shanghai see Hunter, *Shanghai Journal.* There is still no extended, satisfactory study of the Red Guard movement as a political phenomenon.

83. Parris H. Chang, *Radicals and Radical Ideology in China's Cultural Revolution,* p. 19.

84. *Ping-t'uan chan-pao,* no. 5 (December 26, 1966) and no. 11 (March 12, 1967). A leftist (anarchist) organization accused them of conservatism (see *Chung-hsueh feng-pao,* no. 1 [May 27, 1967]; the Flying Tigers, publisher of this journal, seem to include a dissident faction that broke off from the Capital Corps).

85. *Ping-t'uan chan-pao,* no. 3 (November 26, 1966), no. 4 (December 16, 1966).

86. *Shou-tu feng-lei,* no. 5 (March 25, 1967).

87. Miriam London and Ivan D. London, "The Shaping of the 'Red Guard Mind,'" *Freedom at Issue,* November-December 1975.

88. Sa Meng-wu, *Shui-hu chuan yü chung-kuo she-hui,* p. 10. The two ethical systems were perhaps not as clear-cut and mutually exclusive as Sa suggests, however.

89. London and London, "'Red Guard Mind.'"

90. PD, April 2, 1973; Wen P'u, "Talk about letters and other matters," PD, December 6, 1973. The worst assignments are probably with the military-run state farms and construction corps in the border regions, which combine wretched climate and intense discipline in the midst of an often strange and not overly friendly population.

91. PD, February 7, 1964.

92. PD, June 2, 1973. This story tells how a group of youths worked so hard that, despite the lack of rebate from the state, production and hence consumption actually went up. Things surely do not always work out so well.

93. PD, February 7, 1974. Here again it seems we do not have the whole story. The girl herself seems rather obnoxious: the only thing she finds to say about her poor husband is that he is a common peasant. What is considered shameless may be less her marriage than her attitude.

94. *Chung-kuo ch'ing-nien,* no. 21 (November 15, 1954), p. 31. This is morally obtuse in that it suggests the main evil in the seduction of fifteen-year-old girls by public officials is that it takes the girls' minds off their studies.

95. Liang Chiao, "Old K'ung number two at the end of the feudal era," PD, June 28, 1974. This article, part of the criticism of Lin Piao and Confucius campaign, discusses the novel *Dream of the red chamber* and is, I think, one of the articles in that campaign that takes the radical line. The relevant sections are the discussions of Chia Hao's easy ways with the servant girls of the Chia household.

96. *Chung-kung yen-chiu,* no. 82 (October 1973), pp. 93–98.

97. T'an Wen, "Youth is a most active and most spirited strength," PD, March 10, 1973.

98. *Kuang-ming jih-pao,* January 19, 1973.

99. PD, July 23, 1973.

100. PD, December 25, 1974. This girl, however, is not an outsider but a native of the village where she works.

101. *Voice of China*, no. 5 (May 16, 1971), pp. 3, 4.

102. See especially Merle Goldman, *Literary Dissent in Communist China*; also D. W. Fokkema, *Literary Doctrine in China and Soviet Influence, 1956–1960*.

103. Martin Dewhirst and Robert Farrel, eds., *The Soviet Censorship*, p. 1.

104. For excerpts from this speech see Schram, *Political Thought of Mao*, pp. 359–63.

105. Chou Yang, "Let literature and art develop their enormous function in the great enterprise of socialist development," PD, September 26, 1956; Ch'u Lan, "Talking about the problem of depth in works of literature and art," PD, November 2, 1974.

106. Yao Wen-yuan, *Lun wen-hsueh-shang te hsiu-cheng-chu-i ssu-ch'ao* [On the revisionist thought tide in literature], p. 258 (hereafter cited as *Revisionist thought tide*). The quoted passage, of course, contradicts itself.

107. Ibid., p. 15; see also p. 215.

108. Ibid., p. 134 (Morgan is Lewis Henry Morgan [1818–81], the American ethnologist admired so much by Engels); pp. 53, 4.

109. Ibid., pp. 41, 129.

110. Cheng Chia-chen, *Chiang-p'an ch'ao-yang*, p. 17. The novel, to be fair, does contain some nice passages.

111. C. T. Hsia, *A History of Modern Chinese Fiction*.

112. Leo Ou-fan Lee, "The Romantic Temper of May Fourth Writers," in *May Fourth Movement*, ed. Schwartz, pp. 69–84; Tsi-an Hsia, *The Gate of Darkness*.

113. Yao, *Revisionist thought tide*, p. 306.

114. On literary factions see Merle Goldman, *Literary Dissent*, chap. 4.

115. This liberalism, however, is not evident in his public pronouncements, which echo the current line, whatever it may have been. See, e.g., Chou's last speech, "Raise high the red flag of the Thought of Mao Tse-tung, be literary warriors able both to labor and to create," PD, January 1, 1966. Perhaps as one criticism of him had it, "What Chou Yang said at large meetings was one thing; what he said at small meetings and outside talks was something else" (PD, July 29, 1966).

116. Lu Wei-jan, *Hu Feng shih-chien te ch'ien-yin hou-kuo*, p. 48. This book also contains the excerpts from the letters of Hu Feng to his friends, originally published in PD, May 13, May 24, and June 10, 1955.

117. Shu Wu, "Study from the beginning the 'Speech at the Yenan forum on literature and art,'" PD, June 8, 1952; Lu Wei-jan, *Hu Feng*, pp. 47 ff.

118. Lin Mo-han, "Hu Feng's anti-Marxist literary thought," *Wen-i pao*, 1953, no. 2 (January 30), pp. 3–8.

119. Kuo Mo-jo, "Hu Feng's antisocialist program," PD, April 1, 1955.

120. [Hu Feng], *Hu Feng i-chien shu*, p. 38. Hu's letter was originally issued as a supplement to *Wen-i pao*, 1955, nos. 1–2 (January 30). The edition I have used may be this supplement, although it contains no publication data and is much more poorly printed—in places it is unreadable—than is usual for mainland publications. The volume is in the East Asia Collection of the Hoover Institution, Stanford, Ca.

121. Ibid., pp. 29–30, 135.

122. Lu Wei-jan, *Hu Feng*, p. 74.

123. Hu Feng, "Speech," *Wen-i pao*, 1954, no. 22 (November 30), pp. 7–15; quote on p. 9.

124. Chou Yang, "We must fight," *Kuang-ming jih-pao*, December 10, 1954.

125. Hu Feng, "My self-criticism," PD, May 10, 1955.

126. Yuan Shui-po, "Hu Feng's theoretical bankruptcy as seen from his creations," PD, February 20, 1955.

127. Yao Wen-yuan, "Clearly distinguish right from wrong, clearly draw the line," *Wen-i pao*,

1955, nos. 1–2 (January 30), pp. 37–39. Since we are interested in cliques, there is a note of historical interest here. Yao signs his article with the date, adding a romantic *shen-yeh*—"deep night." In attacking Feng Hsueh-feng two and a half years later, Yao's friend Chang Ch'un-ch'iao follows the same practice ("In the midst of great wind and waves," *Jen-min wen-hsueh*, 1957, no. 9 [September], pp. 4–6). Is this a cabalistic sign?

128. *Jen-min wen-hsueh*, 1957, no. 9 (September), p. 1.

129. Ibid., p. 3; Yao, *Revisionist thought tide*, p. 285.

130. K'ang Cho, "Comments on short stories during the past few years," *Wen-i p'ing-lun*, no. 5 (September 1962), pp. 12–29; Merle Goldman, "Party Policies toward the Intellectuals: The Unique Blooming and Contending of 1961–1962," in *Party Leadership*, ed. Lewis, p. 302.

131. Lu Kuei-shan, "To write about middle characters is the manifestation in literary theory of 'two combine into one' and the 'summary' of the spirit of the times," *Wen-i pao*, 1964, nos. 11–12 (December 30), p. 3.

132. Ibid., pp. 3–12 passim; see also the other articles in this dull issue.

133. *Kuan-yü mu-ch'ien nung-ts'un kung-tso-shang jo-kan wen-t'i te chüeh-ting* (*ts'ao-an*) (May 1963), p. 2; Ch'en Yuan-hui, "Pragmatism: truth is nothing but an expedient method," PD, May 30, 1963.

134. Yuan Hsuan-lü, "The Shakespeare business," PD, March 12, 1964. The Shakespeare quote is from *Timon of Athens*, act 5, sc. 1, line 114.

135. Hsu Tsung-wen, "The new conservative political philosophy of the American bourgeoisie," PD, May 12, 1964.

136. Ch'u Lan, "Criticism of the Shansi opera *Three times up peach peak*," PD, February 8, 1974.

137. See, e.g., Hsiang Hui, "Criticizing the Hunan opera *The gardener's song*," PD, August 2, 1974.

138. Jen T'u, "Come out of 'Petersburg,'" PD, April 6, 1975.

139. *Wen-i chan-ku*, no. 2 (May 23, 1967).

140. Ch'u Lan, "Problem of depth."

141. *Chung-yang jih-pao*, January 16, 1974.

142. Jen Wen-ch'in, "Why is the seagull so popular?" *Hsueh-hsi yü p'i-p'an*, 1974, no. 1 (January 16), pp. 41–44; the translation is on pp. 44–49.

143. Shirley Garrett, *Social Reformers in Urban China*.

144. For the two texts together see, conveniently, *China Quarterly*, no. 62 (June 1975), pp. 404–5.

145. Lu Ting-i, "Let a hundred flowers bloom, a hundred schools contend," *Jen-min shou-ts'e*, 1957, p. 567 n.

146. Holmes Welch, *Buddhism under Mao*, p. 300; Chen and Ridley, *Rural People's Communes*, p. 110.

147. *Su-ch'ing ti-kuo-chu-i te wen-hua ch'in-lüeh shih-li*.

148. E. H. Johnson, "Christian Voices from the Church in China: April, 1975," *China Notes* 13 no. 3 (Summer 1975): 26.

149. Wu Yao-tsung, "Some problems in thoroughly carrying out the policy on religion," PD, March 9, 1957.

150. Johnson, "Christian Voices," pp. 27, 29, 30.

151. PD, June 7, 1951.

152. PD, July 5, 1951.

153. Lo Jui-ch'ing, "The people of the whole country must get united and firmly, thoroughly, cleanly, and completely purge all counterrevolutionary elements," PD, July 29, 1955.

154. Tu Mo, *Chung-kuo ta-lu t'ien-chu-chiao chen-hsiang* [True picture of the Catholic church on the China mainland], pp. 171, 174 (hereafter cited as *Catholic church*).

155. Chi Yun, "Under the cover of the cloak of religion," PD, December 11, 1955.

156. Tu, *Catholic church,* p. 183.

157. Ibid., p. 53.

158. Ibid., p. 93.

159. Ibid.; see also PD, August 3, 1957.

160. Tu, *Catholic church,* p. 94.

161. Ibid., p. 152.

162. Kenneth Lierberthal, "The Suppression of Secret Societies in Post-Liberation Tientsin," *China Quarterly,* no. 54 (April/June, 1973), pp. 242–56.

163. Lo Jui-ch'ing, "People of the whole country"; Yen Ching-yao, "The need for the firm suppression of counterrevolutionaries as seen from the situation in eastern Chekiang," PD, July 4, 1955.

164. Oliver J. Caldwell, *A Secret War.*

165. Welch, *Buddhism under Mao,* pp. 100, 169–85, 201–10.

166. *Hsien-tai Fo-hsueh,* 1958, no. 8 (August), pp. 30–31.

167. Welch, *Buddhism under Mao,* p. 347.

168. John and Sarah Strong, "A Post–Cultural Revolution Look at Chinese Buddhism," *China Quarterly,* no. 54 (April/June, 1973), p. 330.

169. *Hui* is an ambiguous term. It means "Moslem" in Chinese, but not all Moslems who are citizens of China—for example, the Turks in Sinkiang—are members of the Hui nationality. And, of course, many members of the Hui nationality are not practicing Moslems—some, for example, belong to the party.

170. PD, October 17, 1958.

171. *China News Service,* no. 586 (October 8, 1975), p. 4, based on a report in the *South China Morning Post,* July 11, 1975.

172. George H. Kerr, *Formosa Betrayed,* p. 340.

173. Cf. Johan Huizinga, *Homo Ludens.*

174. Central Issue (1971) No. 85, in *Chung-kung yen-chiao,* no. 69 (September 1972), p. 103.

175. PD, February 7, 1974.

176. James T. Myers, "Religious Aspects of the Cult of Mao Tse-Tung," *Current Scene* 10, no. 3 (March 10, 1972): 1–11.

177. John Bryan Starr, *Ideology and Culture,* pp. 32 ff.

178. Welch, *Buddhism under Mao,* p. 381.

179. Wu I-lai, "We must pay attention to spreading the common language," PD, December 3, 1975.

180. Chiang Hua, "Firmly support the party's correct line, struggle for the victory of the Rectification movement on every front," PD, December 28, 1957.

181. Ezra Vogel, *Canton under Communism,* p. 104.

182. Teng Hsiao-p'ing, "Report on the rectification movement," *Jen-min shou-ts'e,* 1958, p. 40.

183. Chiang Hua, "Support the party's correct line."

184. Ou Meng-chüeh, "What are the errors of Ku Ta-ts'un and Feng Pai-chü?" *Hsin-hua pan-yueh k'an,* 1958, no. 19 (October 10), p. 44.

185. Audrey Donnithorne, "China's Cellular Economy," *China Quarterly,* no. 52 (October/December 1972), pp. 605–19.

186. *Chui chiu kuan,* no. 4 (May 20, 1967).

187. Ch'en Ch'i-t'ien, *Han Fei-tzu chiao-chi,* p. 290.

188. Ibid., p. 283.

189. Ibid., pp. 181–82.

190. Ibid., p. 195.

191. Ibid., pp. 685 ff.

192. Barry M. Richman, *Industrial Society in Communist China*. Richman likes to call the radical ideology "theology." If words are to be bandied in this way, his own ideas are also theology, the elucidation of the ways of mammon. The issues between the radicals and the moderates cannot, I believe, be settled by technical considerations.

193. Nieh Jung-chen, "Firmly protect the work of socialist science," *Jen-min shou-ts'e*, 1958, pp. 159–60.

194. Liu Shao-ch'i, "Report on the work of the Central Committee of the Communist Party of China to the second session of the Eighth National Congress of the Communist Party of China," PD, May 27, 1958.

195. Moody, *Eighth Central Committee*, p. 127.

196. RF, 1958, no. 7 (September 1), p. 14.

197. Li Hsien-nien, "A look at the people's communes," PD, October 17, 1958.

198. Barnett, *Cadres, Bureaucracy, and Political Power*, p. 8.

199. Cf. Moody, *Eighth Central Committee*, pp. 50–51.

200. Parris H. Chang, "The Changing Loci of Decision-Making in the CCP," *China Quarterly*, no. 44 (October/December 1970), pp. 169–94.

201. Michel Crozier, *The Bureaucratic Phenomenon*, p. 202.

202. *Hsin-wen chan-pao*, no. 3 (May 14, 1967).

203. Liu Shao-ch'i, *Lun tang*, p. 13; Teng Hsiao-p'ing, "Report on the revision of the party constitution," *Jen-min shou-ts'e*, 1957, p. 27.

204. John E. Rue, *Mao Tse-tung in Opposition, 1927–1935*. The unusual 1975 celebrations of the anniversary of the Long March stress the leftism of Mao's pre-1935 opponents (Liu Po-ch'eng, "Remembering the Long March," PD, October 19, 1975 [originally published in 1959]; I Chün, "Remembering the central Red Army's revolutionary deeds in southern Szechwan on the Long March," *Li-shih yen-chiu*, 1975, no. 5 (October 20), p. 45.

205. Ch'en Po-ta, "Under the banner of Comrade Mao Tse-tung," RF, 1958, no. 4 (July 15), pp. 1–12; Max Weber, *The Theory of Social and Economic Organization*, p. 380; PD, December 18, 1958.

206. See the documents collected in *Case of Peng Teh-huai*; for the rekindling of the cult see Wu Chih-p'u, "Study the works of Comrade Mao Tse-tung," PD, January 1, 1960.

207. RF, 1970, no. 9 (September 19), p. 7.

208. PD, April 16, 1971.

209. See, e.g., Hsieh Sheng-wen, "The background of 'apriori perception,'" PD, October 20, 1971.

210. PD, November 7, 1971.

211. Wang Che, "Engels Criticized Duhring's Apriorism."

212. PD, October 15, 1972. "Savior" here is *chiu-hsing;* in the song it is *chiu-shih-chu*.

213. See, e.g., Hsiao Hua, "Propel the mass movement for the living study–living use of the works of Chairman Mao to a new stage," PD, October 10, 1966.

214. Edgar Snow, "A Conversation with Mao Tse-tung," *Life*, April 30, 1971, p. 46.

215. *Chung-yang jih-pao*, November 2, 1972.

216. Yao, "Lin Piao antiparty clique."

217. Chen and Ridley, *Rural People's Communes*, pp. 98, 109.

218. MacFarquhar, *Hundred Flowers Campaign*, pp. 20, 65, 75.

219. [Chung Chih-min], "A report on a request to withdraw from school," PD, January 18, 1974; Yao, "Lin Piao antiparty clique."

220. *Voice of China*, no. 1 (January 15, 1969), p. 19.

221. Wang Jen-chung, "Speech."

222. Chen and Ridley, *Rural People's Communes,* pp. 196–97, quote on p. 196.

223. C. K. Yang, *A Chinese Village in Early Communist Transition,* p. 190.

224. *Nan-hai tung-feng,* no. 5 ([October?] 1967).

225. Early 1976 saw the revival of attacks on Khrushchev's "goulash communism." One critique points out that by material standards it is the United States that comes closest to realizing the second stage of communism (Shu Tung, "The total bankruptcy of phony 'goulash' communism," PD, January 3, 1976). Except that the state does not seem to be withering away, this is true enough. There are, no doubt, all kinds of morals here for any who would care to point to them.

226. Crozier, *Bureaucratic Phenomenon,* p. 4.

227. Samuel P. Huntington, *The Soldier and the State.*

228. *Jen-min shou-ts'e,* 1956, p. 78.

229. Hsiao Hua, "On the problem of the management of educational work in platoons," *Work Bulletin,* 1961, no. 24 (June 18), pp. 1, 2. Prior to the Cultural Revolution the Military Affairs Commission, not the Ministry of Defense, was the main locus of power in the army, but the Minister of Defense was also the effective head of the Military Affairs Commission.

230. *Work Bulletin,* 1961, no. 3 (January 7), pp. 3–4.

231. In 1960 Lin instituted a "purge of counterrevolutionaries (liquidation) movement" in the army (*Work Bulletin,* 1961, no. 1 [January 1], pp. 29–32). In 1964 P'eng Te-huai's supporters began to fill up the labor camps (Bao and Chelminski, *Prisoner of Mao,* p. 301).

232. Yeh Chien-ying, "Speech at the conference on military training," *Work Bulletin,* 1961, no. 10 (February 20), p. 5; Liu Ya-lou, "The need clearly and positively to see the problem of air force training and fighting," ibid., p. 22.

233. *Work Bulletin,* 1961, no. 3, p. 7.

234. PD, February 1, 1964.

235. PD, February 14, 1964.

236. Lin Piao, "Speech at the all-army conference on education management work," *Work Bulletin,* 1961, no. 22 (June 1), p. 4.

237. Lin Piao, *Long Live the Victory.*

238. William L. Parish, Jr., "Factions in Chinese Military Politics," *China Quarterly,* no. 56 (October/December 1973), pp. 667–99. It would seem reasonable to expect, however, that factional relationships will be intertwined with the formal bureaucratic structure.

239. Lo Jui-ch'ing, "Learn from Lei Feng."

240. Lo Jui-ch'ing, "Commemorate the defeat of German Fascism, carry through to the end the struggle against American imperialism," PD, May 11, 1965; idem, "The people were able to defeat Japanese Fascism, the people will certainly be able to defeat American imperialism," PD, September 4, 1965. For a full analysis of this argument see Donald Zagoria, *Vietnam Triangle,* chap. 2.

241. Lin Piao, "Address to the Enlarged Meeting of the CCP Politburo" (May 10, 1966), *Issues and Studies* 6, no. 5 (February 1970): 81–92.

242. William Whitson, "Field Army"; also Whitson, with Chen-hsia Huang, *The Chinese High Command.*

243. Whitson, with Huang, *Chinese High Command,* p. 332; Ellis Joffe, "China's Military Elites," *China Quarterly,* no. 62 (June 1975), p. 314.

244. PD, April 10, 1967.

245. PD, July 31, 1967.

246. Yang Ch'eng-wu, "Very particularly establish the absolute authority of the great generalissimo Chairman Mao, very particularly establish the absolute authority of the great Thought of Mao Tse-tung," PD, November 3, 1967.

247. For a good study of this obscure incident see Hsuan Mo, "The open and hidden story of the Bandit Yang Ch'eng-wu incident," *Fei-ch'ing yen-chiu* 11, no. 8 (August 1968): 43–56.

It is worth mentioning that in the early 1970s Yang, along with Hsiao Hua, Lo Jui-ch'ing, Ho Lung (posthumously), and other soldiers purged in the Cultural Revolution, was rehabilitated. It is difficult to know why. One hopes this is magnanimity but suspects there is more to it.

248. Ling, *Revenge of Heaven,* p. 178; Bennett and Montaperto, *Red Guard,* p. 95.

249. The "unofficial official" version—that which Peking would have us believe (at time of publication) but which it need not commit itself to—is given in Jack Chen, *Inside the Cultural Revolution,* pp. 342–85. Even this account is confused—it is likely the people in Peking are still confused. I prefer to work directly from the original documents, such as they are, rather than follow Chen, except for matters of detail. He presents, in effect, the Chou En-lai version, stressing Lin's affiliation with the ultraleft as opposed to the true left, meaning Mao and Chou; but Chen also must take into account the official radical interpretation of Lin as a man of the right. The whole affair is very messy.

250. Ch'eng Yueh, "Firmly support the party line," PD, January 8, 1976.

251. PD, September 12, 1971.

252. Hsiang Hui, "Sincerely read books and study, raise the awareness of the implementation of Chairman Mao's revolutionary line," PD, October 15, 1971.

253. "Document No. 24 of the CCP Central Committee," *Issues and Studies* 9, no. 3 (December 1972): 94.

254. For a text of Mao's speech see *Chung-yang jih-pao,* August 10, 1972.

255. Jack Chen, *Inside the Cultural Revolution,* p. 370.

256. *Chung-yang jih-pao,* August 10, 1972.

257. From a purported "confession" by one of the plotters, Li Wei-hsin, *Chung-yang jih-pao,* April 13, 1972.

258. [Lin Li-kuo], "'571 engineering' outline."

259. Jack Chen, *Inside the Cultural Revolution,* p. 344.

260. Tien Chih-sung, "The Masses Are the Makers of History," *Peking Review,* July 21, 1972, p. 10.

261. Chu T'ung and Shih Lei, "Read Wang An-shih's 'Answer to Ssu-ma's memorial,'" *Kuang-ming jih-pao,* August 27, 1974.

262. *Hsing-tao jih-pao,* January 19, 1972.

263. T'ang Hsiao-wen, "Refuting the absurd Confucian theories on the cause of the destruction of the Ch'in dynasty," *Kuang-ming jih-pao,* September 1, 1974; Yang Kuang-han, "On the lessons of the experience of the collapse of the Ch'in dynasty," ibid., October 11, 1974.

264. Whitson, with Huang, *Chinese High Command,* p. 415.

265. *Chung-yang jih-pao,* April 13, 1972.

266. Cf. Merle Goldman, "China's Anti-Confucius Campaign, 1973–1974," *China Quarterly,* no. 63 (September 1975), pp. 435–62.

267. Shih Chung, "The pro-Legalist anti-Confucian spirit of 'On feudalism,'" PD, December 25, 1973; Chou I-lang, "Read Liu Tsung-yuan's 'On feudalism,'" RF, 1974, no. 2 (February 1), pp. 32–35.

268. PD, January 2, 1974.

269. Shih Hsueh-ch'ing, "A pro-Legalist anti-Confucian statesman, Sun Ch'üan," *Kuang-ming jih-pao,* December 23, 1974.

270. *Work Bulletin,* 1961, no. 1 (January 1), p. 17.

271. Lo Jui-ch'ing, "Report to the Center of an investigation of a certain division," *Work Bulletin,* 1961, no. 7 (February 1), p. 18.

272. Lo Jui-ch'ing. "Report on an investigation of the condition of the troops in several districts," *Work Bulletin,* 1961, no. 11 (March 2), p. 6.

273. Wakeman, *History and Will,* p. 25.

6: OPPOSITION MOVEMENTS

1. Jacques Ellul, *Hope in a Time of Abandonment,* p. 24.

2. For a detailed study of the intraparty politics of the time see MacFarquhar, *Cultural Revolution,* vol. 1.

3. Chou En-lai, "Report on the question of intellectuals," PD, January 30, 1956; Lu Ting-i, "Let a hundred flowers bloom."

4. Chou, "Question of intellectuals,"

5. MacFarquhar, *Cultural Revolution,* vol. 1, argues P'eng opposed rectification.

6. P'eng Chen, "Upholding the method of gentle breeze and light rain," PD, May 10, 1957.

7. PD, June 11, 1957.

8. PD, June 22, 1957.

9. PD, June 14, 1957.

10. Lu Ting-i, "Our basic divergence from the bourgeois rightists," PD, July 2, 1957.

11. PD, June 22, 1957.

12. MacFarquhar, *Hundred Flowers Campaign.*

13. Ibid., p. 65.

14. Chou En-lai, "Report on the work of the government" (June 26, 1957), *Jen-min shou-ts'e,* 1958, p. 212.

15. Ibid., pp. 204–5.

16. MacFarquhar, *Hundred Flowers Campaign,* p. 72.

17. Chou, "Work of the government" (1957), p. 207.

18. Ibid., pp. 207–8.

19. Ibid., p. 205.

20. MacFarquhar, *Hundred Flowers Campaign,* p. 50.

21. Chou, "Work of the government" (1957), p. 210.

22. MacFarquhar, *Hundred Flowers Campaign,* p. 51.

23. Ibid., p. 10.

24. Chou, "Work of the government" (1957), pp. 210–12.

25. MacFarquhar, *Hundred Flowers Campaign,* p. 25.

26. PD, May 31, 1957.

27. Liu Chia, "'Rejection' and solidarity," PD, June 8, 1957.

28. Doolin, *Communist China.* The passages that follow are taken from pp. 49, 51, 60, 63.

29. MacFarquhar, *Hundred Flowers Campaign,* pp. 145–53.

30. Mei Kung-ping, "The form of Ch'en Ming-shu's reactionary goal," *Kuang-ming jih-pao,* October 29, 1957.

31. MacFarquhar, *Hundred Flowers Campaign,* p. 14.

32. Doolin, *Communist China,* p. 38.

33. Cited in MacFarquhar, *Hundred Flowers Campaign,* p. 88.

34. Doolin, *Communist China,* p. 70.

35. Chang Ch'un-ch'iao, "Great wind and waves," p. 6.

36. Levenson, *Confucian China,* 3: 121.

37. Liberalism hardly flourishes in Taiwan but in that province does (so far) manage to hold its own. Many erstwhile liberals living outside China have become outspoken proponents of the Peking regime, particularly since the late 1960s: their nationalism has taken precedence over their liberalism. See, e.g., Ho Ping-ti, "The characteristics and accomplishments of New China viewed from a historical measurement," *Ch'i-shih nien-tai,* no. 50 (March 1974), pp. 4–14. These people

continue, of course, to berate the Taiwan regime for violations of civil liberties rather less gross than is the norm on the mainland (Yao Li-min, "Critical introduction to the fighter against tradition, Po Yang," in *Po Yang ho t'a-te yuan-yü*, ed. Sun Kuan-han, pp. 242–325). These gentlemen seem in no hurry to return and participate in national construction.

38. *Chung-kung jen-ming lü*, p. 311.

39. Ma Yin-ch'u, "My philosophical thought and economic theory," *Hsin chien-she*, 1959, no. 11 (November), p. 55.

40. Sha Ch'ing, "Dissecting a sophistry," PD, January 30, 1976.

41. Wu Han [Liu Mien-chih], "Hai Jui scolds the emperor."

42. *Ko-ti t'ung hsun*, September 13, 1967, in *Survey of the China Mainland Press*, no. 4081 (December 15, 1967), p. 7.

43. *Ko-ming ch'uan-lien*, August 24, 1967, in *Survey of the China Mainland Press*, no. 4032 (October 2, 1967), pp. 1–4.

44. *Pei-ching hsin wen-i*, 1967, no. 3 (June 8).

45. Wu Han, "On Hai Jui," PD, September 17, 1959. Most of the quotes come from statements by P'eng Te-huai. The business about sun spots and fingers, however, comes from a public pronouncement by T'ao Chu, then first secretary of Kwangtung (T'ao Chu, "The brilliance of the sun," PD, June 3, 1959). T'ao seems to have shared the philosophical and policy preferences of the P'eng Chen group, although in 1966 he allied himself with the radicals, earning rapid promotion and equally rapid purge. In 1960 T'ao's cronies apparently tried to horn in on Hai Jui themselves (see Chang P'ing-hua, "Party publications must stick in the red flag." PD, January 12, 1960).

46. Wu Han, *Hai Jui pa kuan* [Hai Jui is dismissed from office].

47. See Wang Hsueh-wen, *Chung-kung wen-hua ta ko-ming*, pp. 14–18.

48. Teng T'o, *Teng T'o shih-wen hsuan*, p. 74. This collection consists of excerpts from Teng's controversial writings, along with his critics' 1966 glosses, which allegedly reveal Teng's secret meanings.

49. *T'an-t'an P'eng Te-huai che-ko jen*, p. 91.

50. Teng T'o, *Shih-wen hsuan*, p. 107.

51. PD, June 11, 1957.

52. Teng T'o, *Shih-wen hsuan*, pp. 137–40.

53. Lo Keng-mo, "On the question of how to implement correctly the principle of distribution according to labor," *Ta kung pao* (Peking), April 16, 1962.

54. Laurence A. Schneider, *Ku Chieh-kang and China's New History*, p. 217. The Communists can in fact justify this view rather cleverly: Confucius is held to be an ideologist of the slave society who appeared just as that society was becoming feudal. Hence, Confucianism is never the ideology of a rising class and therefore is always reactionary (see Yang Jung-kuo, *Kung-Mo te ssu-hsiang*). This view has perhaps always been the dominant one in the People's Republic but did not become dogma until around 1973.

55. Levenson, *Confucian China*, 3: 80, 114.

56. Robert C. Tucker, *The Marxian Revolutionary Idea*, p. 46.

57. Richard N. Hunt, *The Political Ideas of Marx and Engels*, 1: 131.

58. Hunter, *Shanghai Journal*, p. 275.

59. RF, 1974, no. 1 (January 1), p. 93, with specific reference here, however, to the Soviets.

60. Feng Yu-lan, *Hsin li-hsueh*. Some argue, however, that Feng divorces the virtue of *jen* too much from the moral realm, making it too transcendental and thus falls into a Buddhist or Taoist heresy (Wing-tsit Chan, *Neo-Confucianism*, p. 34).

61. Feng Yu-lan, "Gains and experience from the two anti-movements," *Cheng-ming*, 1958, no. 8 (July), p. 11. It took age and the Cultural Revolution to break this old man's spirit, and we cannot be sure it was completely broken. In one of his banal 1973 essays Feng says he was deceived by Confucianism for so long because he took seriously a statement by the Ming philosopher Wang

Yang-ming, "The streets are full of sages." Feng naïvely thought this was an assertion of human equality and dignity, whereas in reality, of course, it is just a swindle, no different from bourgeois "liberty, equality, fraternity." (Feng, "On the criticism of Confucius.") If Feng can baldly assert that Wang Yang-ming means the opposite of what he says, may he not intend for us to do the same for him?

62. Feng Yu-lan, "The problem of succession to the Chinese philosophical heritage," *Kuang-ming jih-pao,* January 8, 1957.

63. Feng Yu-lan, "On several problems in the study of the history of Chinese philosophy," *Hsin chien-she,* 1959, no. 12 (December), pp. 26–36.

64. Yang Jung-kuo et al., *Chien-ming chung-kuo ssu-hsiang shih,* pp. 15, 21; Kuan Feng and Lin Yü-shih, "On Confucius," *Che-hsueh yen-chiu,* 1961, no. 4 (July 25), pp. 42–70; Feng Yu-lan, "Confucius's thought on '*Jen,*' " ibid., no. 5 (September 25), pp. 63–71, 36.

65. Feng Yu-lan, "On the basic problem of ethics," *Hsin chien-she,* 1961, no. 4 (April), pp. 40–42; Lo Ko, "Discussing several problems of Marxist ethics," *Kuang-ming jih-pao,* December 6, 1961.

66. Chang Yü-lou, "The method of Marxist class analysis and historical research," PD, June 18, 1963. Liu's original essays are apparently not available outside of China.

67. Wu Han, "On Hai Jui." If, as Mao says, "Hai Jui is P'eng Te-huai," might this not be a criticism of P'eng for being reformist in conditions that required basic social change?

68. Wu Han, *Hai Jui pa kuan* [Hai Jui is dismissed from office], pp. 12, 13, 34, 36, 57.

69. Teng T'o, *Shih-wen hsuan,* p. 56.

70. Ibid., pp. 122–23.

71. Ibid., pp. 129–30. For a curiously parallel argument see C. S. Lewis, *The Abolition of Man,* p. 56.

72. Yao Wen-yuan, *Yao Wen-yuan wen-chi,* ed. Liu Ts'un-chih, pp. 4, 25.

73. Wu Han, *Hai Jui pa kuan,* p. iii.

74. Yao, *Wen-chi,* pp. 17, 27.

75. Teng T'o, *Shih-wen hsuan,* pp. 31–32.

76. Ibid., p. 47.

77. Ibid., p. 113.

78. Ibid., p. 44.

79. Ibid., pp. 116, 86; Liang Ch'i-hsiung, "The nature and origins of Han Fei's thought," *Kuang-ming jih-pao,* August 24 and 25, 1961. The critique is on August 25. This interpretation of Han Fei as both progressive and anti-people is not new; other communist writings, however, give more weight than does Liang to Han Fei's good side. See, e.g., Wang I, "Han Fei," *Chung-kuo ch'ing-nien,* 1957, no. 3 (February 1), pp. 26–28. The use of the term *totalitarian* is very unusual.

80. Teng T'o, *Shih-wen hsuan,* p. 134.

81. Yao, *Wen-chi,* p. 60.

82. Teng T'o, *Shih-wen hsuan,* pp. 17, 69 ff., 94.

83. Merle Goldman, "Party Policies toward the Intellectuals: The Unique Blooming and Contending of 1961–1962," in *Party Leadership,* ed. Lewis, p. 300; Teng T'o, *Shih-wen hsuan,* pp. 27, 29, 42; Yao, *Wen-chi,* p. 51.

84. Teng T'o, *Shih-wen hsuan,* pp. 61–62. *Mao-ping,* "hair illness," is a very common colloquial way of saying "defect." The entire phrase may also be a clumsy way of saying "Big Mao is sick." I doubt very much that a pun is intended, however.

85. Ibid., pp. 124–26.

86. Li Yu-ning, *Wu Han chuan,* p. 82. I do not know whether the Ming forces ever used the title *Hung Chün,* "Red Army"; Chu, the surname of the Ming emperors, means "vermillion" and is, of course, a synonym for *hung*.

87. Hong Yung Lee, "The Radical Students in Kwangtung during the Cultural Revolution," *China Quarterly,* no. 64 (December 1975), p. 673.

88. Ibid.

89. Tucker, *Marxian Revolutionary Idea,* p. 182.

90. Dahrendorf, *Theory of Sociology,* p. 169.

91. Chang Ch'un-ch'iao, "Destroy bourgeois legal-rights thought," PD, October 1, 1958. See also Wu Ch'uan-ch'i, "Communism seen from the people's communes," ibid.; Kuan Feng, "The best form of distribution for the transition to communism," PD, October 22, 1958. Wu and Kuan were purged as ultraleftists in 1967. Kuan's 1958 argument, however, is more moderate than Chang's.

92. *Hung yen chan-pao,* no. 2 (June 5, 1967); *China News Analysis,* no. 670 (July 5, 1967); ibid., no. 673 (July 28, 1967), pp. 1–6.

93. Lee, "Radical Students," p. 674.

94. Chao Han, "Obey the party constitution, strengthen party nature," PD, October 17, 1961.

95. [Hsu Chin], "Is this a melon-head?" *Chung-kuo ch'ing-nien,* 1957, no. 3 (February 1), pp. 30–31.

96. [Chang T'ieh-sheng], "An examination that causes people to ponder deeply," PD, August 10, 1973.

97. Jack Chen, *Inside the Cultural Revolution,* p. 331. For domestic consumption, of course, the regime would stress the scoundrels' ambition, not such feudal-bourgeois-idealist drivel as morality and conscience.

98. This is the theme of the story by Wang Meng, "Young newcomer."

99. The proper order should have been, of course, Mao, Liu, Chou. The transposition is no doubt significant, although heaven only knows what was going on. In his answer to the letter Tung tacitly draws our attention to the transposition: "In quoting your original letter I have made no changes at all" (Tung Pi-wu, "On the livelihood of the worker-peasant masses and other matters," *Chung-kuo ch'ing-nien pao,* April 13, 1957).

100. Sun Yü-shan, "A letter to Venerable Tung," *Chung-kuo ch'ing-nien pao,* April 13, 1957.

101. PD, April 26, 1957.

102. Doolin, *Communist China.* This is no longer strictly true, if it ever really was.

103. Lin Hsi-ling, "Tentative discussion of the world views and works of Balzac and Tolstoy," *Wen-i pao,* 1955, no. 21 (November 15), pp. 32–35.

104. Doolin, *Communist China,* p. 23. To keep things in perspective, it would have been difficult to publish anything on literature in 1955 without some nasty words for Hu Feng, and Miss Lin's attack on him is rather ritualistic.

105. Ibid., pp. 27, 28.

106. Ibid., pp. 34, 36–37.

107. Ibid., pp. 30–31, 35, 23–24, 39, 38.

108. Ibid., pp. 38, 41.

109. Liu Shao-ch'i, "Liu Shao-ch'i te tzu-wo p'i-p'ing" (Photocopy of a handwritten copy of a wall poster at Tsinghua University, December 26, 1966), pp. 32–33, East Asia Collection, Hoover Institution, Stanford, Ca.

110. For good popular accounts see Stanley Karnow, *Mao and China*; and Edward E. Rice, *Mao's Way*; for background on this section see Parris H. Chang, *Radicals and Radical Ideology.*

111. Richard Baum and Frederick C. Teiwes, *Ssu-ch'ing.*

112. Chiang Ch'ing, "Speech," *Hung-i chan-pao* [Red Arts War Report], no. 1 (February 15, 1967).

113. K'o Ch'ing-shih, "The brilliant road ahead for modern plays that reflect the new socialist era," PD, December 29, 1963; idem, "Put great effort into developing and making flourish socialist plays, make them serve the socialist economic base even better," PD, August 16, 1964.

114. Ch'i Pen-yü, "Criticism of the confession of Li Hsiu-ch'eng," *Li-shih yen-chiu,* 1963, no. 4 (August), pp. 27–42. The prime exponent of the orthodox thesis defends it in the same issue: Lo Ehr-kang, "Some explanations of what I have written on the textual analysis of the confession of Li Hsiu-ch'eng," ibid., pp. 43–45.

115. *CCP Documents,* pp. 7–10.

116. Peter Moody, "Power and Policy," *China Quarterly,* no. 54 (April/June 1973), pp. 267–93.

117. Mao swam ten miles in one hour and five minutes—backstroke! Jack Chen, *Inside the Cultural Revolution,* p. 221, hints that the treatment given to the swim may have been a "deliberate attempt to lampoon the whole thing" by T'ao Chu and Ch'en Po-ta. There is an undeniable element of farce in reports of the event; but why would T'ao, or especially Ch'en, deliberately ridicule the Chairman?

118. Ch'i Pen-yü, "Patriotism or treason?" PD, April 1, 1967.

119. Ch'i Pen-yü, "Speech at the Peking Mining Academy," *Chan-tou pao,* no. 2 (ca. January 1, 1967).

120. *Hung ch'i* (Peking: Peking Flying Academy Red Flag Fighting Team), nos. 10–11 (February 10, 1967).

121. Fan Chin, "The 'class character of man' is anti–Thought of Mao Tse-tung poison," PD, April 30, 1967.

122. Kao Ko, "Plant and develop revolutionary new-born things," RF, 1972, no. 12 (December 1), p. 9.

123. Lin Piao, "Political report to the Ninth National Congress of the Communist Party of China," PD, April 28, 1969; Ch'ao Yang, "Study well Chairman Mao's theory of continuing revolution under proletarian dictatorship," PD, July 5, 1969.

124. See, e.g., PD, May 6, 1971.

125. Ch'en Po-ta, "The struggle between the proletarian and bourgeois world views," RF, 1959, no. 22 (November 16), pp. 11–16.

126. *Chung-yang jih-pao,* November 4, 1972.

127. Chi P'ing, "Grasp the laws of class struggle in the socialist era," RF, 1972, no. 8 (August 1), p. 7. The use, even if half sarcastic, of Confucian terms in this context is probably significant in view of the later campaign against Confucius.

128. Chung Tso-wen, "Deepen and develop the strong ideological weapon of the struggle between the two lines," PD, March 9, 1972.

129. RF, 1973, no. 4 (April 1), pp. 23, 22.

130. Yao Wen-yuan, "Criticism of two books by T'ao Chu," PD, September 8, 1967.

131. Moody, "Power and Policy," p. 288.

132. Barry Burton, "The Cultural Revolution's Ultraleft Conspiracy," *Asian Survey* 11, no. 11 (November 1971): 1031.

133. A speech by Chou En-lai, *Chu-ying tung-fang-hung,* October 1, 1967, in *Survey of the China Mainland Press,* no. 4066 (November 24, 1967), pp. 2–3.

134. Jack Chen, *Inside the Cultural Revolution,* p. 364, says this, not the Wuhan incident, led to the crackdown on the group.

135. *T'ao Ch'i,* March 1, 1968.

136. Jack Chen, *Inside the Cultural Revolution,* p. 293.

137. Wuhan *Hsin hua kung,* September 16, 1967, in *Survey of the China Mainland Press,* no. 4042 (October 17, 1967), pp. 1–6.

138. Jack Chen, *Inside the Cultural Revolution,* p. 280.

139. Burton, "Ultraleft Conspiracy," pp. 1049–50.

140. Jack Chen, "Treason at the Top," *Far Eastern Economic Review* 73, no. 29 (July 9, 1971): 21–23. Chen does not mention Ch'en Po-ta by name, but he was obviously the target of the purge of the leftists at that time. It was not yet permitted to name Ch'en Po-ta, and Chen always follows the discipline of the movement in giving his astonishing revelations.

141. Jack Chen, *Inside the Cultural Revolution,* p. 364.

142. Burton, "Ultraleft Conspiracy," p. 1052.

143. *Survey of the China Mainland Press,* no. 4042 (October 17, 1967), p. 2.

144. Ibid., p. 5.

145. Hunan Provincial Broadcasting Station, October 18, 1967, in *Chung-kung ko-ti kuang-po tien-t'ai lu-yin hsin-wen* (*Provincial Broadcasting Stations*), (hereafter cited as *Provincial Broadcasting Stations*).

146. Canton *Pa-wu,* February 1968, in *Survey of the China Mainland Press,* no. 4136 (March 12, 1968), pp. 5–15.

147. This brings up a difficult (but, I hope, illusory) problem. A scholar whose opinion is worthy of respect has suggested to me that at least some of the documents purporting to come from the alliance are in fact KMT black propaganda, cooked up on Jen-ai Lu, smuggled onto the mainland, and then smuggled back out. He based his opinion on his impressions of the terminology used. The alliance uses some fashionably "new left" terms in its Taiwan translation, and the language supposedly corresponds to Taiwan, not mainland, usage. I have not seen the Chinese texts and am unable to judge this (the differences in usage would be statistical, not absolute, and I would not have much confidence in any philological analysis of mine on this question anyway). The scholar gave this as his impression but was not willing to be dogmatic.

Several things can be said: (1) While the national media have not, as far as I know, ever mentioned the alliance, there is no question that an ultraleft group of students by that name was active in Hunan during the time concerned. (2) We have two major documents purporting to come from the alliance: a program (*Survey of the China Mainland Press,* no. 4174 [May 9, 1968], pp. 10–13) and a manifesto, "Whither China" (ibid., no. 4190 [June 5, 1968], pp. 1–18). They are both translated from the same issue of the same Red Guard paper *Kuang-yin hung-ch'i,* no. 5 (March 1968). (3) K'ang Sheng quotes extensively from the program (*Survey of the China Mainland Press,* no. 4136 [March 12, 1968], pp. 5 ff.), as do some local official media (see Shanghai Municipal Broadcasting Station, March 27, 1968, *Provincial Broadcasting Stations,* no. 165). This would imply that the Communist authorities accept at least the program as genuine. (4) Since the program and the manifesto both come to us from the same source, this in itself would imply they are equally authentic; but in that case, why was not the more outrageous manifesto quoted as well? These reasons (3 and 4) perhaps cancel each other out. (5) In some respects the manifesto seems to contradict the program; there is at least a difference of emphasis. But they evidently come from different hands, and this need not imply the manifesto is a fake. The manifesto speaks of "Comrade Mao Tse-tung," which is unusual (see pp. 10, 12). It is usually "Chairman Mao," if you please. This "Comrade," however, may be an expression of radical iconoclasm, and a forger would probably follow the established and easily visible usage. Also, the manifesto warns against "bourgeois legal rights," (p. 16); if this document is a forgery, this is a nice touch. I don't think it would have occurred to a forger to insert this in 1968. I am inclined, in the absence of definite evidence, to accept both documents as coming from the alliance, although with misgivings to which this footnote is a testimony.

This does not necessarily mean the KMT had no hand in drawing up the documents. "Students, being inexperienced, are easily misled." The alliance may well have been infiltrated by the KMT. From the point of view of this study, the important point is whether certain mainland youths did accept the documents as statements of their own position, regardless of the genesis of the documents.

For an analysis of the alliance, relating it to the youth movement in other countries at the time, see Klaus Mehnert, *Peking and the New Left*.

148. *Survey of the China Mainland Press,* no. 4136, p. 6.

149. See, e.g., PD, April 22, 1975.

150. *Survey of the China Mainland Press,* no. 4136, p. 13.

151. Ibid., no. 4174, pp. 11, 12.

152. Ibid., no. 4190, pp. 1, 2, 4, 6.

153. Ibid., pp. 7, 5–6.

154. Ibid., pp. 8, 9, 10, 12.

155. Feng Hai, *Kuang-chou ti-ch'ü wen-ko li-ch'eng shu-lüeh* (Hong Kong: Union Research Institute, 1971), pp. 319 ff. Rather strangely, the account of the Center's attack on the alliance seems to come to us through this organization's paper. See note 146, this chap.

156. *Provincial Broadcasting Stations,* no. 165; Chekiang Provincial Broadcasting Station, March 27, 1968, ibid., no. 246. The last quote is a reconstruction of what is garbled in the source. The program of the radicals is called the "two [*sic*: *ehr*] nos and two wholes": "No rebels, no conservatives, no capitalist roaders; [they] want [garbled] whole people, elections by the whole people." The first *two*, as both syntax and context make clear, is a misprint for *three*.

157. *Voice of China,* no. 1 (January 15, 1969), pp. 1, 2; no. 3 (December 20, 1969), p. 2; no. 5 (May 15, 1971), p. 2.

158. *Voice of China,* no. 1, pp. 5–6.

159. *Voice of China,* no. 3, pp. 35–36.

160. *Voice of China,* no. 1, p. 27; no. 5, p. 5.

161. *Voice of China,* no. 1, p. 21.

162. Ibid., p. 15.

163. Ibid., pp. 16, 17, 19, 21.

164. Ibid., p. 7.

165. Ibid., pp. 30–33. Tseng Hsi-sheng had been one of the most outspoken proponents of the radicalism of the Leap, although in his last pronouncement he turned surprisingly moderate. I had assumed that his last statement was a self-criticism and that he had been purged by the "capitalist roaders." (Moody, *Eighth Central Committee,* pp. 149–50.) The *Voice of China*, however, says he was purged for implementing the responsibility fields system. This, and other evidence, makes me think I was wrong.

The program for economic development outlined here, it might be noted, is not much different from at least part of official regime policy.

166. *Voice of China,* no. 5, p. 12.

167. See *China News Analysis,* no. 984 (December 20, 1974), p. 2.

168. Li I-che, "On socialist democracy and the rule of law," *Chung-kung yen-chiu,* no. 107 (November 1975), pp. 117–31. The text presents a few problems. At least two quotations from Marx are garbled. We read, p. 120: "Revolution advances, opening its own road. This is not because it obtains a tragic victory, but, on the contrary, because it produces a united and firm great revolution, since it produces its enemy, and only when a party that advocates change struggles with its enemy is it able to become a true revolutionary party." This should be: "In a word, the revolution made progress, forged ahead, not by its immediate tragicomic achievements, but, on the contrary, by the creation of a powerful, united counterrevolution, by the creation of an opponent in combat with whom only the party in revolt ripened into a really revolutionary party." [Lewis S. Feuer, ed., *Marx and Engels*, p. 281] Less garbled, p. 121, we have: "Hegel says somewhere, 'All great facts and persons in world history can be said to appear twice.' They forget to add, the first time they appear as tragedy, the second time as farce." This should be: "Hegel remarks somewhere that all facts and personages of great importance in world history occur, as it were, twice. He forgot to add: the first time as tragedy, the second as farce." [Feuer, *Marx and Engels,* p. 320] Li I-che says, p. 124, "Obviously, we have read very little of Marx and Lenin." If the copying mistakes were made by Li I-che, this is of no great moment. But if the quotes were garbled somewhere in the transmission of the poster, this could mean there are inaccuracies in our text.

169. Li I-che, "Socialist democracy," p. 122. He also has a kind word here for Chao Tzu-yang, purged with T'ao Chu in 1966 but in 1974 first secretary of Kwangtung. The admiration for persons of the moderate tendency was not reciprocated. Taiwan reports Li Hsien-nien called the poster "manifestly reactionary, malicious in the extreme" (*Chung-kung yen-chiu,* no. 107 [November 1975], p. 116).

170. Cf. Leo Strauss, *Persecution and the Art of Writing*.

171. Li I-che, "Socialist democracy," p. 124. The business about Hungary and Czechoslovakia is a fancy equivocation. The Chinese people do not seem to have been all that thrilled with Soviet intervention in Hungary. In each case it is the attitude of the Chinese government that is relevant. The implication of the phrasing is that in 1968 the government and people were in accord.

172. Ibid., p. 128.

173. Ibid., pp. 125–126.

174. Ibid., p. 126.

175. Ibid., pp. 126–27.

176. Ibid., pp. 127–28.

177. Ibid., pp. 117–19.

178. Ibid., pp. 119–20.

179. Ibid., pp. 121–23. On Huang Shuai see PD, December 28, 1973.

180. Li I-che, "Socialist democracy," p. 123.

181. Ibid., pp. 129–31.

182. Hsuan Chi-wen, "Criticism of 'On socialist democracy and the rule of law,'" *Chung-kung yen-chiu,* no. 107 (November 1975), p. 132.

183. Doolin, *Communist China,* p. 34.

184. Meisner, "Leninism and Maoism," p. 36.

185. [Chou En-lai], "Chou En-lai Talks about the 'February Adverse Current,'" *Issues and Studies* 5, no. 12 (September 1969), p. 104.

186. Ibid.

187. Jack Chen, *Inside the Cultural Revolution,* p. 287. There is an easy irony in the attacks on T'an. T'an, the minister of agriculture, had supported the Great Leap in its most radical phase and had easily the most radical record of all of Chou's supporters.

188. [Lin Li-kuo], "'571 engineering' outline," pp. 98–99.

189. Ibid., pp. 99, 101–2.

190. Ibid., p. 100.

191. Ibid., pp. 99—100.

192. Ibid., pp. 100–101, 102.

193. PD, January 29, 1974.

194. *Wu-ssu i-lai fan-tung-p'ai, ti-chu-tzu-ch'an-chieh-chi hsueh-che tsung-k'ung fu-ku yen-lun chi-lu,* pp. 45, 10, 39–40.

195. Lo Ssu-ting, "Study the thoroughgoing revolutionary spirit of Lu Shun's criticism of Confucius and company," PD, September 25, 1971.

196. Kuo Mo-jo, "Problem of periodization," p. 61.

197. Yang Jung-kuo, "The struggle between the two lines in the thought sphere during the Spring and Fall and Warring States periods," RF, 1972, no. 12 (December 1), pp. 45–54. The two later essays: idem, "Confucius," PD, August 7, 1973; "The struggle between materialism and idealist apriorism in the two Han periods," PD, August 13, 1973.

198. PD, February 2, 1974.

199. Peter R. Moody, Jr., "The New Anti-Confucius Campaign in China," *Asian Survey* 14, no. 4 (April 1974): 307–24; Merle Goldman, "China's Anti-Confucius Campaign."

200. Li I-che, "Socialist democracy," p. 126.

201. Shih Chung, "Pro-Legalist anti-Confucian spirit"; Ch'ing Ssu, "The struggle of Li Chih against the school of reason and the rebellion against the 'Sacred Way,'" *Kuang-ming jih-pao,* November 13, 1973; Shih Hung-ping ("History Red Soldier"), "Thoroughly liquidate Hou Wai-lu's anti–Thought of Mao Tse-tung crimes," ibid., March 26, 1967.

202. Ch'ing Ssu, "Struggle of Li Chih."

203. Some more scholarly radicals, however, wish to save Li Chih, who was, after all, a true iconoclast. Thus, it is held that he was a historical personage with two natures, one progressive and the other conservative or reactionary. His editing of *Water margin* shows his bad side (Ch'en

Hsu-luan, "Tearing down the temple or coming to the aid of heaven?" *Hsueh-hsi yü p'i-p'an,* 1976, no. 2 [February 14], p. 34). But, of course, the 1973 interpretation is correct: Li's editing of *Water margin* is simply one more manifestation of his general iconoclasm. Ch'en's is a rather sad little essay by one who seems to be a true scholar.

204. Chou En-lai, "Report on the work of the government," (1975), PD, January 21, 1975; italics added.

205. PD, January 30, 1974.

206. Lo Ssu-ting, "The process of struggle between restoration and counterrestoration in the Ch'in dynasty," *Kuang-ming jih-pao,* November 9, 1973. This essay also teaches, as do many others, that Ch'in's burning of the books and burying of the scholars was not an act of cruelty but a necessary policy required to eliminate malcontent intellectuals who opposed the consolidation of feudalism. Does Lo, then, advocate the physical extermination of the radicals? A recurring theme in the campaign is that Ch'in fell, not because its emperor was too cruel, but because he was too mild. He did not suppress his enemies sufficiently. This, for what it is worth, is the only thing Stalin could find against another great progressive, Ivan the Terrible (Adam B. Ulam, *Stalin,* p. 673).

207. Li Ch'eng, "We must continue to criticize Confucius," PD, February 13, 1976.

208. PD, February 2, 1974.

209. My speculation, then, is exactly opposite that of Parris H. Chang in "The Anti–Lin Piao and Confucius Campaign," *Asian Survey* 14, no. 10 (October 1974): 884.

210. Che Chün, "Confucius's golden mean is a philosophy that opposes social change," PD, January 13, 1974; Wang Hung-wen, "Report to the central study group," italics added (this would indicate that the phrase "criticism of Lin Piao and Confucius" was in use, at least among radicals, some weeks prior to its open introduction); Honan Provincial Broadcasting Station, April 10, 1974, in *Provincial Broadcasting Stations,* no. 1905.

211. PD, February 2, 1974.

212. Yang Jung-kuo, "Struggle between the two lines," p. 46; idem, "Confucius."

213. Liang Hsiao, "Develop new-born things and limit bourgeois legal rights," PD, February 22, 1976.

214. T'ang Hsiao-wen, "Is Confucius a 'teacher of the whole people'?" PD, September 27, 1973.

215. Yang Jung-kuo, "Confucius." For more than a thousand years Chinese scholars have debated the authenticity of the story of Shao-cheng Mao. The solution turns out to be simple. T'ang Hsiao-wen, whose hobby seems to be transparently specious philological exercises, explains: Doubts have arisen because the story is not found prior to Hsun-tzu, who lived about 200 years after Confucius. Mencius, for example, says nothing of Shao-cheng Mao. But Mencius was an idealist and naturally would cover this up. And—here is the clincher—all the early sources *after* Hsun-tzu do mention the story. ("What is the meaning of Confucius's killing of Shao-cheng Mao?" PD, January 4, 1974.)

216. Yang, "Struggle between the two lines," p. 54.

217. RF, 1972, no. 1 (January 1), p. 21.

218. Yang, "Struggle between the two lines," p. 53.

219. Hung Kuang-ssu, "The peasant wars at the end of the Ch'in and the 'government of Ching and Wen,'" *Kuang-ming jih-pao,* January 16, 1975.

220. Judith Shklar, *Legalism,* p. 209.

221. Yang Jung-kuo, *K'ung-Mo te ssu-hsiang,* p. 92. Yang is at pains to explain that while Mo-tzu said he believed in God, he wasn't really prey to such a crude superstition (p. 99).

222. Confucians have generally felt that if universal love means one loves strangers in the same way as one loves one's own parents, it is unjust (cf. the hippy who loves mankind but can't stand his mother and father), and they have been unhappy with the authoritarian implications of Mohism politically. (Liang Ch'i-hsiung, "Han Fei's thought," identifies the Mohist principle of "identification with the superior" as a source of Legalism, or, in his terms, totalitarianism.) The Confucian view also has been that if morality is identified with utility, morality is a redundant concept.

223. See, e.g., Shih Ting, "Discussion of 'burning books and burying scholars,' " PD, September 28, 1973.

224. PD, November 3, 1975.

225. Hung Kuang-ssu, "Peasant wars."

226. Liu Tsung-yuan, "On feudalism," *Kuang-ming jih-pao,* June 29, 1974.

227. Kuei Chih, "The rightist rehabilitation wind and bourgeois legal rights," PD, March 8, 1976.

228. *Provincial Broadcasting Stations,* no. 1905.

229. Chou En-laï, "Work of the government," (1975).

230. PD, February 9, 1975.

231. Yao, "Lin Piao antiparty clique."

232. Chang Ch'un-ch'iao, "Full-scale dictatorship."

233. PD, March 10, 1976.

234. PD, April 3, 1976.

235. See Ch'ih Heng, "Summarize the criticism of *Water margin,* deepen the study of theory," PD, November 4, 1975, who puts these themes together with each other. The same author, or someone using the same pseudonym, published an attack on the three directives a few months later: "From bourgeois democrat to capitalist roader," PD, March 1, 1976.

236. Liang Hsiao and Jen Ming, "Criticize the 'three directives as the guide,' " PD, February 28, 1976; PD, January 1, 1976; Ch'u Lan, "Support the literary revolution, counterattack the rightist rehabilitation wind," PD, March 4, 1976; Chiang T'ien, " 'Rectification' of literature in name, rehabilitation and restoration in fact," PD, April 7, 1976.

237. The Chairman may not have been that wild about the role his wife played. In 1971 he said of Lin Piao: "I have never approved of making your own old lady the head of an office in your work unit" (*Chung-yang jih-pao,* August 10, 1972).

238. Honan Provincial Broadcasting Station, October 3, 1975, in *Provincial Broadcasting Stations,* no. 2369.

239. Hua Kuo-feng, "The whole party should mobilize, do a lot of work in agriculture, fight to make universal Tachai-like counties," PD, October 21, 1975.

240. PD, August 31, 1975.

241. Wen Ching, "Criticize Chin Sheng-t'an's abridgement of *Water margin,*" PD, October 7, 1975.

242. PD, March 10, 1976. Even at the time there were hints, if only we had known, of Sung Chiang's real identity. "Like all political swindlers, Sung Chiang is superficially staunch and upright, true to his word . . ." (Hsieh Lin, "A thoroughgoing surrenderist," PD, September 11, 1975). This must be a reference to Teng's alleged violation of his alleged oath.

243. There are grounds for speculating that even the criticism of *Water margin* was not entirely univocal. One article notes that the contradiction between Sung Chiang and the court was within the landlord class, although Sung Chiang was more "clever" (Hung Kuang-ssu, "Sung Chiang and Kao Ch'iu," PD, September 22, 1975). The court might be a symbol for the radicals, and the message: a plague on both your houses; Teng Hsiao-p'ing seems better than the radicals, but this is an illusion. Someone using this same pseudonym ("Surging Far-Ranging Thought"?), it will be remembered, seemed to threaten the regime with a peasant rebellion if it did not straighten out ("Peasant wars").

244. PD, December 7, 1975.

245. Mao Tse-tung, "A dialogue of birds," RF, 1976, no. 1 (January 1), p. 4.

246. PD, March 10, 1976.

247. PD, April 8, 1976.

248. New York *Times,* April 14, 1976.

249. *Chung-yang jih-pao,* March 8, 1976.

250. Chang Shu-fang, "Rumor-mongers must fail," PD, April 21, 1976.

251. Eugene D. Genovese, *Roll, Jordan, Roll,* pp. 588, 595.

7: CONCLUSIONS

1. Chalmers Johnson, *An Instance of Treason,* p. 88.

2. Norman Podhoretz, "Making the World Safe for Communism," *Commentary,* April 1976, pp. 31–41.

3. A "federal agency with the acronym of OSHA . . . prevents consenting adults from doing unsafe things to one another, unless they are immoral or subversive, in which case they are protected by the Constitution" (Irving Kristol, "Notes on the Spirit of '76," *Wall Street Journal,* April 23, 1976). This sort of joke must be kept in perspective, of course. Chinese workers would probably find something like OSHA a good idea.

4. I am thinking in particular of Woodhouse, "Revisioning the Future"; also of Heilbroner, *Human Prospect,* although Heilbroner is less tickled by the general implications of his recommendations than is Woodhouse.

5. One need not go to China to figure this out. An American political scientist writes: "If the ratio of resources to population falls below what is needed to maintain life for everyone, equitable distribution could be a disaster; there could be grounds for defending maldistribution even though it increased the number of dead and dying. . . . The tendency in such cases is to 'let nature take its course,' though if starvation occurs at random its consequences may be far worse than starvation controlled by reasoned choice. An outmoded tradition, and an understandable reluctance to make deadly choices, inhibits the development of reasoned arguments for dealing with such situations. But prating against 'playing God' seems in context little more than attribution of responsibility to an actor whose externality removes the stigma of choice from the shoulders of men who actually make such decisions. If the choice lies between saving persons by 'playing God' and saving none, then God must be played, and to the hilt. . . . How can a form of social organization be developed that would be accepted and acceptable as a legitimate source of action in deadly cases? . . . Lotteries may be needed when rational distribution of resources would lead to preposterous results. Ritual celebrations of the norms [which allow us to kill people] may be prescribed on reasoned grounds. To label such recommendations as 'Machiavellian' is to pay tribute to Machiavelli, but say nothing of their defensibility." [Eugene Meehan, *The Foundations of Political Analysis,* pp. 233, 234–35] What is offensive about these suggestions is precisely that they are so sanctimoniously un-Machiavellian. Machiavelli would not doubt that people are willing to kill others for their own advantage, but unlike Meehan, he would not think this had anything to do with ethics. The choice is not between saving persons by playing God and saving none, but, rather, between allowing conditions in which some die and deliberately killing some. More, apparently, will die under conditions of reasoned choice, although, while God is more merciful than men, it is hard to see why this should always be so. It is also hard to see what *reason* means here. The recommendations are a denial of the axioms of moral reasoning of most outmoded traditions I know of (thou shall do no murder; to kill by policy is no different from killing with a knife; etc.). In instrumental terms, *reason* here could only be those actions which assure that those who set the norms retain the power to do so. It is an argument for totalitarianism; and since the factual conditions Meehan adduces seem real enough, this may be where we are heading.

Those marked for death will probably not be happy with the reasoned arrangement, however. (I am not criticizing here any deliberate, autonomous self-sacrifice for the sake of others.) It is conceivable that persons could be conditioned to the point where they no longer mind being killed; so, as hedonists, how could we object to their deaths? But it is also hard to see why we should care about the survival of a society whose members are indifferent to their personal survival. In our terms such beings would be no longer human.

I cannot conceive of any Chinese writing the passage quoted, and it is to avoid giving the impression of slandering the Chinese that it is buried in the obscurity of a footnote. If such an attitude ever develops in China it will be under rational modernist, not radical, auspices. The Chinese do, of course, currently practice abortion but have so far refrained from the ritual celebration of it common in the West. Still, the point is that the Chinese have developed the social techniques that promise to solve the problem Meehan sets himself.

APPENDIX: NOTES ON OPPOSITION ON TAIWAN

1. William E. Bueler, *U.S. China Policy and the Problem of Taiwan,* p. 99. For a good collection of essays on Taiwan politics, generally favorable to the regime, see Paul T. K. Sih, ed., *Taiwan in Modern Times.* For an excellent, although now dated, short study see J. Bruce Jacobs, "Recent Leadership and Political Trends on Taiwan," *China Quarterly,* no. 45 (January/March 1971), pp. 38–67.

2. Starr, *Ideology and Culture,* p. 246. American liberal hostility to the KMT is perhaps easy to understand. There is, of course, the double standard in our perceptions of foreign regimes (a defect conservatives are no doubt guilty of as well) and a tendency to be more harsh on regimes that are allied with us or pretend to share our values—a product, perhaps, of American sanctimony. There is also the liberal lack of confidence whenever faced with disagreement from the left but not the right (although what is so "right" about the KMT?). And, as the Quaker lady said to Dr. Johnson, it is always difficult for us to forgive those whom we have injured.

3. T'ung P'ang, "Reasons for the unfair evaluation of 'freedom,'" *Chung-yang jih-pao,* January 29, 1976.

4. William Armbruster, "Paying the Price of Dissent," *Far Eastern Economic Review* 91, no. 10 (March 25, 1976): 27–28.

5. *Chung-yang jih-pao,* December 31, 1975.

6. Ch'iu Sheng-hsiung, "Two kinds of longing," *Ch'iao-k'an,* nos. 63–64 (January-February 1976), p. 58, reprinted from *T'ai-wan cheng-lun,* 1975, no. 5 (December 1).

7. William Armbruster, "With the Old Familiar Faces," *Far Eastern Economic Review* 91, no. 2 (January 10, 1976): 13.

8. For material on the case see Sun Kuan-han, *Po Yang.*

9. Ibid., p. 72. The translations of the cartoons are also from Sun Kuan-han's book.

10. Hung-mao Tien, "Taiwan in Transition," *China Quarterly,* no. 64 (December 1975), p. 626.

11. Wei Yung, "Modernization Process on Taiwan," *Asian Survey* 12, no. 5 (March 1976): 259; Lester R. Brown, *World without Borders,* p. 329.

12. The 1973 elections to the Taipei city council gave victory to no mainlander, and to no Taiwanese not native to Taipei, who lacked KMT backing. Some independent Taipei natives did win, although not many (some of these may have had tacit KMT support). No KMT candidate lost. For a tabulation of the results see *Chung-yang jih-pao,* December 2, 1973.

13. Some of these works are in fact available on the island. My edition of Feng Yu-lan's *History of Chinese philosophy* was printed on Taiwan with all publication data, even the name of the author, omitted; Lu Hsun's *History of Chinese fiction* is available in a similar format. There is a black market in the older banned literary works (one suspects they are sold mainly to American students, with much whispering and winking, at outrageous prices). There is also a not at all surreptitious market in the back issues of banned periodicals.

14. There is occasional official grumbling about money spent on religious festivals, but not much seems to come of this. There are also objections to the showing of Taiwan operas on television (too vulgar, it is said, but the real reason is probably that they are in Taiwanese), to which, it sometimes seems, the entire population of the island is addicted, particularly on the excruciatingly hot summer middays.

15. Tien, "Taiwan in Transition," p. 628.

16. P'eng Ming-min, *A Taste of Freedom,* pp. 137 ff., 146.

17. Ibid., p. 179.

18. Ibid., p. 190.

19. *Kung-lun pao,* September 18, 1960.

20. On Kao's career see Douglas Mendel, *The Politics of Formosan Nationalism,* p. 102. Mendel does not mention Kao's assiduous cultivation of the American military, which would hardly endear him to the regime but which also probably served to keep him from harm.

21. Schurmann, *Logic of World Power,* pp. 178–79. There is also the extremely strong Japanese economic presence, which may be just as politically touchy.

22. Those who are part of the Taiwan independence movement often prefer *Taiwan* to be rendered *Formosa. Taiwan,* it seems, sounds sort of Chinese. For the sake of consistency I shall not comply. This word-play to me only indicates how Chinese those in the movement really are, how given to *cheng-ming*. Unless the independent state adopts English or Portuguese as its national language, the name of the island will continue to be pronounced *Taiwan,* as it is in Hokkien (and even Japanese) as well as Mandarin.

23. Kerr, *Formosa Betrayed,* pp. 271 ff; Mendel, *Formosan Nationalism,* p. 37.

24. Chang Ching-han, "Extirpate three obstacles to modernization," *Ta hsueh,* no. 31 (January 1971), p. 10.

25. Jacobs, "Recent Leadership," p. 137; Mendel, *Formosan Nationalism,* p. 13.

26. Yang Hsing-ting, "T'ai-wan ch'ing-nien pai-p'i-shu" (Handwritten manuscript on Bank of Taiwan draft paper, 1950), pp. 1–14, East Asia Collection, Hoover Institution, Stanford, Ca.; P'eng, *Taste of Freedom,* p. 153; Sheldon Appleton, "Taiwanese and Mainlanders on Taiwan," *China Quarterly,* no. 44 (October/December 1970), p. 56.

27. Mendel, *Formosan Nationalism,* p. 7.

28. P'eng Ming-min, Hsieh Ts'ung-min, and Wei Ting-ch'ao, "Taiwan declaration of independence," *Taiwan ching-lien,* no. 62 (June 25, 1966), p. 14.

29. Ibid., pp. 15–16.

30. Mendel, *Formosan Nationalism,* p. 111.

31. Ch'en Kuang-hsiung, "From 'overthrow Chiang and gain independence' to 'oppose China and gain self-determination,'" *Ch'i-shih nien-tai,* no. 71 (December 1975), p. 79. Little is heard any more of the canard that Chiang Ching-kuo was planning to sell out to the Communists as soon as his dad was encoffined. One hesitates to say this was never in fact planned and hesitates even more to say it will never happen, particularly as the American guarantees to defend the island become less meaningful; still, the story has always seemed like a Taiwan independence movement pitch to American anticommunism: if you want to keep the island, support us. I did not meet anyone on Taiwan—Taiwanese or mainlander—who considered this other than a joke.

32. Yü Yü, "A chat with Premier Chou," *Tiao-yü-t'ai,* no. 18 (March 1973), p. 10.

33. Tien, "Taiwan in Transition," p. 641.

34. Mendel, *Formosan Nationalism,* p. 245.

35. Thus, in 1953 Wu Kuo-chen, once mayor of Shanghai, was removed as governor of Taiwan and fled to the United States. In 1955 the able General Sun Li-jen, Stilwell's favorite Chinese soldier, was arrested. Unsympathetic observers find these purges part of a power-play by Chiang Ching-kuo (Kerr, *Formosa Betrayed,* pp. 423, 425). The close relations between these men and the Americans were probably also a factor. The regime encourages a rumor that Sun Li-jen planned, in collusion with the CIA, to overthrow Chiang Kai-shek and declare Taiwan independent.

36. *Tzu-yu Chung-kuo* 12, no. 50 (December 16, 1956): 763.

37. See Chu Wen-po, "Mourning for *Tzu-yu Chung-kuo,*" *Min-chu ch'ao,* no. 217 (October 1, 1960), pp. 6–8.

38. P'eng Ming-min, "The emotional factors in pan-African thought," *Wen hsing,* no. 74 (December 1963), pp. 15–18; idem, *Taste of Freedom,* p. 122.

39. Warren Tozer, "Taiwan's 'Cultural Renaissance,'" *China Quarterly,* no. 43 (July/September 1970), pp. 61–99.

40. Chou Chih-ming, ed., *Fei Cheng-ch'ing chi-t'uan tsai T'ai-wan ta yin-mou,* 1:266.

41. Ibid., p. 99. I had thought this must be a gross distortion; it is not entirely so: Li Ao, "The eyeglasses of Chang Fei," *Wen hsing,* no. 62 (February 1963), pp. 61–63.

42. Hu Shih, Mao Tzu-shih, and Li Chi, *Hu Shih yü chung-hsi wen-hua,* pp. 261–66, reprinted from *Wen hsing,* no. 50 (December 1961).

43. Li Ao, "A diagnosis of those who discuss Chinese and Western culture," *Wen hsing,* no. 52 (February 1962), p. 17.

44. Li Ao, "On Methods of distorting contemporary history," *Wen hsing,* no. 67 (May 1963), pp. 4–18.

45. *Far Eastern Economic Review* 76, no. 18 (April 29, 1972): 15.

46. Li Hsueh-jui, "Filial piety," *Ta hsueh,* no. 39 (March 1971), pp. 59–60.

47. Lao Li, "The Taipei city council elections and other matters," *Ch'i-shih nien-tai,* no. 50 (March 1974), p. 17, contends that antigovernment candidates lost the support of students because of their pro-Americanism. This report may be colored by the radical chic of many exiled Chinese, but more generally one might argue that even people unhappy with their rulers do not always enjoy seeing them humiliated by foreigners.

48. Chang Ching-han, "Extirpate three obstacles," p. 8.

49. Sun Kuan-han, *Po Yang,* p. 4.

50. Yin Hai-kuang, "My view of Lei Chen and the new party," *Min-chu ch'ao,* no. 217 (October 1, 1960), p. 5.

51. Sun Kuan-han, *Po Yang,* pp. 139–40.

52. Bueler, *U.S. China Policy,* p. 122.

53. Wei, "Modernization Process on Taiwan," p. 267.

54. Hsu Chün-hsiung, "On the duty of the university and political reform," *Ta hsueh,* no. 31 (January 1971), pp. 40–43.

55. *Hua-fu ch'un-ch'iu,* no. 5 (September 1972), p. 1.

56. Ibid., p. 2.

57. *Hua-fu ch'un-ch'iu,* no. 25 (April 1974), p. 2.

58. Jacobs, "Recent Leadership," pp. 146–47.

59. Chou Chih-ming, *Fei Cheng-ch'ing,* 1: 260.

Bibliography

Titles of longer Chinese works, periodicals, and the like are romanized and then translated (where appropriate). Titles of articles are simply given in English translation, because of their great number (and hence the probability of typographical error), and because the romanization is meaningless to those who do not know Chinese and almost as meaningless to those who do, who would prefer the characters.

NEWSPAPERS AND OTHER SERIAL PUBLICATIONS CONTAINING PRIMARY MATERIAL

Chan-tou pao [War Report]. Peking: Central Drama Academy Mao Tse-tungism Fighting Corps.

Che-hsueh yen-chiu [Studies in Philosophy]. Peking.

Cheng-chih hsueh-hsi [Political Studies]. Peking.

Cheng-ming [Contend]. Peking.

Ch'iao-k'an [The Bridge]. New York.

Chieh-fang jih-pao [Liberation Daily]. Yenan.

China News Analysis. Hong Kong.

China News Service. Hong Kong.

Ching-kang-shan. Peking: Tsinghua University Red Guards.

Ch'i-shih nien-tai [The Seventies]. Hong Kong.

Chui chiu kuan [Pursue the Tottering Foe]. Peking: Planning Department of the Great Committee Thoroughly to Criticize Liu Shao-ch'i's Counterrevolutionary Line.

Chung-hsueh feng-pao [Middle-School Storm]. Peking: Flying Tiger Brigade of the Peking Architectural and Engineering Schools Red Guards. Peking.

Chung-hua hu-sheng [Voice of China]. Hong Kong.

Chung-kung ko-ti kuang-po tien-t'ai lu-yin hsin-wen (*Provincial Broadcasting Stations*). Hong Kong: China News Analysis.

Chung-kung yen-chiu [Studies on Chinese Communism]. Taipei. (Formerly *Fei-ch'ing yen-chiu* [Studies on Bandit Affairs].)

Chung-kuo ch'ing-nien [China Youth]. Peking.

Chung-kuo ch'ing-nien pao [China Youth Daily]. Peking.

Chung-yang jih-pao [Central Daily News]. Taipei.

Current Background. Hong Kong: U.S. Consulate General.

Daily Summary of the Japanese Press. Tokyo: U.S. Embassy.

Far Eastern Economic Review. Hong Kong.

Fei ming ti [Flying Screaming Arrow]. Peking: Propaganda Department of the 915 Revolutionary Rebel Headquarters of the Seventh Machine [-Building] Ministry.

Hsien-tai Fo-hsueh [Modern Buddhism]. Peking.

Hsin chien-she [New Construction]. Peking.

Hsing-tao jih-pao. Hong Kong.

Hsin-hua pan-yueh k'an [New China Half-Monthly]. Peking.

Hsin-wen chan-pao [Journalism War Report]. Peking: Capital News Criticism Liaison Station.

Hsueh-hsi [Study]. Peking.

Hsueh-hsi yü p'i-p'an [Study and Criticism]. Shanghai.

Hua-fu ch'un-ch'iu [Washington Spring and Fall]. Washington, D.C., and College Park, Md.

Hung ch'i [Red Flag]. Peking: Central Committee, Communist Party of China.

Hung-ch'i [Red Flag]. Peking: Peking Flying Academy Red Flag Fighting Team.

Hung-ch'i [Red Flag]. Peking: Peking Red Flag Fighting Team of the Red Representative Assembly.

Hung-i chan-pao [Red Arts War Report]. Peking: First Peking Opera Company East is Red Revolutionary Rebel Corps.

Hung-i chan-pao [Red Medicine War Report]. Peking: Peking Medical and Hygiene Circles Great Alliance Revolutionary Committee.

Hung-yen chan-pao [Red Cliffs War Report]. Peking: Peking Geology College East is Red Commune and the China Youth Publishing Co. Revolutionary Rebel Corps.

Issues and Studies. Taipei.

Jen-min jih-pao [People's Daily]. Peking.

Jen-min shou-ts'e [People's Handbook]. Peking.

Jen-min wen-hsueh [People's Literature]. Peking.

Kuang-ming jih-pao. Peking.

Kung-lun pao [Public Opinion News]. Taipei.

Kung-tso t'ung-hsun [Work Bulletin]. Peking.

Li-shih yen-chiu [Historical Research]. Peking.

Min-chu ch'ao [Democratic Tide]. Taipei.

Nan-hai tung-feng [Southern Seas East Wind]. Canton: Nanhai District Workers' Revolutionary Committee.

Pei-ching hsin wen-i [Peking New Literature and Art]. Peking: Peking Literary Alliance Proletarian Revolutionary Faction Liaison Station.

Peking Review. Peking.

Ping-t'uan chan-pao [Corps War Report]. Peking: Capital Corps Thought of Mao Tse-tung Red Guards.

Shou-tu feng-lei [Capital Storm]. Peking: Capital Storm Editorial Department.

Survey of the China Mainland Press. Hong Kong: U.S. Consulate General.

Ta hsueh [Great Learning, or, alternatively, University; official translation: The Intellectual]. Taipei.

Ta kung pao. Hong Kong.

Ta kung pao. Peking.

Ta kung pao. Tientsin.

Taiwan ching-lien [Taiwan Youth]. Tokyo.

T'ao Ch'i [Punish Ch'i (Pen-yü)]. Canton: Chung-shan University Revolutionary Rebel Committee.

Tiao-yü-t'ai. New York.

T'i-yü chan-pao [Physical Education War Report]. Peking: Peking Worker-Peasant-Soldier Physical Educational School Mao Tse-tungism Corps (Red Representative Assembly).

Tzu-yu Chung-kuo [Free China]. Taipei.

Washington *Post*.

Wen hsing [official translation: *Apollo*]. Taipei.

Wen hui pao. Shanghai.

Wen-i chan-ku [Literature and Art War Drum]. Peking: People's Literature Publishing Co. Revolutionary Alliance Headquarters.

Wen-i pao [Literary Gazette]. Peking.

Wen-i p'ing-lun [Literary Review]. Peking.

PRIMARY SOURCES IN CHINESE

Because of the great number of references to it, *Jen-min jih-pao* [People's Daily] is cited as PD; and to distinguish it from other publications with the same name, *Hung ch'i* [Red Flag: the organ of the CPC Central Committee] is cited as RF.

Ai Ssu-ch'i et al. *Lun ssu-hsiang kai-tsao wen-t'i* [On the problem of thought reform]. Peking: Hsueh-hsi tsa-chih ch'u-pan she, 1951.

An Hsueh-chiang. "Firmly support the principle of 'a cup of water filled to the brim.'" PD, June 23, 1969.

Chang Ching-han. "Extirpate three obstacles to modernization." *Ta hsueh,* no. 31 (January 1971), pp. 8–10.

Chang Ch'un-ch'iao. "Destroy bourgeois legal-rights thought." PD, October 1, 1958.

———. "In the midst of great wind and waves." *Jen-min wen-hsüeh,* 1957, no. 9 (September), pp. 4–6.

———. "On full-scale dictatorship over the bourgeoisie." PD, April 1, 1975.

Chang P'ing-hua. "Party publications must stick in the red flag." PD, January 12, 1960.

Chang Shu-fang. "Rumor-mongers must fail." PD, April 21, 1976.

Chang Te-sheng. "With agriculture as the base, propel our national economic development." PD, December 12, 1960.

[Chang T'ieh-sheng.] "An examination that causes people to ponder deeply." PD, August 10, 1973.

Chang Yao-liang and Sun Shih-k'ai. "Welcoming spring in the home of a nightsoil worker." PD, February 3, 1965.

Chang Yü-lou. "The method of Marxist class analysis and historical research." PD, June 18, 1963.

Chao Han. "Obey the party constitution, strengthen party nature." PD, October 17, 1961.

Chao Hao-sheng. "Three Chinese scholars talk about the criticism of Lin and Confucius." *Ta kung pao* (Hong Kong), July 14–20, 1974.

Ch'ao Yang. "Study well Chairman Mao's theory of continuing revolution under proletarian dictatorship." PD, July 5, 1969.

Che Chün. "Confucius's golden mean is a philosophy that opposes social change." PD, January 13, 1974.

Ch'en Hsu-luan. "Tearing down the temple or coming to the aid of heaven?" *Hsueh-hsi yü p'i-p'an,* 1976, no. 2 (February 14), pp. 29–34.

Ch'en Kuang-hsiung. "From 'overthrow Chiang and gain independence' to 'oppose China and gain self-determination.'" *Ch'i-shih nien-tai,* no. 71 (December 1975), p. 70.

Ch'en Po-ta. "The struggle between the proletarian and bourgeois world views." RF, 1959, no. 22 (November 16), pp. 11–16.

———. "Under the banner of Comrade Mao Tse-tung." RF, 1958, no. 4 (July 15), pp. 1–12.

Ch'en Yuan-hui. "Pragmatism: truth is nothing but an expedient method." PD, May 30, 1963.

Cheng Chia-chen. *Chiang-p'an ch'ao-yang*. Shanghai: Jen-min ch'u-pan she, 1972.

Ch'eng Yueh. "Firmly support the party line." PD, January 8, 1976.

Ch'i Pen-yü. "Criticism of the confession of Li Hsiu-ch'eng. *Li-shih yen-chiu,* 1963, no. 4 (August), pp. 27–43.

———. "Patriotism or treason?" PD, April 1, 1967.

———. "Speech at the Peking Mining Academy." *Chan-tou pao,* no. 2 (ca. January 1, 1967).

Chi P'ing. "Grasp the laws of class struggle in the socialist era." RF, 1972, no. 8 (August 1), pp. 6–10.

Ch'i Wen-i. "A history of coups or a history of class struggle?" PD, September 19, 1972.

Chi Yun. "Under the cover of the cloak of religion." PD, December 11, 1955.

Chiang Ch'ing. "Speech." *Hung-i chan-pao* [Red Arts War Report], no. 1 (February 15, 1967).

———. "Speech." PD, December 4, 1966.

Chiang Chi-yung. "Collect peasant proverbs." PD, May 16, 1961.

Chiang Hua. "Firmly support the party's correct line, struggle for the victory of the Rectification movement on every front." PD, December 28, 1957.

[Chiang Jen-te.] "A secret diary." PD, August 9, 1957.

Chiang T'ien. "'Rectification' of literature in name, rehabilitation and restoration in fact." PD, April 7, 1976.

Ch'ih Heng. "From bourgeois democrat to capitalist roader." PD, March 1, 1976.

———. "Summarize the criticism of *Water margin,* deepen the study of theory." PD, November 4, 1975.

Ch'ing Ssu. "The struggle of Li Chih against the school of reason and the rebellion against the 'Sacred Way.'" *Kuang-ming jih-pao,* November 13, 1973.

Ch'ing Yen. "Go a step further in strengthening party unity." PD, August 8, 1975.

Ch'iu Chiang. "We must have the revolutionary spirit of daring to oppose the tide." PD, November 7, 1973.

Ch'iu Sheng-hsiung. "Two kinds of longing." *Ch'iao-k'an,* nos. 63–64 (January-February 1976), pp. 60–58.

Chou Chih-ming, ed. *Fei Cheng-ch'ing chi-t'uan tsai T'ai-wan ta yin-mou* [The big plot of the John King Fairbank clique on Taiwan]. Taipei: Kuo-chi kung-tang wen-t'i yen-chiu she, 1969.

Chou En-lai. "Report on the question of intellectuals." PD, January 30, 1956.

———. "Report on the work of the government," June 26, 1957. *Jen-min shou-ts'e,* 1958, pp. 201–14.

———. "Report on the work of the government," 1975. PD, January 21, 1975.

———. "Report on the work of the government to the first session of the Third National People's Congress." PD, December 31, 1964.

———. "Report to the Tenth National Congress of the Communist Party of China." PD, September 1, 1973.

Chou I-lang. "Read Liu Tsung-yuan's 'On feudalism.' " RF, 1974, no. 2 (February 1), pp. 32–35.

Chou Yang. "Let literature and art develop their enormous function in the great enterprise of socialist development." PD, September 26, 1956.

———, "Raise high the red flag of the Thought of Mao Tse-tung, be literary warriors able both to labor and to create." PD, January 1, 1966.

———. "We must fight." *Kuang-ming jih-pao,* December 10, 1954.

Ch'u Lan. "Criticism of the Shansi opera *Three times up peach peak.*" PD, February 8, 1974.

———. "Support the literary revolution, counterattack the rightist rehabilitation wind." PD, March 4, 1976.

———. "Talking about the problem of depth in works of literature and art." PD, November 2, 1974.

Chu T'ung and Shih Lei. "Read Wang An-shih's 'Answer to Ssu-ma's memorial.'" *Kuang-ming jih-pao,* August 27, 1974.

Chu Wen-po. "Mourning for *Tzu-yu Chung-kuo.*" *Min-chu ch'ao,* no. 217 (October 1, 1960), pp. 6–8.

[Chung Chih-min.] "A report on a request to withdraw from school." PD, January 18, 1974.

Chung Hsueh-tso. "Lu Ting-i's counterrevolutionary mug revealed by the hawking of the *Story of Wei Cheng.*" PD, November 9, 1967.

Chung Tso-wen. "Deepen and develop the strong ideological weapon of the struggle between the two lines." PD, March 9, 1972.

Ch'un-mei. "Self-criticism." *Ta kung pao* (Peking), December 19, 1964.

Ehr-shih-wu shih ching-hua [Main extracts from the twenty-five histories]. 4 vols. Taipei: Tu-che shu-tien, 1959.

Fan Chin. "The 'class character of man' is anti–Thought of Mao Tse-tung poison." PD, April 30, 1967.

Fan Chung-liu. "What kind of parents should we be?" *Hsueh-hsi yü p'i-p'an,* 1975, no. 7 (July 18), p. 55.

Feng Yu-lan. "Confucius's thought on 'jen.'" *Che-hsueh yen-chiu,* 1961, no. 5 (September 25), pp. 63–71, 36.

———. "Gains and experiences from the two anti-movements." *Cheng-ming,* 1958, no. 8 (July), pp. 11–15.

———. *Hsin li-hsueh* [Neo-rationalism]. Shanghai: Shang-wu yin-shu kuan, 1946.

———. "On several problems in the study of the history of Chinese philosophy." *Hsin chien-she,* 1959, no. 12 (December), pp. 26–36.

———. "On the basic problem of ethics." *Hsin chien-she,* 1961, no. 4 (April), pp. 40–43.

———. "On the criticism of Confucius and on my self-criticism of my former ideology of revering Confucius." *Kuang-ming jih-pao,* December 3, 1973.

———. "The problem of succession to the Chinese philosophical heritage." *Kuang-ming jih-pao,* January 8, 1957.

———. "Speaking from the point of view of personal understanding on the relationship of the criticism of Lin and Confucius to the unity, education, and reform of intellectuals." *Kuang-ming jih-pao,* February 1, 1974.

———. "Whether to restore the old or to oppose restoration of the old is a struggle between two lines." *Kuang-ming jih-pao,* December 4, 1973.

Ho Ping-ti. "The characteristics and accomplishments of New China viewed from a historical measurement." *Ch'i-shih nien-tai,* no. 50 (March 1974), pp. 4–14.

Hsiang Hui. "Criticizing the Hunan opera *The gardener's song.*" PD, August 2, 1974.

———. "Sincerely read books and study, raise the awareness of the implementation of Chairman Mao's revolutionary line." PD, October 15, 1971.

Hsiao Hua. "On the problem of the management of educational work in platoons." *Kung-tso t'ung-hsun,* 1961, no. 24 (June 18), pp. 1–21.

———. "Propel the mass movement for the living study–living use of the works of Chairman Mao to a new stage." PD, October 10, 1966.

Hsieh Lin. "A thoroughgoing surrenderist." PD, September 11, 1975.

Hsieh Sheng-wen. "The background of 'apriori perception.'" PD, October 20, 1971.

[Hsu Chin.] "Is this a melon-head?" *Chung-kuo ch'ing-nien,* 1957, no. 3 (February 1), pp. 30–31.

Hsu Chün-hsiung. "On the duty of the university and political reform." *Ta hsueh,* no. 37 (January 1971), pp. 40–43.

Hsu Tsung-wen. "The new conservative political philosophy of the American bourgeoisie." PD, May 12, 1964.

Hsu Yun-hsi. "Informal view of some literary history." *Hsueh-hsi yü p'i-p'an,* 1975, no. 8 (August 18), pp. 58–61.

Hsuan Chi-wen. "Criticism of 'On socialist democracy and the rule of law.'" *Chung-kung yen-chiu,* no. 107 (November 1975), pp. 131–41.

Hu Feng. "My self-criticism." PD, May 10, 1955.

———. "Speech." *Wen-i pao,* 1954, no. 22 (November 30), pp. 7–15.

Hu Shih, Mao Tzu-shui, and Li Chi. *Hu Shih yü chung-hsi wen-hua: Chung-kuo hsien-tai-hua chih chien-t'ao yü chan-wang* [Hu Shih and the culture of China and the

West: examinations and prospects of the modernization of China]. Taipei: Shui-niu ch'u-pan she, 1967.

Hu Yao-pang. "Struggle for the revolutionization of the youth of our country." PD, July 7, 1964.

Hua Kuo-feng. "The whole party should mobilize, do a lot of work in agriculture, fight to make universal Tachai-like counties." PD, October 21, 1975.

Huang Huo-ch'ing. "On the reform of capitalist industry and commerce and of the understanding of the capitalists." PD, September 30, 1956.

Hung Kuang-ssu. "The peasant wars at the end of the Ch'in and the 'government of Ching and Wen.'" *Kuang-ming jih-pao,* January 16, 1975.

———. "Sung Chiang and Kao Ch'iu: foxes on the same hill." PD, September 22, 1975.

I Chün. "Remembering the central Red Army's revolutionary deeds in southern Szechwan on the Long March." *Li-shih yen-chiu,* 1975, no. 5 (October 20), pp. 43–49.

Jen T'u. "Come out of 'Petersburg.'" PD, April 6, 1975.

Jen Wen-ch'in. "Why is the seagull so popular?" *Hsueh-hsi yü p'i-p'an,* 1974, no. 1 (January 16), pp. 41–44.

Kan Wen. "Consolidate the great basic law of proletarian dictatorship." PD, January 24, 1975.

K'ang Cho. "Comments on short stories during the past few years." *Wen-i p'ing-lun,* no. 5 (September 1962), pp. 12–29.

Kao Ko. "Plant and develop revolutionary new-born things." RF, 1972, no. 12 (December 1), pp. 9–12.

K'o Ch'ing-shih. "The brilliant road ahead for modern plays that reflect the new socialist era." PD, December 29, 1963.

———. "Put great effort into developing and making flourish socialist plays, make them serve the socialist economic base even better." PD, August 16, 1964.

Kuan Feng. "The best form of distribution for the transition to communism." PD, October 22, 1958.

Kuan Feng and Lin Yü-shih. "On Confucius." *Che-hsueh yen-chiu,* 1961, no. 4 (July 25), pp. 42–70.

Kuan-yü mu-ch'ien nung-ts'un kung-tso-shang jo-kan wen-t'i te Chüeh-ting (ts'ao-an) [Resolution on certain current problems in rural work (draft)], May 1963. Taipei: Bureau of State Security, 1965.

Kuei Chih. "The rightist rehabilitation wind and bourgeois legal rights." PD, March 8, 1976.

Kuo Chia-hsiung. "Accusation." *Ching-kang-shan,* no. 21 (March 22, 1967).

Kuo Hui and Chang Pao-chiang. "Develop the revolutionary spirit of opposing the tide," PD, October 12, 1973.

Kuo Mo-jo. "Hu Feng's antisocialist program." PD, April 1, 1955.

———. "The problem of periodization in ancient Chinese history." RF, 1972, no. 7 (July 1), pp. 56–62.

Lai Jo-yü. "Go a step further in directing the functions of trade unions in building socialism." PD, September 24, 1956.

Lao Li. "The Taipei city council elections and other matters." *Ch'i-shih nien-tai,* no. 50 (March 1974), pp. 16–17.

Li Ao. "A diagnosis of those who discuss Chinese and Western culture." *Wen hsing*, no. 52 (February 1962), pp. 1–17.

———. "The eyeglasses of Chang Fei." *Wen hsing*, no. 62 (February 1963), pp. 61–63.

———. "On the methods of distorting contemporary history." *Wen hsing*, no. 67 (May 1963), pp. 4–18.

Li Ch'eng. "We must continue to criticize Confucius." PD, February 13, 1976.

Li Fu-ch'un. "Continue to advance, holding high the red flag of the general line." PD, August 17, 1960.

Li Hsien-nien. "How to look at reform in the management system of finance and trade in the rural areas." PD, January 17, 1959.

———. "A look at the people's communes." PD, October 17, 1958.

Li Hsueh-jui. "Filial piety." *Ta hsueh*, no. 39 (March 1971), pp. 59–60.

Li I-che. "On socialist democracy and the rule of law." *Chung-kung yen-chiu*, no. 107 (November 1975), pp. 117–31.

Li Kuo-wen. "Reelection." *Jen-min wen-hsueh*, 1957, no. 7 (July), pp. 1–6.

Li Wei-hsin. "Confession." *Chung-yang jih-pao*, April 13, 1972.

Liang Chiao. "Old K'ung number two at the end of the feudal era." PD, June 28, 1974.

Liang Ch'i-hsiung. "The nature and origins of Han Fei's thought." *Kuang-ming jih-pao*, August 24, 25, 1961.

Liang Hsiao. "Develop new-born things and limit bourgeois legal rights." PD. February 22, 1976.

Liang Hsiao and Jen Ming. "Criticize the 'three directives as the guide.'" PD, February 28, 1976.

Lin Chieh. "Down with slavism, strictly observe proletarian revolutionary discipline." PD, June 16, 1967.

Lin Hsi-ling. "Tentative discussion of the world views and works of Balzác and Tolstoy." *Wen-i pao*, 1955, no. 21 (November 15), pp. 32–35.

[Lin Li-kuo.] "'571 engineering' outline." *Chung-kung yen-chiu*, no. 67 (July 1972), pp. 98–102.

Lin Mo-han. "Hu Feng's anti-Marxist literary thought." *Wen-i pao*, 1953, no. 2 (January 30), pp. 3–8.

Lin Piao. "Political report to the Ninth National Congress of the Communist Party of China." PD, April 28, 1969.

———. "Speech at the all-army conference on education management work." *Kung-tso t'ung-hsun*, 1961, no. 22 (June 1), pp. 1–5.

Liu Chia. "'Rejection' and solidarity." PD, June 8, 1957.

Liu Po-ch'eng. "Remembering the Long March." PD, October 19, 1975.

Liu Shao-ch'i. *Lun kung-ch'an-tang-yuan te hsiu-yang* [On the cultivation of a Communist Party member]. Chang-chia-k'ou: Hsin-hua shu-tien, 1946.

———. *Lun tang*. [On the party]. N.p., 1948.

———. "On intraparty struggle." *Chieh-fang jih-pao*, October 9, 1942.

———. "Report on the work of the Central Committee of the Communist Party of China to the second session of the Eighth National Congress of the Communist Party of China." PD, May 27, 1958.

Liu Tsung-yuan. "On feudalism." *Kuang-ming jih-pao,* June 29, 1974.

Liu Ya-lou. "The need clearly and positively to see the problem of air force training and fighting." *Kung-tso t'ung-hsun,* 1961, no. 10 (February 20), pp. 19–27.

Lo Ehr-kang. "Some explanations of what I have written on the textual analysis of the confession of Li Hsiu-ch'eng." *Li-shih yen-chiu,* 1963, no. 4 (August), pp. 43–45.

Lo Jui-ch'ing. "Commemorate the defeat of German Fascism, carry through to the end the struggle against American imperialism." PD, May 11, 1965.

———. Explanation of the draft statute on labor reform in the People's Republic of China." *Jen-min shou-ts'e,* 1955, pp. 363–65.

———. "Learn from Lei Feng." PD, March 5, 1963.

———. "The people of the whole country must get united and firmly, thoroughly, cleanly, and completely purge all counterrevolutionary elements." PD, July 29, 1955.

———. "The people were able to defeat Japanese Fascism, the people will certainly be able to defeat American imperialism." PD, September 4, 1965.

———. "Raise vigilance, oppose numbness." *Jen-min shou-ts'e,* 1956, pp. 351–53.

———. "Report on an investigation of the condition of the troops in several districts." *Kung-tso t'ung-hsun,* 1961, no. 11 (March 2), pp. 2–18.

———. "Report to the Center of an investigation of a certain division." *Kung-tso t'ung-hsun,* 1961, no. 7 (February 1), pp. 18–22.

———. "The success of our country's struggle to purge counterrevolutionaries and the future tasks." *Hsueh-hsi,* 1958, no. 1 (January 3), pp. 2–9.

Lo Keng-mo. "On the question of how to implement correctly the principle of distribution according to labor." *Ta kung pao* (Peking), April 16, 1962.

Lo Ko. "Discussing several problems of Marxist ethics." *Kuang-ming jih-pao,* December 6, 1961.

Lo Ssu-ting. "The process of struggle between restoration and counterrestoration in the Ch'in dynasty." *Kuang-ming jih-pao,* November 9, 1973.

———. "Study the thoroughgoing revolutionary spirit of Lu Hsun's criticism of Confucius and company." PD, September 25, 1971.

Lu Kuei-shan. "To write about middle characters is the manifestation in literary theory of 'two combine into one' and the 'summary' of the spirit of the times." *Wen-i pao,* 1964, nos. 11–12 (December 30), pp. 3–12.

Lu Li. "Leadership of agriculture must begin from reality." PD, November 12, 1960.

Lu Ting-i. "Let a hundred flowers bloom, a hundred schools contend." *Jen-min shou-ts'e,* 1957, pp. 565–71.

———. "Our basic divergence from the bourgeois rightists." PD, July 2, 1957.

Ma Yin-ch'u. "My philosophical thought and economic theory." *Hsin chien-she,* 1959, no. 11 (November), pp. 21–55.

Mao Tse-tung. "Bombard the headquarters." PD, August 5, 1967.

———. "A dialogue of birds." RF, 1976, no. 1 (January 1), p. 4.

———. "Introducing a cooperative." RF, 1958, no. 1 (June 1), pp. 3–4.

———. *Kuan-yü cheng-ch'üeh ch'u-li jen-min nei-pu mao-tun te wen-t'i* [On the correct handling of contradictions among the people]. Peking: Jen-min ch'u-pan she, 1957.

Mei Kung-ping. "The form of Ch'en Ming-shu's reactionary goal." *Kuang-ming jih-pao,* October 29, 1957.

Nieh Jung-chen. "Firmly protect the work of socialist science." *Jen-min shou-ts'e,* 1958, pp. 159–60.

Ou Meng-chüeh. "What are the errors of Ku Ta-ts'un and Feng Pai-chü?" *Hsin hua pan-yueh k'an,* 1958, no. 19 (October 10), pp. 43–45.

P'eng Chen. "Speech at the meeting of actors in the modern Peking opera." RF, 1964, no. 14 (July 31), pp. 18–24.

———. "Upholding the method of gentle breeze and light rain." PD, May 10, 1957.

P'eng Ming-min. "The emotional factors in pan-African thought." *Wen hsing,* no. 74 (December 1963), pp. 15–18.

P'eng Ming-min, Hsieh Ts'ung-min, and Wei Ting-ch'ao. "Taiwan declaration of independence." *Taiwan ching-lien,* no. 62 (June 25, 1966), pp. 12–16.

Sha Ch'ing. "Dissecting a sophistry." PD, January 30, 1976.

Shen Hsin. "The struggle between the two lines in the process of consolidating the people's communes." *Cheng-chih hsueh-hsi,* 1958, no. 10 (October), pp. 40–43.

Shih Chung. "The pro-Legalist anti-Confucian spirit of 'On feudalism,'" PD, December 25, 1973.

Shih Hsueh-ch'ing. "A pro-Legalist anti-Confucian statesman, Sun Ch'üan." *Kuang-ming jih-pao,* December 23, 1974.

Shih Hung-ping. "Thoroughly liquidate Hou Wai-lu's anti–Thought of Mao Tse-tung crimes." *Kuang-ming jih-pao,* March 26, 1967.

Shih Ting. "Discussion of 'burning books and burying scholars.'" PD, September 28, 1973.

Shu Tung. "The total bankruptcy of phony 'goulash' communism." PD, January 3, 1976.

Shu Wu. "Study from the beginning the 'Speech at the Yenan forum on literature and art.'" PD, June 8, 1952.

Stanford, Ca. Hoover Institution on War, Revolution, and Peace. East Asia Collection. 4292.3/4271.47. *Hu Feng i-chien shu* [Hu Feng's letter of opinion]. [by Hu Feng, n.p., n.d.].

———. 4292.3/7294.1. "Liu Shao-ch'i te tzu-wo p'i-p'ing" [Liu Shao-ch'i's self-criticism] [by Liu Shao-ch'i, n.d.].

———. 3071.1/4240. "T'ai-wan ch'ing-nien pai-p'i-shu" [Taiwan youth white paper] [handwritten manuscript by Yang Hsing-ting, 1950, Taipei].

Su-ch'ing ti-kuo-chu-i te wen-hua ch'in-lüeh shih-li [Purge the influences of cultural imperialist aggression]. Shanghai: Jen-min chiao-yü ch'u-pan she, 1951.

Sun Sheng-fu. "Criticism of several poisonous weeds in the seventh issue of *Jen-min wen-hsueh.*" *Jen-min wen-hsueh,* 1957, no. 10 (October), pp. 32–34.

Sun Yü-shan. "A letter to Venerable Tung." *Chung-kuo ch'ing-nien pao,* April 13, 1957.

T'an Fu-jen. "Speech at the Yunnan province agricultural work conference," August 1967. *Chung-kung yen-chiu,* no. 46 (October 1970), pp. 118–32.

T'an I-wu. "The fanatical activities of counterrevolutionary elements in Hunan." PD, July 5, 1955.

T'an Wen. "Youth is a most active and most spirited strength." PD, March 10, 1973.

T'ang Hsiao-wen. "Is Confucius a 'teacher of the whole people'?" PD, September 27, 1973.

———. "Refuting the absurd Confucian theories on the cause of the destruction of the Ch'in dynasty." *Kuang-ming jih-pao,* September 1, 1974.

———. "What is the meaning of Confucius's killing of Shao-cheng Mao?" PD, January 4, 1974.

T'ang Sheng-p'ing. "Actively cultivate female party members and female cadres." PD, May 18, 1973.

T'ao Chu. "The brilliance of the sun." PD, June 3, 1959.

Teng Hsiao-p'ing. "Report on the Rectification movement." *Jen-min shou-ts'e,* 1958, pp. 33–42.

———. "Report on the revision of the party constitution." *Jen-min shou-ts'e,* 1957, pp. 26–37.

Teng T'o. *Teng T'o shih-wen hsuan* [Selected poetry and prose of Teng T'o]. Hong Kong: Pao-chen ch'u-pan she, 1966.

Teng Tzu-hui. "Do a good job in managing public mess halls, sincerely carry through the principle of voluntariness." *Chung-kuo ch'ing-nien,* 1959, no. 12 (June 1), pp. 5–6.

Tsen-yang kai-tsao ssu-hsiang [How to reform thought]. Chungking: Hsi-nan ch'ing-nien ch'u-pan she, 1952.

T'ung P'ang. "Reasons for the unfair evaluation of 'freedom.'" *Chung-yang jih-pao,* January 29, 1976.

Tung Pi-wu. "On the livelihood of the worker-peasant masses and other matters." *Chung-kuo ch'ing-nien pao,* April 13, 1957.

Wang Hung-wen. "Report on the revision of the party constitution." PD, September 2, 1973.

———. "Report to the central study group." *Chung-yang jih-pao,* December 5, 1974.

Wang I. "Han Fei." *Chung-kuo ch'ing-nien,* 1957, no. 3 (February 1), pp. 26–28.

Wang Jen-chung. "Speech." PD, July 28, 1955.

Wang Meng. "The young newcomer at the organization department." *Jen-min wen-hsueh,* 1956, no. 9 (September), pp. 29–43.

Wen Ch'ien. "That the rate of increase in wages should be lower than the rate of increase in productivity is an objective demand for the speeding up of the realization of national socialist industrialization." *Ta kung pao* (Tientsin), February 3, 1955.

Wen Ching. "Criticize Chin Sheng-t'an's abridgement of *Water margin.*" PD, October 7, 1975.

Wen P'u. "Talk about letters and other matters." PD, December 6, 1973.

Wu Chih-p'u. "Study the works of Comrade Mao Tse-tung." PD, January 1, 1960.

Wu Ch'uan-ch'i. "Communism seen from the people's communes." PD, October 1, 1958.

Wu Han. *Hai Jui pa kuan* [Hai Jui is dismissed from office]. Peking: Pei-ching ch'u-pan she, 1961.

———. "On Hai Jui." PD, September 17, 1959.

———. [Liu Mien-chi]. "Hai Jui scolds the emperor." PD, June 16, 1959.

Wu I-lai. "We must pay attention to spreading the common language." PD, December 3, 1975.

Wu-ssu i-lai fan-tung-p'ai, ti-chu-tzu-ch'an-chieh-chi hsueh-che tsung-k'ung fu-ku yen-lun chi-lu [Record of the pronouncements of reactionary and landlord-bourgeois scholars praising Confucius and advocating the restoration of the old since the May fourth period]. Peking: Jen-min ch'u-pan she, 1973.

Wu Te. "We must resolutely and thoroughly carry out party policy." PD, December 22, 1960.

Wu Yao-tsung. "Some problems in thoroughly carrying out the policy on religion." PD, March 9, 1957.

Yang Ch'eng-wu. "Speech at the January 12 telephone conference." *Kung-tso t'ung-hsun,* 1961, no. 6 (January 26), pp. 6–15.

———. "Very particularly establish the absolute authority of the great generalissimo Chairman Mao, very particularly establish the absolute authority of the great Thought of Mao Tse-tung." PD, November 3, 1967.

Yang Hsiu. "This is the kind of communist spirit we should cultivate." *Chung-kuo ch'ing-nien,* 1960, no. 5 (March 1), pp. 5–6, 35.

Yang Jung-kuo. "Confucius: a thinker who stubbornly upheld the slave system." PD, August 7, 1973.

———. *K'ung-Mo te ssu-hsiang* [The thought of Confucius and Mo-tzu]. Peking: San-ho shu-tien, 1950.

———. "The struggle between materialism and idealist apriorism in the two Han periods." PD, August 13, 1973.

———. "The struggle between the two lines in the thought sphere during the Spring and Fall and Warring States periods." RF, 1972, no. 12 (December 1), pp. 45–54.

Yan Jung-kuo et al. *Chien-ming chung-kuo ssu-hsiang shih* [Simple history of Chinese thought]. Peking: Chung-kuo ch'ing-nien ch'u-pan she, 1962.

Yang Kuang-han. "On the lessons of the experience of the collapse of the Ch'in dynasty." *Kuang-ming jih-pao,* October 11, 1974.

Yang P'u. "The spirit of opposing the tide." PD, August 16, 1973.

Yao Wen-yuan. "Clearly distinguish right from wrong, clearly draw the line." *Wen-i pao,* 1955, nos. 1–2 (January 30), pp. 37–39.

———. "Criticism of two books by T'ao Chu." PD, September 8, 1967.

———. *Lun wen-hsueh-shang te hsiu-cheng-chu-i ssu-ch'ao* [On the revisionist thought tide in literature]. Shanghai: Hsin wen-i ch'u-pan she, 1958.

———. "On the social base of the Lin Piao antiparty clique." PD, March 1, 1975.

———. "The working class must take the lead in everything." PD, August 6, 1968.

———. *Yao Wen-yuan wen-chi: Kuan-yü wen-hua ta ko-ming (1965–1968)* [Collected works of Yao Wen-yuan: on the cultural revolution (1965–1968)]. Edited by Liu Ts'un-chi. Hong Kong: Li-shih tzu-liao ch'u-pan she, 1971.

Yeh Chien-ying. "Speech at the conference on military training." *Kung-tso t'ung-hsun,* 1961, no. 10 (February 20), pp. 1–9.

Yen Ching-yao. "The need for the firm suppression of counterrevolutionaries as seen from the situation in eastern Chekiang." PD, July 4, 1955.

Yin Hai-kuang. "My view of Lei Chen and the new party." *Min-chu ch'ao,* no. 217 (October 1, 1960), pp. 4–5.

Yü Yü. "A chat with Premier Chou." *Tiao-yü-t'ai,* no. 18 (March 1973), p. 10.

Yuan Hsian-lü. "The Shakespeare business." PD, March 12, 1964.

Yuan Shui-po. "Hu Feng's theoretical bankruptcy as seen from his creations." PD, February 20, 1955.

TRANSLATED PRIMARY SOURCES AND PRIMARY SOURCES ORIGINALLY IN ENGLISH

Bao Ruo-wang [Pasqualani, Jean] and Chelminski, Rudolph. *Prisoner of Mao*. New York: Coward, McCann and Geoghan, 1973.

Baum, Richard, and Teiwes, Frederick C. *Ssu-ch'ing: The Socialist Education Movement of 1962–1966*. Berkeley and Los Angeles: University of California Press, 1968.

Bennett, Gordon A., and Montaperto, Ronald N. *Red Guard: The Political Biography of Dai Hsiao-ai*. Garden City, N.Y.: Anchor Books, 1972.

Caldwell, Oliver J. *A Secret War: Americans in China, 1944–1945*. Carbondale: Southern Illinois University Press, 1972.

The Case of P'eng Teh-huai, 1959–1968. Hong Kong: Union Research Institute, 1968.

CCP Documents of the Great Proletarian Cultural Revolution, 1966–1967. Hong Kong: Union Research Institute, 1968.

Chen, C. S., and Ridley, Charles Price. *Rural People's Communes in Lien-chiang: Documents concerning Communes in Lien-chiang County, Fukien Province, 1962–1963*. Stanford: Hoover Institution Press, 1969.

Chen, Jack. *Inside the Cultural Revolution*. New York: Macmillan Co., 1975.

———. "Treason at the Top." *Far Eastern Economic Review* 73, no. 29 (July 9, 1971): 21–23.

[Chou En-lai.] "Chou En-lai Talks About the 'February Adverse Current.'" *Issues and Studies* 5, no. 12 (September 1969): 103–4.

Cooper, Gene. "An Interview with Chinese Anthropologists." *Current Anthropology* 14, no. 4 (October 1973): 480–83.

Doolin, Dennis J. *Communist China: The Politics of Student Opposition*. Stanford: Hoover Institution Press, 1964.

"Emancipation of Philosophy." *Current Background,* no. 932 (May 21, 1971).

Hunter, Neal. *Shanghai Journal: An Eyewitness Account of the Cultural Revolution*. New York: Praeger Publishers, 1969.

Johnson, E. H. "Christian Voices from the Church in China: April, 1975." *China Notes* 13, no. 3 (Summer 1975): 25–30.

Lin Piao. "Address to the Enlarged Meeting of the CCP Politburo," May 10, 1966. *Issues and Studies* 6, no. 5 (February 1970): 81–92.

———. *Long Live the Victory of People's War*. Peking: Foreign Languages Publishing Co., 1965.

Ling, Ken. *The Revenge of Heaven: Journal of a Young Chinese*. New York: Ballantine Books, 1972.

MacFarquhar, Roderick. *The Hundred Flowers Campaign and the Chinese Intellectuals*. New York: Praeger Publishers, 1960.

Mu Fu-sheng. *The Wilting of the Hundred Flowers: The Chinese Intellectuals under Mao*. New York: Praeger Publishers, 1963.

P'eng Ming-min. *A Taste of Freedom: Memoirs of a Formosan Independence Leader*. New York: Holt, Rinehart & Winston, 1972.

Ruge, Gerd. "An Interview with Chinese Legal Officials." *China Quarterly,* no. 61 (March 1975), pp. 118–26.

Schram, Stuart R. *Chairman Mao Talks to the People: Talks and Letters, 1956–1971.* New York: Pantheon Books, 1974.

———. *The Political Thought of Mao Tse-tung.* Rev. and enl. ed. New York: Praeger Publishers, 1969.

Snow, Edgar. "A Conversation with Mao Tse-tung." *Life,* April 30, 1971, pp. 46–48.

Tien Chih-sung. "The Masses Are the Makers of History." *Peking Review,* July 21, 1972, pp. 7–11.

Tung Chi-ping and Evans, Humphrey. *The Thought Revolution.* New York: Coward, McCann, 1966.

Walker, Richard L. *Letters from the Communes.* 2 pts. New York: New Leader, 1959, 1960.

Wang Che. "How Engels Criticized Duhring's Apriorism." *Peking Review,* March 10, 1972, pp. 5–9.

SECONDARY SOURCES IN CHINESE

Ch'en Ch'i-t'ien. *Chung-kuo fa-chia kai-lun* [Outline of Chinese Legalism]. Taipei: T'ai-wan Chung-kuo shu-chü, 1970.

———. *Han Fei-tzu chiao-chi* [Textual explication of Han Fei-tzu]. Taipei: T'ai-wan shu-tien, 1958.

Chung-kung jen-ming lü [Roster of Chinese Communist personnel]. Taipei: Institute of International Relations, 1968.

Feng Hai. *Kuang-chou ti-ch'ü wen-ko li-ch'eng shu-lüeh* [An account of the Cultural Revolution in the Canton area]. Hong Kong: Union Research Institute, 1971.

[Feng Yu-lan.] *Chung-kuo che-hsueh shih* [A history of Chinese philosophy]. N.p., n.d.

Hsiao Hui. "Analysis of the current chaotic situation on the mainland." *Chung-kung yen-chiu,* no. 105 (September 1975), pp. 8–15.

Hsuan Mo. "The open and hidden story of the Bandit Yang Ch'eng-wu incident." *Fei-ch'ing yen-chiu* 11, no. 8 (August 1968): 43–56.

I-chiu-ch'i-ssu-nien chung-kung nien-pao [Yearbook on Chinese Communism, 1974]. Taipei: Chung-kung yen-chiu she, 1974.

Li Yu-ning. *Wu Han chuan* [Biography of Wu Han]. Hong Kong: Ming-pao yueh-k'an ch'u-pan she, 1973.

Lu Wei-jan. *Hu Feng shih-chien te ch'ien-yin hou-kuo* [The causes and consequences of the Hu Feng incident]. Hong Kong: Nan-feng ch'u-pan she, 1956.

Sa Meng-wu. *Shui-hu chuan yü chung-kuo she-hui* [*Water margin* and Chinese society]. Taipei: San-min ch'u-pan she, 1970.

Sun Kuan-han, ed. *Po Yang ho t'a te yuan-yü* [Po Yang and his unjust imprisonment]. Hong Kong: Wen-i shu-chü, 1974.

T'an-t'an P'eng Te-huai che-ko jen [Talk about this fellow P'eng Te-huai]. Taipei: Intelligence Staff Office, Ministry of Defense, 1968.

Tu Mo. *Chung-kuo ta-lu t'ien-chu-chiao chen-hsiang* [True picture of the Catholic church on the China mainland]. Hong Kong: Chiu chen hsueh she, 1966.

Wang Hsueh-wen. *Chung-kung wen-hua ta ko-ming yü hung-wei-ping* [The Chinese

Communist Cultural Revolution and the Red Guards]. Taipei: Institute of International Relations, 1969.

Wang Shuo-ch'i. "Social order on the mainland viewed from the case of the suppression of counterrevolutionary sabotage activities in Yunnan." *Chung-kung yen-chiu,* no. 106 (October 1975), pp. 66–79.

OTHER SECONDARY SOURCES

Appleton, Sheldon. "Taiwanese and Mainlanders on Taiwan: A Survey of Student Attitudes." *China Quarterly,* no. 44 (October/December 1970), pp. 38–67.

Apter, David. *The Politics of Modernization*. Chicago: University of Chicago Press, 1965.

Arendt, Hannah. *Between Past and Future: Six Exercises in Political Thought*. New York: Viking Press, 1961.

———. *The Origins of Totalitarianism*. 2d enl. ed. New York: Meridian Books, 1958.

Armbruster, William. "Paying the Price of Dissent." *Far Eastern Economic Review* 91, no. 10 (March 25, 1976): 27–28.

———. "With the Old Familiar Faces." *Far Eastern Economic Review* 91, no. 2 (January 10, 1976): 12–13.

Armstrong, John A. *The European Administrative Elite*. Princeton: Princeton University Press, 1973.

Baerwald, Hans H. *The Purge of Japanese Leaders under the Occupation*. Berkeley and Los Angeles: University of California Press, 1959.

Bailey, F. G. *Stratagems and Spoils: A Social Anthropology of Politics*. New York: Schocken Books, 1969.

Balazs, Etienne. *Chinese Civilization and Bureaucracy*. New Haven: Yale University Press, 1964.

Barghoorn, Frederick C. "Soviet Political Doctrines and the Problem of Opposition." *Bucknell Review* 12, no. 2 (May 1964): 1–29.

Barnett, A. Doak, with a contribution by Ezra Vogel. *Cadres, Bureaucracy, and Political Power in Communist China*. New York: Columbia University Press, 1967.

Bauer, Wolfgang. *China und die hoffnung auf Glück: Paradiese, Utopien, Idealvorstellungen*. Munich: C. Hanser, 1971.

Bay, Christian. "Politics and Pseudopolitics: A Critical Evaluation of Some Behavioral Literature." *American Political Science Review 59,* no. 1 (March 1965): 39–51.

Bernstein, Thomas P. "Problems of Village Leadership after Land Reform." *China Quarterly,* no. 36 (October/December 1968), pp. 1–22.

Bodde, Derk, and Morris, Clarence. *Law in Imperial China*. Cambridge: Harvard University Press, 1967.

Boorstin, Daniel J. *The Image: A Guide to Pseudo-events in America*. New York: Atheneum, 1971.

Boyle, John Hunter. *China and Japan at War, 1937–1945: The Politics of Collaboration*. Stanford: Stanford University Press, 1972.

Bradsher, Harry S. "China: The Radical Offensive." *Asian Survey* 13, no. 11 (November 1973): 989–1009.

Brown, Lester R. *World without Borders*. New York: Vintage Books, 1973.

Buchheim, Hans. *Totalitarian Rule: Its Nature and Characteristics*. (Middletown: Wesleyan University Press, 1968.

Bueler, William E. *U.S. China Policy and the Problem of Taiwan*. Boulder: Colorado Associated University Press, 1971.

Burrows, Robert. "Totalitarianism: The Revised Standard Version." *World Politics* 21, no. 2 (January 1969): 272–94.

Burton, Barry. "The Cultural Revolution's Ultraleft Conspiracy: The 'May 16 Group.'" *Asian Survey* 11, no. 11 (November 1971): 1029–53.

Castles, Francis C. "Interest Articulation: A Totalitarian Paradox." *Survey,* no. 73 (Autumn 1969), pp. 116–32.

Chan, Wing-tsit. *Neo-Confucianism*. Hanover, N.H.: Oriental Society, 1969.

Chang Hao. *Liang Ch'i-ch'ao and Intellectual Transition in 1890–1907*. Cambridge: Harvard University Press, 1971.

Chang, Parris H. "The Anti–Lin Piao and Confucius Campaign: Its Meaning and Purpose." *Asian Survey* 14, no. 10 (October 1974): 871–94.

———. "The Changing Loci of Decision-Making in the CCP." *China Quarterly,* no. 44 (October/December 1970), pp. 169–94.

———. *Radicals and Radical Ideology in China's Cultural Revolution*. New York: Research Institute on Communist Affairs, School of International Affairs, Columbia University, 1973.

Chen, Theodore H. E. [Hsi-en]. *The Maoist Educational Revolution*. New York: Praeger Publishers, 1974.

———. *Thought Reform of the Chinese Intellectuals*. Hong Kong: University of Hong Kong Press, 1960.

Chesneaux, Jean. *Peasant Revolts in China, 1840–1949*. New York: W. W. Norton & Co., 1973.

Chien Yu-shen. *China's Fading Revolution: Army Dissent and Military Division, 1967–1968*. Hong Kong: Centre for Contemporary Chinese Studies, 1968.

Chow Tse-tsung. *The May Fourth Movement: Intellectual Revolution in Modern China*. Cambridge: Harvard University Press, 1960.

Cobban, Alfred. *The Social Interpretation of the French Revolution*. London: Cambridge University Press, 1964.

Coleman, James S. "Foundations for a Theory of Collective Decisions." *American Journal of Sociology* 71, no. 6 (May 1966): 615–27.

Confucius. *The Analects of Confucius*. Edited and translated by Arthur Waley. London: G. Allen & Unwin, 1938.

Couborn, Rushton. *Feudalism and History*. Princeton: Princeton University Press, 1956.

Crick, Bernard. *The American Science of Politics: Its Origins and Conditions*. Berkeley and Los Angeles: University of California Press, 1959.

Crozier, Michel. *The Bureaucratic Phenomenon*. Chicago: University of Chicago Press, 1964.

Dahl, Robert, ed. *Political Opposition in Western Democracies*. New Haven: Yale University Press, 1966.

———. *Regimes and Oppositions*. New Haven: Yale University Press, 1973.

Dahrendorf, Ralf. *Essays in the Theory of Sociology*. Stanford: Stanford University Press, 1968.

Dallin, Alexander, and Breslauer, George. *Political Terror in Communist Systems*. Stanford: Stanford University Press, 1970.

Dewhirst, Martin, and Farrel, Robert, eds. *The Soviet Censorship*. Metuchen, N.J.: Scarecrow Press, 1973.

Dirlik, Arif. "The Ideological Foundations of the New Life Movement: A Study in Counterrevolution." *Journal of Asian Studies* 34 (1974–75): 945–80.

Domes, Jürgen. "New Course in Chinese Domestic Politics: The Anatomy of Readjustment." *Asian Survey* 13, no. 7 (July 1973): 633–46.

Donnithorne, Audrey. "China's Cellular Economy: Some Economic Trends since the Cultural Revolution." *China Quarterly*, no. 52 (October/December 1972), pp. 605–19.

Douglas Jackson, W. A., ed. *Agrarian Policies in Communist and Non-Communist Countries*. Seattle: University of Washington Press, 1971.

Downs, Anthony. *An Economic Theory of Democracy*. New York: Harper, 1957.

Dunn, John. *Modern Revolutions: An Introduction to the Analysis of a Political Phenomenon*. London: Cambridge University Press, 1972.

Duverger, Maurice. *Les parties politiques*. Paris: Colin, 1951.

Eastman, Lloyd E. "Fascism in Kuomintang China: The Blue Shirts." *China Quarterly*, no. 49 (January/March 1972), pp. 1–31.

Eberhard, Wolfram. *Conquerors and Rulers: Social Forces in Medieval China*. 2d rev. ed. Leiden: E. J. Brill, 1965.

Eckstein, Alexander, ed. *The Cultural Revolution: 1967 in Review*. Michigan Papers in Chinese Studies No. 2. Ann Arbor: Center for Chinese Studies, University of Michigan, 1968.

Eisenstadt, S. N. *The Political Systems of Empires*. New York: Macmillan Co., Free Press, 1963.

Ellul, Jacques. *The Autopsy of Revolution*. New York: Alfred A. Knopf, 1971.

———. *Hope in a Time of Abandonment*. New York: Seabury Press, 1973.

———. *The Political Illusion*. New York: Alfred A. Knopf, 1967.

———. *Propaganda: The Formation of Men's Attitudes*. New York: Alfred A. Knopf, 1965.

———. *The Technological Society*. New York: Alfred A. Knopf, 1967.

Elvin, Mark. *The Pattern of the Chinese Past*. Stanford: Stanford University Press, 1973.

Fairbank, John King, ed. *Chinese Thought and Institutions*. Chicago: University of Chicago Press, 1957.

———. *The Chinese World Order*. Cambridge: Harvard University Press, 1968.

Fehl, Noah Edward. *Rites and Propriety in Literature and Life: A Perspective for a Cultural History of Ancient China*. Hong Kong: Chinese University of Hong Kong Press, 1971.

Festinger, Leon. *A Theory of Cognitive Dissonance*. Evanston, Ill.: Row, Peterson, 1957.

Feuer, Lewis S., ed. *Marx and Engels: Basic Writings in Politics and Philosophy*. Garden City, N.Y.: Anchor Books, 1959.

Fleischer, Martin, ed. *Machiavelli and the Nature of Political Thought*. New York: Atheneum, 1972.

Fokkema, D. W. *Literary Doctrine in China and Soviet Influence, 1956–1960*. The Hague: Mouton, 1965.

Friedrich, Carl J., and Brzezinski, Zbigniew. *Totalitarian Dictatorship and Autocracy*. 2d ed. Cambridge: Harvard University Press, 1966.

Friedrich, Carl J.; Curtis, Michael; and Barber, Benjamin. *Totalitarianism in Perspective: Three Views*. New York: Praeger Publishers, 1969.

Garrett, Shirley. *Social Reformers in Urban China: The Chinese YMCA, 1895–1926*. Cambridge: Harvard University Press, 1970.

Gasster, Michael. *Chinese Intellectuals and the Revolution of 1911: The Birth of Modern Chinese Radicalism*. Seattle: University of Washington Press, 1969.

Gehlen, Michael P., and MacBride, Michael. "The Soviet Central Committee: An Elite Analysis." *American Political Science Review* 62, no. 4 (December 1968): 1232–41.

Genovese, Eugene D. *Roll, Jordan, Roll: The World the Slaves Made*. New York: Pantheon Books, 1974.

Gillian, Donald G. "'Peasant Nationalism' in the History of Chinese Communism." *Journal of Asian Studies* 23 (1963–64): 269–89.

———. *Warlord: Yen Hsi-shan in Shansi Province, 1911–1949*. Princeton: Princeton University Press, 1967.

Goldman, Merle. "China's Anti-Confucius Campaign, 1973–1974." *China Quarterly*, no. 63 (September 1975), pp. 435–62.

———. *Literary Dissent in Communist China*. Cambridge: Harvard University Press, 1967.

Goodrich, Luther Carrington. *The Literary Inquisition of Ch'ien-Lung*. Baltimore: Waverly Press, 1935.

Gregor, A. James. *The Fascist Persuasion in Radical Politics*. Princeton: Princeton University Press, 1974.

———. *The Ideology of Fascism: The Rationale of Totalitarianism*. New York: Macmillan Co., Free Press, 1969.

Grieder, Jerome. *Hu Shih and the Chinese Renaissance: Liberalism in the Chinese Revolution*. Cambridge: Harvard University Press, 1970.

Guinness Book of World Records. Edited by Norris and Ross MacWhister. 21st ed. London: Guinness Superlatives, 1974.

Gurr, Ted Robert. *Why Men Rebel*. Princeton: Princeton University Press, 1970.

Harrison, James P. *The Communists and Chinese Peasant Rebellions: A Study in the Rewriting of Chinese History*. New York: Atheneum, 1969.

Heilbroner, Robert L. *An Inquiry into the Human Prospect*. New York: W. W. Norton & Co., 1974.

Ho, Ping-ti. *The Ladder of Success in Imperial China: Aspects of Social Mobility, 1368–1911*. New York: Columbia University Press, 1962.

Ho, Ping-ti, and Tsou, Tang, eds. *China in Crisis*. Vol. 1, *China's Heritage and the Communist Political System*. Chicago: University of Chicago Press, 1968.

Hobsbawm, Eric. *Primitive Rebels: Studies in Archaic Forms of Social Movement in the 19th and 20th Centuries*. Manchester: University of Manchester Press, 1959.

Hsia, C. T. *A History of Modern Chinese Fiction*. 2d ed. New Haven: Yale University Press, 1971.

Hsia, Tsi-an. *The Gate of Darkness: Studies on the Leftist Literary Movement in China*. Seattle: University of Washington Press, 1968.

Hsiao Kung-chuan. *Rural China: Imperial Control in the Nineteenth Century*. Seattle: University of Washington Press, 1960.

Hsiung, James Chieh. *Ideology and Practice: The Evolution of Chinese Communism*. New York: Praeger Publishers, 1970.

———, ed. *The Logic of 'Maoism': Critiques and Explications*. New York: Praeger Publishers, 1974.

Hsu Cho-yun. *Ancient China in Transition: An Analysis of Social Mobility, 722–222* B.C. Stanford: Stanford University Press, 1965.

Hsueh, Chün-tu, ed. *Revolutionary Leaders of Modern China*. London: Oxford University Press, 1971.

Hucker, Charles O., ed. *Chinese Government in Ming Times: Seven Studies*. New York: Columbia University Press, 1969.

Huizinga, Johan. *Homo Ludens: A Study of the Play Element in Culture*. Boston: Beacon Press, 1955.

Hunt, Richard N. *The Political Ideas of Marx and Engels*. Vol. 1, *Marxism and Totalitarian Democracy, 1818–1850*. Pittsburgh: University of Pittsburgh Press, 1974.

Huntington, Samuel P. *The Soldier and the State*. Cambridge: Harvard University Press, Belknap Press, 1957.

Huntington, Samuel, and Moore, Clement H., eds. *Authoritarian Politics in Modern Society: The Dynamics of Established One-Party Systems*. New York: Basic Books, 1970.

Irwin, Richard Gregg. *The Evolution of a Chinese Novel: "Shui-hu-chuan."* Cambridge: Harvard University Press, 1953.

Isaacs, Harold R. *Scratches on Our Minds*. Cambridge, Mass.: M.I.T. Press, 1958.

Israel, John. *Student Nationalism in China, 1927–1937*. Stanford: Stanford University Press, 1966.

Jacobs, J. Bruce. "Recent Leadership and Political Trends on Taiwan." *China Quarterly*, no. 45 (January/March 1971), pp. 38–67.

Joffe, Ellis. "China's Military Elites." *China Quarterly*, no. 62 (June 1975), pp. 310–17.

Johnson, Chalmers. *An Instance of Treason: Ozaki Hotsumi and the Sorge Spy Ring*. Stanford: Stanford University Press, 1964.

———. *Peasant Nationalism and Communist Power: The Emergence of Revolutionary China, 1937–1945*. Stanford: Stanford University Press, 1962.

Kapp, Robert A. *Szechwan and the Chinese Republic: Provincial Militarism and Central Power, 1911–1938*. New Haven: Yale University Press, 1973.

Kariel, Henry S. *Open Systems: Arenas for Political Action*. Itasca, Ill.: F. E. Peacock Publishers, 1969.

Karnow, Stanley. *Mao and China: From Revolution to Revolution*. New York: Viking Press, 1972.

Kataoka, Tetsuya. "Communist Power in a War of National Liberation: The Case of China." *World Politics* 24, no. 3 (April 1972): 410–27.

Kendall, Willmoore. "The 'Open Society' and Its Fallacies." *American Political Science Review* 54, no. 4 (December 1960): 972–79.

Kerr, George H. *Formosa Betrayed*. Boston: Houghton Mifflin Co., 1964.

Kim, Ipjong J. *The Politics of Chinese Communism: Kiangsi under Soviet Rule*. Berkeley and Los Angeles: University of California Press, 1973.

Klein, Donald, and Hager, Lois B. "The Ninth Central Committee." *China Quarterly,* no. 45 (January/March 1971), pp. 37–56.

Kornhauser, William. *The Politics of Mass Society*. Glencoe, Ill.: Free Press, 1959.

Kristol, Irving. "Notes on the Spirit of '76." *Wall Street Journal,* April 23, 1976.

Lasswell, Harold D., and Lerner, Daniel, eds. *World Revolutionary Elites: Studies in Coercive Ideological Movements*. Cambridge, Mass.: M.I.T. Press, 1966.

Lee, Hong Yung. "The Radical Students in Kwangtung during the Cultural Revolution." *China Quarterly,* no. 64 (December 1975), pp. 645–83.

Leng Shao-chuan. *Justice in Communist China: A Survey of the Judicial System of the Chinese People's Republic*. Dobbs Ferry, N.Y.: Oceana Publications, 1967.

Lenin, V. I. *What Is to Be Done? Burning Questions of Our Movement*. New York: International Publishers, 1929.

Levenson, Joseph. *Confucian China and Its Modern Fate: A Trilogy*. Berkeley and Los Angeles: University of California Press, 1968.

Lewis, C. S. *The Abolition of Man*. London: Macmillan & Co., 1947.

Lewis, John Wilson, ed. *The City in Communist China*. Stanford: Stanford University Press, 1971.

———. *Party Leadership and Revolutionary Power in China*. London: Cambridge University Press, 1970.

———. *Peasant Rebellion and Communist Revolution in Asia*. Stanford: Stanford University Press, 1974.

Liao, Thomas W., trans. and ed. *Han Fei-tzu: Works from the Chinese*. 2 vols. London: A. Probsthian, 1959.

Lieberthal, Kenneth. "The Suppression of Secret Societies in Post-Liberation Tientsin." *China Quarterly,* no. 54 (April/June 1973), pp. 242–56.

Lifton, Robert Jay. *Thought Reform and the Psychology of Totalism: A Study of "Brainwashing" in China*. New York: W. W. Norton & Co., 1959.

Lindbeck, John M. H., ed. *China: Management of a Revolutionary Society*. Seattle: University of Washington Press, 1971.

Liu, Alan P. K. *Communications and National Integration in Communist China*. Berkeley and Los Angeles: University of California Press, 1974.

Liu, James T. C. *Reform in Sung China: Wang An-shih (1021–1086) and His New Policies*. Cambridge: Harvard University Press, 1959.

London, Miriam, and London, Ivan D. "The Shaping of the 'Red Guard Mind.'" *Freedom at Issue,* November-December 1975.

Lowi, Theodore J. *The End of Liberalism*. New York: W. W. Norton & Co., 1969.

MacFarquhar, Roderick. *Origins of the Cultural Revolution*. Vol. 1, *Contradictions among the People*. New York: Columbia University Press, 1974.

Machiavelli, Niccolò. *The Prince and the Discourses*. New York: Modern Library, 1950.

Marcuse, Herbert; Moore, Barrington; and Wolff, Robert Paul. *A Critique of Pure Tolerance*. Boston: Beacon Press, 1965.

Meadows, Thomas Taylor. *The Chinese and Their Rebellions*. London: Smith, Elder and Co., 1856.

Medvedev, Roy A. *Let History Judge: The Origins and Consequences of Stalinism*. New York: Vintage Books, 1973.

Meehan, Eugene. *The Foundations of Political Analysis: Empirical and Normative*. Homewood, Ill.: Dorsey Press, 1971.

Mehnert, Klaus. *Peking and the New Left*. Berkeley: Center for Chinese Studies, 1970.

Meisner, Maurice. "Leninism and Maoism: Some Populist Perspectives on Marxism-Leninism in China." *China Quarterly*, no. 45 (January/March 1971), pp. 1–36.

Meisner, Mitch. "The Shenyang Transformer Factory: A Profile." *China Quarterly*, no. 52 (October/December 1972), pp. 717–37.

Mendel, Douglas. *The Politics of Formosan Nationalism*. Berkeley and Los Angeles: University of California Press, 1970.

Michels, Robert. *Political Parties*. New York: Hearst's International Library Co., 1915.

Moody, Peter R., Jr. "The New Anti-Confucius Campaign in China: The First Round." *Asian Survey* 14, no. 4 (April 1974): 307–24.

———. *The Politics of the Eighth Central Committee of the Communist Party of China*. Hamden, Conn.: Shoestring Press, 1973.

———. "Power and Policy: The Career of T'ao Chu, 1956–1966." *China Quarterly*, no. 54 (April/June 1973), pp. 267–93.

Moore, Barrington, Jr. *Political Power and Social Theory: Seven Studies*. Cambridge: Harvard University Press, 1958.

———. *Social Origins of Dictatorship and Democracy: Lord and Peasant in the Making of the Modern World*. Boston: Beacon Press, 1966.

Munro, Donald. *The Concept of Man in Early China*. Stanford: Stanford University Press, 1969.

———. "The Malleability of Man in Chinese Marxism." *China Quarterly*, no. 48 (October/December 1971), pp. 609–40.

Myers, James T. "Religious Aspects of the Cult of Mao Tse-tung." *Current Scene* 10, no. 3 (March 10, 1972): 1–11.

Nathan, Andrew J. "A Factionalism Model for CCP Politics." *China Quarterly*, no. 53 (January/March 1973), pp. 34–66.

Nivison, David S. "Communist Ethics and the Chinese Tradition." *Journal of Asian Studies* 16 (1956–57): 51–74.

Nyomarkay, Joseph. *Charisma and Factionalism in the Nazi Party*. Minneapolis: University of Minnesota Press, 1967.

Oksenberg, Michael. "Policy-Making under Mao Tse-tung, 1949–1968." *Comparative Politics* 3, no. 3 (April 1971): 323–60.

Parish, William H., Jr. "Factions in Chinese Military Politics." *China Quarterly*, no. 56 (October/December 1973), pp. 667–99.

———. "Socialism and the Chinese Peasant Family." *Journal of Asian Studies* 34 (1974–75): 613–30.

Perkins, Dwight L. *Agricultural Development in China, 1368–1968*. Chicago: Aldine, 1969.

Pfeffer, Richard M. "Serving the People and Continuing the Revolution." *China Quarterly*, no. 52 (October/December 1972), pp. 620–53.

Plamenatz, John. *Man and Society: A Critical Examination of Some Important Social and Political Theories from Machiavelli to Marx*. 2 vols. New York: McGraw-Hill Book Co., 1963.

Podhoretz, Norman. "Making the World Safe for Communism." *Commentary*, April 1976, pp. 31–41.

Prittie, Terrence. *Germans against Hitler*. Boston: Little, Brown & Co., 1964.

Pryblya, Jan S. "Notes on Chinese Higher Education, 1975." *China Quarterly*, no. 62 (June 1975), pp. 271–96.

Pye, Lucian. *The Spirit of Chinese Politics: A Psychocultural Study of the Authority Crisis in Political Development*. Cambridge, Mass.: M.I.T. Press, 1968.

Rice, Edward E. *Mao's Way*. Berkeley and Los Angeles: University of California Press, 1972.

Richman, Barry M. *Industrial Society in Communist China*. New York: Random House, 1969.

Rigby, T. H. "Crypto-Politics." *Survey*, no. 50 (January 1964), pp. 183–94.

———. "'Totalitarianism' and Change in Communist Systems." *Comparative Politics* 4, no. 3 (April 1972): 433–53.

Rothfels, Hans. *The German Opposition to Hitler: An Appraisal*. New, rev. ed. Chicago: Henry Regnery Co., 1966.

Rue, John E. *Mao Tse-tung in Opposition, 1927–1935*. Stanford: Stanford University Press, 1966.

Sanchez, A. R., and Wong, S. L. "On 'An Interview with Chinese Anthropologists.'" *China Quarterly*, no. 60 (October/December 1974), pp. 775–90.

Sansom, Robert L. *The Economics of Insurgency in the Mekong Delta of Vietnam*. Cambridge, Mass.: M.I.T. Press, 1970.

Sartori, Giovanni. "Concept Misinformation in Comparative Politics." *American Political Science Review* 54, no. 4 (December 1970): 1033–53.

Scalapino, Robert. *Democracy and the Party Movement in Prewar Japan*. Berkeley and Los Angeles: University of California Press, 1953.

———, ed. *Elites in the People's Republic of China*. Seattle: University of Washington Press, 1972.

Scalapino, Robert, and Lee, Chong-sik. *Communism in Korea*. 2 vols. Berkeley and Los Angeles: University of California Press, 1972.

Schapiro, Leonard. "The Concept of Totalitarianism." *Survey*, no. 73 (Autumn 1969), pp. 93–113.

———. *The Origin of the Communist Autocracy: Political Opposition in the Soviet State, First Phase, 1917–1922*. Cambridge: Cambridge University Press, 1955.

———. *Totalitarianism*. New York: Praeger Publishers, 1972.

Schneider, Laurence A. *Ku Chieh-kang and China's New History: Nationalism and the Quest for Alternative Traditions*. Berkeley and Los Angeles: University of California Press, 1971.

Schurmann, Franz. *The Logic of World Power: An Inquiry into the Origins, Currents, and Contradictions of World Politics*. New York: Pantheon Books, 1974.

Schuster, George N., ed. *Freedom and Authority in the West*. Notre Dame, Ind.: University of Notre Dame Press, 1967.

Schwartz, Benjamin I. *Chinese Communism and the Rise of Mao*. Cambridge: Harvard University Press, 1951.

———. *In Search of Wealth and Power: Yen Fu and the West*. Cambridge: Harvard University Press, 1964.

———, ed. *Reflections on the May Fourth Movement: A Symposium*. Cambridge: Harvard University Press, 1972.

Selden, Mark. *The Yenan Way in Revolutionary China*. Cambridge: Harvard University Press, 1971.

Shih, Vincent J. C. "Some Chinese Rebel Ideologies." *T'oung pao* 44 (1956): 150–226.

Shklar, Judith. *Legalism*. Cambridge: Harvard University Press, 1964.

Sih, Paul T. K., ed. *Taiwan in Modern Times*. Jamaica, N.Y.: St. John's University Press, 1973.

Skilling, H. Gordon. "Background to the Study of Opposition in Communist Eastern Europe." *Government and Opposition* 3, no. 2 (Spring 1968): 294–324.

———, ed. *Interest Groups in Soviet Politics*. Princeton: Princeton University Press, 1971.

Skinner, B. F. *Beyond Freedom and Dignity*. New York: Alfred A. Knopf, 1972.

Solomon, Richard. *Mao's Revolution and the Chinese Political Culture*. Berkeley and Los Angeles: University of California Press, 1971.

———. "One Party and 'One Hundred Schools': Leadership, Lethargy, or *Luan*?" *Current Scene* 7, nos. 19–20 (October 1, 1969).

Starr, John Bryan. *Ideology and Culture: An Introduction to the Dialectic of Contemporary Chinese Politics*. New York: Harper & Row Publishers, 1973.

Strauss, Leo. *Persecution and the Art of Writing*. Glencoe, Ill.: Free Press, 1952.

———. *Thoughts on Machiavelli*. Glencoe, Ill.: Free Press, 1958.

Strong, John and Sarah. "A Post-Cultural Revolution Look at Chinese Buddhism." *China Quarterly*, no. 54 (April/June 1973), pp. 301–30.

Tang, Peter S. H., and Maloney, Joan M. *Communist China: The Domestic Scene, 1949–1967*. New York: Seaton Hall University Press, 1967.

Teiwes, Frederick C. "The Evolution of Leadership Purges in Communist China." *China Quarterly*, no. 41 (January/March 1970), pp. 122–35.

Thaxton, Ralph. "Some Critical Comments on Peasant Revolts and Revolutionary Politics in China." *Journal of Asian Studies* 33 (1973–74): 279–88.

———. "Tenants in Revolution: The Tenacity of Traditional Morality." *Modern China* 1, no. 3 (July 1975): 323–57.

Thornton, Richard. *The Comintern and the Chinese Communists, 1928–1931*. Seattle: University of Washington Press, 1969.

———. "The Structure of Communist Politics." *World Politics* 24, no. 4 (July 1972): 495–517.

Tien Hung-mao. *Government and Politics in Kuomintang China, 1927–1937*. Stanford: Stanford University Press, 1972.

———. "Taiwan in Transition: Prospects for Socio-Political Change." *China Quarterly*, no. 64 (December 1975), pp. 615–44.

Tilly, Charles. *The Vendee*. Cambridge: Harvard University Press, 1964.

Tinbergen, J. *Economic Policy: Principles and Design*. Amsterdam: North Holland Publishing Co., 1966.

Townsend, James R. *Political Participation in Communist China*. New ed. Berkeley and Los Angeles: University of California Press, 1969.

Tozer, Warren. "Taiwan's 'Cultural Renaissance': A Preliminary Survey." *China Quarterly,* no. 43 (July/September, 1970), pp. 61–99.

Treadgold, Donald W., ed. *Soviet and Chinese Communism: Similarities and Differences*. Seattle: University of Washington Press, 1967.

Truman, David B. *The Governmental Process: Political Interests and Public Opinion.* New York: Alfred A. Knopf, 1951.

Tucker, Robert C. "The Dictator and Totalitarianism." *World Politics* 17, no. 4 (July 1965): 555–83.

———. *The Marxian Revolutionary Idea*. New York: W. W. Norton & Co., 1968.

———. "Toward a Comparative Politics of Movement Regimes." *American Political Science Review* 55, no. 2 (June 1961): 281–89.

Ulam, Adam B. *Stalin: The Man and His Era*. London: Allen Lane, 1974.

Unger, Aryeh L. *The Totalitarian Party: Party and People in Nazi Germany and Soviet Russia*. London: Cambridge University Press, 1974.

van Etten Casey, William, S. J. "Mao's China." *Holy Cross Quarterly* 7, nos. 1–4 (1975): 5–12.

Verba, Sidney. *Small Groups and Political Behavior: A Study of Leadership*. Princeton: Princeton University Press, 1961.

Voegelin, Eric. *The New Science of Politics: An Introduction*. Chicago: University of Chicago Press, 1952.

———. *Order and History*. Vol. 1, *Israel and Revelation*. Baton Rouge: Louisiana State University Press, 1956.

Vogel, Ezra. *Canton under Communism: Programs and Politics in a Provincial Capital, 1949–1968*. Cambridge: Harvard University Press, 1969.

———. "From Friendship to Comradeship: The Change in Personal Relations in Communist China." *China Quarterly,* no. 21 (January/March 1965), pp. 46–60.

Vohra, Ranbir. *Lao She and the Chinese Revolution*. Cambridge: Harvard University Press, 1974.

Wakeman, Frederick, Jr. *History and Will: Philosophical Perspectives on Mao Tse-tung's Thought*. Berkeley and Los Angeles: University of California Press, 1973.

———. "The Use and Abuse of Ideology in the Study of Contemporary China." *China Quarterly,* no. 61 (March 1975), pp. 127–52.

Walker, Richard L. *The Human Cost of Communism in China*. Washington, D.C.: U.S. Government Printing Office, 1973.

Walzer, Michael. *The Revolution of the Saints: A Study of the Origins of Radical Politics*. New York: Atheneum, 1973.

Wang, John. *Land Reform in the People's Republic of China: Institutional Transformation in Agriculture*. New York: Praeger Publishers, 1973.

Weber, Max. *The Theory of Social and Economic Organization*. New York: Oxford University Press, 1947.

Wei Yung. "Modernization Process on Taiwan: An Allocative Analysis." *Asian Survey* 12, no. 5 (March 1976): 249–69.

Welch, Holmes. *Buddhism under Mao*. Cambridge: Harvard University Press, 1972.

Whitson, William. "The Field Army in Chinese Communist Politics." *China Quarterly,* no. 37 (January/March 1969), pp. 1–30.

Whitson, William, with Huang, Chen-hsia. *The Chinese High Command: A History of Communist Military Politics*. New York: Praeger Publishers, 1973.

Whyte, Martin King. "Corrective Labor Camps in China." *Asian Survey* 13, no. 3 (March 1973): 253–69.

———. *Small Groups and Political Rituals in China*. Berkeley and Los Angeles: University of California Press, 1974.

———. "The Tachai Brigade and Incentives for the Peasant." *Current Scene* 6, no. 16 (August 1969).

Wills, Garry. *Nixon Agonistes: The Crisis of the Self-Made Man*. Boston: Houghton Mifflin Co., 1970.

Wilson, Richard W. *Learning to Be Chinese: The Political Socialization of Children in Taiwan*. Cambridge, Mass.: M.I.T. Press, 1970.

Wittfogel, Karl A. "Chinese Society: An Historical Survey." *Journal of Asian Studies* 16 (1956–57): 343–64.

———. *Oriental Despotism*. New Haven: Yale University Press, 1957.

Woodhouse, Edward J. "Revisioning the Future of the Third World: An Ecological Perspective on Development." *World Politics* 25, no. 1 (October 1972): 1–33.

Wright, Mary C. *The Last Stand of Chinese Conservatism: The T'ung-chih Restoration, 1862–1874*. New preface and additional notes. New York: Atheneum, 1966.

Yang, C. K. *The Chinese Family in the Communist Revolution*. Cambridge, Mass.: M.I.T. Press, 1959.

———. *A Chinese Village in Early Communist Transition*. Cambridge, Mass.: M.I.T. Press, 1959.

Zagoria, Donald. *Vietnam Triangle: Moscow, Peking, Hanoi*. New York: Praeger Publishers, 1967.

Index